Jesus in a World of Colliding Empires

Jesus in a World of Colliding Empires

Mark's Jesus from the Perspective of Power and Expectations

Volume One: Introduction and Mark 1:1—8:29

MARK J. KEOWN

WIPF & STOCK · Eugene, Oregon

JESUS IN A WORLD OF COLLIDING EMPIRES, VOLUME ONE:
INTRODUCTION AND MARK 1:1—8:29
Mark's Jesus from the Perspective of Power and Expectations

Copyright © 2018 Mark J. Keown. All rights reserved. Except for brief quotations in critical publications or reviews, no part of this book may be reproduced in any manner without prior written permission from the publisher. Write: Permissions, Wipf and Stock Publishers, 199 W. 8th Ave., Suite 3, Eugene, OR 97401.

Wipf & Stock
An Imprint of Wipf and Stock Publishers
199 W. 8th Ave., Suite 3
Eugene, OR 97401

www.wipfandstock.com

PAPERBACK ISBN: 978-1-5326-4133-6
HARDCOVER ISBN: 978-1-5326-4134-3
EBOOK ISBN: 978-1-5326-4135-0

Manufactured in the U.S.A.   FEBRUARY 7, 2018

Scripture quotations marked (ESV) are from The Holy Bible, English Standard Version® (ESV®). Copyright © 2001 by Crossway, a publishing ministry of Good News Publishers. Used by permission. All rights reserved.

Contents

Dedication and Acknowledgments | *xi*
Abbreviations | *xiii*

Introduction | 1

1. The Background of Mark | 6

   The Setting for Mark
   The Importance of Mark
   Approach

2. A World of Colliding Empires: The Roman World | 12

   Rome
   Greece (Macedonia)
   The Persians
   The Babylonians
   Before the Babylonians
   Beyond the Mediterranean
   Augustus and Tiberius
   Nero

3. A World of Colliding Empires: The Rest of the Known World at the Time of Christ | 20

    China's Dynasties
    Central Asia
    India's Dynasties
    Southeast Asia
    Southern Russian Region (The Scythian Kingdoms)
    Iran (the Parthian Empire)
    Middle East
    Africa
    Europe
    The Rest of the World
    Conclusion

4. Israel in this Clashing World | 46

    War, Violence, and Empires in the Old Testament
        Wilderness
        Conquest
        The Time of the Judges
        United Monarchy
            The Desire for a King
            Saul
            David
            Solomon
        Divided Monarchy
        The Decline and Exile of the North
        The Decline and Exile of the South
        Foreign Rule
        The Maccabean Revolt

5. The Hope of a Deliverer ("Theo" = "the Expected One") | 76

    The Old Testament
        Genesis
        Numbers

Isaiah 1–39
  Isaiah 40–55
  Isaiah 56–66
  Jeremiah
  Ezekiel
  Daniel
  Hosea
  Amos
  Micah
  Haggai
  Zechariah
  Malachi
  The Psalms
The Apocrypha, Pseudepigrapha, Philo, Josephus, and the Rabbis
  God as Theo in a Direct Sense
  Theo as a Human/semi-divine Messianic Agent of Some Sort
    Jubilees
    Assumption of Moses
    1 Enoch
    2 Baruch
    4 Ezra
    Testament of the Twelve Patriarchs
      Testament of Levi
      Testament of Reuben
      Testament of Judah
      Testament of Gad
    Psalms of Solomon
    3 Enoch
    Sibylline Oracles 3
    Pseudo-Philo
    Apocalypse of Abraham
    The Dead Sea Scrolls
  Philo
  Josephus

>>>> Rabbinic Literature
>>>>> Talmud and Midrashim
>>>> Messianic Movements and the New Testament
>>>>> Messianic Movements
>>>>> The New Testament
>>>>>> The Synoptics
>>>>>> John
>>>>>> Acts
>>>>>> Paul
>>> A Composite Picture of Theo
>>>> The Coming of the Divinely Empowered Warrior-King Leader
>>>> The Restoration of Israel by Military Force
>>>> The Vanquishing of the Gentiles by Military Force
>>>> The Establishment of Jerusalem and Zion as the Capital of the World
>>>> Law
>>>> The Establishment of Cosmic Shalom
>>>> How it Might Have Looked
>>>> The Problem with This Perspective

6. The Messiah Revealed (Mark 1:1—8:29) | 141

>>> The Prologue (Mark 1:1–13)
>>>> The Title of the Gospel (Mark 1:1)
>>>> The "Last" Prophet and Crowner of the King, John the Baptist (Mark 1:2–8)
>>>> Jesus' Coronation, John's Baptism (Mark 1:9–11)
>>>> Jesus Resists Satan (Mark 1:12–13)
>>> Jesus the Davidic Messiah King Revealed (Mark 1:14—8:29)
>>>> God's Deliverance is Imminent (Mark 1:14–15)
>>>> Calling Disciples, Conscription to an Army? (Mark 1:16–20; 2:13–17; 3:13–19)
>>>> Jesus' Miracles and Teaching: Demon-Possessed, Prophet, or Messiah?
>>>> Jesus and Israel's Leaders
>>>>> Leaders a Theo-Figure May Oppose

The Herodians
The Sadducees
The Priests
The Sanhedrin
The Romans
Leaders a Theo-Figure Would Potentially Work With
The Pharisees
The Scribes
The Essenes
Summary
The Moment of Truth: The Disciples Recognize Jesus Messiah (Mark 8:27–29)

Works Referenced | *207*
Author Index | *215*
Scripture Index | *219*

Dedication and Acknowledgments

I DEDICATE THIS WORK TO the Lord Jesus Christ who, although being God and fully equal with God, did not plunder our world to claim it as his own; rather, he became one of us and poured himself out in our service. He allowed himself to be utterly humiliated dying on a cross to save us. His voluntary decision to leave eternity and the fullness of deity to come to us in this way and to live as he did shows us what it means to be God and what it means to be human. I thank you, Lord Jesus, and pray you use this book for your glory.

I also thank my beloved wife Emma and my three children for being who you are. May you live out of the Christ-pattern, for there is no other real way to live.

I thank my wonderful mum, Nolarae, for teaching me to read and think and especially for reading me Lewis's *The Lion, the Witch and the Wardrobe* as a boy. Love you, Mum. Rest in peace, Dad.

I thank Laidlaw College for believing in me, employing me, and supporting me in so many ways. May the college ever live out of the cruciform pattern we have received in Christ. May all Christians renounce the patterns of this dark world and live this way.

Abbreviations

AB	Anchor Bible
ABD	Freedman, David Noel, Gary A. Herion, David F. Graf, John David Pleins, and Astrid B. Beck, eds. *The Anchor Yale Bible Dictionary.* New York: Doubleday, 1992.
ABRL	Anchor Bible Reference Library
ANET	*Ancient Near Eastern Texts Relating to the Old Testament.* Edited by James B. Pritchard. 3rd ed. Princeton: Princeton University Press, 1969.
ANF	The Ante-Nicene Fathers
ATR	*Australasian Theological Review*
BA	*Britannica Academic*, Encyclopædia Britannica.
BAGD	Arndt, William, F. Wilbur Gingrich, Frederick W. Danker, and Walter Bauer. *A Greek-English Lexicon of the New Testament and Other Early Christian Literature: A Translation and Adaption of the Fourth Revised and Augmented Edition of Walter Bauer's Griechisch-Deutsches Worterbuch Zu Den Schrift En Des Neuen Testaments Und Der Ubrigen Urchristlichen Literatur.* Chicago: University of Chicago, 1979.
BBB	Bonner biblische Beiträge
BDAG	Arndt, William, Frederick W. Danker, and Walter Bauer. *A Greek-English Lexicon of the New Testament and Other Early Christian Literature.* Chicago: University of Chicago, 2000.

BDF	Blass, Friedrich, Albert Debrunner, and Robert Walter Funk. *A Greek Grammar of the New Testament and Other Early Christian Literature*. Chicago: University of Chicago, 1961.
BEB	Elwell, Walter A., and Barry J. Beitzel. *Baker Encyclopedia of the Bible*. Grand Rapids: Baker Book House, 1988.
BECNT	Baker Exegetical Commentary on the New Testament
BJRL	*Bulletin of the John Rylands University Library of Manchester*
BNTC	Black's New Testament Commentary
CBC	Cornerstone Biblical Commentary
CD	Cairo Genizah copy of the Damascus Document
CGTC	Cambridge Greek Testament Commentary
CCGNT	Classic Commentaries on the Greek New Testament
Colloq	*Colloquium*
COQG	Christian Origins and the Question of God
CPNIVC	The College Press NIV Commentary
DBLH	Swanson, James. *Dictionary of Biblical Languages with Semantic Domains: Hebrew (Old Testament)*. Oak Harbor: Logos Research Systems, Inc., 1997.
DNTB	Porter, Stanley E., and Craig A. Evans. *Dictionary of New Testament Background: A Compendium of Contemporary Biblical Scholarship*. Electronic ed. Downers Grove, IL: InterVarsity, 2000.
DJG	*Dictionary of Jesus and the Gospels*
EDB	Freedman, David Noel, Allen C. Myers, and Astrid B. Beck. *Eerdmans Dictionary of the Bible*. Grand Rapids: W.B. Eerdmans, 2000.
EDNT	Balz, Horst Robert, and Gerhard Schneider. *Exegetical Dictionary of the New Testament*. Grand Rapids: Eerdmans, 1990.
EEC	Evangelical Exegetical Commentary
EKK	Evangelisch-Katholischer Kommentar zum Neuen Testament

ERE	Matthew Bunson, *The Encyclopedia of the Roman Empire*. Revised Edition. New York: Facts on File Books, 1994, 2002.
ESV	English Standard Version
ExpTim	*Expository Times*
FBBS	Facet Books. Biblical Series.
HBM	Hebrew Biblical Monographs
HNT	Handbuch zum Neuen Testament
HNTC	Holman New Testament Commentary
HTKNT	Herders theologischer Kommentar zum NT
HTR	*Harvard Theological Review*
HUCA	*Hebrew Union College Annual*
ISBE	*The International Standard Bible Encyclopedia, Revised*. Edited by Geoffrey W. Bromiley. Grand Rapids: Eerdmans, 1979–1988.
ISBE (1)	Orr, James, John L. Nuelsen, Edgar Y. Mullins, and Morris O. Evans, eds. *The International Standard Bible Encyclopaedia*. Chicago: The Howard-Severance Company, 1915.
ITC	International Theological Commentary
JBL	*Journal of Biblical Literature*
JETS	*Journal of the Evangelical Theological Society*
JQR	*Jewish Quarterly Review*
JRS	*Journal of Roman Studies*
JSNTSup	Journal for the Study of New Testament Supplement Series
JSP	*Journal for the Study of the Pseudepigrapha*
JTS	*Journal of Theological Studies*
KJV	King James Version
LAD	Liber Antiquitatum Biblicarum
LBD	Barry, John D., David Bomar, Derek R. Brown, Rachel Klippenstein, Douglas Mangum, Carrie Sinclair Wolcott, Lazarus Wentz, Elliot Ritzema, and Wendy Widder, eds. *The Lexham Bible Dictionary*. Bellingham, WA: Lexham, 2016.

LNTS	Library of New Testament Studies
LSJ	Liddell, Henry George, Robert Scott, Henry Stuart Jones, and Roderick McKenzie. *A Greek-English Lexicon*. Oxford: Clarendon, 1996.
LXX	The Greek Old Testament, the Septuagint
MS(S)	*Manuscript(s)*
NAC	New American Commentary
NASB	New American Standard Bible
NICNT	New International Commentary on the New Testament
NIV	New International Version
NKJV	New King James Version
NRSV	New Revised Standard Version
NovT	*Novum Testamentum*
NTS	*New Testament Studies*
OTSS	Old Testament Survey Series
PNTC	Pillar New Testament Commentary
P.Oxy.	Oxyrhynchus papyri
RB	*Revue Biblique*
REB	Revised English Bible
Rev Qum	*Revue de Qumran*
RSV	Revised Standard Version
SBT	Studies in Biblical Theology
s.a.	See also
SNTSMS	Society for New Testament Studies Monograph Series
SNTW	Studies in the New Testament and Its World
SP	Sacra Pagina
SSEJC	Studies in Scripture in Early Judaism and Christianity
Str-B	Strack, H. L., and P. Billerbeck, *Kommentar zum Neuen Testament aus Talmud und Midrasch*. 6 vols. Munich, 1922–1961.

SVTP	*Studia in Veteris Testamenti Pseudepigrapha*
TDNT	Kittel, Gerhard, Geoffrey W. Bromiley, and Gerhard Friedrich, eds. *Theological Dictionary of the New Testament.* Grand Rapids: Eerdmans, 1964.
Theo	The Expected One
Tijd. Theol.	*Tijdschrift voor Theologie*
UBSHS	United Bible Society Handbook Series
WBC	Word Bible Commentary
WissWeis	*Wissenschaft und Weisheit*
ZNW	*Zeitschrift für die neutestamentliche Wissenschaft und die Kunde der älteren Kirche*

Introduction

THE IDEA FOR THIS book on Mark's Gospel came as I taught the subject in one of my New Testament classes at Laidlaw College, Auckland, NZ; and as I was working on my EEC commentary on Philippians, and especially spending time thinking about Philippians 2:6–8.[1] As he wrote the letter to "little Rome," Paul was likely sitting in prison in Rome chained to a Roman guard. The Philippians were a great bunch, loving Jesus, giving generously, and sharing the gospel—truly one of Paul's "best" churches. However, there was a problem in their midst; namely, that they had allowed their Roman culture to mar their mindsets and affect their behavior away from a life formed in the gospel of a crucified messiah (e.g. Phil 2:1–4, 15–16; 4:1–3[2]). Put simply; they were seeking to elevate their position within their church structures. They were vying for position.

We should not be hard on them for this; it is common in many churches, denominations, and human life. In fact, whether we recognize it or not, we are all, to some extent or another, infected by our culture. Anyway, that aside, these Philippians were falling prey to patterns of power which are found in the Roman world (and all worlds). They were looking to increase their status and esteem through selfish ambition and some good old-fashioned envy and pride. Paul understandably was concerned and wrote the letter to remedy things so that they didn't become like the almost-out-of-control Corinthian church down the road in Achaia (see 1 Cor 1—4; 11:18). So, Paul wrote to them, and placed in the center of his letter a reminder of

---

1. For discussions defending the ideas in this introduction related to Philippians, please see the Introduction to Keown, *Philippians* 1–92. See also my earlier book *Congregational Evangelism in Philippians*, 37–70.

2. Unless otherwise noted, the author uses the ESV throughout this volume.

the pattern of life Jesus laid down for them to emulate. Perhaps using or adapting an old hymn written in the first days of the Palestinian church, he gives a nice summary of this pattern:

> **5** Have this attitude in you, which was also in Christ Jesus,
> **6** Who, being in form God,
> did not consider equality with God something to be exploited,
> **7** but he emptied himself,
> taking the form of a slave,
> being born in human likeness
> and found in appearance as a man,
> **8** he humbled himself,
> becoming obedient to the point of death,
> even death on a cross.
> **9** Therefore, God highly exalted him and gave him the name above all names.
> **10** That at the name of Jesus,
> every knee will bow in heaven and on earth and under the earth,
> **11** and every tongue acknowledge that Jesus Christ is Lord,
> to the glory of God the Father.

This hymn has got me (and not a few others) thinking about patterns of power then and now. Having also taught Mark for a few years I have noticed that central to Mark is the question of whether Jesus is Messiah and the way in which Jesus redefines the idea of messiah away from presumed patterns of power in the ancient world. The world then, and to a considerable extent, now, revolves around power through political intrigue, status, wealth, and force. The ancient world was ruled by empires wielding spear and sword. Its story is one of clashing empires seeking dominance. Where one empire did not dominate, tribalism and territorialism were strong with rivalry and imperialism waxing and waning.

In Jesus' day, the dominant force in the Mediterranean region was Rome (27 BC–476 AD).[3] Before Rome, there was a series of empires such as the Macedonians/Greeks, the Medo-Persians, the Babylonians, the Assyrians, and the Egyptians. Outside of the Mediterranean region, the world was

---

3. In this book, I choose to use BC and AD ("before Christ," and *Anno Domini*, "in the year of our Lord") rather than the increasingly common BCE (Before the Common Era) and CE (Common Era). This is due not only to my own convictions concerning Jesus Christship and Lordship, but because I believe that even if some in the world are seeking to distance themselves from Christianity, Jesus still reigns as Lord and is the ultimate divider of history.

mostly tribal with a range of dynasties, empires, and tribal contention across Southern Russia, Asia, Africa, and Europe.

Since Christ, the quest for power has gone on endlessly, with Rome eventually overthrown (AD 476). There have been many invaders and empires since that time. Of prominence are the many Chinese dynasties, the Byzantine Empire (330–1453), Holy Roman Empire (962–1806), the Aztecs (1428–1521), the Ottoman Empire (1299–1922), the British Empire (1603–1997), the colonial powers of Europe, Communism (particularly the Soviet Union and China), Islam, the Reiches of Germany, the empire of capitalism and consumerism, and more. The spread of western culture today suggests a kind of ongoing cultural imperialism from dominant western nations.

As recently as last century, there were two massive world wars between collectives of nations forming competing forces within Europe, North Africa, America, Asia, and the Middle East, the rise and fall of communism (especially the Soviet Union), despotic local rulers such as Idi Amin (Uganda), Pol Pot (Cambodia), Robert Mugabe (Zimbabwe), the North Korean dynasty, and the rise of Islamic powers. Today, ironically, all that seems to hold humanity back from continuing this desperate fight for dominance is the immense power of weapons of mass destruction, meaning that the cost of conflict is so great that such forces are withheld. It seems only a matter of time before someone decides to unleash ultimate force and the world will descend into what might be the final conflict of human history.

The point is this; humanity continues to be held captive by a lust for power and a desire to dominate. Some would see this as a product of our evolutionary development. Most Christians would explain it by the fall of Adam and Eve. However we explain its origins; we are a world in conflict vying for power. Power is wielded in many ways, usually linked with brute force, wealth, attractiveness, charisma, shrewdness, and the philosophical, ideological, and religious constructs that undergird it.

Where Philippians 2 is concerned, the immediate backdrop is Roman might. As we consider Mark, we will see that Jesus completely and utterly clashes with the Roman story. Where Israel's story is concerned, as this book will show, her history was based on similar patterns, with most placing their hope on God's spiritual and military intervention, whether directly through God himself, a transcendent supernatural semi-divine kingly figure, or a Davidic Messiah. God would intervene to put things right. He would vanquish these Roman upstarts, and take the world for Yahweh.

Jesus turned the world on its head. Jesus came and simply refused to play the "Game of Thrones" which dominated the ancient world. Or better yet, he played it in a unique way. He did not allow himself to become a player in the game of world domination. He did not seek to win the world through this pattern. He knew that this blueprint had its origins in hell itself, the master plan of Satan. Satan knows that if he can get the world to keep playing these games, humanity will ultimately self-destruct. Rather, Jesus came and showed humanity where real power lies, and what it looks like. Real power is not found in governments, tanks, bombs, WMDs, looks, money, wisdom, giftedness, political intrigue, force, etc. Rather, it is found in *the appearance* of weakness and powerlessness; namely, selflessness, service, sacrifice, suffering, and humility, i.e. love! This is seen most vividly in the "Theomorph" or "form of God," Jesus, pre-existent, in the flesh, and on a cross. The "deep magic before the dawn of time" is that the real power is love (C. S. Lewis).

Jesus came to put to an end all power games and establish a new paradigm of being that renounced force. He came to set humanity free from its inability to live any other way and to live out of love. He came to end war. He came to establish peace. He came to show all people, leaders and otherwise, how to live and lead. Leadership is not about coercive force to get people to see things our way and conform to the vision and strategy we concoct in our hubris; rather, it is to take up a cross and towel and follow Jesus in the path of humility, self-denial, sacrifice, service, suffering, and, if need be, even death.

Some pit Paul against Jesus and suggest Paul created a new religion. This is far from the truth—Paul "got it" better than anyone. But that is another story. As I have pondered Mark in the light of rereading Paul again and again and noticing that this Christ-pattern to some extent or another undergirds every letter, I realized that Mark fully understood what Jesus was about, too. Set against the backdrop of the power patterns of the world, Mark's story is laced with what is, at times, hilarious, yet bitter irony. In a nation that anticipated "The Expected One" (Theo)[4] to be a man of war, a warrior-king to establish a dynastic empire, he came as Servant and died to save the world. More than that, he lived and died to show the world how to live. All this I will explore in diverse ways through the book.

I will begin in chapter 1 by putting Mark in its context to ensure that we grasp more firmly the forces that were at work at the time of its writing. In chapter 2, I will briefly sum the colliding empires which had affected Israel in the centuries before the time of Christ. In chapter 3, I will examine what was going on at the time of Christ beyond the Roman Empire showing that the whole known world was caught up in a battle for power based around powerful men with armies. Jesus came in vivid contrast to an entire

---

4. This is an acronym I have coined for "the one Israel expected"—which is a composite core of a range of ideas from the direct intervention of God himself, a Messiah, a Prophet, Elijah, a Son of Man, an Elect One, and so on.

world of colliding empires. In chapter 4, I discuss Israel's story which shows that she too was caught up in this same pattern of kingship, violence, and power. In chapter 5, I will summarize Israel's hope of intervention which, while varied, inevitably involved violent military intervention and the establishment of God's reign. Common to this story was the expectation of an expected ruler (Theo = "The Expected One") who would be God's key instrument in establishing his reign. After this background work, in chapters 6–8, I will explore Mark, reading it against the backdrop of the pattern of a warrior-king and a military/religious empire, and drawing out the deep irony in the story as read against this backdrop. In so doing, we will realize why many Jews did not understand the story (and still don't). We will see how utterly subversive, world-changing, and monumental it is. Then in chapter 9 I will draw conclusions and implications of this for Christian life in a range of ways. I will suggest that what is needed is a new "revolution" whereby the global church rediscovers its call to live the essential principles of Christianity, a renunciation of paradigms of power based on might and force and living out of the pattern of the cross.

Essentially, we need to rediscover this Jesus and recognize what he was about. He died to save the world, yes! We cannot downplay this; his death and resurrection is the salvation of the world, if people would only believe! God's offer in Christ is a gift of grace with no strings attached![5] But that's not all. Jesus died not only to save us (priority one though this was), but to show us what true life looks like. That is, true life is living out of love seen in sacrifice, self-denial, selflessness, service, and suffering to the point at which it hurts.

If believers can only grasp this truth, and seek to live it out *with unwavering intent*, the church will look more and more like it was always intended to be. This will spread from us to the world. This is God's dream for us: to live out the Christ-pattern and see the world transformed. What is needed is an "army"[6] of Christians who rediscover the fullness of the Christ-story and live it in the power of the Spirit with the only weapons in our hand being the story itself and lives of love and service. We need to lay down our false reliance on human patterns of power in church and beyond, and we will see a new world dawn. My prayer for this book is that people will read it and, like Paul and Mark, get it and live it. Amen. Shalom!

---

5. You can get my take on the Christian story in Keown, *What's God Up to On Planet Earth*.

6. Throughout this work, if referring to military imagery for Christian life, I am using it in a non-military and non-violent sense. In one sense, it is anything but a war and we anything but an army. But we can use the imagery, if we recognize its limitations.

1

The Background of Mark

Before setting out on this journey, it is important to get a good grip on the setting of Mark's Gospel. Understanding when an ancient document was written, where it was written, the audience the writer has in mind, who wrote it, the influences on the writer, their possible sources, and other background questions, helps us grasp its force. In this short section, I will establish a setting for the Gospel of Mark. This need only be done in general terms, as the details are secondary to the discussion that will follow.

THE SETTING FOR MARK

Most of the background details of Mark's gospel are disputable. Based on the tradition of Papias, the Bishop of Hierapolis around AD 130, some argue that Mark's Gospel is a record of the essence of the message preached by Simon Peter.[1] If so, it was written somewhere either before or after Peter's death at the hands of Nero in the mid-to-late 60s AD. Supported by a wide range of early church tradition,[2] it is argued that the writer is John Mark of Jerusalem, a traveling companion of Paul and, in later life, Peter (Acts 12:12, 25; 15:37, 39; Col 4:10; Phlm 24; 1 Pet 5:13). If this is correct, Mark was written in Rome where Peter died at the hands of Nero,[3] and where Mark was his companion (ca. 64–68 AD). This would mean that it was penned

---

1. For example, Edwards, *Mark*, 3–6.
2. See for details Cranfield, *The Gospel according to St Mark*, 3–4, who notes, aside from Papias, Justin Martyr (*Dial.* 106), the "Anti-Marcionite Prologue," Irenaeus (*Haer.* 3.1.1), the Muratorian Canon, Clement of Alexandria, and Eusebius who records Papias's testimony (*Hist. eccl.* 3:39, cf. 2.15; 6.14).
3. Origen cited in Eusebius, *Hist. eccl.* 3.1.2.

near the end of the Roman emperor Nero's reign. In this period, Rome was witness to the horrific persecution of Christians amidst Nero's other acts of brutality and madness.[4] In many ways, Nero represents the limits of absolute power. So then, Mark was written with the Roman context in mind, seeking to preserve Peter's memory of Jesus and give a base for the faith and its spread. It would also have sought to encourage Christians under Nero's lunacy. The pattern of Jesus' kingship stands in stark contrast to the living example of Nero in Rome the time. It is likely that Rome had a substantial Christian population at the end of the 60s.[5] The backdrop for Mark's Gospel would then be Rome and Nero's despotism.

Others dispute the reliability of Papias and claim that Mark is better placed during or after the time of the Roman destruction of Jerusalem in AD 70. Such thinkers argue that that the author is not necessarily the John Mark of the New Testament, but is an unknown writer perhaps with the

---

4. The first five years of Nero's reign were "moderate" (Tacitus, *Ann.* 13), although he was likely complicit in Claudius's death and the killing of his brother Britannicus (Suetonius, *Nero*, 33; Tacitus, *Ann.* 8.16; Josephus, *Ant.* 20.153). He enjoyed going out at night to beat people up, rob them, and debauch the proceeds away, until a senator beat him up! He also feasted and engaged in sex with boys and women, including a Vestal Virgin. He married a boy after castrating him. He dressed in wild animals' skins and attacked people's privates (Suetonius, *Nero*, 26–30). Josephus, *Ant.* 20. 154–57 treats Nero in a more favorable light due to his positive attitude toward the Jews. However, in *J.W.*, 2.250 he alludes to his conduct. After this initial period, he plunged into despotism after farcically "organizing" the murder of his mother Agrippina in a collapsing ship in AD 59 (Tacitus, *Ann.* 14.1–8; Dio Cassius, *Hist*, 62.12–14; Suetonius, *Nero*, 34). He then killed his aunt (Suetonius, *Nero*, 35.5). He likely poisoned his advisor and head of the Praetorian Guard Burrus (Dio Cassius, *Hist*, 62.13.3; Suetonius, *Nero*, 35; Tacitus, *Ann.* 14.51). Seneca (his tutor) and his other advisor retired and "committed suicide" after plotting against him in AD 62 (Tacitus, *Ann.* 14.52–56; Dio Cassius, *Hist*, 62.24–25; Suetonius, *Nero*, 35). He crushed Senate opposition, expelled and then killed his wife Octavia (Claudius's daughter) and married the unscrupulous, ambitious, and God-fearing Jewish proselyte Poppaea Sabina (Tacitus, *Ann.* 60–64; Dio Cassius, *Hist*, 62.13.1–2; Suetonius, *Nero*, 35, cf. Josephus, *Ant.* 20.195; *Life*, 16). He appointed new advisors, the weak Faenius Rufus (Lightfoot, *Saint Paul's Epistle*, 24) and the dominant, debauched, and ruthless Ofonius Tigellinus as Praetorian head (Tacitus, *Ann.* 14.51, Dio Cassius, *Hist*, 62.27). See further Dio Cassius, *Hist*, 61.17.1–21; 62.14–15; Tacitus, *Ann.* 14.30–50; Suetonius, "Nero," 25–35. See also on Nero: Malitz, *Nero*.; Griffen, *Nero*, and Griffen, "Nero," 4:1076–1081; Grant, *Nero*; Champlin, *Nero*; and Holland, *Nero: The Man Behind the Myth*.

5. The expulsion of Jews by Claudius due to conflict over *Chrestus* in Rome in AD 49 suggests a strong Christian presence by this time (Acts 18:2; Suetonius, *Claudius*, 25.4). It is likely that there was an increased gentile presence in the church after this time, and on the return of the Jews after Claudius's death in AD 54 a significant growth in numbers. Romans indicates a good number of house churches (Rom 16). Nero's choice to target the Christians for the fire suggests a strong presence. The martyrdom of Paul and Peter adds to this picture.

common name "Marcus" and of non-Palestinian origin. That he is argued to be non-Palestinian is due to perceived errors in detail concerning Palestine.[6] It is also postulated that the accurate details of Mark 13 suggest it was written *after* the destruction of Jerusalem, a kind of "prophecy after the event" (postdiction or *vaticinium ex eventu*). If so, the precise setting for Mark is unclear with any non-Palestinian setting possible. If this perspective is correct, Mark is set after Nero's reign in the time of Vespasian, perhaps (AD 69–79), during which Rome was wielding considerable military force. This included the ransacking of Judea to quash the Jewish rebellion with the proceeds of this plundering used to begin building the Colosseum, The Temple of Peace, a massive statue of Apollo, and other monuments to the glory of Rome.

Another possible angle is that the name "Mark" is a cipher for an unknown author, a name chosen because of its meaning and the ironical nature of the Markan material. Being named Mark myself, I am well aware that the name Latin name *Marcus* derives from the Roman god *Mars*, the god of war.[7] Tentatively, I have pondered whether Mark was chosen as a title for this book because of its irony. Set in a world defined by military force and expansion through war, the Jesus' story turns this on its head with Jesus waging "war" with "weapons" such as healing, preaching, service, and his sacrificial death. He raised an "army" of disciples to combat Satan and his power, and to overcome human hubris with cross-bearing service. It could be in the sovereignty of God that the Gospel of Mark was written by a disciple of that name, but that his name has a double-barreled edge.

While I quite like the latter idea because of its novelty and intrigue, the first perspective that the writer is John Mark of Jerusalem writing "Peter's gospel" somewhere near his point of death is to be favored. I believe we can be utterly confident it was written during the period of Nero's reign or in the subsequent period during or after his death in the early years of Vespasian and the destruction of Jerusalem. Mark's Gospel then is set during a time of Roman rule by might and force. More broadly, (as I will show), it is unquestionably set during a period in which human history was built around men vying for power through military might. It is the period of the warrior-ruler and his dynastic successors. It is into this world that Jesus enters. As such, I will use the name Mark for the writer of the Gospel and assume it is written sometime during the period AD 60–72. I will explore Mark in the context of colliding imperial forces.

---

6. See the summary in Reddish, *An Introduction to the Gospels*, 35–36.

7. It is from the old Latin *Martkos*, meaning "consecrated to the god Mars" and so can mean "God of war" or "to be warlike." It was very common in Rome. See "Mark (name)," https://en.wikipedia.org/wiki/Mark_(name).

THE IMPORTANCE OF MARK

Grasping the importance of Mark's Gospel is vital. While it is traditional to see Matthew as the first Gospel, a view held by a small group of scholars today (the so-called Griesbach hypothesis),[8] the overwhelming majority of contemporary scholars from all theological persuasions hold that Mark's Gospel is the first Gospel.[9] As such, Mark has a certain historical primacy being the *first recorded and surviving story of Jesus*.[10] The importance of Mark is seen through a cursory glance at the material in the other three Gospels. Clearly, both Matthew and Luke have used Mark's account as the basis for their accounts of Jesus. Of the four Gospels, only John diverges from this pattern as he utilized his own independent sources and/or perspective.[11]

It is clear then that Luke and Matthew supplemented Mark's material with other sources. Some material is unique to Matthew and Luke, and this indicates that they gathered some of their own data independently (so-called M and L material). Other material is common to both Matthew and Luke but not found in Mark. Scholars debate the nature of this material and whether it originally existed as some written document—a collection of sayings, ethical teachings, and parables. Some argue it is even an earlier written gospel. Others prefer to see it not as a written source but as oral material, or a combination thereof. Some argue Q never existed at all, and that Matthew used Mark and Luke used both Matthew and Luke, or vice versa. Indeed, there are a multiplicity of theories on all this.[12] The majority, however, agree that Matthew and Luke had access to material that was passed down in written and oral form and give it the label Q, from the German *Quelle*, meaning "source." It could be that Q is one of the sources Luke refers to in Luke 1:1 when he says, "many have undertaken to draw up an account of the things that have been fulfilled among us."

---

8. Farmer, *The Gospel of Jesus*.
9. E.g. Blomberg, *Jesus and the Gospels*, 79.
10. The letters of Paul of course precede Mark's Gospel, but are not "stories of Jesus" in any sense; although they give us great insight into who Jesus was for Paul. The view that the Gospel of Thomas is to be dated around this time is spurious; see Hartin, "The Gospel of Thomas." While Q may or may not have existed, its content hardly constitutes a Gospel, but a range of sayings and parables (see Paul Foster, "Q Source," who writes, "The Q document . . . is a compendium of Jesus material—mainly sayings, but also narratives—that appear to be directed toward those who identify themselves as followers of Jesus."
11. My personal view is that John knew of at least Mark and possibly Luke. However, this is not important to this discussion.
12. See, for a recent discussion, Tuckett, "The Current State," 9–50.

If this is correct, what matters is that both Matthew and Luke in their subsequent accounts of Jesus utilize Mark's material as the basis for their Gospels. Its use shows that Mark's Gospel was held in very great esteem by these authors and in some sense seen as a primary and vital record of the Jesus-story. It also supports that the material originated from Simon Peter.

Leaving this and other nuances of the debate about source aside, what matters is that Mark is highly important and seen as the primary source for the narrative of Jesus. Luke and Matthew effectively leave Mark's shape to the Jesus-story intact but add in other material as they work it toward their own goals. This all means that understanding Mark's Gospel is utterly critical for people who want to make sense of Jesus. As such, this study will initially focus on Mark's Gospel. After this, we will notice how Matthew and Luke have the irony implicit in Mark and amplified and moved it in different directions for their purposes.

APPROACH

Aside from accepting that Mark is the first full Gospel of Jesus we have, I will take the text as is without concern for the complexities of debates over its historicity. I will approach the text as found deemed to be the best text by *Nestle Aland* 28 with trust, assuming that Mark's record of events is "true" in the sense that he has sought to faithfully give an account of Jesus. Of course, what is written in Mark's Gospel is one moment in time from one man with all his biases. It is his take on the Jesus-story and so not complete. Even Luke felt this, as he took Mark and reshaped it for Theophilus (Luke 1:1–4). Yet, in my view, despite the significant efforts of decades of biblical scholarship with all its criteria for authenticity, we still have no absolute means of testing the veracity of Mark's component parts. Such analyses often reflect the biases of those who argue for or against this or that part of Mark's story being true or otherwise. I am accepting that what we have reflects a real situation in which the events, as Mark has summarized, happened. As such I will read Mark as a literary whole with a hermeneutic of trust.[13]

My approach to reading the text will be eclectic, a blend of form, redaction, and narrative critical approaches.[14] Regarding background, my

---

13. Whereby one approaches the text accepting its final form and the integrity of the author. It contrasts with a hermeneutic of suspicion where one comes with historical skepticism. I accept that this reflects my own bias as a confessing Christian with a high view of Scripture.

14. On these approaches to Scripture see Klein et al., *Introduction to Biblical Interpretation*, 52–70.

interest is to read the text from the perspective of the political and military perspective of ancient imperialism which dominated the milieu. That is, as Mark's Jesus went about his business and finally went to the cross, how was he being experienced by the disciples and others who fully and justifiably (considering Israel's ancient writings and a world of colliding empires) expected a military intervention from God or his agent (Theo)? How was Jesus being interpreted? Why did they not understand him? Why did his people kill him? Why did it take the resurrection for them to "get it"?

Because of this approach, much about Mark will be glossed over. That is the nature of writing a book like this. I am also not seeking to write an academic work such as a doctoral thesis or pure New Testament scholarship with masses of supporting footnotes and engagement with the full field. Rather, I am seeking to write a book that an educated Christian can understand. There will be footnotes, but I hope they are not too complex and serve only to give some justification at times and fill things out for readers. My prayer and hope are that all who find Jesus an interesting figure will be stimulated to live lives that reflect his desire to see a world shaped by love, humility, non-violence, justice, and service.

2

A World of Colliding Empires: The Roman World

As I have noted in the introduction above, the world in which Mark wrote was a world of conflict where empires and powerful rulers fought for dominance. Setting this in its context is important.

ROME

At the time of Mark's account, Rome held sway over the region. Over the previous three hundred or so years, Rome had expanded its influence through military might.[1] Important in this were the Punic wars in which Rome clashed with the Carthaginian Empire led by great military leaders such as Hannibal (see on this later). In three great conflicts, Rome assumed control of North Africa, Spain, and parts of Gaul (France). The maps below show the astonishing expansion:[2]

---

1. A nice summary is found in 1 Macc 8:1–16 of early Roman exploits.

2. "The Roman Empire," http://www.worldhistory.timemaps.com/roman-empire/AD1.htm.

The Expansion of the Roman Empire

Roman Empire 200 BC

Roman Empire AD 1

Roman Empire AD 200

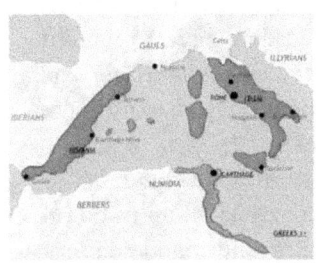
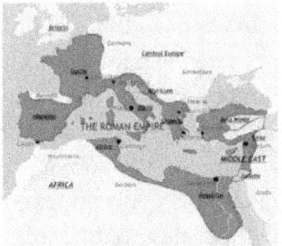
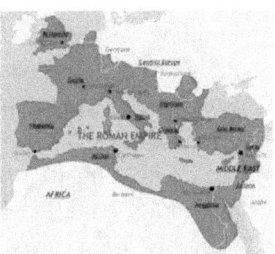

In the latter half of the first century BC, through Julius Caesar (100–44 BC) and the civil war that followed his assassination, the Roman Republic was ended. Then, through Octavian (Augustus Caesar, 63 BC–AD 14), who ruled from 27 BC to his death, the Roman Empire was formed under a dictator, the emperor, and Roman rule was extended. In the first century AD, this expansion was in full sway, expanding into Britain, and would culminate in the early second century and hold into the third century, after which Rome declined. Israel, in which Mark's Gospel is set, came under Roman rule after Pompey conquered Jerusalem in 63 BC; his entry into Jerusalem was achieved through a political split in the Jewish ranks, with some allowing Pompey's army in to secure the city. He then assaulted the temple with a ramp, eventually entering and butchering twelve thousand within. He then restored the high priest Hyrcanus. Josephus wrote, "for now we lost our liberty, and became subject to the Romans."[3] From this point on, Rome ruled Israel. At the time of Christ's ministry some seventy or so years later, Tiberius was emperor, and Roman rule was unquestioned. We see Rome's dominance in the Gospels themselves with references to Romans being quite common;[4] and at Rome's climax, Pilate, as the Roman prefect, sentenced Jesus to death.[5] Whatever the precise background to Mark's Gospel before or during Nero's reign another thirty or so years later, it is written into a region completely dominated by Roman might.

---

3. Josephus, *Ant.* 14.54–79. Quote from page 77.

4. See, e.g. Mark 12:14–17 and parr.; 15:39, 44–45 and parr.; Matt 8:5–13 and par.; Luke 2:1; 3:1; 23:2; John 11:48; 19:12, 15, etc.

5. Evans notes that Pilate was prefect rather than procurator, as prior to Agrippa I (41–44 AD), Roman governors were prefects (*Mark 8:27—16:20*, 476).

GREECE (MACEDONIA)

Prior to Rome's dominion, Greece had dominated the region after the blitzkrieg of the Macedonian Alexander the Great between 334 and 323 BC.[6] Building on the work of his father Phillip II of Macedon, he had achieved the great Greek dream of moving east from Greece into Asia Minor, the Fertile Crescent, Egypt, and even as far as India, conquering all in his path. This was achieved through military force and cunning.

According to Josephus, Israel was subjugated to Alexander after his father Philip was killed by Pausanias. Alexander entered Asia Minor (modern western Turkey) crossing the Hellespont (Dardanelles) and conquered Asia Minor and the whole of modern Turkey, Damascus, Sidon, and besieged Tyre. Alexander sought support for his army, as he attacked Tyre, from Jaddua, the Jewish high priest. Jaddua refused because he was pledged to Darius III Codommanus (336–331 BC), the then (and final) Persian ruler. Sadly, Jaddua had backed the wrong horse (playing the Game of Thrones involves dangerous gambles!). Alexander was infuriated and, after destroying Tyre, besieged Gaza. The high priest Jaddua, purportedly warned in a dream, ensured that Jerusalem was adorned, the people dressed in white, and the priests dressed in full clerical clothing. With priests and citizens, he welcomed Alexander into the city without violence, due to Alexander supposedly earlier receiving a vision of the high priest (Josephus, *Ant.* 11.304–47). Israel chose subjugation rather than destruction.

After his death in 323 BC, after a period of vying for power (as there often is in such cases), the Macedonian Empire was divided into four blocks: the Ptolemaic Kingdom of Egypt, the Seleucid Empire in the East, the Kingdom of Pergamon in Asia Minor, and Macedon. These more or less held reign until the Romans broke up their rule in the second to first centuries BC. This was not a time of peace and security, however, with constant skirmishes and wars across the region. Hellenization dominance was so great that, even into the time of Roman rule, the Greek language and culture remained dominant. Indeed, the impact of Greek reign would be felt for centuries. This influence is seen in that the New Testament documents are written in Koine Greek, the *lingua franca* of the Roman Empire.

---

6. There is a nice little summary of Alexander in 1 Macc 1:1–9 which speaks of his glorious victories and death.

THE PERSIANS

Prior to Greece, Israel was subjugated to the second Persian Empire (550–330 BC). True to Isaiah's prophecy (Isa 44:28; 45:1),[7] the ruler Cyrus had liberated Israel from bondage to the Babylonians. Cyrus was originally the son of a nomadic tribal ruler who revolted and conquered the Medes. He forged together Medes and Persians (so Medo-Persia), and they dominated the Near East for two hundred years. Like all imperial leaders, he sought to extend his rule. He overthrew Lydia and then Babylon in 539 BC, ultimately entering Babylon without resistance.[8] Cyrus allowed those in exile to return and rebuild the temple, albeit while still in bondage to Medo-Persian rule (2 Chr 36:22–23; Ezra 1:1, 7–8; 3:7; 4:3, 5; 5:13–17; 6:3, 14; Dan 1:21; 6:28; 10:1).

THE BABYLONIANS

Before the Medo-Persians, Israel was subdued by the neo-Babylonians (636–539 BC). The destruction of Jerusalem is recorded in biblical history. In 2 Kings 24–25, Nebuchadnezzar subjugated Judah's kin Jehoiakim for three years (609–598 BC), after which Jehoiakim rebelled against him. This led to war, with Chaldeans, Syrians, Moabites, and Ammonites devastating Judah. After Jehoiachin succeeded as king (598/597 BC), Nebuchadnezzar besieged Jerusalem, pillaging the temple, and Jehoiachin was taken into exile (2 Kgs 24:1–17). Zedekiah (597–586 BC) succeeded Jehoiachin, but ultimately rebelled against Babylon. This led to Jerusalem being besieged, utter starvation for those in the city, an escape by the Zedekiah and others, and Zedekiah's capture. Zedekiah's sons were killed before him and his eyes taken out. He was then taken in chains to Babylon. The goods from the

---

7. Some see this as an example of *Vaticinium ex eventu* ("prophecy after the event") which is possible but not able to be proven. Robinson and Harrison, "Isaiah," 1508, very perceptively state: "There is really no valid objection to the prediction of Cyrus. For the one outstanding differentiating characteristic of Israel's religion is predictive prophecy. The Hebrews certainly predicted the coming of a messiah. Indeed, the Hebrews were the only people of antiquity whose 'Golden Age' lay in the future rather than in the past. Accordingly, to predict the coming of a Cyrus as the *human* agent of Israel's salvation is but the reverse side of the same prophet's picture of the *Divine* agent, namely, the obedient, Suffering Servant of Yahweh, who would redeem Israel from its sin. Deny to Isaiah the son of Amoz the prediction concerning Cyrus, and it is but logical to go farther and to deny to him the messianic hope which is usually associated with his name. Deny to Isaiah the son of Amoz the predictions concerning a *return* from captivity, and the prophecies of his book are robbed of their essential character and unique perspective. Emasculate those portions of the Book of Isaiah which unveil the future, and they are reduced to a mere *vaticinium ex eventu*, and their religious value as Divine oracles is largely lost."

8. Hoglund, "Cyrus," 306.

temple were taken to Babylon and the temple destroyed by fire. Israel was subjugated violently by the Babylonians (2 Kgs 25:1–30).[9]

BEFORE THE BABYLONIANS

Before the Babylonian destruction and exile, the dominant force was the Neo-Assyrians (934–609 BC). Shalmanesar V (726–722 BC) besieged Samaria with the city falling in 722/721 BC with many taken into exile (2 Kgs 17:1–6; 18:10–11).[10] The Assyrian ruler Sennacherib (704–681 BC) also invaded Judah during Hezekiah's reign. As is often the case in dynastic succession, Sennacherib rebuilt Nineveh. He also engaged in war, destroying Babylon (689 BC). Following a rebellion against Assyrian rule in 701 BC and defeating the Philistines, he led an invasion of Judah. After defeating many of the cities of Judah, he besieged Jerusalem but failed to defeat it (2 Kgs 18:13—19:36; 2 Chr 32:1–22; Isa 36:1—37:38). In the period before this, the region was dominated by a range of empires including the Egyptians (1570–1070 BC), the Hittites (1460–1180 BC), the Babylonians (1900–1600 BC), and the Akkadians (2300–2200 BC).

BEYOND THE MEDITERRANEAN

As we will see in more detail in chapter 3, in other parts of the world, little was different. There were the great dynasties, such as in China, that ultimately extended for nearly five millennia, and a number in India. Others included the Carthaginian Empire in North Africa (650–146 BC), the Parthian Empire (247 BC–224 AD), the Armenian Empire (190 BC–428 AD), the Goguryeo Empire of Korea (37 BC–AD 678), and so on. More importantly, as both the Greeks and Romans found as they expanded, they met strong violent resistance from the barbarians wherever they went—the world was run by men with political power and weapons.

What stands out through human history until the emergence of Jesus is the way in which the world was defined by power through despot, sword, bow, and spear. Power was achieved through military force and dynastic succession; it was maintained through force and gaining sufficient wealth. This was realized through expansion and exacting tribute. Power

---

9. See also on Nebuchadnezzar: 2 Chr 36; Jer 21:2, 7; 22:24; 24:1; 25:1, 9; 27:6, 8, 20; 28:3, 11, 14; 29:1, 3, 21; 32:1, 28; 34:1; 35:11; 37:1; 39:1, 5, 11; 43:10; 44:30; 46:2, 13, 26, 28; 49:30; 50:17; 51:34; 52:4, 12, 28–30; Ezek 26:7, 18–19; 30:10; Dan 1:1, 18; 2:1, 28, 46; 3:1–28; 4:1, 4, 18, 28–37; 5:2, 11, 18.

10. See Kuan, "Shalmaneser," 1195–96.

was reflected in glorious monuments to self and gods, multitudes of women (wives, concubines), and supposed wisdom. It was a survival of the fittest world. Power was gained by warrior-kings and their dynastic successors—many of whom were not at all warrior-like, but built monuments to themselves and basked in opulent obesity in the glory of the victories of yesteryear. At times these dynasties were broken through a coup or invasion in which another warrior-figure assumed control and destroyed anyone from the previous reign, setting in place another dynastic order. At yet other times, there would be a period of instability as rival forces fought for control until one or other became dominant, wiped out their enemies, and assumed leadership. Always, military power was central. Reign was established and maintained with severe force with enemies removed and friends rewarded. It was a "dog-eat-dog" world.

AUGUSTUS AND TIBERIUS

Mark sets his Gospel in the life of Jesus. Jesus was born while Augustus was emperor (27 BC–AD 14). He ministered while Tiberius ruled (AD 14–37). It was Julius Caesar who functioned as warrior-king, as the Roman Republic disintegrated and reestablished the conditions for Augustus to be the first emperor of the Roman Empire and to launch the Julio–Claudian dynastic period. After Julius Caesar's murder, Augustus defeated all claimants to power and established the Empire. Through a series of wars and shrewd politicking, he brought "peace" (*Pax Augustus*). Rome's peace was due to her prodigious influence and power. It was a stratified society, with the emperor supreme, power in the hands of those with wealth and power, and citizenship highly valued and sought after, with much of the empire run by slaves. Tiberius inherited a strong, peaceful empire, and generally speaking, continued the "good" work of Augustus.

NERO

At the time of the writing of Mark, it is during or just after the reign of Nero (AD 54–68), the last of the Julio-Claudian dynasty begun by Augustus. Like Caligula (AD 37–41), Nero represents the ultimate archetype to Jesus, his reign demonstrating well the limits of ultimate power against which Jesus vividly stands. His mother Agrippina, the great-granddaughter of Augustus, poisoned her second husband and helped organize the murder of Claudius's wife, Valeria Messalina. She then married her uncle Claudius (incest is a feature of much imperialism). After Claudius had adopted

Nero, she devoted herself to ensuring Nero ascended the throne, persuading Claudius that Nero should succeed him over his son Britannicus. Nero married Claudius's daughter Octavia. Agrippina eliminated opposition and likely poisoned Claudius, after which Nero was proclaimed emperor at age seventeen by the Praetorian Guard under her ally Burrus. Nero assumed control of Rome with his advisors Burrus and his tutor Seneca.[11] Nero, like his predecessor Claudius (41–54 AD), was initially a reasonable dictator (if such a thing exists), and "Up to the year 59, Nero's biographers cite only acts of generosity and clemency on his account. His government, mainly in the hands of Burrus and Seneca, forbade contests in the circus involving bloodshed, banned capital punishment, reduced taxes, and accorded permission to slaves to bring civil complaints against unjust masters."[12] He also removed secret imperial trials, corrupt freedmen, and granted more independence to the Senate. He sponsored the arts and sport. He granted assistance after disasters, including giving aid to the Jews on one occasion. However, during this time Nero lived to satiate his pleasures, including delighting in fighting on the streets at night.

In AD 59 Nero became an altogether different leader. First, after a comedy of errors including seeking and failing to kill his mother Agrippina with a collapsing ship, he sent assassins to kill her. He murdered Octavia in AD 62 after falling in love with Poppaea Sabina, a young wife of a senator and the future emperor, Otho. He then married Poppaea, who died, purportedly kicked to death by Nero, and married again. In AD 59, he also began to give arranged and public performances in chariots and on the lyre. In AD 63 he became enamored with religion and novel cults. His two advisors, Burrus (who died likely by poison) and Seneca (who retired), were replaced by the brutal head of the Praetorian Guard, Tigellinus. After the fire of Rome, which may have been orchestrated by Nero himself, he blamed the Christians and put many to death. After the fire, he also built an enormous Golden House, including a monument like the Colossus of Rhodes, topped with an image of his head. The home was enormous, designed to fill a third of the city ultimately. After his death, it was destroyed and the Colosseum built in its place. It is likely he had Paul and Peter put to death sometime in his later years. During revolts, and after being sentenced to death by the Senate by crucifixion (the ultimate humiliation), Nero fled and either killed

---

11. Biblical readers will be interested to note that Gallio, proconsul of Corinth at the time of Paul's evangelization (Acts 18:12–17, AD 50–52, see the Gallio Inscription from Delphi) was Seneca's (the then tutor of Nero) older brother linking Paul to Roman politics. See Nash, "Gallio," 481.

12. "Nero." http://www.britannica.com/EBchecked/topic/409505/Nero, para 4.

himself by cutting his throat or was killed on Cynthos.[13] After his death, Rome had a period of instability as men vied for power in the so-called year of the four emperors. Vespasian (AD 69–79) then assumed control, launching the period of the Flavians.

Nero is one of those despots of history who represents the zenith of humanity's lust for debauchery, glory, and power. It is against this backdrop that Mark is to be understood.

---

13. See "Nero," http://academic.eb.com/levels/collegiate/article/Nero/55320. See also "Ofonius Tigellinus," http://academic.eb.com/levels/collegiate/article/Ofonius-Tigellinus/72438. See also "Ancient Rome," http://academic.eb.com/levels/collegiate/article/ancient-Rome/106272.

3

A World of Colliding Empires: The Rest of the Known World at the Time of Christ

THE PURPOSE OF THIS chapter is to explore what was going on in the world outside the Roman Empire in the years leading up to the coming of Christ. In particular, I will demonstrate that, broadly speaking, the same exercise of political and military force and the clashing of empires were not limited to the flow of events in regions around the Mediterranean Sea. Rather, it was a universal state of affairs as humans vied for power across humanity. This can be easily demonstrated.

CHINA'S DYNASTIES

China's history leading to the time of Christ demonstrates well how military imperial force defined the world. Although records are uncertain, they likely indicate a series of dynasties from 2100 BC until the early twentieth-century and the emergence of modern China. Before the time of Christ, the third and second millennia "were marked by the appearance of increasing warfare, complex urban settlements, intense status differentiation, and administrative and religious hierarchies that legitimated and controlled the mobilization of Labor for dynastic work or warfare."[1] These included the Xia Dynasty (ca. 2100–1600 BC) (disputed), the Shang Dynasty (ca. 1600–1046 BC), the Zhou Dynasty (ca. 1046–256 BC), and the Qin Dynasty (221–207 BC).[2] The Zhou Dynasty lasted some eight centuries after overcoming the

---

1. Hucker and Chan, "China," http://academic.eb.com/levels/collegiate/article/China/117321.

2. Dates from ibid. For further descriptions see this article, and for more detail see

Shang Dynasty over three generations of conflict, in which the Zhou were led by Wenwang, the conqueror Wuwang, and Zhougong. It featured feudal states vying for power. The Qin Dynasty period is also called Imperial China, as the Qin emperor took control of large sections of the Han Chinese area and united them together around the center of Xianyang and a doctrine of legalism based on a legal code and the emperor's absolute authority. This assumption of power aided military expansion with political opposition savagely subdued, and the burning of books and killing of intellectuals who in any way opposed the Qin doctrine.[3]

The link between religion and the dynastic rule is also central. In the first millennium before Christ, the term "Hua-Zia" was used of the Zhou-ruled region. It denotes the Sinitic people and their territory, commonly called "All Under Heaven" ruled by a "Son of Heaven." It involved yielding to the Zhou mandate of Heaven, worship of the Zhou ancestors, participation in the spoken and written Chinese language community, and even certain standards of conduct, ritual, manners, and dress.[4]

It was expected that imperial claimants would continue the tradition of a "Son of Heaven." The emperors stood in this tradition, their political rule buttressed by religion.

At the time of Christ, China was under the Han Dynasty (206/202 BC–AD 220), which Major and Cook divide into the Western Han Dynasty (206 BC–AD 7) and Eastern (or later) Han Dynasty (AD 25–220). Jesus was then born in the final days of the Western Han period, and his resurrection and growth of the Christian faith began in the early days of the Eastern Han era.

The Dynasty developed through rebellion against the Qin. Liu Bang assumed the title "king of Han" in 206 BC and there followed intense war to secure power. Qin armies were devastated, rivals were murdered or committed suicide, until Bang became the undisputed ruler of China.[5] Five rulers

---

Major and Cook, *Ancient China*, "Eras, Cultures, Nations, States, and Dynasties." They note that "dynasty" is hard to define, and prefer "era" or "age." The "three dynasties" are Xia, Shang, and Zhou kingdoms, although the Zhou dynasty is disputed. However, through the whole ancient history of China we see the world of colliding empires at play.

3. In this time, "Millions of people were dragooned to the huge construction jobs, many dying on the long journey to their destination . . . Weapons were confiscated. Hundreds of intellectuals were massacred for daring to criticize the emperor's policies. Books . . . were kept out of public circulation because the emperor considered such knowledge to be dangerous and unsettling. These things have contributed to make Shihuangdi appear the arch tyrant of Chinese history" (see Hucker and Chan, "China," http://academic.eb.com/levels/collegiate/article/China/117321). While possibly exaggerated, this is classic stuff of empires and power.

4. Major and Cook, *Ancient China*, "Introduction" to "The Western Zhou Period."

5. Ibid., "The Struggle to Succeed Qin."

led the Western Han Empire from 202 to 87 BC. This was a period involving territorial expansion, economic and military power, cultural expression, and controlling mothers seeking power for sons.[6]

During the later Western Han Dynasty, from 87 BC to AD 6, six emperors reigned and the period was unstable. Jesus was born into the world just after the relatively stable reign of Emperor Cheng (33–7 BC). As is common in a world of clashing powers, in an established dynasty, Cheng is renowned for licentious behavior and showed little concern for the government. He was infatuated with a certain woman named Zhao Feiyan ("Flying Swallow Zhao") from the royal harem, whom he married. She did not produce an heir, so other children born of his concubines were brutally murdered to ensure they did not seize the throne after his death. He was succeeded in 7 BC by his chosen heir, Emperor Ai. Emperor Ai continued the sexual licentiousness of Cheng, notorious for a sexual relationship with another man, Dong Xian. He went as far as preparing to abdicate to grant Dong the throne. Dong committed suicide after Grand Empress Dowager Wang stripped him of power.[7]

The Western Han Dynasty was throughout marked by fights for power including the challenge in AD 9 by another claimant of the Mandate of Heaven, Wang Mang, who became emperor after Ai. He led the short-lived attempt at a Xin Dynasty. He is vilified in history as a "nepotistic conspirator, a rebel, a usurper who deserved his ugly death."[8] So, when Christ was in his teens, we have a classic demonstration of a world of colliding empires. Mang was a bright, charismatic man, ambitious for power, deceitful and ruthless. He buttressed his claims with supposed omens pointing to his divine sonship. He introduced China's first income tax. He marginalized aristocrats—a mistake, for this created deep antagonism. He sought the submission of the Han, but in the end, as is expected, he had to use force, which ultimately weakened his power. The cataclysmic flood of AD 11 was seen as a bad omen. It led to famine and revolts. Ultimately, Wang died in battle in AD 23 as the Han Dynasty fought back. The Han Dynasty was reaffirmed in AD 25 by Guangwu, who reigned until AD 57, and his descendants to AD 220.[9] After Guangwu's death, his son Ming became emperor, and a time of peace prevailed.

During the Han period:

---

6. Ibid., "Challenges to Imperial Authority."
7. Ibid., "The Fate of the Huo Clan."
8. Ibid., "Disruption and Usurpation: The Xin Dynasty."
9. For detail, see ibid., "The Han Restoration, the Eastern Han Dynasty, and the Three Kingdoms Period."

there were only a few short periods marked by dynastic strength, stable government, and intensive administration. Several reigns were characterized by palace intrigue and corrupt influences at court, and on a number of occasions the future of the dynasty was seriously endangered by outbreaks of violence, seizure of political power, or a crisis in the imperial succession.[10]

During the Han dynasty, China extended its empire, taking territory from the Xiongnu (Huns) including Gansu, Ningxia, and Qinghai. This opened up the Silk Road for trade with the West. It also expanded conquest to the shores of the Caspian Sea. There is evidence of Roman embassies to China in Chinese writings in AD 166 and 284.

There is also evidence of internal conflict with Wang Mang leading a revolt seeking land and economic reform to weaken the power of the elite and forming the Xin ("New") Dynasty in AD 9. This led to a period of chaos and uprisings. Ultimately, Emperor Guangwu restored the Han Dynasty with the support of the wealthy. Eventually, the Han Dynasty declined until the Yellow Turban Rebellion of AD 184 and the period of the warlords. After this time, successive Dynasties reigned up until 1911. The period is full of wars and invasions, and it is fair to say that political rule was maintained by military force.

CENTRAL ASIA

The region of Xiongnu was peopled by nomads; they had numerous military clashes with the Chinese dynasties of Shang and Zhou, who would often conquer and enslave them. In 215 BC, driven by a military ambition to extend the Qin Empire, the Chinese invaded Xiongnu and drove them to the Mongolian Plateau. This led to the formation under Touman of a tribal confederacy in 209 BC, forming the first large Steppe Empire, the Xiongnu. This empire covered much of present Siberia and Mongolia. They were fierce horseback warriors. This enabled them to be better prepared to counter the Chinese. The Great Wall of China was constructed as a barrier between China and the Xiongnu. Under Modu Chanyu, who first killed off his father Touman, the empire was expanded with the conquering of nomadic people such as the Dingling to the north in southern Siberia, the Donghu in eastern Mongolia and Manchuria, and the Yuezhi, and the reoccupation of the land taken by the Qin general Meng Tian. They even threatened the

10. Hucker and Chan, "China."

Hun Dynasty. When they overthrew the Yuezhi in Gansu, Modu's son Jizhu made a cup out of the skull of the Yuezhi king.[11]

In 200 BC, the Han Dynasty launched a campaign to subdue Xiongnu. However, the Xiongnu forces ambushed them and surrounded the Han emperor Gao for seven days, forcing his submission and, ultimately, a treaty signed in 198 BC—peace through violent force. This also involved the Chinese paying annual tribute to Xiongnu and royal intermarriage (two features of ancient politics). After Modu's death in 174 BC, the empire was divided up left and right. The supreme ruler was labeled "Son of Heaven" (chanyu), and the empire was highly and precisely stratified. The Xiongnu-Chinese treaty held for sixty years until full-scale war again broke out in 129 BC and lasted on and off for some years, with the Chinese taking back significant territory. Between 60–53 BC, civil war broke out in Xiongnu due to claims of power among the descendants of the twelfth Chanyu at his death. In the ensuing years after 53 BC, into the early part of the first-century AD, the leader of Xiongnu submitted to Han China with Xiongnu agreeing to send representatives to pay homage, send a hostage prince, and pay tribute to the Han emperor.

INDIA'S DYNASTIES

The Indian story shows similar kinds of political and military patterns.[12] During the Vedic period (ca. 1500–500 BC), those in the Indus region were mainly agricultural with a move to settled villages. However, there were a series of kingdoms, including the Kurus and the Mahajanapadas, which involved sixteen powerful kingdoms and republics across the Indo-Gangetic plains. There were also smaller kingdoms across the whole region. In some, kingship was hereditary, while in others, rulers were elected.

As in the world of the Bible, the Empires of the Mediterranean clashed with the eastern peoples in the region we call Pakistan and India.[13] From ca. 520 to 326 BC, much of what we would know as Eastern Afghanistan and Pakistan came under the rule of the Achaemenid Kingdom during the

---

11. See "Xiongnu People," http://academic.eb.com/levels/collegiate/article/Xiongnu/41305.

12. Interestingly, the Hindu tradition, as with that of Judaism and Christianity, begins with the Flood in the *Satapatha Brahmana*, cf. Gen 6—9. It is dated by some at 3102 BC, while others see this as the date for the great Bharata War, and others 1400 BC (see Keay, *India: A History*, "The Harappan World C3000–1700 BC").

13. The first use of the term "Hindu" is found in an inscription in Persepolis in Iran, the capital of the Persian or Achaemenid empire led by Darius. See ibid., 56–78.

reign of Darius the Great.[14] Some of the Indians served in the Achaemenid forces as archers, cavalry, and chariots, and fought against the Spartans at Thermopylae and the Greeks at Plataea.[15] Indeed, Cyrus, Israel's deliverer after exile, was killed there in battle around 530 BC.

Sometime in the mid-fifth century, in the context of rival holy men traveling the country giving physical and spiritual evidence of their prowess to gain patronage, Siddhartha Gautama or "Buddha" emerged. He encountered the king of Magadha, Bimbisara. Magadha had a well-organized and well-equipped military. Bimbisara and other kings patronized Bhudda's teaching. An example of standard brutal imperialism is the demise of Bimbisara. One of his sons, Ajatashatru, likely seized the throne by force and starved his father to death—a standard situation in ancient Indian history.[16] Ajatashatru then went to war with the likes of Koshala and the Licchavis to extend the Magadha empire through wars provoked by political marriage, dowries, land-claims, and such things. Succession struggles were also normative, with Ajatashatru fighting his brother over a priceless necklace. After Ajatashatru's death, history is vague but involved "mainly court intrigues and murders" with "the throne changing hands frequently."[17] Ultimately, Mahapadma Nanda of low-caste origins remarkably gained power and extended his kingdom to include the entire Ganga Valley, Orissa, and parts of the central regions of India. Importantly, he was the first to be entitled "one-umbrella sovereign" and "the first great historical emperor of northern India." As one expects of imperial dominance, Nada had an enormous military, including twenty thousand cavalries, two hundred thousand infantries, two thousand chariots, and up to six thousand elephants.[18] The empire also developed a catapult for firing rocks, which enabled many victories.

Around this time, in 326 BC, Alexander reached the northwest frontier of the Indian subcontinent and conquered a large part of the Punjab, defeating King Puru in the Battle of Hydaspes (modern Jhelum, Pakistan). The accounts speak of bloody wars as Alexander sought to extend Macedonian rule. However, after his army (exhausted from marching twenty-five thousand kilometers over eight years and fighting endless wars) mutinied at Hyphasis (modern Beas), they turned back before facing the Nanda Empire of Magadha and that of Gangaridai in Bengal. As they returned, Alexander was badly wounded by an arrow in the chest. He would die two years later.

14. Keay, *India*, "Out of the Myth-Smoke"—the region of Gandhara or Gadara.
15. Ibid.
16. Ibid., "The March of Magadha."
17. Ibid.
18. Ibid.

These invasions may have affected India's political system, especially in the Mauryan dynasty, while Gandhara (Afghanistan, NW Pakistan) became what is known as Greco-Buddhist, a fusion of Indian, Persian, Central Asian, and Greek cultures until the fifth century AD[19]

Important to this discussion is the expansive Maurya Empire (321–185 BC)[20] ruled by the Mauryan Dynasty. This was established by Chandragupta Maurya, who is described as "an Indian Julius Caesar."[21] After a failed *coup* d'état, the Nandas were defeated militarily. Chandragupta also made peace with Seleucus I Nicator who, after Alexander, ruled the eastern half of the Macedonian Empire. The empire was continued by Bindusara, the relatively unknown son of Chandragupta. He was known to the Greeks as "Amitrochates," meaning "slayer of enemies," suggesting he continued his father's military conquests.[22] His son was the renowned Ashoka, "Beloved of God," a licentious and ruthless young man who killed all rivals, including his ninety-nine brothers! Legend has it he visited hell to gain torture ideas! He also conquered the Kalinga, with one hundred thousand people killed in the conflict, and many more after the war. Another one hundred fifty thousand were deported. Supposedly, repulsed by the carnage, Ashoka took on Buddhism, renounced violence and war, and became what many consider a great leader.[23] He focused his life on *dhamma*, "mercy, charity, truthfulness and purity."[24] This was considered revolutionary, for one of the core sacred duties of an Indian king was the conquest of neighboring regions. Ashoka sent envoys to five Greek kings and had close relations with Sri Lanka. At its peak, his empire extended from the boundary of the Himalayas in the north, to the east in modern Assam, and in the west beyond modern Pakistan and much of Afghanistan. It extended into central and southern India through Chandragupta and Bindusara.[25] The forested tribal area of Kalinga remained under the rule of Ashoka, who was important in the spread of Buddhism. The last Maurya leader was killed around AD 180, unsurprisingly murdered by the commander of his armies, Pushyamitra. The Shunga

---

19. Ibid., "The Macedonian Intrusion," notes that for Indian historians, Alexander's incursion was barely a blip and that his great achievement was reaching India at all. See Keay's account for details.

20. Ibid., "An Indian Julius Caesar," dates it 320–200 BC.

21. Ibid. Keay makes the excellent point that, chronologically, Julius Caesar is "a Roman Changragupta."

22. Ibid., "The Greatest of Kings."

23. Ibid.

24. Ibid.

25. See further, ibid., "An Indian Julius Caesar," for discussion over the southern extent of the kingdom, which is disputed.

dynasty ruled for one hundred and ten years, ending with the assassination of its final king by one of his many female consorts, and the Kanva ruled what was left of the empire for another fifty years.

As the time of Christ approached, there was a range of kings such as Kharavela of Kalinga, Shatavahana of the Deccan, a Tamil confederation in the south, and the Yavanas (Greeks) who infiltrated due to the weakness of the Mauryas. The Greeks include Demetrius II (ca. 180 BC) followed by Menander and Antialcidas (ca. 110 BC). There were also incursions by the Parthians in the first century BC.[26]

There were also wars, including the defeat of the Sunga Empire in the north by Satakarni. Kharavela, the warrior-king of Kalinga, also ruled a large area and was important in the spread of Jainism. His empire, the Kharavela Jain Empire, was a powerful trader across Southeast Asia. There is also evidence that the empired colonized Sri Lanka, Burma, the Maldives, and the Malay Archipelago.

The Kuninda Kingdom formed a huge empire from Tajikistan to the mid-Ganges. There were also a few different empires in the south during the period leading to the time of Christ which warred regularly, seeking to gain dominance. These included the Pandyans, Cholas, Cheras, Kadambas, Western Gangas, Pallavas, and Chalukyas. In the north, there were a number of hybrid cultures formed after invasions. These include the Indo-Greek Kingdom formed after the Greco-Bactrian Demetrius invaded in 180 BC, and which lasted almost two hundred years under over thirty conflicting Greek kings, i.e. almost to the time of Christ, as well as the Indo-Scythian, Indo-Parthian, and Indo-Sassanid empires at various times across the continent. There is evidence of Roman trade as early as AD 1 after Augustus, with up to one hundred twenty ships, sailed from Myos Hormos to India, the Romans exchanging vast amounts of money for luxuries.

While this history is clouded, there is good evidence that the Indian subcontinent was also a scene of massive turmoil and conflict between empires based on war, wealth, and power.[27]

SOUTHEAST ASIA

From what we know of Southeast Asia at the time of Christ, the quest for power through political and military might was little different than the rest of the world.

26. See ibid., "In the Dynastic Wilderness."
27. See further Subrahmanyam and Alam, "India," http://academic.eb.com/levels/collegiate/article/India/111197.

The history of Burma (Myanmar) until recent times was premised on struggles between kingdoms in the interior and those of the Irrawaddy Delta. There were also ongoing dynastic disruptions in Lower and Upper Burma.[28] The earliest kingdom in Burma was the Tagaung, founded by the Indian prince Abhiraja (ninth century BC). Surprisingly, after his death, rather than civil war, his two sons engaged in a contest of strength allowing one to succeed him. However, Tagaung was razed, and another Indian prince, Dhajaraja, rebuilt it. The kingdom was subsequently destroyed by the Pyu and the final king, Bhinnakaraja, moved south, and three groups emerged.[29]

In Indonesia, around 2000 BC, Austronesians, who now dominate the Indonesian population, migrated to Southeast Asia from Taiwan or China. They pushed the Melanesian peoples to the east, likely through military dominance. Small kingdoms flourished in Indonesia from the eighth to first-century BC. One example is the Kingdom of Funan around the first century AD, which was located in the Mekong Delta of southern Vietnam and southern Indochina. This may have been a collective of city-states who warred at times and at other times formed a single political unit.

From the second to fifteenth century, the kingdom of Langkasuka dominated the northern area of the Malay Peninsula. In the southern part of the peninsula, the Srivijaya Kingdom, which flourished between the seventh and thirteenth centuries, was dominant.

In the Philippines, there were four distinct kinds of peoples, including forest hunter-gatherer tribal groups, the Ifugao Cordillera Highlanders in the mountains, trading harbor principalities, and stratified warrior societies who practiced ritual warfare and roamed the plains.[30]

In Vietnam, according to legend, the Hong Bang Period/Dynasty ran for two and a half millennia from 2879 to 258 BC. Loc Tuc became ruler of Vietnam in 2879 BC and was declared king by the other tribal leaders, and the dynasty ran for eighteen generations. He ruled over a wide area of Northern Vietnam and parts of southeastern China. Legends indicate war using armor, horses, staffs, and archery were important aspects of life. The dynasty came to an end in 258 BC with conflict, overthrown by Thuc Phan, the ruler of the neighboring Au Viet tribes. In alliance with the Lac Viet tribes, the Thục Dynasty (257–207 BC) formed, centered on a fortified Co Loa, just north of present-day Hanoi.

In 207 BC, the Thục Dynasty was succeeded by the Trieu Dynasty (207–111 BC) when Qin warlord Zhao Tuo defeated the Thuc ruler. This was

---

28. Cotterell, *A History*, 4.
29. Ibid., 4–8.
30. Legarda, "Cultural Landmarks," 40.

made possible because of information gained when Zhao's son married the daughter of An Dương Vương. Zhao Tuo annexed Au Lac and established himself king of Nan Yue from his base in Guangdong in southern China. He was disdainful toward the Chinese Han ruler. However, when he learned that the Han would kill his entire family, he yielded.[31] His son drowned himself when his wife was killed in the war that ensued. The story of colliding empires goes on!

In 111 BC, armies of China's Han Dynasty invaded Nanyue and divided Vietnam up, mostly under Chinese officials. Chinese culture, language, Taoism, and Confucianism were imposed. Their rule lasted until 39 AD[32] when a revolt led by the Trung sisters (Trung Trac, Trung Nhi), who were ferocious warrior, succeeded in overcoming the Han. Trungg Trac became Queen, but she and her sister committed suicide when the Han counter-attacked under General Ma Yuan. Their heads were then sent to China, and there was a mass surrender to the Chinese.[33] The Han regained control and imposed Chinese culture, including sending many Chinese immigrants, brutally eliminating the power of the Vietnamese nobles. They reigned until AD 544, although they had to quell further revolts, including one led by another woman, (Lady) Trieu Thi Trinh in AD 248.

SOUTHERN RUSSIAN REGION (THE SCYTHIAN KINGDOMS)

To the east in Southern Russia, we get good evidence of the clashing of kingdoms. In prehistoric times, Southern Russia's vast steppes were peopled by nomadic herders. The earliest traces of mounted warfare have been discovered in these areas, indicating that these were a warring people.

In the period leading up to the New Testament, the Pontic-Caspian Steppe was labeled Scythia. The Greeks traded with the Scythians as early as the eighth century BC. The Romans also stretched their empire to the southwestern region of the Caspian Sea in the second-century AD.

The Scythians were likely Iranian-raced people from Turkestan and western Siberia. From as early as the eighth century BC, they penetrated across the Caucasus Mountains, which stretch between the Black and Caspian Seas, and established a kingdom. They were renowned horseback warriors and archers. This involved the subjugation of rural populations (Cimmerians) including allying with the Assyrians to brutally destroy the

31. Cotterell, *A History*, 70.
32. Cotterell suggests a date between AD 40 and 42 (ibid., 72).
33. Ibid., 72.

last Cimmerians in Pontis.³⁴ They took plunder and taxes from as far east as Syria, Media, Assyria, and Egypt. Grousset says of the Scythians, "the great Indo-European barbarians were the terror of the Old World."³⁵ This dynasty was likely founded by a certain Koloksai (Alcman, seventh-century BC) and ran for a few generations dominating its early period.³⁶ They were then defeated and driven out of the Near East by the Chinese in the first half of the sixth-century BC, a further example of the clash of empires across pre-Christ history. They then reconquered the lands north of the Black Sea in the second half of the sixth century, and again forced tribute. They clashed with Darius who sought to invade their regions, but he withdrew.³⁷

The second Scythian Kingdom then arose, reaching its peak in the fourth century BC. In the fifth and fourth centuries BC the Scythians traded with the Greeks. An important aspect of this was the sale of slaves captured in many wars to the Greeks. The Greek rhetorician Isocrates (436–338 BC) considered the Scythians, Thracians, and Persians "the most able to power, and the peoples with the greatest might."³⁸

Under King Ateas, in the fifth century BC, the Scythians expanded west, subjugating the Thracian Triballi tribe (modern Serbia, western Bulgaria), and they were taxed heavily. They also fought the Bosporian Kingdom, which flanked the Bosporus River and the Black Sea. The kingdom included the exploitation of the nomadic and indigenous agricultural tribes who did not participate in the wars.

The clash of kingdoms is seen as the Scythians were defeated by Philip II of Macedon (339 BC) and Ateas was killed. They did, however, defeat Zopyrian at Olbia (northern coast the Black Sea) in 331 BC. The kingdom fell in the second half of the third century BC through attacks from the Celts, Thracians, and particularly the Sarmatians from the east who wreaked havoc in Scythia, reducing much of the empire to a desert.³⁹ Some then settled in Scythia Minor in Thrace, and a third Scythian empire developed around the northern Black Sea and Crimea. This third kingdom overthrew Olvia to the east, but ultimately became subject to Parthia.

---

34. For more on the Scythians, see Grousset, *The Empire*, 7.
35. Ibid., 9.
36. Herodotus, *Hist.* 4.76.
37. Grousset, *The Empire*, 9.
38. Isocrates, *Paneg.* 67.
39. On the Sarmartians, see ibid., 16. Unlike the Scythian mounted archers, they preferred the lance and wore conical caps with coats of mail.

IRAN (THE PARTHIAN EMPIRE)

Between 247 BC and AD 224, the Parthian (or Arsacid) Empire dominated the area known today as Iran (ancient Persia). The empire's origins came when Andragoras, the Seleucid governor of Parthia in 247 BC, declared independence from the Seleucids—one empire declines and another emerges. Arsaces I then led an invasion by the Parni tribe, and they seized control of Parthia. Mithridates I (ca. 171–138 BC) and, as empires must do, expanded, wresting Media and Mesopotamia from the Seleucids.

At its zenith, it stretched into southeastern Turkey. It stood between Rome and China on the Silk Road and was a center for trade. Their rulers were titled "king of kings" and claimed continuity from the Persian or Achaemenid Empire (ca. 550–330 BC). They subjugated other local kings and established satrapies outside of Parthia. They clashed with the Armenian Kingdom and especially the Romans in the Roman-Parthian wars (66 BC–AD 217). These included the Parthians defeating Marcus Licinius Crassus in the Battle of Carrhae (53 BC) and capturing almost all the region along the eastern Mediterranean coast (40–39 BC). The Romans took Seleucia on the Tigris River many times, but could not hold it.

In the leadup to the time of Christ, Parthia was extremely unstable. Orodes II ruled from 57 to 37 BC, and he came to power after a fierce struggle with his brother Mithridates, the "rightful" heir. This involved Mithridates fleeing to Syria, returning to invade Parthia and reclaim the throne briefly, and, upon capture, being killed. Orodes's rule was ended by his son Phraates II, who claimed the throne in 37 BC, murdering his father and his thirty brothers!

On assuming the throne, Phraates II was attacked by the Romans, led by Mark Antony, in 36 BC. The Parthians were defeated, but when Roman civil war with Octavian broke out, Phraates regained rule. Phraates was a ruthless leader. He was briefly usurped by Tiridates II in 37 BC, but regained control with the help of the Scythians. When he assumed rule, Augustus established a treaty with the Parthians, and Phraates continued this rule. To ensure his safe rule, at the instigation of his favored wife, Musa ("Theamusa"), a Roman concubine gifted by Augustus, Phraates sent five of his sons to Rome as hostages. However, his rule ended in 2 BC when his wife and son poisoned him, and she ruled with her son Phraates V from 2 BC to AD 4. She married her son, and this angered the Parthians. Consequently, they rebelled and overthrew Musa, and installed Orodes III, who ruled briefly in AD 4–6.

The Romans established Vonones I, the eldest son of Phraates IV, as king (AD 8–10). However, he was an extremely cruel man and despised as a Roman appointee. Civil war broke out, with Vonones fleeing and becoming king of Armenia, then moving to Syria and then Cilicia, where he was murdered by his guards.

After the defeat of Vonones, Artabanus III (AD 10–40), the son of an Arsacid Parthian princess and a relative of Vonones and Darius, assumed the throne under the protection of Rome. He too was cruel, killing as many of the Arsacid princes as possible. Ultimately, war with Rome broke out, and he ultimately fled, with Tiridates III appointed king, only to return and reassume rule. He made peace with Rome in 37, only to be deposed briefly by Cinnamus and restored to the throne again until his death in AD 40.

After the death of Artabanus, Parthia was ruled by a range of rulers, who superintended turbulent times. At the time of the writing of Mark, Vologases I ruled (AD 51–78). During his reign, Vologases invaded Armenia and, thumbing his nose to Rome, proclaimed his brother Tiridates I king. After instability over this action, Nero sent General Corbulo in AD 58 to restore Roman sovereignty. The Romans drove Tiridates out of Armenia and established Tigranes as ruler, he a descendant of the Herods. Vologases sought to reinstate his brother to the throne and attacked the Romans. Ultimately, after much conflict and political negotiation, Tiridates I was vindicated as ruler of Armenia with Nero's blessing in AD 62. Vologases remained in good relations with Rome after Nero and supported Vespasian.

After this time, within Parthia, there was a string of civil wars, where usurpers sought to gain control of the empire, and eventually Ardashir I led a revolt, killing the last of the Arsacids in AD 224 and establishing the Sassanid Empire (224–651 AD), which ruled until the Muslim conquest. The Arsacid Dynasty continued in Armenia (54–428 AD).

The Parthian Empire illustrates well the usual imperial concerns of dynastic rule, political and military machinations, civil war, threats from one's own family, and cruelty.[40]

MIDDLE EAST

What is now called Saudi Arabia, and previously Arabia, was peopled by nomadic tribes with a few urban settlements. The Nabatean Kingdom sat at the juncture of the Sinai and Arabian peninsulas, with Judea to the north, and Egypt to the southwest. Its capital was Petra, which was an important trade center, especially for spices. It peaked under Aretas III (87–62 BC) and

---

40. See further "Parthia," http://academic.eb.com/levels/collegiate/article/Parthia/58588; "List of Parthian Kings," https://en.wikipedia.org/wiki/List_of_Parthian_kings; Bimson et al., "Parthian Empire," 99; Trost, "Parthia," in *LBD*, n.p.; Debevoise, *A Political History of Parthia*; Porter, "Parthians," 2251–53.

was defeated by the Roman Republic, who besieged Petra. They then paid tribute to Rome. Petra remained independent under the Roman Empire until annexed by Trajan in AD 106.

AFRICA

The periods leading up to Christ give ample evidence of a world dominated by people (usually men), seeking to extend their power, subjugate other peoples, plunder resources, and establish a dynastic rule.

Although it peaked before the time of the New Testament, due to its clashes with the Romans in the centuries leading up to Christ, of interest to my study is the Carthaginian Empire in North Africa. Carthage's dominance starts with the Phoenicians who lived in northern Canaan; modern Lebanon and southern Syria. They extended their influence along the northern African littoral, powerfully independent from 1200 to 850 BC. They founded Utica (Tunisia) at this time. It is believed that they traveled the whole coast of Africa, according to Herodotus.

As the Phoenicians declined, power shifted from Tyre to Sidon and then to Carthage (Tunis) in modern Tunisia. It is argued that Carthage was the first city-state to seek to rule an empire, and was successful for centuries.[41]

By the fifth century BC, Carthage was the commercial center of the Western Mediterranean until defeated by Rome. The armies of Carthage conquered the older Phoenician colonies, the Libyan tribes, and had control of the North African coast from Morocco to Egypt. They fought the Greeks with fierceness, controlling Sardinia, Malta, west Sicily, the Balearic Islands, and had colonies on the Iberian Peninsula. In the fifth and fourth centuries BC, Carthage engaged in a series of conflicts to capture all of Sicily, only to be ultimately driven out by the Greeks. Herodotus records that this led to King Hamilcar incinerating himself while sacrificing to the gods.[42] Subsequently, Carthage remained dominant in the region until the end of the fifth century BC. War continued with the Greeks, with Agathocles invading North Africa late in the fourth century BC, only to be repelled by the Carthaginians with help from the Berbers.[43]

Then, in the mid-third and second centuries BC, the Carthaginians clashed with Rome in the three Punic wars. The first war (264–241 BC) saw

---

41. Naylor, *North Africa*, 26.

42. Ibid., 27.

43. The Berbers (or Amazigh) were Arabs of North Africa. They lived across Morocco, Algeria, Tunisia, Libya, Egypt, Mali, Niger, and Mauretania. See Brett, "Berber People," https://www.britannica.com/topic/Berber.

Rome seek to land soldiers near Carthage, only to be resisted. However, in fierce naval battles, the Romans were dominant and forced a peace treaty in which Carthage gave up its territories in Sicily. The Carthaginian forces then rebelled (the "Mercenary War") due to a lack of pay, and the Romans seized Corsica and Sardinia. Carthage responded by seizing territory in Spain under Hamilcar Barca and Hasdrubal. This led to conflict with Rome, the second war (218–202 BC). With a huge army of some twenty-six thousand, including Berber cavalry and Celts of Gaul, Hannibal attacked Italy in 218 BC. The Romans were quickly on the backfoot, and the Greeks also revolted. However, the Romans were able to repel the enemy forces and forced Hannibal to return to defend Carthage. Scipio led the Roman forces, defeating the Carthaginians in Spain and Hannibal at Zama in Sicily in 202 BC. Hannibal ultimately committed suicide. After this, Carthage retained its independence but was no longer a threat. With the Numidians led by King Masinissa, the Romans, fearing a Carthaginian resurgence, attacked, and in the third Punic War (149–146 BC), entered the city. They enslaved the survivors and destroyed the city completely, even salting the ground to stop its regeneration.

Egypt was unified in ca. 3150 BC by King Menes and a series of dynasties ruled until the thirtieth dynasty fell to the Persians in 343 BC.[44] The Hyksos infiltrated Egypt and gained control around the middle of the second millennium before Christ. They introduced the horse, chariot, and composite bow. Thebes revolted around this time.[45] Kamose and Ahmose (1550–1525 BC) rebelled, and drove out the Hyksos and Kushites. Egypt's power was extended, and the pharaohs emerged. In 1473 BC, Queen Hatshepsut overthrew Tuthmosis II. Tuthmosis II (1479–1425 BC) was renowned for destructive military incursions into Asia.

During this period, especially in the thirteenth century BC, Egypt is heavily involved in the story of Israel, including the period leading into Exodus and beyond in which Israel was subjugated (Gen 37—Exod 15).[46] The story of the Exodus, when God destroyed Egypt's forces by divine intervention, is the pivotal historical event which defined Israel.

---

44. For a brief account of the Egyptian dynasties until the Greek period, see Naylor, *North Africa*, 18–22.

45. Ibid., 19.

46. For more on the date, see Kitchen, "The Exodus," 702–3. While it may be dated in the fifteenth-century (ca. 1446 BC) based on the four hundred eighty years of 1 Kings 1:6. However, four hundred eighty years may be a schematic figure (twelve times forty years, or similar) and reference to Rameses is likely Rameses II (1279–1213 BC). The Exodus likely fell between ca. 1279 and 1209 BC, something supported by archaeological evidence and the form of the Sinai covenant, which fits the period 1380–1200 BC.

Between 1184 and 1153 BC, Rameses II asserted political power over Canaan. In the first half of the first-millennium BC (third intermediate period), Egypt declined and was dominated politically and militarily by Libyans. The Kushites then invaded and established rule (twenty-fifth dynasty, 945–715 BC), only for the Assyrians to force them to retreat to Nubia. The Persians under Cambyses II defeated Egypt in 525 BC, a reign which lasted two thousand years.

Greek interest in North Africa dates back some one thousand years before Christ, especially, initially, Libya. There, the Greeks colonized areas, including establishing Cyrene in 631 BC. Greek influence accelerated in 332 BC when Alexander claimed Egypt and, in 331, established Alexandria as a center for Greek trade and culture.[47] After his death and the Wars of the Diadochi, the Ptolemies ruled from Syria to Cyrene and south to the frontier with Nubia. Until the Roman period, they clashed with the Seleucids of western Asia. They remained in power until the Roman civil war, when Cleopatra VII committed suicide after the suicidal death and burial of her lover Mark Antony following Alexandria's capture by Octavius's forces (30 BC).

In northern Africa, by the second century BC, several large Berber kingdoms had emerged. Masinissa became the first king of Numidia after fighting in the Second Punic War (218–201 BC). He initially fought against the Romans, but switched sides (political expediency!) and, following the war, was supported by the Romans to establish the Kingdom of Numidia. The kingdom, as is customary, was based on dynastic succession, and was divided in two due to conflicts over succession. In 104 BC, then-ruler Jugurtha was executed after the war with Rome. Numidia ultimately became part of the province Africa Nova.

Another African Empire was the Kushite Kingdom (1070 BC–AD 350), an ancient Nubian state in modern Sudan. In the eighth century BC, King Kashta, "the Kushite," invaded Egypt and the Kushites ruled as pharaohs in the twenty-fifth Egyptian dynasty until expelled in 656 BC. In Greek geography, the area was known as Ethiopia, and it is believed by some to be connected to Cush in Gen 10:6–11 (see also 1 Chr 1:10). In this passage, Kush (Cush) fathered Nimrod, purportedly the first empire builder (see chapter 4 of this manuscript). One Kushite king, Piye, sought to expand the empire into the Near East but was held back by Sargon II of Assyria. Assyrian kings drove the Kushites out of Egypt and ended all hopes of a revival of the kingdom.

---

47. See Naylor, *North Africa*, 31–33, who notes the amazing cultural development, especially philosophy, literature, medicine, science, and religion. Many Jews also settled in Alexandria.

The Kushites also fought the Romans in the first century BC and were defeated, and the capital Napata sacked (further below). They continued to challenge the Romans until peace was negotiated. Kush's power waned in the first and second centuries AD, and the Kushites feature in the Old Testament narrative among Israel's historic enemies.

In the eighth century BC, a kingdom called D'mt formed in northern Ethiopia and Eritrea, based on Yeha, perhaps influenced by Sabaeans. This kingdom fell in the fourth century BC, broken up into smaller kingdoms led by rival successors. At the same time the Christian movement was becoming prominent, the Kingdom of Axum (or Aksum) united the northern Ethiopian peoples and moved south. It dominated modern northern Ethiopia, Eritrea, and at times extended to Yemen. It ran for almost one thousand years. A leading Persian religious figure Mani (ca. 216–276 AD) listed Axum with Rome, Persia, and China as the four great powers of his time.

The Roman involvement in North Africa drew local rulers into conflict. A Massyli prince, Masinissa (ca. 240–148 BC) had fought the Romans with the Carthaginians in Spain. After the death of his father, Masinissa was overthrown, and the Romans helped him overthrow his rival, Syphax. He fought with the Romans against Hannibal in the second Carthaginian conflict and was subsequently appointed king of "Numidia." He was highly regarded by the Romans. Supported by Rome, with his capital in Cirta, and with a strong military, he established a significant kingdom from the west of Tunisia to Algeria. He clashed with Carthage and determined to overcome it; he aided the Romans in their destruction of the city. However, more Romans came, and they weakened Numidia.

After Masinissa's death, his sons ruled until his great-grandson, Jugurtha, assisted the Romans in Spain in wars against the Iberians. This forced the then-Numidian ruler, Micipsa, to accept him as co-heir with his two sons, Adherbal and Hiempsal. However, as is normal in a world of clashing powers, after Micipisa's death, there ensued a power struggle. Jugurtha ordered the death of Hiempsal and defeated Adherbal. With Jugurtha seeking his death, Adherbal lobbied Rome for help, as did Jugurtha. The Roman Senate divided the Numidian Kingdom between the two men. As one might expect, this did not last, and Jugurtha besieged the capital, in which Adherbal was in refuge, and killed many of the citizens, including some Romans. The Romans were infuriated, and they attacked, claiming Numidian cities and, aided by King Bocchus of Mauretania (Jugurtha's father-in-law), they seized Jugurtha in 106 BC. This ended Numidian rule.

As one expects, Bocchus was rewarded by the Romans with significant Numidian land, while Gauda, Jugurtha's half-brother, acted as client king over what was left of Numidia. However, when Bocchus died, his sons vied for power, with one joining Marius and the other (Hiempsal) Sulla, two conflicting Roman leaders. Sulla prevailed, and Hiempsal was rewarded with charge of Numidia. His son, Juba I, then supported Pompey against Julius Caesar. In 46 BC, at the battle of Thapsus, Juba was vanquished and ordered his own forces to kill him. Caesar then created an African province—Africa Nova, including much of Numidia. Juba II was a great friend of Augustus.[48]

In AD 48, after Pompey's death, Caesar came to Africa and supported the brilliant and beautiful Cleopatra, and when she became queen, he brought her to Rome. He was assassinated, and Cleopatra returned to Egypt. She supported those who sought revenge for Caesar and married Mark Antony. As per a world of contending forces, she and Antony dreamed of the conquest of the whole Mediterranean region, which would be ruled from Alexandria. However, the Second Triumvirate, led by Octavian and Lepidus, gained dominance. After a brutal war, which culminated in the Battle of Actium (AD 31), Antony and Cleopatra were defeated and, as is common in such situations, committed suicide. Egypt came fully under Rome.[49]

After Octavian's inauguration as emperor in 27 BC, he arranged the marriage of Cleopatra Selene, the daughter of Mark Antony and Cleopatra, to Juba II, who had grown up in his household. The couple ruled Mauretania from its capital Iol, a region including Central Algeria and Morocco. Juba was a much-admired intellectual. The Berbers revolted during the life of Christ in AD 17–24; the rebellion was quashed with difficulty. Juba II was succeeded by Ptolemy who was executed by the brutal Caligula. The Berbers again revolted, and Mauretania was split into two. To the west, Garamantes in Libya remained independent of Rome. The Romans also clashed with the Kushites and Queen "Candace," destroying the capital, Napata, in 25 BC. Augustus made peace with them, and they engaged in trade.[50] Africa was critical for Roman grain.

As this brief summary has shown, Africa, like the rest of the ancient world, was a region of colliding empires.

EUROPE

What we call Europe, north of the Roman areas of influence, was made up of organized tribal groups under a chieftain. In Britain during the Iron Age period (800–43 BC), as population pressure grew, war with neighboring tribes

---

48. See further ibid., 40–43.
49. See further, ibid., 43–44.
50. See further, ibid., 44–46.

was common; particularly in southern and western Britain,[51] hill forts were developed partly for the defense of people and food.[52] At Danebury Hill, Iron Age weaponry has been discovered, including swords, hammers, and iron spearheads made up of "long slender shanks culminating in triangular points as big as beech leaves."[53] An enormous number of butchered human skulls and other body parts have also been uncovered from charnel pits. Oliver writes of the battle that must have ensued:

> Although we have no name or date for the Iron Age battle that filled a charnel pit with a heap of slain, it is reasonable to imagine the scarred survivors telling and retelling their stories with all the pride of any that stood with Henry at Agincourt [two thousand] years later. Limbless or not, scarred or battered, they lived in a society that learned to value the warrior, so that such men would have carried their wounds with a bearing won only in combat. A charnel pit is indisputable proof, that, for at least part of the Iron Age, might was right.[54]

Oliver goes on to note the discovery of a range of other digs which provide evidence of the importance of the warrior and a range of weapons, even chariots.[55] He suggests that in this period, as tribes clashed, power was held in the hands of strong warriors who fought for "overall control, for power and prestige."[56] He goes on, "The leaders were warriors now, chieftains controlling grain and people alike."[57] It was the time of the "Celtic Chieftain."[58]

---

51. In Scotland and Ireland, they tended to dwell in crannogs, fortified dwellings constructed in a lake or marsh; again, ideal for defense.

52. See Oliver, *A History*, "Warriors." He notes that the earliest of these is on Crickley Hill in Gloucestershire, the scene of a bloody Neolithic battle. He discusses their use which is debated. While their importance may be overstated, their existence suggests that the people faced aggressive threat and they were used in such times for central defense. The Danebury Hill Fort is a formidable place, well designed to ward off attackers. He suggests that Danebury should be called a "mega hill fort."

53. Ibid.

54. Ibid.

55. Ibid. He notes archeological finds such as the Gristhorpe Man, a six-foot skeleton with many broken bones, presumably from war, which supports this content. Similarly, a warrior and a number of swords were discovered at Fortevoit, Scotland. He also makes mention of Celtic weaponry: the River Thames Spearhead (200–50 BC), the "Battersea Shield" (350–50 BC), the Kirkburn Sword found in the grave of the Kirkburn Warrior ("a great man, a man of war") (300–200 BC), and the Newbridge Chariot. Commonly, knives, spearheads, axes, and arrowheads have been found.

56. Ibid.

57. Ibid.

58. Ibid.

So, in the Iron Age, a "warrior elite" formed, "regional chieftains, those who controlled the land and the food it produced." Although they were not numerous, "each controlled so much land and so much trade they became the first of the super-rich."[59] Movement across the English Channel became commonplace in the century before Christ. This includes Caesar seeking to conquer Brittanica. While the British defended their land from the Romans in 55–54 BC, Britain was ultimately invaded by Rome in AD 43.

The Phoenicians arrived on the Iberian Peninsula around 1100 BC, founding colonies in Malaga, Adra, and Cadiz. Others were established by the Greeks. Large portions were conquered by the Carthaginians. The region was invaded by Rome in the third century BC in the Celtiberian Wars. Three emperors of Rome, just after the New Testament period, were Spanish in origin; Trajan (AD 98–117), Hadrian (AD 117–138), and Marcus Aurelius (AD 161–180).[60]

The region termed Transalpine Gaul defeated Rome in the fourth century BC and raided Italy to Sicily. In the third century BC, they moved east (281–279 BC), invading Thrace, Macedon, and Illyria, and settled in ancient Galatia. They sacked Delphi and killed the Macedonian king Ptolemy Keranos. They were held back by Antiochus I in 275 BC. In the second century before Christ, Rome formed "the Province," enabling movement between Italy and Spain. Between 58 and 50 BC, due to internal rivalries, Gaul was easily conquered by the Roman Republic, led by Julius Caeser. Later, Augustus divided the country into four provinces.[61]

The tribes of Germany likely came from the Scandinavian regions moving into northern Germany over several millennia before the time of Christ. Little is known of this early period, except through interactions with Rome. In 113 BC, several hundred thousand Cimbrians and Teutons made their way through the Alps into Roman territory and clashed with the Romans. They were designated "barbarians," and were large men with blond hair who "wore breastplates of iron and helmets crowned with the heads of wild beasts, and carried white shields." Egged on by the women, "they first hurled double-headed spears in battle, but at close quarters fought with heavy swords."[62] They moved on into Gaul, wreaking havoc, and returned

---

59. Ibid. There is also evidence of human slavery, hence, they controlled people.

60. See, "Spain—History," http://www.expatfocus.com/expatriate-spain-history?gclid=CNeSwNrcttICFYwDKgodLuoB6w. See also Harrison et al., "Spain," http://academic.eb.com/levels/collegiate/article/Spain/108580.

61. See John E. Flower, et al., "France," http://academic.eb.com/levels/collegiate/article/France/110436.

62. Taylor, *A History of Germany*, "The Ancient Germans and their Country (330 BC–70 BC)."

to Italy wherein 102 BC they met Marius in battle and were defeated. Five centuries later, German tribes would return to overthrow Rome.

The German tribes occupied a large part of central Europe, separated from the Gauls by the Rhine in the west, and the Vistula and Danube in the east and south, and had penetrated Sweden, and perhaps Norway. A range of fierce polytheistic tribes filled the region, renowned for "indolence, drunkenness and love of gaming."[63] These tribes were distinct, and war was not frequent until occasioned by the Romans, which led to alliances for the sake of defense.

In 70 BC, the German Ariovistus, chief of the Suevi, with fifteen thousand men, assisted the Gallic Arveni and Sequani to take control of a region in Gaul. As a result, Ariovistus gained a third of the area of the Sequani, and it was filled with one hundred twenty thousand Germans. As this was on Roman land, in 57 BC, Caesar summoned Ariovistus, only to be refused; Ariovistus responded that the land was won in war. This led to Caesar attacking the Suevi, and despite his soldiers being very fearful of the Barbarians, the Romans vanquished them and sent them packing. Two years later, fearing a revolt of the Gauls, Caesar was forced to attack and defeat two other German tribes (the Usipetes and Tencteres) who had crossed the Rhine near modern Cologne. He then built his famous wooden bridge and had control of the western bank of the Rhine to its river mouth. Further attempts were made by Celtic and German alliances to overthrow the Romans, but they were resisted. Some Germans developed a high regard for Caesar, and six thousand fought with him against Pompey.

From the time of Caesar to Augustus, the Germans were pushed back from the Alps to the Danube, which in AD 15 became the boundary between Rome and the German tribes. Augustus sought to extend Rome's rule to North and Baltic Seas first led by Drusus, and then by Tiberius. They gained substantial areas west of the Rhine, as far as the Weser. However, the tribes of the region revolted, forming alliances to overcome the Romans. An alliance of seventy thousand infantry and four thousand cavalry soldiers formed under Marbod, forcing Augustus to send twelve legions. However, insurrection in Dalmatia and Pannonia forced the Romans to offer peace terms to Marbod.

At this point, Quinctilius Varus imposed brutal taxation and ruthless justice on the Germans. This led to the German tribes to the west, especially the Cherusci, forming a strategic alliance. One of the Cherusci, Hermann (also Arminius), was a German member of the Roman military. In AD 9, he instigated a revolt with great shrewdness. He tricked Varus into believing

---

63. For detail see ibid.

there was an insurrection to the east, causing Varus to move east, and leaving Hermann to gather troops and join him. Hermann gathered troops alright, but then moved west, and rather than helping Varus in the supposed revolt, attacked his forces. Varus eventually killed himself, and the Roman forces were decimated in the so-called Battle of the Teutoburger Forest. Only a few made it over the Rhine.

However, the Germans, including some in his own family, opposed him, and Tiberius returned and regained control. After Tiberius became emperor in AD 14, Germanicus, son of Drusus, was in charge, re-entering Germany in the following year. Hermann then instigated the second revolt, and a second battle ensued in the Teutoberger Forest, and the Romans were forced to withdraw. Germanicus was not done, however, and raised eight legions to subjugate the Germans as far as the Elbe River. The Romans crossed the Weser, and two great battles ensued, with neither side completely victorious.

Although he claimed to have conquered Germany to the Elbe, Germanicus returned east in AD 16. He was determined to finish the job, but was recalled to Rome by Tiberius in the hope that the Germans would self-destruct internally. In AD 19, war broke out among the Germans between two alliances, one led by Marbod of the Marcomanni, and one by Hermann, the head of the Cherusci. Hermann's greater popularity gave him ascendency, and Marbod fled to Rome. Hermann sought to unite the Germans, only to be assassinated by his family in AD 21 at the age of thirty-seven. Tacitus writes of him:

> He was undoubtedly the liberator of Germany, having dared to grapple with the Roman power, not in its beginnings, like the other kinds and commanders, but in the maturity of its strength. He was not always victorious in battle, but in *war* he was never subdued. He still lives in the songs of the Barbarians, unknown to the annals of the Greeks, who only admire that which belongs to themselves—nor celebrated as he deserves by the Romans, who, in praising the olden times, neglect the events of the later years.[64]

After Hermann's resistance, a sort of truce remained between Rome and the German tribes, which was broken on occasion. German soldiers continued to serve in the Roman army, and military colonies formed a triangular region from the Danube to the Rhine at Cologne, including Vienna. A stockade with a ditch was built marking the border, something that held

---

64. See ibid., "Hermann: The First German Leader (AD 9–21)." The translation of Tacitus comes from Taylor (see further on the details of Hermann's resistance in this work). See also Tacitus, *Germanicus*.

for two hundred years.⁶⁵ It was not until the reign of Marcus Aurelius (AD 161–180) that another significant uprising occurred.

In modern Austria and parts of Slovenia, a Celtic kingdom or federation of twelve tribes, the Noricum developed (800–400 BC). They were warlike and fought alongside Caesar against Pompey in 48 BC. It became a province but retained its name *regnum Noricum*. Before the Classical period, two periods of Greek history are of interest. First the Minoans, who dominated from twenty-seventh to fifteenth centuries BC.⁶⁶ They originated in Crete, formed around a mythic "king" Minos. They are the first well-known literate civilization in Europe. The Minoans were traders. Their involvement in warfare is disputed, with some believing that they were involved in war and others that they were a peace-loving people whose only interest in weaponry was ceremonial. If the latter, they were exceptional in the ancient world. However, more likely, "the absence of trenches, walls, and parapets surrounding the urban centers suggests that the Minoans were confident of their dominance in the region. Moreover, it indicates that the various cities on the island of Crete did not compete with each in a way that led to armed aggression or civil war."⁶⁷

The demise of the Minoans came between about 1500 and 1400 BC, precipitated by natural disaster: a volcanic eruption.⁶⁸ Weakened by this event, they were they were overcome by the Mycenaeans, who were located especially in modern Greece, Crete, Macedonia, the Aegean, western Asia Minor, the Levant, Cyprus, and Italy. They were a warring people who advanced their interests with military conquest, and were led by a warrior aristocracy. Their weapons of choice included helmets, bronze swords and shields, and chariots.⁶⁹ Their influence was greatest at the time of the Trojan War, when thousands attacked the Anatolian city of Troy sometime between 1334 and 1183 BC.⁷⁰ They eventually waned through the Dorian invasion and/or natural disasters.⁷¹

In Bulgaria, the Odrysian Kingdom—a union of Thracian tribes—formed under the first king of Thrace, Teres, in the fifth to third centuries BC. This kingdom spanned present-day Bulgaria, parts of Romania, Greece,

---

65. See further Taylor, *A History of Germany*, "Germany During the First Three Centuries (AD 21–300)."

66. On the Minoans, see Charles River Editors, *The Minoans*.

67. Ibid., "The Chronology of Minoan Civilization."

68. Ibid., "The End of Minoan Culture."

69. Ibid., "The Modern Discovery of Mycenaean Culture."

70. Ibid., "The Trojan War." The historicity is no longer debated; but, the extent and impact remains uncertain. They opt for 1220 BC.

71. See ibid., "The Collapse of Mycenaean Culture."

and Turkey. The Odrysians are important, as they were the first to move from tribalism to a state entity in the eastern Balkans. However, tribalism meant that it lacked consistent cohesion, and the central military power was inadequate to hold itself together. It ultimately split into three parts in the fourth century BC, leading to political and military decline. Under Teres's son Sitalces in 429 BC, they allied with the Athenians to fight the Macedonians, although the campaign ended through lack of provisions and winter. As it weakened, it became subject to Alexander and others who followed. Rome annexed it in 46 AD.

Ancient Dacia is an area corresponding to modern Romania, Moldova, and small parts of Bulgaria, Serbia, Hungary, and the Ukraine. The Dacian Kingdom existed between 82 BC and AD 106. It is mentioned by Herodotus, who describes the Dacians (or Getae) as "the noblest as well as the most just of all the Thracian tribes."[72] They, like the Scythians, were mounted archers.[73] They fought with the falx, which is like a sickle and was particularly destructive.

The Romans also engaged with the Dacians. The initial key figure was Burebista, who became king in 61 BC. He formed a strong alliance and sought to conquer surrounding peoples of Thrace, the Danube, and the Black Sea with great success. Pompey sought his support, and Julius Caesar planned his destruction, but both were killed before carrying through their plans. Octavian was concerned about Burebista's allying with Marc Antony, but his victory at Actium left the question of Dacia unresolved. Dacians crossed the Danube into Pannonia and Moesia and ultimately, in AD 85, Decebalus attacked Moesia, killing the Moesian governor. This led to war, and Domitian led legions into Moesia with a plan to attack Dacia. However, the Romans were ambushed and overcome at Tapae. The Romans attacked again, defeating the Dacians and their king Decebalus, who sought peace, only to be initially refused and then later accepted due to Germanic threats. In AD 101, Trajan led the Romans against Dacia. They marched into Dacia, defeating them at the Battle of Tapae. Decebalus again sought to end the hostilities. However, after another uprising, the king committed suicide, the capital Sarmizegetusa was destroyed by the Romans in AD 106, and it became the capital of the Roman province of Dacia. Tens of thousands of slaves were taken to Rome, and the riches of Dacia's gold mines became an important source of Roman finance.[74]

---

72. *Hist.* 4.43.
73. Thucydides, *Peloponnesian Wars*, 2.
74. See Bunson, "Dacia," 165–67.

THE REST OF THE WORLD

At the time of Christ, the North American native population had likely originated from North Asia, crossing the Bering Land Bridge during earlier ice ages or by boat, and formed the Native Americans, Inuit, and Aleuts.[75] These peoples ranged from small bands of a few families to large empires. They were hunter-gatherers who lived in socio-linguistic groups based on common culture, geography, and biological zones, such as bison hunters, the Great Plains, etc.

As with North America, South America was probably similarly inhabited by migrants crossing the Bering Land Bridge from Asia. There is evidence of sophisticated human organization, such as the Norte Chico (or Caral, Caral-Supe) civilization (ca. 3500–1800 BC), in what we call modern Peru. They produced some amazing architecture. In addition, a powerful religious elite controlled agriculture, cotton, and fishing. They worshiped the Staff God, often pictured with a headdress of snakes with clawed feet, fanged teeth, and staff. There is little evidence of warfare, which is highly unusual in ancient times.[76]

Some of the nations of Oceania were populated at the time of Christ (e.g. Australia, ca. 70,000–40,000 BC; Fiji and Samoa, ca. 1500 BC; Tonga, 1500–1000 BC). Although there was a range of cultures, the peoples of Oceania lived in tribes and were fierce warriors; many of them practiced cannibalism. One example is Rarotonga, where I grew up as a child. Before the coming of the missionaries in 1823, the island was made up of tribes who lived in the highlands for security. They were warlike and cannibalistic. When the gospel came to the island, the Christianized tribes renounced cannibalism and war, buried their weapons, and relocated to the coast.

CONCLUSION

The short and limited analysis above makes it abundantly clear that humanity at the time of Christ understood power in terms of land, resources, and military might. Much of the world was tribal, with small collectives based on a common ancestry, culture, and language protecting their own territory and people. Across the world, however, from Europe, North Africa, the Middle East, Southern Russia, Central Asia, and Southeast Asia, kingdoms

---

75. Thornton, "Population History," 9. It is likely that there were three migrations; Paleo-Indians, forty thousand years ago; Na-Dine, twelve thousand years ago; and Inuit (Eskimo)-Aleut (Aleutian Islands), nine thousand to ten thousand years ago. See also Johansen, *Native Peoples*, 11–14.

76. Haas et al., "Power and the Emergence," 37–52.

and empires formed with men of power, their allies and armies seeking to dominate their neighbors in their quest for wealth and glory.

In common, these empires were launched by a warrior-king who initially seized control of his own region with intrigue and force, and then extended this reign into neighboring areas with military power and intrigue. Most often, this either involved violent overthrow or voluntary subjugation—the easy way or the hard way. The subjugated people then paid tribute and provided people-power for the kingdom, including resources, wealth, warriors, women, and slaves. The initial warrior-king was usually succeeded by a son, forming a dynasty, although often succession was disputed with internal conflict to establish the succession, or the kingdom/empire was broken up under various rulers. When this occurred, threats were wiped out, especially those from the family or inner circle of the defeated former monarch. The successor may or may not continue the expansion, but ultimately decline would begin and the kingdom/empire would weaken and eventually break up or be succeeded by another, either internally or from a neighboring empire or nation. Although there were periods of "peace and security," people were inevitably swept up again and again in this ongoing struggle for power.

In the case of Israel, a succession of empires mentioned above dominated—the Assyrians, the Babylonians, the Medo-Persians, the Macedonian/Greeks, the Seleucids, and finally the Romans. For those reading Mark's Gospel in Italy and the wider region, Rome is totally dominant. For Israel, the hope of the messiah's intervention to set up a Theocratic Empire based in Jerusalem is the dream. For those in the Greco-Roman world, talk of Jesus as Lord conjured up thoughts of God's intervention to overthrow Caesar. It is important to press further into Israel's story to see whether she was any different to the surrounding world. As we explore her story, we find that they were little different. To this, I now turn.

4

Israel in this Clashing World

ISRAEL'S STORY, FROM WHICH Jesus emerged, born a Jew of the tribe of Judah in Bethlehem, cannot be isolated or understood apart from these competing forces. Not only was Israel buffeted here and there by great powers in their world, but they too thought of power through military might terms. Here, I will go through Israel's story in the Old Testament and explore her attitude.

WAR, VIOLENCE, AND EMPIRES IN THE OLD TESTAMENT

The Old Testament accounts for the introduction of evil and violence through the sin of Eve and Adam (Gen 3).[1] The result of their disobedience was initially marital conflict (Gen 3:16), and, after the birth of their first sons, the first murder or fratricide. Adam and Eve's oldest son Cain, inflamed with jealousy because his younger brother Abel's offering was more pleasing to God than his own, killed Abel (Gen 4:1–16). We read then of the violence of Lamech, who also kills a man and speaks of avenging himself seven times more than Cain, which itself deserves seven-fold restitution. This violates the *lex talionis*,[2] i.e., "a life for life, eye for eye, tooth for tooth, hand for hand, foot for foot, burn for burn, wound for wound, bruise

---

1. Some contemporary Christians would argue that war and violence existed in the process of human development rather than because of the Fall. Either way, we have the same problem in human history—humanity beset with desire for power and a preparedness to use violence to get it.

2. Wenham, *Genesis 1–15*, 114.

for bruise" (Exod 21:25), and clearly indicates the intensification of human violence (Gen 4:23–24). The writer of Genesis in the rest of the Primeval Prologue (Gen 1—11) writes of how humanity plunged into deeper and deeper decay. The account speaks of cohabitation of spiritual beings with women, and the presence of Nephilim who fathered mighty "heroes" of old (Gen 6:1–5). While this is very difficult to interpret,[3] what is clear is that from these relationships came great hunters and warriors, the forerunners of the warrior-kings. Ultimately, due to the universal total corruption of humanity (Gen 6:5–7), God moved to wipe humanity out through a flood and start again with Noah's family.

Sadly, restored humanity proved to be little better. Before long we read of Ham's grandson Nimrod (son of Cush) who is then described as "a mighty *warrior*[4] on the earth." He is a legendary hunter credited with the building of a great empire and cities encompassing the region of Mesopotamia, including Assyria and Babylon (Gen 10:8–11).[5] What we have in the story is the first empire in the region and the first great warrior-king. Whoever Nimrod is or represents,[6] in the narrative he is an important figure, as he prefigures what is to come, where others create such kingdoms and reign with power. In the biblical narrative, he is the prototypical warrior-king. Before long, these kingdoms will collide across the known world. This story of empires will go on unabated until the coming of Jesus—and sadly, unabated ever since.

Human hubris climaxes at Babel, where they seek to storm heaven itself and usurp God (Gen 11:1–9). The tower symbolizes human corporate

---

3. This is variously understood as a remnant of an old myth with the "Sons of God," lesser deities under El or the Canaanite pantheon, but that this section refutes this, and these are ancient tyrannical people thought to be divine giants but were mortal, angels, the descendants of Seth, demoniacs possessed by fallen angels, or human judges or rulers. The Nephilim may be the indigenous population of Canaan who are "fallen" either morally or in battle, or are the giants of Numbers 13:33. However, identification of either is fraught. See the discussion in Mathews, *Genesis 1–11:26*, 323–39.

4. While the Hebrew ṣā·yiḏ means "hunter" (ESV), in the context of the establishment of God's kingdom in the following verse, "warrior" (NIV) would seem an appropriate translation.

5. Mathews notes, "Moreover, the means by which Nimrod achieves his ascendancy suggests that his distinction came by aggressive force rather than the gradual diffusion of peoples as shown elsewhere by the table" (ibid., 448).

6. Nimrod is variously understood as: 1) The Babylon patron deity Marduk; 2) The Babylon god of war and hunting Ninurta; 3) The divine hero Gilgamesh of Erech; 4) Sargon of Akkad; 5) Naram-Sin, king of Akkad and grandson of Sargo; 6) Egyptian ruler Amenhotep III; 7) or Tukulti-Ninurta I (1243–1207 BC). See ibid., 449.

evil and defiance of God.[7] The center of the passage's chiastic structure[8] is God's response to come down and scatter humanity. Over time, this scattering ensures that language diverged to limit humanity's lust for corporate evil to challenge God and goodness. However, the subsequent story of human history is one of ongoing contention between these nations claiming common ancestry for resources and power. Some were driven by a need to survive, but most were motivated by a desire for power and dominance.

The story of Israel is embedded in the clash of world powers. At the time of Jacob, due to a famine that threatened his family's existence, and out of necessity, he took them into Egypt to come under the power of the dominant force of that period (either mid-fifteenth or thirteenth century BC).[9] Initially, due to a blend of sin and God's providence (ensuring one of Joseph's sons was in a position of political power in Egypt), Israel was favored (Gen 37–50). However, over time the Pharaoh turned nasty and put the Hebrews into slavery, using them on his building programs. This king follows the pattern of the dynastic kingdom whose kings rule with might and force. Slavery is utilized as the workforce of the empire in question. Order is maintained at the end of a whip. Monuments are built to glorify the king and empire.

This pattern will recur now and ever more. Indeed, when one travels the great archaeological sites of Egypt, Rome, Greece, Turkey, and beyond, as I have done, the monuments are almost without exception built by enforced labor or slaves, using tribute gained from military success and built for the "glory" of the patron or deified monarch. They symbolize the "greatness" of these kings. That they become ruins indicates that such empires inevitably fall.[10]

Israel's subsequent story includes, first, the victory and deliverance from Egypt through God's miraculous power (Exod 12). This salvation involved the violent defeat of Pharaoh's military power, without the use of direct human intervention. The first song of the Bible celebrates this defining event (Exod 15:1–21), and the Passover celebration ensures it remains

---

7. Mathews notes many parallels to the Garden narrative in Gen 3, the Cain narrative in Gen 4, and the post-flood narrative of Gen 6—9 (ibid., 467).

8. Ibid., 468.

9. For a brief summary of the discussion on the date of the Exodus see La Sor et al., *Old Testament Survey*, 125–28. They favor a date in the first half of the thirteenth-century with the Pharaoh of the oppression Seti I (1305–1290 BC) and the Pharaoh of the Exodus Ramases II (1290–1224 BC). Alternatively, Thutmoses III (1479–1425 BC) was the Pharaoh in question.

10. The poem "Ozymandias" sums this up. See Shelley, "Ozymandias," http://www.online-literature.com/shelley_percy/672/.

in the psyche as Israel's formative event (Exod 12:43–49). Israel's history is built on military victory, albeit a miracle by God.

From this point on, Israel's security will be maintained by an alliance of military power and spiritual force and vindication. Their God El, then revealed as Yahweh (Exod 3:14), entered a treaty (covenant) with Israel whereby he would be their God, their king, and they would be his people. The heart of the Law, the Ten Commandments (or Decalogue), gives the terms of the relationship (Exod 20:1–17). Scholars of the ancient world recognize the form of the Ten Commandments as that of a Suzerain-Vassal (King-Servant) Treaty.[11] Such treaties are found in the documents of the surrounding nations. This version is the agreement between a God-King and a people. The King promises to care for the people. Their part is to keep the terms of the covenant. The curses and blessings of the covenant relate to Israel's fidelity to these commands. Obedience will bring security, progeny, peace, and prosperity. Conversely, disobedience will see Israel experience struggle and suffering, poverty, barrenness, and war, and, if there is no repentance, subjugation at the hands of the military might of enemies, i.e. exile (Deut 28; Lev 26). As such, this formative document is critical to this discussion. At Sinai, Israel entered an agreement with God that he would be their sole sovereign. He would reign over them and care for them. They would, in turn, keep the covenant. If so, peace would prevail. If not, they would face their King's judgment. The subsequent history shows that their preference for a human warrior-king and a dynastic monarchy led to Israel's downfall and subjugation. Ironically, this defeat will be at the hands of other kingdoms—those who live by the sword. Jesus must be understood in terms of the big picture: God the King coming to establish his rightful reign as it should be.

In the Law, murder is ruled out with the imperative "you shall not murder" (Exod 20:13). This is further explained in Exod 21 with clarifications of the law around murder and violence (e.g. Exod 21:12–15, 18–27; Lev 24:17, 21, 23; Num 35:16–24, 30–32). Central to the law is the principle of exact retribution (*lex talionis*). This is an advance on non-Israelite biblical era law which favored the "superior person" over the "inferior" by impartially limiting retribution to fit the crime. Where violence is concerned, violence is appropriate but with real equity. So, a murderer was put to death for murder.[12]

---

11. See La Sor et al., *Old Testament Survey*, 144–46.

12. Stuart notes that it was never literally applied to an eye for an eye or a tooth for a tooth—rather, it was an idiomatic for "someone who permanently injured another person ought to be fully punished in a way that really 'hurt'" (*Exodus*, 492).

What matters for this discussion is that this limitation is for internal issues *within Israel's covenant community*. It is not a general imperative. Jesus explicitly went further; his appeal to love for all people (even one's enemies) and to turn the other cheek transcends the *lex talionis*, which thus falls short of the ethic we see in the New Testament, where there is no partiality on the limitation of violence (see later).

In Israel, where the purity of the covenant people is concerned, in terms of freeing the nation of idolatry, sexual sin, Sabbath violation, familial breakdown, driving out foreign invaders, violating the Tabernacle, false prophets, theft of people, etc., the narrative and law vindicates the use of violent force even to the point of death (e.g. Gen 34:24–29; Exod 21:15–17; 22:19; 31:16; 35:2; Lev 20:2, 4, 9–16, 27; 24:14, 16; Num 1:51; 15:35–36; 25:5, 8; 26:61; Deut 13:5–10; 17:1–7, 12; 18:20; 21:18–22; 22:1, 22–25; 24:7).[13]

War is seen as just if it rids Israel of idolatry and foreign subjugation. As such, the wilderness-wandering Israelites (Num 31:7–8, 17); judges like Deborah (Judg 4–5), Gideon (Judg 6–8), and Samson (Judg 14–16); King David (e.g., 1 Sam 17) and his mighty men (Judg 23:8–39); and, later in history, the Maccabees (e.g. 1 Macc 2), are not seen negatively for their use of force. Rather, their violence is celebrated.

God using violence is also seen as just and right, such as when holiness laws are violated (Exod 19:12), when there is complaint against God (Num 21:6), the destruction of the firstborn of Egypt and of Pharaoh's forces in the sea (Exod 11–15), the conquest of the land (Joshua), and his interventions at various points in history to give victory to Israel, such as David's victory over Goliath (1 Sam 16). This justified use of violent force by God is seen too in his intervention *against* Israel herself. This is found throughout the Old Testament in the Judges period, where nations rise up against Israel due to her sin. This is interpreted by the writer of Judges as a result of Israel's failure to completely eradicate the Canaanites (Judg 1:27–36). These include the Philistines in the initial phases of the monarchy (e.g. 1 Sam 4), and even more dramatically with the Assyrians and Babylonians bringing Israel to exile (2 Kgs 15:29–31). After the exile, the Medo-Persians act on God's and Israel's behalf, in turn overthrowing the Babylonians (2 Chr 36:22–23; Ezra 1). In the period after the final work in the Old Testament, Malachi, this pattern stands firm, seen in the heroic status accorded the Maccabees.[14]

---

13. In Leviticus, aside from the application of the *lex talionis* (Lev 20:2; 24:17, 21, 23), the death penalty is prescribed for blasphemy (Lev 24:14–16; 1 Kgs 21:9–14), cursing of the parents (Lev 20:9; Deut 21:18–21), sexual infidelities (Lev 20:10–20), and consulting the dead (Lev 20:7); those devoted to the Lord for death (e.g., someone captured in battle, or a murderer; see Rooker, *Leviticus*, 327 [Lev 27:29]).

14. This status is seen in the celebration of Hanukah commemorating the

Violence and war are endorsed where the purity of the people of God is concerned, whether by God or his divinely endorsed agents. This appears to be the standard understanding in Israel at the time of Christ (see Matt 5:21). This left wide open the expectation of a messiah figure who would use force to subdue the world to Yahweh, his covenant, law, and the supremacy of Israel as God's chosen nation.

I will now look at this a little more closely through the Old Testament narrative. Israel's history from Sinai can be broken up into nine phases: 1) Wilderness, 2) Conquest, 3) the Time of the Judges, 4) United Monarchy, 5) Divided Monarchy, 6) the Decline and Exile of the North, 7) the Decline and Exile of the South, 8) Restoration, and 9) Israel under Foreign Rule. Each of the three phases involves the use of military power to establish control, maintain it, or to subjugate Israel.

Wilderness

In the Wilderness period, Israel met some opponents and, with the vindication and empowering of Yahweh, gained victories over their opponents. The first victory is over the Amalekites, who attack the Israelites at Rephidim but are defeated through military engagement and God's power as Moses intercedes with Aaron and Hur's intercessory (raised arm) support (Exod 17:8–16). We see here the alliance of human military force and prayer, which leads to divine vindication, support, and action, bringing victory. The victory demonstrates the superiority of Yahweh and vindicates Israel as his elect. Exodus 23:20–32 sees the same pattern with God sending his angel ahead to drive out Israel's enemies and bring Israel into the Promised Land. In the subsequent narrative, Arad (Num 21:1–3), the Amorites (Num 21:21–35), and the Midianites are defeated (Num 31:1–20). These victories indicated Yahweh's superiority and came through military conquest.

Aside from the military engagements with other people, there are internal points of contention where God moves in judgment against rebellious and idolatrous Israelites. These are characterized by legitimized death and destruction demonstrating God's vindication of Moses and the faithful (Exod 32; Num 12; 14; 15:32–36; 25).

---

rededication of the Second Temple through the Maccabean Revolt on the twenty-fifth day of Kislev, usually in late November to late December.

Conquest

In Israel's story, the conquest of Canaan was achieved by the blend of military force with divine power and vindication. The promise is the land (Gen 12:1–3). The command was the complete extermination of the peoples of the land. The justification is their complete and utter depravity, which must be removed. The endorsement is from God and his promise. The political and military leader is Joshua (Greek: Jesus). He is not the son of Moses and so not some dynastic successor to a king. Rather, he is a personally chosen right-hand man who is trained at Moses' side for the role of King. Israel has not yet taken on the patterns of dynastic succession seen in the surrounding nations such as Egypt. Rather, Joshua is the one selected with God's promise of victory if he is faithful to the covenant and has complete trust in Yahweh (e.g. Josh 1:1–9).

The story of Joshua is one of war involving reconnaissance, spying, treachery (Josh 2), the miraculous action of God on behalf of Israel, spiritual leadership, and vindication (e.g. Josh 3:1–8, 13–17; 4:15–24). Victory is due to divine promise, trust, and obedience to God, and is applied with ruthless and divinely legitimized brutality. Alliance of ruler and priest is central to victory; the priest gives spiritual vindication to the ruler. Memorial sites for worship are established at points of God's activity on their behalf (Josh 4:4–9). Military victory is etched into the religious psyche. Ritual action such as circumcision (Josh 5:1–9) and festival (Josh 5:9–12) are right responses to God's action on Israel's behalf reinforcing the cult and endorsing the ruler. Through the narrative, victory is found through divine power in alliance with military power. Victory is a result of complete obedience to divine command (e.g., Jericho, Josh 6). Failure is due to disobedience and the loss of God's favor (e.g., Ai, Josh 7). This is resolved through repentance and ritual action. Violence is justified to purify God's people where the covenant is violated as in the killing of Achan's family (Josh 7). This leads to the subsequent victory as the sin is remedied and purity restored (Josh 8). The covenant is renewed, bringing assurance of the divine support for the campaign (Josh 8:30–35).

These patterns are found throughout the ancient world as one tracks the clash of empires, with rulers allying with priests' spiritual power and endorsement to win great victories. The assumption is that where divine favor is found, victory is assured. Victory then proves this was right—a kind of circularity of logic. Defeat sends the religious leaders to their death for failure, or back to their divinities for a fresh approach. Divine favor comes through obedience to the terms of the cult. A ritual such as sacrifice and purification restores divine favor. Military victory then is linked intimately to the religious system. If one wins, the God or gods are pleased. If one loses, then the gods or God are displeased and the people are seemingly guilty of some failure or sin and cursed. Later this will be a problem for Jesus in the eyes of some, as he is put to death by Romans, suggesting that the Roman pantheon is superior to Yahweh. This will be turned on its head at the resurrection, where Jesus is vindicated. The subsequent spread of the Christian faith through the Roman world ironically turns this upside down.

The Gibeonite deception of Joshua 9 illustrates ancient thinking. Because of Israel's blazing military success as they enter the land, the Gibeonites recognized the spiritual vindication and so the invincibility of the Israelites. They wisely and shrewdly chose deceit and submission rather than military engagement, and they thus deceived Joshua and the Israelites, effectively selling themselves into slavery to ensure their survival. This pattern of subjugation and voluntary submission is seen in the ancient world, whereby city rulers, rather than face defeat, effectively hand over their cities to invading forces. One example of this I came across on my recent trip through Europe is Pergamum (modern Bergama). In 133 BC, Attalus III, the last king of the Attalic dynasty, in the context of civil war with no male heir and under Roman imperial power, chose to hand over his whole kingdom (aside from Pergamum) to Rome rather than see it destroyed. Because of this, Pergamum and other Greek cities were spared, allowed independent administration, and were exempted from tribute.[15] The same pattern was seen in the capitulation of Jerusalem to Alexander the Great (see chapter 3). At the time of the Jewish revolt, coterminous with the writing of Mark's Gospel, the city of Sepphoris refused to support the rebels, throwing their support behind Rome and withstanding Jewish attacks.[16]

The subsequent narrative of Joshua endorses the pattern of military victory and divine vindication, empowerment, and action. For example, in Joshua 10 it is recorded that the Lord confused the enemies, intervened with weather events (hailstones), and the sun stood still. This ensured a great victory for Israel over an alliance of kings who had formed to defeat the invaders. Another example is Joshua 11, where God directs Joshua to be unafraid and to win over another huge alliance of northern kings with specific instructions to hamstring the horses and burn their chariots, giving them a great victory (Josh 11:6–8). Weather events are interpreted spiritually, and are seen as an endorsement of the invading force's supremacy. Destruction was total (e.g.

15. "Pergamum, Pergamos," 2:1644.

16. Strange ("Sepphoris," 1091) notes that, while a Jewish city, Sepphoris remained pro-Roman, and refused even to aid Jerusalem when the temple was threatened (Josephus, *Life*, 65). They cut a deal with Vespasian at Ptolemais and he helped them defeat a force led by Josephus (*J.W.* 3.4).

Josh 10:20, 30) in north and south. Consequently, the whole land was taken (Josh 11:16). The somewhat ironical consequence of this is peace gained through violent force; "the land had rest from war" (Josh 11:23).

This is the pattern of the ancient world (and much of the present); "peace" is gained through conquest and subjugation of enemies within and without, no matter how brutal (*Pax Augusta*)—it is peace through brutal subjugation. As the account continues, however, there are large pockets of the land unconquered (Josh 13:1–5). This inability to purge the land completely will lead to ongoing problems. The implication is that anything less than total extermination is a failure, disobedience to the divine, and it sows the seeds of future problems. The land, however, is at peace in the hands of Abraham's descendants, and can now be split up across the twelve tribes. The irony of the ancient world (and on into today, e.g., WWII) is that *peace was achieved through military conquest*. Indeed, failure to exterminate the inhabitants with their idolatrous practices will effectively be seen as the root of Israel's decline into idolatry. This effectively shifts the blame from Israel to others. Jesus will directly and surprisingly confront this when he targets Israel and not the nations for her sins (more on this later).

For our purposes, as we turn later to Mark, the name "Joshua" will be of immense importance. "Jesus" is the Greek for the Hebrew *Yehoshua* or *Yeshua* and God's choice of name for Jesus (Matt 1:21). Hence, while it is true that Jesus is the new Moses and Davidic king, Jesus is also the new *Joshua*. The first Joshua led the conquest of the Promised Land through spiritual and military power. He was a great military leader. Jesus was endorsed and empowered by Yahweh, and God acted around and through him. Joshua performed great miracles. He was a fearless and courageous warrior leader. He was not a king who claimed absolute power and set up a dynasty, but he would have made a good one by ancient standards. Religiously, he was obedient to the Law, the terms of the covenant. His endorsement by Yahweh was seen in his victories. He was ruthless, determined to obey God's call for extermination and removing those who violated the terms of holy war, such as the destruction of Achan's whole family for failure to uphold the command not to take any plunder (Josh 7). He led a collective of twelve tribes with twelve tribal leaders (cf. the twelve disciples). He purified the land, removing the pagans with their abominable practices. He brought Israel God's "Shalom." The Markan account of Jesus is set against this backdrop. However, as we will see, Jesus does not conform to the pattern or expectations of this first Joshua; at least, not in literal terms—watch this space.

The Time of the Judges

During the Judges period, power is defined by military might linked to spiritual obedience. After Joshua died, the people sought to purge the land, taking Jerusalem (Judg 1). As in Joshua's time, the attacks were endorsed by God, and victory is due to his guidance, vindication, empowering, and action (Judg 1:2, 4, 19–20). For example, "the Lord gave the Canaanites and Perizzites into their hands" (Judg 1:4). Victory indicated God's presence: "the Lord was with the men[17] of Judah" (Judg 1:19). However, Israel was not able to annihilate the inhabitants (e.g., Judg 1:21, 27–36). As one might expect, this is interpreted spiritually as a result of disobedience to the covenant, the consequence being perpetual problems from the pagan population and defeat (Judg 2:1–5).

After this, Israel's life became a cycle as this diagram demonstrates.

The Cycle of the Judges

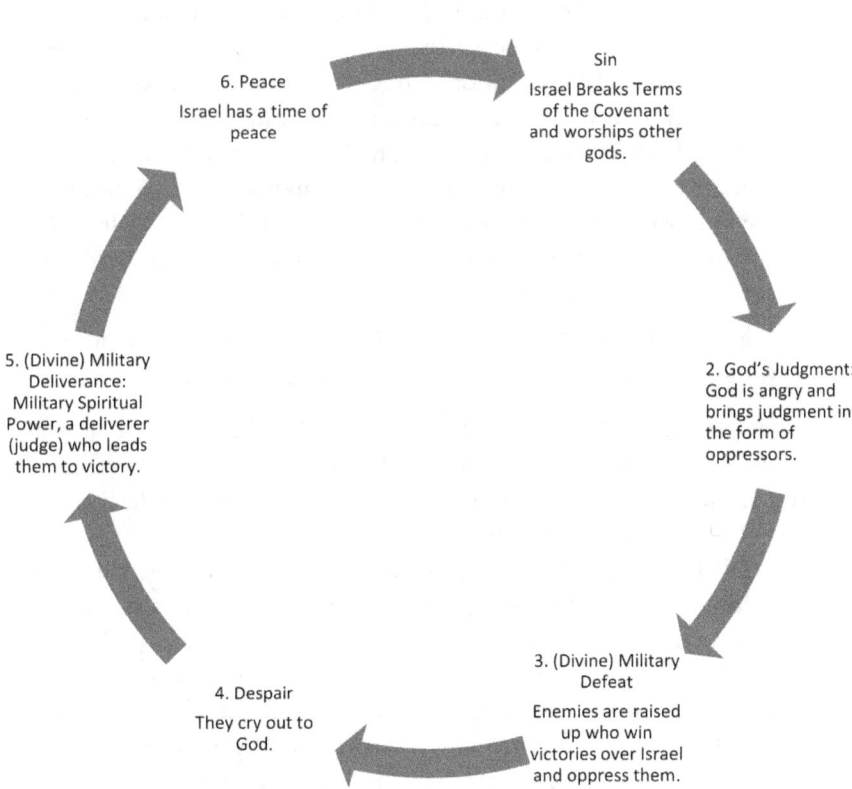

---

17. I have kept "men" here as it is appropriate as war was mainly the sphere of the men back in the day (and in the main today, actually).

The pattern recurs either explicitly or implicitly through the Judges accounts; namely, Othniel, Ehud, Shamgar, Deborah, Gideon, Tola, Jair, Jephthah, Ibzan, Abdon, and Samson, with varying levels of detail:

1. Sin: Israel sins through idolatry. Critically, it is military failure that is the cause of their sin as they fall into worship of the gods of their neighbors, especially Baal and the Ashtaroths (Judg 2:11–13; 3:7, 12; 4:1; 6:1; 8:33–35; 10:6; 13:1).

2. God's Judgment: God acts against Israe, due to his anger at their idolatry and sin (Judg 2:14; 3:8, 12; 4:2; 6:1; 10:7; 13:1).

3. Divine Military Defeat: Enemies are allowed by God to invade parts of the nation and assume political power, oppressing Israel for a period (Judg 2:14–15; 3:8, 12–14; 4:2–3; 6:1–6; 10:8–9; 13:1).

4. Despair: Israel is in despair and cries out to God for deliverance (Judg 2:15; 3:8, 15; 4:3; 6:6; 10:10).

5. Divine Military Deliverance: God raises judges who lead Israel to victory over their enemies. This person is spiritually empowered through the rushing Spirit of God. Often this is an unlikely person, or the victory is unusual or unexpected, indicating God's vindication and involvement, e.g., left-handed Ehud, a woman Deborah, an insignificant timid man Gideon, or a blinded and weakened Samson. In the interplay of the human and the divine, it is the divine who is the empowering force (Judg 2:16; 3:9–10, 15–29, 31; 4:4–24; 6:7—8:27; 11:1—12:7; 13:2—16:31).

6. Peace: After the deliverance of the Judge, Israel has a time of peace without threat from enemies (Judg 3:11, 30; 5:31; 8:28).

However, after these moments of salvation, Israel repeatedly falls back into idolatry usually after the death of the judge, and the cycle resumes. Through the story of Judges over time, there is a progressive decline into almost complete idolatrous anarchy.

While the judge is alive, God is with him or her. However, after the judge's death, the people turned quickly to idolatry, and the pattern recurs (Judg 1:17–23). This is probably part of the reason for the later desire for a monarch. Israel falsely believed a dynasty would halt this process of decline. The nations who oppress Israel are seen as a consequence of sin and Israel's failure to drive them out. While they are enemies, they are instruments of God in his work with his people. Thus, military engagement, defeat/victory, and divine rejection/divine favor are intimately linked. Israel's whole existence is defined with reference to war and peace, and all of history is viewed through the spectacles of their own existence.

The story of Abimelech in Judges 9 cannot pass without comment. It illustrates the patterns of power from the ancient world which would become more prevalent in Israel after the monarchy. It anticipates what will happen later as the monarchy is established and declines. After the death of the "great" judge Gideon (Jerub-baal), his son Abimelech sought to gain total control. This was essentially a move toward dynastic monarchy. To do so, he called for the support of the people, raised funds, and employed a small army (Judg 9:1–4). This is classic military posturing in the ancient world. Recalling Cain's fratricide (Gen 4:1–16), he then murdered his *seventy* brothers (Judg 9:5). While breaking Jewish law (e.g. Exod 20:13; Deut 5:17), Abimelech here is acting in accordance with dynastic imperial principles. This act of brutal violence is typical of the ancient world, to assume power required removing all political threats of which brothers are the greatest. Abimelech is then crowned as king, a despotic dictator (Judg 9:6). Such rulers dominate the story of the ancient world. Jotham, the youngest son of Gideon, escaped (Judg 9:5), and he proved to be Abimelech's undoing, predicting what will occur with a parable (Judg 9:7–21). The story that ensues is typical of the ancient world of military and political collision and intrigue, full of violence, treachery, rivalry, and war between Shechem, led by Gaal (who also seeks power), and her "king" Abimelech. For the writer of Judges, it is God who brings Abimelech's downfall as justice for Gideon's family, sending an evil spirit to incite the conflict between Abimelech and Shechem (Judg 9:23–24). Similarly, his death is attributed to God and the curse given by his brother Jotham (Judg 9:56). As such, even in Israel, power was becoming increasingly attached to the model of the warrior-king and applied brutally to remove all obstacles.

Judges 17 focuses around the continuing decay of Israel into sin and anarchy. The key theme is that Israel has no king (Judg 18:1; 19:1; 21:25), preparing the way for the monarchy to come. This decay is seen in the story of Micah, his idols, the idolatrous Levite and Danites who invade "peaceful and unsuspecting" Laish, and the Levite with the concubine and her Sodom-like rape (Judg 17–19). This act leads to civil war against the Benjaminites (Judg 20). Again, we have the alliance of divine authority and war with God directing the battle against Benjamin (Judg 20:18, 23, 28).

The cycle of Judges revolves around military power. Military power is related to fidelity, to the covenant, and so to God's blessing and vindication. Military defeat is related to sin, and so to God's anger and judgment. This pattern shapes the ancient world and Israel's understanding before Christ comes.

United Monarchy

The Desire for a King

The failure of the twelve-tribe confederacy, the resultant internal anarchy, and the oppression of foreign nations, especially the Philistines (1 Sam 4–5), all led to a desire in Israel for monarchy. The bridge between the two systems was the Prophet-Judge Samuel, whose story dominates the first sixteen chapters of 1 Samuel, leading to the beginning of the Davidic dynasty. Samuel was born to a desperate barren woman Hannah due to divine intervention (1 Sam 1—2:11). He is specifically dedicated and called by God (1 Sam 1; 3) as a replacement for the failed Eli and family (1 Sam 2:12–36) who reflect the corrupted state of Israel. Samuel enters a situation where the word of the Lord was rare and brings God's word to Israel (3:1, 7, 19, 21; 4:1). He is the last of the Judges delivering Israel from Philistine reign (1 Sam 7).

Incidentally, there are astonishing consistencies with Luke's account of John the Baptist, who also arrives on the scene when prophets were a distant memory. John bridges the gap between the old system and the kingship of Christ, he is born of a barren woman, and he anoints the new Davidic king, the Christ (Luke 1–2). As Samuel legitimizes Saul and then David, John legitimizes Jesus as per the same pattern.

Returning to Samuel, as is the case throughout the Judges period, his sons do not maintain the covenant but turn to evil and injustice (1 Sam 8:1–3). This is the straw that broke the camel's back for the people of Israel, and they cry out for a new political system: monarchy. The desire was to emulate the political system of the surrounding nations, a single monarch. They somehow thought that a dynastic system would resolve the problem of spiritual, moral, and political decline. How wrong they were! From the ashes of this system will come Jesus, who inverts it utterly—God is in control despite appearances.

Samuel's response to the desire for a king is understandably one of reluctance. As noted above, the covenant relationship with God was based on a kingship model with Yahweh as King, and Israel his people (Suzerain-Vassal). The request for a king was then a rejection of God as King (see 1 Sam 10:19). Indeed, the lesson of Abimelech from Judges 19 should have warned them off monarchy! Anyway, Samuel is deeply perturbed (1 Sam 8:6). He receives a word from God that this is indeed a rejection of God's kingship, but God is prepared to allow them to go ahead with a warning of the implications of monarchy (1 Sam 8:7–9). With the privilege of hindsight, we can now see that God had a plan which would culminate in Christ. They had no such privilege nor knew of their need.

Subsequently, Samuel warns them of the consequences of this choice. He tells them that monarchy will see power in the hands of one (always a dangerous situation). This will include the conscription of the best young men in the military, the taking of the best young women of the nation for the king's service and pleasure, and the accumulation of the best of the harvest to feed his bureaucracy—all the trappings of imperialism then and now! Indeed, the oppression would be so great that Samuel predicted Israel would eventually cry out to God for release from the system. However, Samuel warned them that the consequence would be that God would not answer this cry but let it run its inevitable course (1 Sam 8:10–18).

The people, however, are determined that monarchy is better than the mess they were in under the system of Judges and shared rule.[18] However, Samuel's warning is rejected. The people respond: "'No!' they said. "We want a king over us. Then we will be *like all the other nations*, with a king to lead us and to go out before us and *fight our battles*'" (1 Sam 8:19–20). These verses sums up the situation. They were clearly impressed by the warrior-king dynastic model and believed that their best hope was to adopt it. This, they believed, would give them the stability they yearned for. Power through military might and dynastic succession defined their perspective. Perhaps they even have hopes of regional supremacy under a warrior-king, an "Israelite Empire." Through such a ruler, with God's absolute power, they would have peace and stability. Whether this is right or not (and it is not of course), God's response through Samuel is to allow the establishment of a monarchy (1 Sam 8:21–22).

This is a critical moment in our inquiry. It sets the scene for Jesus in many ways. The desire for a king is a rejection of God as King. It is selling out to the patterns of the world around them which are profoundly flawed, and, dare I say, evil. True power is found in trust in God rather than military power based around one man and his family. Dynastic imperialism leads to subjugation and oppression, for "power corrupts, and absolute power corrupts absolutely."[19] Indeed, even where we find a "benevolent dictator" (an oxymoron), it is rare that his son carries on in the same vein. The desire for a king, then, is a form of idolatry reflecting the rejection of God in the garden, the hubris of Babel, and trust in human power and might. God's permissive approach is also critical, as it sets the scene for the next thousand years

---

18. This all goes to show that it is not always the system that is the problem—the people and their hearts make the system work. The problem with communism is the people involved. The problem with capitalism is the people. The problem too with Presbyterianism, Catholicism, Anglicanism, Pentecostalism, etc., is the people, not the systems.

19. See "Power Corrupts," http://www.phrases.org.uk/meanings/absolute-power-corrupts-absolutely.html.

of Israel's history, which will be defined by monarchy one way or another, whether it be their own, the oppressive power of others who dominate Israel, or their yearning for political liberation. This time is vital, as it sets the scene for the growing hope of a redeemer who, it is believed, will be the ultimate warrior-king and deliver Israel. It is important for understanding this figure when he comes.

Saul

Reluctantly, but seemingly under the guidance of God (1 Sam 9:15–16), Samuel then anoints Saul of Benjamin as king. He is an appropriate pick—a tall, standout young man who appears perfect to lead Israel as king (1 Sam 9:2, 22–23). As with the Judges, he is empowered by God's Spirit (1 Sam 9:6, 9–11). There were danger signs immediately, however, when Saul hid himself at his coronation (1 Sam 10:21–22). He instantly attracted supporters who are described as men of valor (1 Sam 10:26). However, initially, others also reject him (1 Sam 10:27).

In 1 Samuel 11, Saul's career as warrior-king begins well. Empowered by the Spirit and so endorsed by God, he takes up the challenge laid down by the Ammonites to free Jabesh Gilead and calls Israel to support him, warning them of the severe consequences for not doing so (he will cut their oxen up!). Three hundred thirty thousand of Israel's best men came to fight with their new king, and Saul led them to a great victory. The people then rallied around Saul, calling for all opponents to be killed. Saul, however, gives the glory to the Lord for the victory, showing impressive benevolence toward these opponents, and Saul's kingship is affirmed (1 Sam 11:12–15). What a great start for a warrior-king!

The remainder of the account of Saul's career in 1 Samuel 13–15 is full of violence and war, particularly with the Philistines (e.g., 1 Sam 13:1–15; especially 1 Sam 13:3–7, 23; 14:23, 47–52; 15:1–9). He also broke the treaty with the Gibeonites and sought to annihilate them (2 Sam 21:1–3). In this section, Saul and his son Jonathan lead with gallantry and valor, embodying courage as warrior-leaders. It seems Jonathan is a worthy dynastic heir.

However, Saul's failure is spiritual, he is usurping the role of the priest and refusing to obey Samuel's instructions; hence, he and his family are supplanted. The corruption of Saul is seen in his murder of the eighty-five priests of Nob and the townspeople for supposedly supporting David (1 Sam 22:10–19) and in his consultation of the medium of Endor (1 Sam 28). This shows that the ancient model could not be torn away from its religious and spiritual vindication.

Ultimately, Saul and Jonathan died in war (how appropriate) along with all his sons, ending the Sauline kingship (1 Sam 31:1–4). Interestingly, the Philistines displayed his head and armor in the temple of their gods, the Ashtaroths, to demonstrate the superiority of their deities over Yahweh. The Saul story shows us that it was not merely a warrior-king that was idealized, but one who was fully faithful to the nation's religious system. Saul had a lot of the attributes required, but was deeply and spiritually flawed.

David

David is particularly important as the expectations of a messiah are framed around the Davidic kingship and monarchy (e.g. Matt 1:1; Luke 1:32; Rom 1:3; 2 Tim 2:8; Rev 5:5). A large portion of 1 Samuel (1 Sam 16–31), all of 2 Samuel's twenty-four chapters, and 1 Kings 1–2, are devoted to David's rise to power and kingship. The account of the monarchy in the Chronicles begins with Saul's death and then gives the remainder of 1 Chronicles 11–29 to David's kingship. Here is not the time to attempt a full account of this material. Rather, I will seek to highlight the emphasis on military power which lies at the heart of these passages.

In the accounts, God's choice of David as Saul's replacement is surprising to Samuel in that, like Saul, Eliab, the *eldest* son of Jesse, is more impressive in height (1 Sam 16:6). This time the *youngest* David is God's choice based on his character ("the heart," 1 Sam 16:7). David is a man of worship. He is described by a servant as "a brave man and *a man of war*. He speaks well and is a fine-looking man. And the Lord is with him" (1 Sam 16:18). He thus appeals as an ideal, potential, ancient, sovereign warrior-king. He is also a shepherd, and as such, knows how to care for and protect his flock. As Moses was prepared in part for leadership in Pharaoh's court, David is prepared in Saul's court as his armor bearer and harpist.

David's greatness is soon seen in that, despite his youth (esp. 1 Sam 17:33), while all the army of Israel cowered in fear, against extraordinary odds, through complete faith in his deity Yahweh, and with great courage and skill (1 Sam 17), he defeated the prodigious Goliath (esp. 1 Sam 17:26, 44–47). For David, such courage was another day at the shepherd boy's office; he had driven off lions and bears from his flocks (1 Sam 17:34–36). This led to a glorious victory over the Philistines.

Such a victory is the stuff of the glorious ancient warrior-king: complete trust in his God, courage, and ruthless efficiency in war. David then was taken into the royal court and quickly promoted (1 Sam 18:5). On return from the war, David was venerated above Saul (1 Sam 18:7). As is unsurprising in the ancient world where royal power was always vulnerable to overthrow, this made David a genuine threat to Saul, and so Saul sought to kill him directly (1 Sam 18:8-12; 19:1-17; 23:7—24:22; 26:1-25) and in battle (1 Sam 18:17, 24-25).

This is typical of ancient political machinations; one is always looking over one's shoulder and trying to kill off any potential threat (cf. Herod, Matt 2). However, the account speaks of David's extraordinary military success (e.g., 1 Sam 18:13-14, 30). He marries Saul's daughter, strengthening his political position and increasing Saul's paranoia (1 Sam 18:27-29). Here are another two features of the ancient political construct; first, paranoia; second, intermarriage to cement political alliances and strengthen power.

The importance of the war motif is found in 1 Sam 22:10, where even in Gath of Philistia, with whom David fought and to which he fled, David was sung of as a great warrior (1 Sam 21:11). Led by God, he defeated the Philistines who attacked the Judean town of Keilah (1 Sam 23:1-6). In 1 Samuel 27:2-12, David led raids in which he determined to kill every person to ensure no one betrayed him (esp. 1 Sam 27:8-9, 11). This is seen as legitimate as it is in Philistine territory, demonstrating that violence outside Israel was deemed legitimate for the good of Israel. He then offers to fight with the Philistines, but this is rejected (1 Sam 28-29). Then, guided by God through priest and ephod, he defeats the Amalekites, rescuing his men's kidnapped wives and children (1 Sam 30). We see violence justified with the brutal killing of the Amalekite who delivers Saul's crown and armband and tells David of his death (2 Sam 1:15).

After Saul's death, we see the problem of rule by military power with an outbreak of intrigue and violent conflict. This was initiated by the house of Saul, which preferred Ish-Bosheth over David. Ultimately, David triumphed, Ish-Bosheth was murdered, and his killers slaughtered (2 Sam 2-4). This sort of battle for power is par for the course in the ancient world. For example, after the death of Alexander the Great, with no legitimate heir, there were forty years of war between "the successors" which eventually settled into four seats of power, including the murders of Alexander IV and Philip III. Similarly, the death of Julius Caesar in 44 BC triggered fifteen years of Roman civil war until Octavian established the *pax*-Augustus and ruled as emperor.

David's first act as king is war. He attacked the Jebusites in the fortress of Zion in Jerusalem and claimed it. Having gained the key cultic center of Jerusalem, as is typical of an ancient king, he built up its defenses (2 Sam 5). Again, as is usual, he took more concubines and wives and had many children (2 Sam 5:13-15, cf. 20:3). After consulting God, he then overcame the Philistines (2 Sam 5:17-25). He established the main religious symbol of Israel, the Ark of the Covenant in the city, the throne of God, replacing the local deities (2 Sam 6). David then sought to build a temple for the Ark, a temple palace for the throne of God (2 Sam 7:1-2). All this is typical behavior for ancient kings who, upon winning battles, use the spoils of war to build sanctuaries to honor their deities who had given them success. This humiliates the opponents and demonstrates the superiority of the conqueror's deity. This then led to the foundation of the Davidic covenant given through Nathan (2 Sam 7:5-16).

2 Samuel 8 and 10 give an account of further victories of David, the subjugation of Israel's enemies, the plundering of their wealth, and the extension of the kingdom, reinforcing his status as a great warrior-king. In all this, David acts like a typical king taking control of his world. Those defeated included the Philistines, the Moabites, Hadadezer, the Arameans, Edom, the Amalekites, and the Ammonites. Others, like Tou, the king of Hamath, avoid destruction by war through yielding and paying honorum and tribute (2 Sam 8:9-10). Given the choice of the easy way (surrender), or the hard way (defeat), he took the easy way.

The writer of Samuel records, "The Lord gave David victory wherever he went" (2 Sam 8:14). He was then the ideal king, "doing what was just and right for all his people" with a strong, stable administrative structure and even showing generosity to Saul's descendants—a risky, merciful, and self-confident attitude (2 Sam 8:15—9:14). All this anticipates what the ultimate Davidic king should do. Like David, a messiah will lead Israel to glorious victories and will extend Israel's reign and the worship of God. Such is the expected pattern of the redeemer Theo. However, Jesus' way of doing this utterly subverts the ancient expectation of military and political subjugation.

In 2 Samuel 11, however, the wheels come off the ideal start to David's reign. It gives an account of David's taking of Bathsheba and the setting up of her husband Uriah to die in military combat to cover his tracks after her pregnancy. Again, we see the corruption of power where it is confined to one man, no matter how talented and how good a start he makes. There is further military engagement with the Ammonites in 2 Samuel 12. In 2 Samuel 13-18, we have an account full of intrigue and violence in a failed attempt of David's son Absalom to wrest power from David by force. This is again the stuff of empires and kingships whereby a king is never safe from challenge, especially from one's own son.

David then had to deal with another threat, Sheba, from the same tribe as Saul (Benjamin), who also seeks to establish himself as king (2 Sam 20:1-5). Here we have the previous dynasty flexing its muscles, trying to regain control, another typical feature of ancient politics (and modern). David sent his men after Sheba. Joab, David's army commander, then tricked Sheba's main man Amasa and ruthlessly stabbed him (2 Sam 20:8–10). This led to Sheba hiding in Abel Beth Maacah with the inhabitants of the town choosing to kill him and cut his head off to avoid destruction. This story illustrates the problem of ruling by coercive power: one is forced to deal with others who seek to usurp the ruler's place of power with ruthless brutality (2 Sam 20). It shows too how the people must function in such an environment; fear controls them and they make choices purely for self-preservation, even the choice to kill. Such a story adds legitimacy to a ruler being utterly ruthless when one assumes power; one *must* remove *all* enemies and leave no vestige of opposition. Sheba proves this point.

There are glimmers of light in the story of David. Within the framework of the war motif, David shows mercy to Saul several times by refusing to kill him (1 Sam 24, 26) and ensuring a just distribution of the plunder (1 Sam 30:26–31). He also sought to make reparation for Saul's slaughter of the Gibeonites (2 Sam 21:2–3). However, the means of doing this was to hand over seven male descendants of Saul to be slaughtered and exposed to public view (2 Sam 21:5–9). Such brutality is the stuff of ancient monarchies.

The military career of David the warrior-king concludes in 2 Samuel 21:15 with his rescue from death by Abishai, David now being too old to continue to lead his people in battle. The song of David in 2 Samuel 22 is full of references to God's salvation in battle (e.g. vv. 15, 18–43). David always honored his deity. Some of the words of the song demonstrate the spiritual endorsement, ruthlessness, and objectification of one's enemies that is required (vv. 38–43):

> I pursued my enemies and *crushed them*; I did not turn back till they were *destroyed*. I *crushed them* completely, and they could not rise; they fell beneath my feet. You armed me with strength for battle; you made my adversaries *bow at my feet*. You made my enemies turn their backs in *flight*, and I destroyed my foes. They cried for help, but there was no one to save them—to the Lord, but he did not answer. I *beat them* as fine as the dust of the earth; I *pounded* and *trampled* them like mud in the streets.

Second Samuel 23–24 give further evidence of the centrality of war to David's reign. First, in 2 Samuel 23:8–39 the writer gives us a list of his greatest warriors, David's mighty men. What is emphasized is their ability to kill multitudes of opponents. For example, Josheb-Basshebeth, who was chief of David's inner circle of three (cf. Jesus' inner circle of Peter, James and John), killed eight hundred men in one encounter (2 Sam 24:8)! Similarly, Abishai killed three hundred (2 Sam 24:18). These and the other thirty-five leading warriors of Israel were held in great honor. Their loyalty to David shows his greatness as a leader.

In ancient terms, then, David was a great warrior-king, leading his people into battle, ruthlessly and justly dealing with internal and external threat. He united his people, he subdued their enemies, and he secured the nation. He honored his deity. This is how ancient nations were established and maintained. He headed up the dynasty that would follow. He is viewed with great adoration in the subsequent history of Israel. So much so, in fact, that the long-hoped-for messiah would be his descendant. All that was lacking in David's reign was the desire and attempt to expand and begin to assume the territories of those surrounding them. Such ideas, I will argue (at least implicitly), are associated with the Davidic descendant who would bring ultimate peace.

Solomon

In 1 Kings 1, as one would expect in a dynastic context, the power plays for the throne of David began between his sons. There are two main claimants: Adonijah and Solomon.[20] Adonijah takes the direct approach, preparing a force and gathering support from some of David's administration to assume power (1 Kgs 1:5–10). Meanwhile, the prophet Nathan and Solomon's mother Bathsheba take a more subtle "spiritual" approach and seek David's support from his deathbed for Solomon. David grants his favor and, with the support of the priest (Zadok), the prophet (Nathan), and David's elite troops (the mighty men, e.g., Benaniah), Solomon becomes king (1 Kgs 1:11–53). Somewhat surprisingly for the ancient world and Israel's subsequent history, this occurred without bloodshed. It is notable how Solomon is clever in ensuring he has full spiritual (priest and prophet) and military endorsement. Adonijah is a victim of his political naivety (as many good and not-so-good men and women often are!).

Solomon's reign is the heyday of Israel's history, the peak of the dynasty. After David's reign of establishing the monarchy securely and giving Israel

20. Adonijah is listed in 2 Samuel 3:2 as David's fourth son. Amnon his first, born from Ahinoam, was murdered by Absalom's men (2 Sam 13:28–29). Chileab (or Daniel), his second (2 Sam 3:3; 1 Chr 3:2) born of Abigail, is not mentioned again, but must be out of the running. Absalom (2 Sam 3:3), the son of Maacah, is the third and led a revolt against David which saw Absalom's demise (2 Sam 18:9–15). This left Adonijah as legitimate heir to David's throne (1 Kgs 1:6). If we trust the Chronicler, after Adonijah were born Shephatiah by Abital; Ithream by Eglah; Shimea; Shobab; Nathan; and then Solomon, who is then the tenth son. Yet he had the support of David himself, the favored wife Bathsheba, the priest Zadok, prophet Nathan, and David's mighty fighting men. Hence, Solomon is king. Such is the way of dynastic succession.

stability, Solomon's reign represents a different phase. Externally, through David, Israel has subdued her enemies, and so war is not required, at least initially. The writer of 1 Kings states that he "had peace on all sides" (1 Kgs 4:24). Internally, the people were secure (1 Kgs 4:25), and all rebellion has been quashed. This is common in the ancient world. For example, after the conquests and establishment of the Roman Empire through Julius Caesar and Augustus, Rome lives in relative peace for over a century (aside from the mess after Nero's death). In that time, successive emperors such as Vespasian, Domitian, Trajan, and Hadrian in particular, built glorious monuments to themselves and their deities in Rome and all over their empire, e.g. the Colosseum, palaces, arches, temples, forums, etc. This is the phase of *pax* and the building of monuments.

Solomon, then, was not a warrior-king like David; as is often the case in the second of a dynasty, he didn't need to be. Rather, as he was not preoccupied with war, he pursued wisdom (what else do you do but become an intellectual?) and demonstrated it (1 Kgs 3; 4:29–34). After all, it is to Solomon that much of the Wisdom Literature of the Old Testament is attributed.[21] Solomon expanded David's minimalist bureaucracy with priests, administrators, military leaders, palace managers, labor managers, and district governors to provide food for the king and household; all to maintain rule throughout the nation (1 Kgs 4, cf. 9:22). He kept an army with officers, captains, and commanders of chariot and charioteers (1 Kgs 9:22), along with a navy manned by men of Tyre (1 Kgs 9:26–28). This paid for itself with trips to places like Ophir and pillaging for (in this case) four hundred twenty talents of gold, almugwood, and precious stones (1 Kgs 9:28; 10:11–12). 1 Kings 10:26 suggests that he had one thousand four hundred chariots (all worth six hundred shekels of silver) and twelve thousand horses, all the very best, imported from Egypt, to the value of one hundred fifty shekels—which would require a fair number of staff and feeding! He also built towns to house them!

An expanding royal and governmental retinue requires feeding, and so rule necessarily involved taking tribute from the region (1 Kgs 4:20–26). Without the specter of war, Solomon turned his attention to building a temple for the God who had blessed them and of which David had dreamed. King Hiram of Tyre provided the timber in exchange for food, and twenty Galilean towns were simply handed over (forget the poor inhabitants) (1 Kgs 9:10). This added further to the requirements of tribute from the people both in Israel and Tyre (1 Kgs 5:1–12). Of course, with the temple to be built, Solomon required labor. As with most kings, he got them from those of non-Israelite descent; the remnant of the Canaanites, the Amorites,

---

21. See for a good discussion Crenshaw, *Old Testament Wisdom*, 31–43.

Hittites, Perizzites, Hivites, and Jebusites (1 Kgs 9:20–21). This is the pattern of enlisting slaves from one's enemies, something that is prevalent where empires rule the world. This, of course, breeds enmity, and often the seeds of future overthrow are sown through this oppression.

These included thirty thousand men to bring timber from Lebanon (1 Kgs 5:13), seventy thousand carriers, eighty thousand stone cutters, and thirty-three thousand foremen to supervise the workmen. He employed five hundred fifty Jewish officials to oversee the laborers (1 Kgs 9:23). He also employed Huram of Tyre to oversee the creation of the furnishings—a workforce of some two hundred thirteen thousand people! While those who were slaves would not be well paid, feeding nearly a quarter of a million people for a project is a massive drain on a nation's resources, especially when the project lasted seven years. As if that were not enough, his own palace took another thirteen years to build, it being twice the size of the temple[22]—a grand total of twenty years of construction! He also built supporting terraces for the temple and palace, the wall of Jerusalem, the towns of Hazor, Megiddo (which would be the place of the last stand against the Romans), and Gezer (this final town had been destroyed by Egyptians and gifted to Solomon's wife, who was Pharaoh's daughter. Such building projects are the pattern of dictatorships; people are pawns in political intrigue and alliances. He also built Lower Beth Horon, Baalath, Tadmor, store cities, and towns for chariots and horses (1 Kgs 9:15–19). He also had a fleet of trading ships (1 Kgs 10:22).

While the building of the temple was an act of devotion to Yahweh, it is surely significant that the temple (the palace in which God was enthroned on the ark, see 1 Kgs 8) was *only half the size* of the palace of the King. It shows how power in the hands of one man corrupts. Anyone who trips through Rome, Greece, and Turkey, viewing the glorious monuments (as I have done), realizes that these were all built in much the same way. It also costs a lot to maintain the rituals of the temple itself with the expectations of the Jewish sacrifice system and priesthood. As such, these monuments are glorious at one level, but at another, they represent the subjugation and exploitation of people for a monarch's ends.

Other trappings of power are seen in Solomon's reign. As is the wont of monarchs, Solomon also hosted foreign dignitaries such as the Queen of Sheba, who arrived bearing gifts of spices, gold, and stones (1 Kgs 10:1–10,

---

22. The temple was sixty cubits long (twenty-eight meters, ninety feet), twenty cubits wide (nine meters, thirty feet), and thirty cubits high (fourteen meters, thirty-five feet). The palace was one hundred cubits long (forty-five meters, one hundred fifty feet), fifty cubits wide (twenty-three meters, 34.5 feet) and thirty high (fourteen meters, forty-five feet).

24–25). He also became greatly wealthy with an income of six hundred sixty-six talents of gold per year (twenty-three metric tons worth approximately nine hundred million US dollars in 2010),[23] plus other revenues from merchants, traders, Arabian kings, and the governors who gathered the food (1 Kgs 10:14–15). He used the gold to make shields, a glorious throne for his palace, and goblets (1 Kgs 10:16–25). He also had huge numbers of chariots and horses, as discussed previously. Usually valuable materials like silver, precious stones, and cedar were a dime a dozen. The writer of Kings suggests that Solomon was the wealthiest and wisest king in the world (1 Kgs 10:23). As with most kings, Solomon liked women and gathered an array of wives and concubine. These included a range of non-Israelites, for which the writer of Kings criticizes him for breaking Mosaic Law and being led astray into idolatry. This is seen as the beginning of the decline of Israel under monarchy and the reason for the split that will follow his death (1 Kgs 11:1–13). Overall, he had seven hundred wives and three hundred concubines! Along with the other trappings of power, this would no doubt have been a heavy drain on the resources of the nation.

At this point in his reign, Solomon began to have issues with opponents. For the writer of Kings, the problem was Solomon's idolatry. Without ruling this out, Solomon was also paying the price for the previous bloodshed. The Edomite Hadad had as a boy witnessed the Israelite forces' six-month invasion of Edom in which they had killed "all the men" (1 Kgs 10:15–16). He had found refuge in Egypt, married Pharaoh's sister-in-law Queen Tahphenes in an act of political alliance, and was no doubt motivated to vent his vengeance on the Israel (1 Kgs 10:17–22). Similarly, Rezon was motivated by David's destruction of his nation's forces under Zobah, and he opposed Solomon from Aram (1 Kgs 10:23–25).

The problem with rule by force is that it creates enemies who will take any opportunity for revenge when the opportunity arises—and people have long memories for this sort of thing. The most important opponent was Jeroboam, one of Solomon's own young hotshot officials overseeing the many laborers. No doubt, like Moses who got enraged watching the subjugation of Israel by Pharaoh, Jeroboam was angered by the treatment of his own northern people in Solomon's programs. He received a divine oracle from the prophet Ahijah that he would be king over ten tribes—again we see the fusion of politics and religion: "God is on our side." Solomon's response is what one would expect in the ancient world. He gets wind of this and seeks to kill Jeroboam, forcing him to flee. Enemies must be destroyed by force

---

23. See "Only Gold," http://www.onlygold.com/tutorialpages/value_of_gold.asp.

when one is a ruler (see 1 Kgs 10:27–40). After Solomon's death, this prophetic oracle is fulfilled, further endorsing Jeroboam's self-belief.

Divided Monarchy

The reign of Solomon was at face value a glorious time for Israel. In reality, it was the beginning of the decline. The massive national infrastructure propping up the royal household, the temple, the palace, the cult, the military, Solomon's harem, and he and his entourage's greed, took its toll. It was simply unworkable to maintain what Solomon had established unless the empire expanded to gain more resources—both people and wealth. That is the problem of empires. They must keep growing (like modern market economies [kingdoms?]).

The problem for Solomon was that he had achieved glorious things, but did so at the expense of his own people. Similarly, the religious cult that held the nation together was unraveling into syncretism. It is the philosophical and religious world-view that undergirds ancient empires. The disintegration of Yahwism would see the ethical and theological basis for Israel's breakdown, so that she fell into idolatry and social chaos. Such is the pattern in the ancient world; the cult must be maintained to keep stability (arguably we are seeing this today in western society; as it has rejected Christianity, its moral climate and power is in decline!).

The problems Solomon had created all came home to roost in the aftermath of Solomon's death. 1 Kings 12 records that Rehoboam, the natural heir, seems set to be enthroned. However, when Jeroboam and leaders of Israel (the northern ten tribes) request that Rehoboam lightens their load, he rather stupidly rejects their request, promising even worse. This is typical of an arrogant young king who thinks he knows better. Again, we see here an example of the way power and greed corrupt, with hubris and lust for power and the inevitable subjugation of peoples. This decision leads to the rupture of the nation into two kingdoms: Israel in the north and Judah in the south (including Benjamin) (1 Kgs 12:1–17). As predicted by the Ahijah, Jeroboam is made the king of Israel and Rehoboam over Judah. Rehoboam prepares for war, as one might expect; however, after divine intervention, he desists (1 Kgs 12:21–24).

The Decline and Exile of the North

The subsequent story is one of two dynastic realms, the northern and southern kingdoms. In the north, a new cult was established to give legitimacy to the new kingship. This included idols of golden calves (see Exod 32), shrines and high places, sacrificial system, and a new priesthood (1 Kgs 12:25–33). This also ensured ongoing southern abhorrence of the north, something that lingers in the New Testament with attitudes toward the Samaritans in particular. In the south, the center remained Jerusalem, the temple, and the existing cult. The subsequent narrative is one of spiritual decline until the point of the subjugation of the north by Assyria, and the south by Babylon. Each has a succession of kings; but unlike the southern monarchs, the biblical description of the northern kings is exclusively corrupt.

Through the period of the divided monarchy, war and violence punctuate the narrative. There are wars between north and south (e.g. 1 Kgs 15:6, 16; 2 Kgs 14:8–14) sometimes involving foreign alliances with Syria (e.g. 1 Kgs 15:18–22). In the north, kingships were often interrupted with violent coups, meaning that a strong dynasty could not form. It was commonplace when this happened to kill off the remnant of former royal households (1 Kgs 15:27–30; 16:9–12, 15–18; 2 Kgs 8:7–15; 9:1–13; 15:10, 14, 25, 30). For example, Baasha, after killing Nebat the son of Jeroboam (1 Kgs 15:28), "killed Jeroboam's whole family. He did not leave Jeroboam anyone that breathed but destroyed them all" (1 Kgs 15:29). In turn, Zimri, one of Baasha's officials, killed Baasha and his whole family (1 Kgs 16:9–12). He then killed himself when the army preferred Omri as king! (1 Kgs 16:15–18). Omri was then challenged by Tibni, but prevailed! (1 Kgs 16:21–23). And so, it goes on.

Through the narrative, prophets (especially Elijah and Elisha) arose who challenged royal behavior, but they were more often than not killed or harassed and threatened with death (e.g. 1 Kgs 17:4, 9–15; 19:1–3). In line with the Law, violence, however, is endorsed by the prophets to purge Israel of idolatry and to end evil rule (1 Kgs 17:40; 19:15–18, cf. 2 Kgs 2:23–25; 9:1–3). Wars with foreign nations also punctuate the accounts (1 Kgs 20:1–43; 2 Kgs 6:8–23; 8:20–24; 15:19, 29). At times, north and south form alliances to fight surrounding nations (1 Kgs 22; 2 Kgs 3:4–27). Corruption was rife, including the killing of innocent people and the taking of their property by the king at his will (1 Kgs 21). The writings of the northern eighth-century prophets Amos and Hosea affirm the utter corruption and social decay of the north. Finally, the north is invaded by Assyria, defeated, their best young people killed or exiled, and Samaria resettled (2 Kgs 17).

The Decline and Exile of the South

The story of Judah in the south matches the decline of the north, but takes a little longer. The Davidic dynasty stands firm through a series of kings until exile. While there are bright points in the reigns of Asa, Jehoshaphat, Joash, Amaziah, Azariah, Jotham, Hezekiah, and Josiah, the nation steadily goes into decline. The accounts are littered with rule by military might and force, betrayal, and corruption.

There are wars with foreign powers (e.g. 1 Kgs 14:25–28; 2 Kgs 8:20–22, 28–29; 12:17–19; 14:7; 16:5–18; 18:9—19:37; 23:29–30, 33–35; 24:1–2), sometimes with the north, and others between north and south. Ahaziah was killed in battle by Jehu (2 Kgs 9:14–28).

There were also some instances of internal dynastic violence to claim the throne. After Ahaziah's death in battle, his wife Athaliah sought to gain control by murdering the whole family, including all heirs to the throne. (Wives are very much caught up in the political machinations of ancient politics; look to Rome for example, in Agrippina, Nero's mother, or to Salome, the mother of James and John, Matt 20:20). However, Joash was secreted away while Athaliah reigned for six years. Joash was crowned (at age seven), and Athaliah killed by military forces (2 Kgs 11:1–21). Joash himself was killed by his officials (2 Kgs 12:20–21). Subsequently, Amaziah was enthroned and killed off the executives! (2 Kgs 14:5–6). (Note that he did not kill their sons, based on the law stating that a child should not be put to death for the sins of the fathers). Amaziah was subsequently killed (2 Kgs 14:19–20). Others were also assassinated, including Amon (2 Kgs 21:19). Another example of brutality is Ahaz's sacrifice of his own son (2 Kgs 16:3).

Foreign Rule

The period of monarchy culminated with the Babylonian invasion, destruction, the plundering of Jerusalem and the deity's palace, the temple, and the carrying of Israel's finest into exile (2 Kgs 25). Israel lived for seventy years in exile until the defeat of Babylon by the Medo-Persians led by Cyrus. This deliverance by Cyrus was predicted by Isaiah (Isa 44:28; 45:1) and again was achieved through spiritual endorsement and military power. Ironically, Babylon pays the price for her brutality to Israel at the hands of another enemy. The cycle of colliding kingdoms which wax and wane goes on.

Israel returns to her land, the temple is restored, Jerusalem is rebuilt, and life continues. As noted earlier, from this point on, aside from the

Maccabean period, Israel is under foreign rule; first the Persians, then the Greeks and her daughter empires, and finally the Romans.

The Maccabean Revolt

For one short period of their time under foreign rule, Israel experienced a degree of freedom. This is important for our study because it ended with Roman invasion and so leads into the New Testament period. What occurred illustrates the militaristic and imperial mindset of the time.

It began with a revolt around 167 BC, after Antiochus Epiphanes IV, the Seleucid king of Syria and Hellenized Jewish factions in Judah, deeply offended many other Jews. 1 Maccabees 1 speaks of Hellenized Jews making a deal with Epiphanes and taking on Hellenistic culture. They built a gymnasium in Jerusalem, removed the marks of circumcision (epispasm or infibulation,[24] cf. 1 Cor 7:18), and rejected the covenant. In this period, Epiphanes invaded and plundered Egypt and "defiled" Jerusalem. He took away the temple utensils and sacred items. He also killed opponents, causing great grief in Israel. He then demanded tribute, plundered, killed, and established Jerusalem as a fort. He raided the nation and caused people to flee. He demanded worship of Greek deities, built altars for worship, and oversaw the sacrifice of pigs and other offensive animals. He also rejected the Sabbath and festivals, burned Jewish books, and banned the sacrifice system, circumcision, and the eating of unclean food on the threat of death. A figure of Zeus was placed in the Jerusalem Temple. Some collaborated. However, others were deeply violated, and this led to revolt.

The rebellion was violent, as one would expect (1 Macc 2). It began when Mattathias refused to yield to pressure from a Seleucid army official to make a sacrifice at a pagan altar in Modein near Jerusalem. Mattathias killed the first Jew to make a sacrifice and the official in question. Then Mattathias and his five sons John (Gaddi), Simon (Thassi), Judas (Maccabeus), Eleazer (Avaran), and Jonathan (Apphus), fled into the hill country and gathered an army of

---

24. Epispasm is briefly described in Hall ("Circumcision," 1027) who writes, "Greeks considered a bare glans so repugnant, perhaps indecent, that those born with a defectively short foreskin frequently submitted to epispasm, surgery designed to restore the foreskin to its natural shape (Celsus *Med.* 7.25.1; Soranus *Gynecology* 2.34; Dioscorides 4.153; Hall 1988). Even those adequately endowed frequently secured the foreskin in place with a string or a pin (fibula), a practice called *kunodesme* in Greek, *infibulation* in Latin (Kreuls 1985; Celsus *Med.* 7.25.2), lest the glans inadvertently be revealed. Since the Romans shared the Greek repugnance toward circumcision, circumcision became the target of horror, contempt, scorn, and ridicule (Martial *Epigrams* 7.35, 82) throughout the period."

"freedom fighters"—one person's freedom fighter is another's terrorist! Some were Hasidim, who are described in 1 Macc 2:42–48 as "mighty warriors of Israel,"[25] zealous for Torah, organized an army, angrily killed sinners and renegades, tore down altars, forcibly circumcised uncircumcised boys (painful), and hunted down those who opposed Yahwism. The writer of 1 Maccabees states: "they rescued the law out of the hands of the Gentiles and kings, and they never let the sinner gain the upper hand" (1 Macc 2:48, NRSV). We get a picture of a group here that is ruthlessly violent. However, despite murder and enforced circumcision, in Israel's pre-Christ thought, this is justified in that it defends and purifies Yahwism and drives out the gentiles.

As one might expect, the movement developed into a dynasty with Mattathias succeeded by Judas "the hammer" (Maccabeus), after whom the family and revolt are named. In his final words, Mattathias commends Judas to lead them in the tradition of the great Israelites of the past as he has

> been *a mighty warrior* from his youth; he shall *command the army* for you and *fight the battle* against the peoples. You shall rally around you all who observe the law, and *avenge* the wrong done to your people. *Pay back the Gentiles in full*, and obey the commands of the law. (1 Macc 2:66–68, emphasis added)

This shows the militaristic and vengeful nature of their attitude and that they saw themselves as divinely endorsed defenders of their religious tradition. Judas led as a political and military ruler (1 Macc 3:55). 1 Maccabees speaks positively of his military leadership (e.g. 1 Macc 3:3–9). Judas won a series of battles over the Syrian forces and defeated far superior numbers utilizing guerilla warfare techniques.

Notably, 1 Macc 3–4 speaks in glowing terms of this, reflecting a strong anti-gentile sentiment and celebrating their routing. Judas then led his forces into Jerusalem, cleansing and rebuilding the temple, and attacking the Akra (a fortress or area in Jerusalem). This was then memorialized as the annual Jewish festival Hanukah (1 Macc 4:56–59). (Note how often such days are critical for defining a nation, war blended into history. In Israel's history, Passover. In western history, Bastille Day, Independence Day, Armistice Day, Veterans Day, and Anzac Day in New Zealand/Australia.) That this is found as an active festival at the time of Christ indicates ongoing Jewish celebration of this event; i.e., successful rebellion to overthrow idolatrous pagans is a positive and good thing to be remembered and endorsed (cf. John 10:22).

---

25. The Greek *ischyroi dynamei* can read "mighty men" in the sense of leading citizens. Some believe that from this group of Hasidim came the Essenes and Pharisees.

Under Judas, war for independence continued in Israel and neighboring areas. This included Galilee (1 Macc 5:14–23, 55). After Epiphanes's death, he was succeeded by Antiochus V Eupator, and war continued, with the Syrians inflicting defeats and attacking Jerusalem. However, the Syrians withdrew to deal with internal conflict and agreed to peace terms (1 Macc 6:18–63). In Antioch, Demetrius I Soter overthrew Eupator and sought to gain control of Judah, installing Alcimus as high priest (1 Macc 7:1–5). Judas then defeated Nicanor's forces killing their leader (1 Macc 7:26–50). Judas then sought an alliance with Rome (1 Macc 8:1–32). Demetrius then renewed his attack, and Judas was killed at Eleasa in 161–160 BC (1 Macc 9:1–22).

After Judas's death, the problem of Hellenistic Jews reemerged, and Jonathan Mattathias's youngest son was chosen to succeed Judas (1 Macc 9:23–31). The militaristic mindset is found in the record: "Since the death of your brother Judas there has been no one like him to go *against our enemies* and Bacchides, and to deal with those of our nation who hate us. Now therefore we have chosen you today to take his place as our ruler and leader, *to fight our battle*." Jonathan was popular and succeeded in driving out the Syrians and establishing "peace" (1 Macc 9:32–73).

With the help of Demetrius seeking to strengthen his position against Alexander Epiphanes, the position of Jonathan, the son of Antiochus, was enhanced (1 Macc 10:1–17). However, Alexander then moved to make Jonathan high priest in 153 BC and killed Demetrius[26] and the provincial governor in 150 BC. However, he, in turn, was murdered by the Syrians in 143 or 142 BC—"those who live by the sword, fall by the sword!" (Matt 26:52).

Jonathan was followed by Simon, who expanded the state taking the Akra in 141. He was then confirmed by the Seleucid King as high priest, commander-in-chief, and ethnarch of the Jews (1 Macc 14:41–43). The State became autonomous under Seleucid rule (not independent) and did not need to pay tribute (see Josephus, *J.W.* 1.53; *Ant.* 13.211).

The violence, however, did not end there. Simon and his two sons Judas and Mattathias were murdered by Simon's son-in-law Ptolemy in 134 BC (1 Macc 16:11–17). This is another example of how ancient power worked—your family was your greatest threat! However, Simon's remaining son John Hyrcanus was then confirmed as high priest and ruled for twenty years from 134 to 104 BC. He managed to extend Israel almost to the same extent as in Solomon's day. After his death, as is most often the case in dynasties, his son Aristobulus took power and then entitled himself "king." This is that same old pattern emerging; what began as a military move to overthrow power

---

26. Read 1 Macc 10:25–50 and see how Demetrius tried to get Jonathan back onside with huge offers of freedom for Israel. Jonathan shrewdly rejected it and sided with Alexander, and it proved a good choice.

and purify the nation becomes itself corrupt imperial power! After his death a year later in 103 BC, his wife Alexandria married his brother Alexander Janneus (political and family unions again), and he reigned from 103 to 76 BC. He was successful in extending Israel through military engagement and overcame religious conflict among Sadducees and Pharisees. On his death, Alexandra became ruler with Pharisaic support and established Hyrcanus II as high priest.

After Alexandra's death in 66 BC, Aristobulus II and Hyrcanus II fought a civil war in which the Roman Pompey the Great intervened in 64 BC, culminating with Pompey capturing Jerusalem for the Romans. Hyrcanus was installed as high priest and ethnarch, but not king. Aristobulus, on the other hand, was paraded in Jerusalem as a prisoner. The Hasmoneans continued to rule under Roman authority until Herod became client king in 37 BC.[27]

This period illustrates the patterns of rule by force in the ancient world. Power is seized and extended by military force. The movement is identified with the key warrior-leader. His sons inherit power and either extend it or maintain it by dynastic succession. Key to this is the continual removal of enemies and maintenance of the religious cult which supports the dynasty. This dynasty itself ultimately becomes corrupted, declines, and falls prey to other military and political forces.

The point of the above discussion is to demonstrate that, despite her glorious covenant relationship with Yahweh, Israel was little different than the surrounding nations. The choice for monarchy condemned Israel to the same forces vying for power: military might, alliances, expansion, wealth, monuments, dynastic succession, violence, vying for power, and more.

---

27. See Mandell, "Hasmoneans," 555–56 for detail.

5

The Hope of a Deliverer ("Theo" = "the Expected One")

THE WRITINGS OF THE Old Testament, the Apocrypha, and the Pseudepigrapha indicate a rising tide of hope for the intervention of God to save his chosen people trapped under foreign rule. Among these expectations is the hope of an agent of God who will act on his behalf to bring about his deliverance. Summarizing these expectations is notoriously difficult, as there is a range of ideas across the literature. Some had no interest in such a person. Across the literature that does include such a hope, there are varied designations and expectations. Because no one concept can fully describe this person, I will use the term "Theo", which is an acronym for "the Expected One" (intentionally a loaded name as *Theos* is Greek for God and Jesus is the Son of *Theos* and, as we Christians believe, *Theos* the Son).

A wide range of designations is used of this figure, including notions that relate to the Davidic dynasty. Some of these include "the branch," implying or stating a branch of the dynastic reign of David;[1] similarly, "a shoot from the stump of Jesse";[2] "a holy seed";[3] and a Davidic shepherd.[4] Another frequently used term is the Hebrew term rendered in English "messiah," meaning "anointed" (Greek *Christos* = "Christ").[5] The notion was used of

---

1. See for example, Isa 4:2; 11:1; Jer 23:5; 33:15; Zech 6:12; T. Jud. 24:4, cf. Zech 3:8; Dan 11:7; 4Q285 f7; 4Q174, 1–3 I, 10; 4Q252. 1, 5.

2. See for example, Isa 11:1; 4Q285 f7.

3. See for example, Isa 6:13; 4Q174, 1–3 I, 10.

4. See for example, Ezek 34:23–24; 37:24.

5. See for example, Isa 9:7; 16:5; 1 En. 48:10; 52:4; Pss. Sol. 17:32; 18:5, 7; 4 Ezra 32:28, 29; 12:32; 2 Bar 29:3; 30:1; 39:7; 40:1; 72:2; 1QS 9:10–11; CD 12:22–23; 14:19; 4Q252. 1, 5; *Frg. Tg.* Gen 49:1; *Tg. Onq.* Gen 49:10–12; *Tg. Ps.-J.* Exod 17:16; *Tg. Isa.*

THE HOPE OF A DELIVERER ("THEO" = "THE EXPECTED ONE") 77

the divine commissioning of prophets, priests, and kings. In the main, it is used in the literature in a kingly way. However, in Qumran, there may have been the expectation of two messiahs, a kingly and a priestly messiah.[6] Another notion is "the Son of Man," which originates in Daniel 7:13-14 and speaks of a being like a son of man who meets God and has eternal rule and complete authority over all the earth.[7] He is thus another kingly figure, although in Daniel, not necessarily Davidic.[8] The idea of the Son of God is usually used of angels, Israel, and of kings.[9] It is linked to the hope of Theo through the longing for a Davidic king.[10] In a few other places, it is linked to the idea of a messiah-king.[11]

Another less common royal idea is that of "a ruler" (scepter) from Judah, most likely based on Genesis 49:10.[12] Another common notion is that

---

4:1-6; 9:5-6; 10:24-27; 11:1-16; 14:29-30; 16:1-5; 28:5-6; 42:1-9; 43:10; 52:13—53:12; *Tg. Neb.* 1 Sam 2.7-10; 2:35; 2 Sam 22:28-32; 23:1-5; 1 Kgs 5:13; Jer 23:1-8; 30:8-11; 30:12; 33:12-26; Ezek 17:22-24; 34:20-31; 37:21-28; Hos 3:3-5; 14:5-8; Mic 4:8; 5:1-3; Hab 3:17-18; Zech 3:8; 4:7; 6:12-13; 10:3; *Tg. Ps.* 19:28-32 (Eng. vv. 27-31); 89:51-52; 132:10-18; *Tg. Song* 4:5; *Tg. Qoh* 7:24; *Tg. Esth II* 1:1; *m. Sota* 9.15; *m. Ber.* 1:5; *y. Ketubot* 12.3: cf. Isa 45:1; 61:1-2; Dan 9:26, cf. Ps 2:2. In the Targums, "kingly Messiah" is often used, e.g. *Tg. Ps.-J.* Gen 3:16; 35:21, 41; 49:1, 10-12; Exod 40:9-11; Num 23:21; 24:17-24; Deut 25:19; 30:4-9; *Frg. Tg.* Gen 3:15; 49:10-12; Exod 12:42; Num 11:26; 24:7; *Tg. Neof.* Gen 3:15; 49:10-12; Exod 12:42; Num 11:26; 24:7; 24:17-24; *Tg. Ps.* 21:1-8; 47:7-18; 61:7-9; 72:1-20; 80:15-18 (Eng. vv. 14-17); *Tg. Song* 1:8, 17; 7:12-14; 8:1-4; *Tg. Ruth* 1:1; 3:15; *Tg. Lam* 2:22; 4:22; *Tg. Qoh* 1:11; *Tg. 1 Chr* 3:24.

6. See for example, 1QS 9:10-11; CD 12:22-23; 14:19, cf. 4Q285 f7.

7. See for example, Dan 7:13; 1 En. 46:1-4; 48:2; 62:5-9, 14, 29; 63:11; 69:26—70:1; 71:13-17; 4 Ezra 13 (does not use name, dependent on Dan 7), cf. Ezek 8:2).

8. We can't completely rule out that Daniel had a Davidic monarchy in mind—all we are sure of is that he didn't mention it.

9. Angels (Gen 6:2; Job 1:6; Dan 3:25; 1 En. 69:4-5; 71:1; Jub. 1:24-25), Israel (Exod 4:22-23; Hos 11:1; Mal 2:10), kings (2 Sam 7:14; Ps 2:7; 89:26-27). It is also used in non-biblical Jewish texts to miracle workers, especially Honi the circle-drawer or Hanina ben Dosa (*b. Ta'an.* 24b, 3:8; *b. Ber.* 17b; *b. ḥul.* 86a).

10. See esp. 2 Sam 7:14; Ps 2:7; 89:26-27.

11. See 4 Ezra 7:27, 29 ("my son the Messiah"), cf. 4 Ezra 13:37, 52; 14:9; 1 En. 105:2 ("my son" = Messiah, Son of Man, Elect One, Righteous One); DSS: 1) 4QFlor 1:10-14 (links 2 Sam 7:11-14 to Messiah); 2) 1QSa 2:11-12 suggests God begetting the Messiah; 3) 4Q246 II speaks of the Son of God, the son of the Most High, cf. Dan 7:13-14.

12. See especially the LXX version of Gen 49:10, which amplifies the idea of an expected one adding "ruler" and "prince"; cf. T. Jud. 24:5; 4Q252. 1, 5).

of "king" or "ruler," often with further explanation.[13] First Enoch utilizes "the elect one"[14] and "the righteous one."[15]

Other less common notions include: "me whom they pierced";[16] "the prophet Elijah";[17] a "signet ring";[18] a star from Jacob;[19] a "lord" (*kyrios*);[20] a prophet;[21] a "new priest";[22] a fountain;[23] a root;[24] one uniquely born of God (before the morning star);[25] or "a man."[26] In the Hebrew of Isaiah 9:7, he is given a four-fold designation: "wonderful counselor, almighty God (*el*), everlasting Father, prince of peace." This is softened in the LXX.[27] Aside from the divine implications of "almighty God," what is most significant here is the reference to this person being a king and most usually a descendant of David.[28] We can thus be confident that many in Israel hoped for this Theo figure and that this person would come as a king. Often, but not always, he would be Davidic.

The question now to address is whether this expectation included the idea of the imposition of power through military force, i.e., the vanquishing of Israel's enemies. As noted thus far, the prevailing understanding of kingship in the ancient world at the time of Christ was a political ruler who would establish their reign and "peace" by military force. Subsequently, sons would reign

---

13. See, for example, Isa 32:1; Zech 9:9–10; Pss. Sol. 17:12, 32–24, 42; Sib. Or. 3:285, 652–55; 5:108–10, cf. Num 24:7, 17 (esp. LXX, which amplifies the idea of a man who will reign); Ps 72:5, 7 (LXX amplifies).

14. See, for example, 1 En. 39:6a; 40:5; 49:2, 4; 51:5a, 3; 52:6, 9; 53:6; 61:5, 8, 10; 62:1.

15. See, for example, 1 En. 38:1: clearly the Son of Man; 53:6 ("righteous and elect one"); 92:3 (raised from the dead?).

16. Zech 12:10.

17. Mal 4:5.

18. It is possible that Hag 2:23 refers to Zerubbabel, who is in the direct line of David, as the fulfillment of the hope of a Davidic king.

19. See Num 24:17; T. Jud. 24:1.

20. Ps 110:1.

21. See T. Benj. 5:2, cf. 1 Macc 4:46; 14:41; 1QS Col IX, 11.

22. T. Levi 18:2–14, cf. 1QS 9:10–11; CD 12:22–23; 14:19; 4Q285 f7.

23. T. Jud. 24:5.

24. See Mal 4:2; T. Jud. 24:5.

25. See Ps 110:3, LXX (109:3).

26. A favorite of Philo for a king (Philo, *Moses I.*, 290; *Rewards*, 95).

27. It reads, "Because a child was born to us; a son was given to us whose leadership came upon his shoulder; and his name is called 'Messenger of the Great Council,' for I will bring peace upon the rulers and health to him" (LES). This is likely to remove the implications of deity ascribed to this figure in the Hebrew text.

28. See Isa 55:3; Jer 33:17; Ezek 34:23–24; 37:24–25; Hos 3:5; Amos 9:11; Zech 12:8, 10, 12; 13:1; Pss 18:50; 89:50; 4 Ezra 12:32; Pss. Sol. 17:21; 4Q174 1–3 I, 10; 4Q252. 1, 5.

THE HOPE OF A DELIVERER ("THEO" = "THE EXPECTED ONE") 79

dynastically, maintaining or extending the "peace" with force and intrigue. This penchant for military force, whether ruled by a monarchy or not, is seen in Israel's history, especially in the Conquest, the Judges, the monarchies of Saul, David, the northern kings, and the Maccabean revolt. The broader context demonstrates the same in the Egyptian, Assyrian, Babylonian, Medo-Persian, Greek, and Roman imperial periods. As we noted in chapter 2, the same applied to the world beyond the Mediterranean. We have shown in chapter 3 that this was the pattern in the non-Roman world as well.

Aside from the Hasmonean/Maccabean period, Israel had been subject to each of these military empires in the previous six hundred or so years. At the time of Christ, it was the Romans who dominated Israel through sheer might, despite many in Israel being deeply offended by their presence. It stands to reason, then, that where an expectation of a king at the time of Christ existed, it would most *necessarily* include the ideas of military conquest—what other way was there? Further, if God himself directly intervened, he would use violent force to achieve his ends, as he had done at other points (e.g., the Exodus). So, whatever else is involved in the coming of this Theo-figure, military dominance would come with his arrival, whether through the direct intervention of God's mighty power, or through a blend of divine power manifest through this king in some way, along with human military engagement. The more specific expectations associated with Theo demonstrate that this is indeed the case.

THE OLD TESTAMENT

Genesis

The early vision of a king from Judah in Genesis 49:8–12 is replete with violent war images.[29] This passage was interpreted messianically in Israel (e.g., 4Q252; *Tgs. Gen., Rab.* 98.8; *b. Sanh.* 98b; *Tanḥ. Wayyeḥi* 10). It speaks of his hand on the neck of enemies; he is like a lion ready to attack ("crouches, lies down") who returns from the prey. The image of a lion is very violent indeed. Verse 10 refers to the perpetual reign of a descendant of Judah until the reign comes to "whom it belongs" (later interpreted as the Davidic messiah). It says of this ruler that "the obedience of the nations is his," indicating their complete subjugation. Verses 11–12 tell of glorious peace and prosperity. The LXX amplifies this messianic hope, speaking of a "prince from his

---

29. Even the protoevangelium of Gen 3:16 hints at violence with the use of *šûp*, "crush."

loins" (v. 10). The vision here is of a ruler from the line of Judah who will subdue the nations through his power and establish Shalom.

Numbers

The oracles of Balaam in Numbers 24 carry a strong nuance of the warrior-king, particularly in the LXX. The context is military, with Israel entering Moabite territory en route to the Promised Land (Num 22:1). Due to Israel's previous military exploits, the Moabites are terrified (Num 22:3–4). Balaam, a spiritual leader, is summoned by the king Balak to curse Israel and ensure victory—again we see the alliance of the spiritual and political leadership endorsing (or not) a particular action (Num 22:5–6). Balaam is instructed by God not to curse Israel, and so refuses to come (Num 22:8–12). The process is repeated with the enticement of money, and Balaam this time goes to Balak, the king, with clear instructions to say what God directs (Num 22:13–20). After an encounter with God repeating his warning to say only what he directs through a donkey (Num 22:21–35), Balaam comes to Balak, and after worship, Balaam brings a series of oracles, in which he refuses to curse Israel (Num 22:36—24:25). The oracles confirm God's vindication of Israel and the assuredness of their victory. Thus, even the enemy's holy man endorses their divine authority. The second oracle endorses this because of the Exodus (Num 23:22) and speaks of their military power as that of a lion who "*devours* his prey and *drinks the blood* of his victims" (Num 23:24, emphasis added).

The main interest lies in two passages viewed messianically in Numbers 24:7 and 17. First, in Numbers 24:7, Balaam predicts that Israel's king will be greater than Agag and their kingdom exalted. Agag here is most likely a dynastic name among the Amalekites (see Exod 17:8–13; Num 24:20; 1 Sam 15:7–9, 32–33).[30] Being mightier than Agag supposes, then, stronger military force—violent power. In vv. 8–9, the Exodus violent deliverance is again mentioned along with Israel having "the strength of a wild ox," that "they *devour* hostile nations and *break* their bones in pieces; with their arrows they *pierce* them" (emphasis added). Israel is again likened to a lion that crouches and lies down in preparation to attack. The LXX version is overtly messianic, amending v. 7 to read "there shall come a man of his seed, and he shall rule over many nations; and that kingdom of Gog shall be exalted, and his kingdom shall be increased." In v. 8 it reads, "he shall *consume* the nations of his enemies, and he shall *drain* their marrow" (emphasis added). This speaks of Israel's military superiority and in the LXX; a military messiah.

30. Cole, *Numbers*, 421.

Balaam's fourth oracle predicts a "star will come out of Jacob; a scepter will rise out of Israel," indicating a monarch who will come from the Israelites. The description of this king's activities is directly militaristic: "he will *crush* the foreheads of Moab, the skulls of the sons of Sheth. Edom will be *conquered*, Seir, his enemy, will be *conquered*, but Israel *will grow strong*. A ruler will come out of Jacob and *destroy* the survivors of the city" (Num 24:17–19, emphasis added). In the LXX, "a scepter will rise out of Israel" is replaced by "a man shall spring out of Israel" adding to the messianic dynamic in the text. As with vv. 7–8, this is a picture of a warrior-king, a military messiah, who will be endorsed and empowered by God to vanquish Israel's enemies.

Isaiah 1–39

In Isaiah 1–39 it is hoped in Israel that the coming time of God's intervention will see an ultimate cessation of war (Isa 2:4, cf. Mic 4:3). This vision of a final peaceful state follows Isaiah's sharp critique of Israel's sin and reference to God's judgment, with the language of severe judgment and violence (esp. Isa 1:4–7). This judgment includes the desolation of the country, burning with fire, stripping by foreigners, being laid waste, minimal survivors, comparisons with Sodom and Gomorrah (which was totally destroyed by a direct act of God) (Isa 1:9–10), the breaking of rebels and sinners (Isa 1:28), and God's destruction of the mighty (Isa 1:31). This is total military devastation. God is the agent of all this (Isa 1:25) and of the restoration (Isa 1:26–27).

After this vision of peace there follows further reference to destruction which God will bring on all the arrogant (Isa 2:9–22). This will involve the destruction of Jerusalem and Judah and the humiliation of its leaders and women as prisoners of war (Isa 3) and defeat in battle of Israel's finest with the destruction of Zion (Isa 3:25). War is assumed.

The Branch of the Lord (Messiah) in Isaiah 4 has a role in the restoration of Mount Zion. He will do so with a "spirit of *judgment* and a spirit of *fire*" (emphasis added). It is likely that this phrase refers to "God's purification of Zion by destroying the remaining sinful people in Jerusalem" (see Isa 1:31; 28:6; 30:27–28; 66:15–16).[31] The "peace" established, then, is through conquest.

Further reference to destruction is found in the song of the vineyard in Isaiah 5 (esp. 5:5–6, 8–10, 13–15, 25–30). God uses distant nations to achieve his ends (Isa 5:26–30). Isaiah's vision likewise involves the desolation of the cities of the nation (Isa 6:11–13). While foreign armies are the

---

31. Smith, *Isaiah 1–39*, 158.

agent, God works in history through political and military force, particularly, in Isaiah 1–39, Assyria and Babylon.

The vision of a glorious Davidic king who will establish justice and righteousness in Isa 9:6–7 includes the shattering of the yoke of burden and the destruction of war apparel as during the days of Midian's defeat (Isa 9:4–5). This recalls Gideon's defeat of the Midianites in Judges 6–7. While it is the zeal of God which will achieve it (Isa 9:7), the parallel suggests the military conquest of Israel's enemies by this Davidic king aided by divine power. After this vision, there is a further reference to God acting through military destruction (see Isa 9:10—10:4). Assyria itself will suffer the same fate (Isa 10:5–19). Only a remnant of Israel will be left (Isa 10:20–34).

The Branch in Isaiah 11 again pictures conquest through God's power and military might. He is a Davidic king ("a shoot from the stump of Jesse," Isa 11:1), will be imbued with God's Spirit (Isa 11:2), will be devoted to Yahweh (Isa 11:3), and will bring justice (Isa 11:4). Isaiah 11:4 indicates he will "*strike* the earth with the *rod* of his mouth; with the breath of his lips he will *slay* the wicked." The agency of his power is then his words and breath. "Slay (*mût*) the wicked" indicates the use of violent force. Through this, he will establish "peace" in the whole created order (Isa 11:5–9), bring the world under his reign (Isa 11:10), bring exiles back to Israel (Isa 11:10–12), and unite north and south (Isa 11:13–14). United Israel will then attack the surrounding nations, defeating the historic gentile enemies of Israel (Isa 11:14–16). While peace is established by God's power, it is extended through divinely empowered invasion. This is the language of imperial extension, so prevalent in the ancient world.

In Isaiah 16:4–5, there is another expression of the hope of a Davidic king. There will be an end to oppression, destruction, and invasion. In love and faithfulness, a man from the line of David will reign, establishing justice and righteousness. Significantly, while this statement mentions only peace and not war, it, and other notes of hope of Israel's restoration (see Isa 14:1–3), it is set among a series of oracles concerning the nations and their destruction at the hands of God and his armies. Specifically, it is nestled in oracles against one of Israel's key enemies, the Moabites.

These oracles against the nations are dripping with references to God's destruction of these nations. For example, of Babylon: "The LORD Almighty is mustering an *army for war* . . . to *destroy* the *whole* country" (Isa 13:4–5, emphasis added). This war will "make the land desolate and *destroy the sinners* within it" (Isa 13:9). It will involve the utter extermination and destruction of infants (Isa 13:15–16, cf. vv. 18–19). Israel will then mock her enemy (Isa 14:3–4). This will involve much death from war (Isa 14:9, 11, 19, cf. Isa 21:1–10). Of Assyria, Isaiah writes of her being crushed and trampled (Isa

14:25). The Philistine survivors will be killed by God (Isa 14:30). Moab too is destroyed (esp. Isa 15:1; 16:13-14; 25:10), the rivers running with blood (Isa 15:9), and the people lamenting (Isa 16:7). Damascus will be destroyed (Isa 17:1-2, 9). Cush will bring tribute to Zion (Isa 18:7). Egypt will be subjugated to a powerful king (Isa 19:4). The people will be powerless, Judah will terrify them (Isa 19:15-17), and the Egyptians will worship God (Isa 19:18-25). Both Cush and Egypt will be subjugated to Assyria (Isa 20). There are also warnings to Edom and Arabia of her defeat in battle (Isa 21:11-17). Jerusalem too is not spared (Isa 22, esp. vv. 5-11; 29:1-4). However, her enemies will be devastated (Isa 29:5-8). Tyre will also be destroyed (Isa 23:1-18).

In Isa 24, the vision becomes a whole world devastated by God (Isa 24 esp. vv. 1, 3, 10, 12, 21-22). Isaiah writes, "in that day the Lord will punish the powers in the heavens above and the kings on the earth below" (Isa 24:21). The hope of the Davidic ruler and peace is the result of the Lord's military conquest of the world. The ultimate peace in Isaiah 25 (see Isa 26:12), including the eschatological feast and the end of death and suffering (vv. 6-8), is due to God's conquering through force and power. This leads to praise for his deliverance (Isa 25:9; 26:1-21), including his victory over his enemies (Isa 26:4, 11, 13-15, cf. 27:1, 12). Ephraim is also condemned with God moving against her (Isa 28:2, 6).

The coming of God is associated with wrath, fire, the shaking of the nations and their subjugation, leading to Israel's peace and celebration (Isa 30:27-29, 30-33; 31:4, 8-9). Israel is to rely on God alone and not the other nations (e.g. Isa 31:1-3). A righteous monarch will reign (Isa 32:1). Isaiah, in chapter 34, pictures a court scene in which God judges the nations, is angry with them, and destroys them, leaving rotten corpses littering the blood-soaked ground (Isa 34:2). God's sword is pictured bathed in blood and fat (Isa 34:4). It is a day of vengeance in which Edom is destroyed (Isa 34:8-15). This is followed by a vision of return from exile, great rejoicing, and cosmic peace (Isa 35:1-10). All in all, it is a gross, violent picture of the complete subjugation of the nations to God.

Isaiah 40-55

Isaiah 40-55 is considered a unit by most scholars (Deutero-Isaiah). These chapters picture the release of Israel from Babylonian exile through God's anointed, the Medo-Persian King Cyrus. In Isaiah 40, the prophet begins with a declaration from God that Jerusalem's warfare is ended (Isa 40:2). This is followed by an oracle which forms a core part of Mark 1:2-3 (with Malachi 3:1), announcing the coming of God (Isa 40:3). This is heralded by Zion/Jerusalem in Isaiah 40:9–11, including "the Lord God comes with might, and his arm rules for him," speaking of God's coming in sovereign military power (Isa 40:10). This is balanced by the picture of God as the gentle shepherd, caring for his flock, Israel (Isa 40:11). In Isaiah 40:12–17, a series of rhetorical questions consider God's supreme creative power while, before him, the nations are merely a drop of water, a speck of dust. The nations are written off as nothing and emptiness before him. Idols are mocked before God's supreme rule (Isa 40:17–22). Not only are the nations nothing, but he "brings princes to nothing, and makes the rulers of the earth as emptiness." He "blows on them, and they wither, and the tempest carries them off like stubble." speaking of their subjugation (Isa 40:23–24). On the other hand, Israel will be strengthened; her young men renewed in strength to sour as eagles (Isa 40:28–31).

In Isaiah 41, God is judge, and one is stirred up from the east (later revealed as Cyrus), and his every step meets victory. God "gives up nations before him," "he tramples kings underfoot; he makes them like dust with his sword, like driven stubble with his bow" (Isa 41:2). This is the word of God (Isa 41:4)—this is the language of divinely empowered political and military subjugation. The world trembles, but Israel is called home, strengthened. Her enemies are shamed (Isa 41:5–13). Israel need not fear, for God will "make you a threshing sledge" which will thresh and crush the mountains into chaff, only to be carried away by the wind.[32] This is a vivid picture of the military destruction of the nations, including Babylon.[33]

After oracles of God's renewal of the deserts (Isa 41:17–20) and another repudiation of idolatry (Isa 41:21–24), Cyrus is again referenced as "one from the north," stirred up by God, who "shall trample on rulers as on mortar, as the potter treads clay" (Isa 41:25). This is another figurative description of the demolition of the nations. This military subjugation is good news heralded to Israel (Isa 41:27).

Isaiah 42:1–9 is the first of the so-called "Servant Songs" of Isaiah.[34] It pictures a servant, upheld by God, Spirit-imbued, who brings justice in

---

32. Knight (*Servant Theology*, 37) notes that "The threshing sledge was a flat piece of wood studded on the underside with *teeth*, or spikes. Domestic animals dragged this implement over the wheat piled on the ground of the farmyard."

33. Watts, *Isaiah 34–66*, 107: "Yahweh is saying that he could have appointed Israel to be his *threshing sled* to do the work that Cyrus is now performing. He could have, and if he had, she would be the glorious victor over all. The *mountains* and the *hills* may well have political meaning in terms of the powers of the earth including Babylon" (emphasis his). This is not merely psychological obstacles (Smith, *Isaiah 40–66*, 137.

34. For a discussion on the identity of the Servant, see Smith, *Isaiah 40–66*, 152–56. Options in context include Israel (Isa 41:8, 9); an Old Testament individual, e.g., Isaiah, Deutero-Isaiah, Moses, Cyrus, Jehoiakim, or David. He argues that it is not yet clear,

quietness and gentleness. He will not be discouraged but will establish justice throughout the world, even to the coastlands—the nations. God will keep this figure and give him "as a covenant for the people, a light for the nations" (Isa 42:6), to heal and release people. In the New Testament, including Mark's Gospel (as well as cited by Matthew [Matt 12:18-21]), this figure prefigures Christ.[35] However, in Jewish thought at the time of Christ, this figure was not seen as a reference to the expected one in any form. Significantly, there is no reference to the use of violence in this. Yet, if one reads the wider context, one would be forgiven to simply expect it, as the context is dripping with images of war.

This is followed by the peoples, including the nations, singing praises (Isa 42:10-12). God is then described in military terms: "The LORD goes out like a mighty man, like a man of war he stirs up his zeal; he cries out, he shouts aloud, he shows himself mighty against his foes." The description "mighty man" (*gib·bôr*) is used throughout the Old Testament of warrior heroes.[36] It is also used of God. So, in Psalm 24:8, the psalmist asks, "Who is this King of glory? The LORD, strong and mighty, the LORD, mighty in battle." Jeremiah says of God: "But the Lord is with me as a dread warrior; therefore my persecutors will stumble; they will not overcome me" (Jer 20:11). Similarly, Zephaniah 3:17 says, "The LORD your God is in your midst, a *mighty one* who gives victory." The designation "man of war" recalls the song of Miriam at Exodus where God is described in this way (Exod 15:3)—through Cyrus, God is again bringing Israel to the land from bondage (a new Exodus). God, the warrior, is essential to Israel's theology and eschatological expectations. Deliverance from the nations will involve military might. In Isaiah 42:14 he "will lay waste mountains and hills," while transforming creation, leading the blind to sight, and shaming idolaters (Isa 42:15-17).

In Isaiah 42:18-25, God calls deaf and blind Israel to see that it is time for her restoration. It was God who in "the heat of his anger and the might of battle" gave up Israel to violent destruction (Isa 42:24-25).

In Isaiah 43, Israel's creator is redeeming her, and she need not fear. To do so, he gives nations such as Egypt, Cush, and Seba in exchange for

---

and can only be assessed when the passages are all considered.

35. See Mark 1:11, s.a. Matt 3:17; Luke 2:32; 9:35; Acts 17:24-25; 26:18, 23. See Jones, *Old Testament Quotations*, "Isa 42."

36. Including Nimrod, the first warrior-king of Scripture (Gen 10:8-9); Israel's armed warriors at the Conquest (Josh 1:14; 1 Chr 1:10) and Jericho (Josh 6:2); David (1 Sam 16:18); Goliath (1 Sam 17:51); David's "mighty men" (2 Sam 23:8, 9; 1 Chr 11:11-12). See also Gen 6:4; 1 Chr 5:24; 7:2; 27:6; Jer 51:30. Isaiah uses it of warriors (Isa 3:2; 5:22; 13:3; 21:17), of "mighty" God (Isa 9:6; 10:21) (s.a. Isa 49:24, 25). Jeremiah also uses it of God (Jer 20:11; 32:18).

his precious people (Isa 43:1–4). Before the nations, he declares that he will gather Israel from east, west, north, and south (Isa 43:5–11). The Babylonians will become fugitives (Isa 43:14), another image of its destruction.[37] Before God, chariot, horse, army, and warrior fall but cannot rise; "they are extinguished, quenched like a wick" (Isa 43:17)—any talk of redemption is profoundly military. This is followed by oracles speaking of God's transformation of the wilderness and forgiveness and redemption of Israel, despite her failings (Isa 43:18—44:5).

God's supremacy is declared (Isa 44:6–8), idolatry is ridiculed (Isa 44:9–20), but Israel is redeemed, her sins forgiven (Isa 44:21–25). Then, Jerusalem and Judah will be restored, and Cyrus is named (Isa 44:27–28).[38] He is the LORD's anointed, his Messiah (Isa 45:1). His right hand has been taken by God "to subdue nations before him," another picture of divinely mandated and empowered political and military domination. God speaks with the first person "I," declaring that he, the creator of light and darkness (Gen 1), will go before him and ensure his victory for the sake of Israel (Isa 45:2–7). Woe is declared over anyone who resists (Isa 45:9–10)—the creator will set his people free (Isa 45:11–13).

This is followed by images of the nations in chains—their wealth and possessions will come over to Israel, yielding to her God, shamed before him (Isa 45:14–17). The nations are challenged to gather with their idols and argue their futile case (Isa 45:20–21), and they are called to turn to him and be saved, which they do, bowing and swearing allegiance (Isa 45:21–23). Isaiah 45:23 is cited in Philippians 2:10 and Romans 14:11; this text points to the ultimate universal subjugation of humanity to Christ, willing or otherwise. The nations then will yield to God, and in context, this will involve war (or so one would think).

In Isaiah 46, two idols, Bel and Nebo,[39] yield in subjugation and are exiled, another picture of subjugation, anticipating the conquest of Babylon (Isa 46:1–2). Israel is called to remember her God and repudiate such idols, for he will accomplish his purpose (Isa 46:3–10). He will do so by "calling a

---

37. Some take this eschatologically of the defeat of all Israel's enemies, while others take it as the defeat of Sennacherib. However, in my view, Westermann is correct to state, "This refers beyond question to Cyrus's capture of Babylon" (see Westermann, *Isaiah 40–66*, 125).

38. See chapter 2 on the question of whether this is a *Vaticinium ex eventu*.

39. Smith (*Isaiah 40–66*, 287–88) notes that Bel is similar to Baal and means "lord," a name used of Enlil in early Mesopotamian texts, which in 1800 BC became a designation of Marduk, the main god of the city of Babylon. Marduk is king of the gods, having defeated Tiamat in Enuma Elish, Babylon's creation myth. Nebo, the god of wisdom, writing, and future, was Marduk's son and the chief god of Borsippa, a city near Babylon. The verses are a picture of their subjugation and exile.

bird of prey from the east," another image of violent war.[40] He will thus save Zion (Isa 46:13).

Isaiah 47:1–15 continues descriptions of Babylon's political and military humiliation, including sitting in the dust rather than a throne, servitude, silence, nakedness, the death of children, widowhood, and cold. In Isaiah 47:3, God, Israel's redeemer and the Holy One, "will take vengeance, and I will spare no one"—a brutal picture of God's retribution for Babylon's destruction of his people.

After Isaiah 48, in which Isaiah again prophesies the release of Israel from Babylon, in Isaiah 49 we have the second of the Servant Songs, in which the nations are called to pay attention to his Servant. This faithful Servant will bring back Israel and will be a "light for the nations that my salvation may reach to the end of the earth" (Isa 49:4–6). Despite his being despised and abhorred by the nation, rulers will come and pay homage to him. Unlike Jewish thinkers of the time, for early Christian thinkers, again Christ is in mind.[41] Again, there is no indication of this figure using violent force.

The remainder of Isaiah 49 speaks of Israel's redemption on the day of salvation (Isa 49:8). Prisoners shall "come out" (Isa 49:9), shall travel through the wilderness, yet be well-fed and protected from the blistering heat (Isa 49:10–11). Indeed, God's people will come from afar (Isa 49:12), so that the heavens and earth burst forth in song (Isa 49:13). Just as a mother cannot forget her nursing child, God has not forgotten Israel (Isa 49:14–15). She will gather from afar (Isa 49:16–21). The nations in subjugation will bring the children of Israel home (Isa 49:22), and kings and queens shall care for them and bow down to God's people, while those who do not will be shamed (Isa 49:23). Again, we have the nations yielding to God. While some have argued this is not military,[42] aside from reading back through

---

40. Scholarship is divided on who this is (see Smith, *Isaiah 40–66*, 293). The compiler of these oracles has place them here, just after reference to Cyrus, hence, although one can argue that the details of Babylon's defeat do not fit the picture, Cyrus fits this picture well and the arranger of Isaiah's oracles places it here amidst references to Babylon, making it certain that he is in mind. As Knight (*Servant Theology*, 104) says, "There is no reason to doubt that Cyrus, pagan bird of prey as he was, could not fit into God's plan." Interestingly, Xenophon (*Cyrop*. 7.1.4) notes "And his ensign was a golden eagle lifted up on a long shaft" (translation mine, s.a. *Anab*. 1.10.12). Whoever is in mind, we have another bloody picture of a bird of prey, such as an eagle or falcon, swooping in and destroying.

41. Allusions to the song include Luke 2:32; John 8:12; 9:5; Acts 13:47; 26:23; Gal 1:15; Eph 6:17; Phil 3:16; 2 Thess 1:10; Heb 4:12; Rev 1:16; 2:12, 16; 19:15. See Jones, *Old Testament Quotations*, "Isa 49."

42. Smith (*Isaiah 40–66*), 371 suggests that the bowing here is not "ugly revengeful domination of foreigners by Israelites." The context would suggest otherwise. The "man of war" has acted through Cyrus, Babylon is humiliated, and Israel is free.

the lens of Christ, the context speaks of military victory. In Isaiah 49:24–26 this is clear where God speaks of "prey [being] taken from the mighty," "the captives of a tyrant being rescued,"

> for I will contend with those who contend with you, and I will save your children. I will make your oppressors eat their own flesh, and they shall be drunk with their own blood as with wine. Then all flesh shall know that I am the LORD your Savior, and your Redeemer, the Mighty One of Jacob.

In fact, this is one of the most brutal pictures of destruction in Scripture. God will act violently against those who oppressed his people, and they will be destroyed. Little wonder that when Jesus was identified as Christ, war was expected.

Isaiah 50 begins with the image of God as Israel's husband, Israel's rejection, and his power to restore. We then have the third of the Servant Songs in Isaiah 50:4–11. He sustains the weary with a word from God and does not retaliate, although mistreated.[43] Knowing God is near, he stands firm knowing God will help him. Israel is called to obey the servant and walk in the light.

Isaiah 51:1–8 speaks of God's comforting of Zion, the coming of his justice, righteousness, and salvation. Isaiah 51:9 is a call to God to arise in war and conquer Israel's enemies, as he cut Rahab to pieces and pierced the dragon (the defeat of Egypt at Exodus, cf. v. 10).[44] As such, Israel will return (v. 11). In Isaiah 51:12–23, whereas she had drunk from the hand of God's wrath" (v. 17), experienced "devastation and destruction, famine and sword" (v. 19), and her sons had been "full of the wrath of the LORD, the rebuke of your God (v. 20), Israel will not again drink from "the cup of staggering" (v. 22). Rather, God will place this cup into the hands of Israel's tormentors—in other words, Babylon will drink the wrath of God. As Israel was destroyed and plundered by Nebuchadnezzar, so now shall the Babylonians be destroyed.

As such, in Isaiah 52:1–12, Israel is to awaken, for the good news of her redemption is declared, and her people are returning to Zion. Then, we have the final and most famous of Isaiah's Servant Song, linked to Jesus' death

---

43. Isaiah 50:6 is echoed in Matt 26:67; 27:30; Isa 50:8 in Rom 8:33.

44. On Rahab, see Day, "Rahab," 610–11. Rahab was a mythological sea serpent mentioned across the Old Testament (Ps 87:4; 89:1; Job 9:13; 26:12; Isa 30:7). It was originally a Canaanite chaos monster, and is a monster defeated at creation and a metaphorical name for Egypt (Isa 30:7). The monster Rahab is used as a metaphor for Egypt in her oppression. This likely recalls the Exodus. On the dragon, see Day, "Dragon and Sea," 228–31. As with Rahab, the Dragon finds its origin in Canaanite myth. Here, it recalls the Exodus deliverance (see also Ps 77:16–20).

in the New Testament (Isa 52:13—53:12). In it, Isaiah speaks of a Servant who acts wisely, is exalted up, is marred in appearance, who will sprinkle many nations, and before whom kings are silent at the sight and thought of him. This one grows up without any particular honor, is despised, rejected, sorrowful, grieving, and a disgrace to others. Yet, he has borne the grief and sorrows of Israel (ours, too), although seen as smitten and afflicted by God. He will be pierced for Israel's transgressions, crushed for her sin, punished for Israel's peace, and wounded for her healing. On him is laid Israel's sin. When oppressed and afflicted, he remains silent, led to his slaughter like a sacrificial lamb. He is removed by oppression and judgment, killed, stricken for the sins of God's people. He is buried with the wicked and wealthy, despite his having done no violence or speaking deceit. It is God's will that he is crushed, put to grief, as an offering for guilt. And yet, he shall see his descendants, lengthen his days, and in his hand, God's will shall prosper. He, the Righteous One, will be satisfied despite his anguish, and the will of God shall prosper in his hand. Through him, many will be counted righteous, and he shall bear their sins. God will reward him and others, because "poured out his soul to death," and was numbered with the transgressors, despite bearing the sin of many and interceding for transgressors.

In context, the meaning of this compelling vision in its initial setting is hotly debated. Yet, in the New Testament, including Mark's Gospel, it provides the shape of Jesus' whole earthly existence. In whatever ways Israel interpreted this text, for the New Testament writers, this Servant is Jesus. Notably, this figure is not an agent of political or military violence, rather, he is the recipient of horrendous suffering. This figure gives himself vicariously for Israel. The connections with the non-violent Jesus are uncanny.

In Isaiah 54, Israel is to sing, for she is extended, her offspring possessing the nations and people its cities—another indicator of the hope of the subjugation of the nations (Isa 54:1-3). Like a deserted wife restored to her husband, Israel will be restored in a covenant of Shalom in accordance with the Noahic covenant (Isa 54:4-10). Israel will know prosperity (54:11-12) and security (54:13-14), all enemies that arise will be vanquished (54:15-17)—a picture of Israel's military dominance.

The second part of Isaiah (Deutero-Isaiah) culminates in chapter 55 with the restoration of Israel. All are invited to dine, with a surfeit of food available to diners. An everlasting Davidic covenant is made, and God makes him (a Davidic heir) "a witness to the peoples, a leader and commander for the peoples" (Isa 55:4). Nations will run to Israel, again a picture of Israel and her king's dominance (Christ?). God, who is beyond human comprehension, has spoken, and so this will happen, and Israel will rejoice, as will creation itself (Isa 55:7-13). Thus, peace is established.

Isaiah 56–66

Many consider that Isaiah 56–66 is a post-exilic work. It begins in chapter 56, with Israel summoned to act justly as they await God's salvation (Isa 56:1). The one who does this receives God's favor, as does the person who keeps the Sabbath (Isa 56:2). Foreigners who are joined to the LORD are welcomed. However, this says nothing of the welcome of those who do not. Similarly, eunuchs too are welcomed with an everlasting name (Isa 56:3–5). The foreigner joined to God's people and maintains the Sabbath and covenant is welcomed to the temple, which will be called a house of prayer for all nations (Isa 56:6–7). Years later, in Mark, Jesus will recite these verses while standing in the temple, repudiating its corruption and marginalization of the gentiles (Mark 11:17, s.a. Matt 21:13; Luke 19:46).

After this, in language reminiscent of Isaiah's rebuke of Israel in the first part of the book, Israel's leaders are powerfully rebuked as blind, ignorant shepherds who, like insatiable dogs, seek their own gain and wine (Isa 56:9–12). In chapter 57, Isaiah's rebuke continues as the righteous are taken away, but Israel's leaders are further rebuked for their idolatry. The rest of the chapter focuses on God's healing of the contrite, but the punishment of the wicked is also referenced (Isa 57:20–21).

Isaiah 58 is an appeal to the people of Israel who fast regularly but treat each other contemptuously to humble themselves and fast with social concern for those in need (Isa 58:6–7). In his Nazareth reading of Isaiah 61:1–2a (Luke 4:18–19), Jesus will include a line of this text, suggesting that this passage helped shape his ministry of feeding the hungry and healing the sick (Isa 58:6; Luke 4:18). Such fasting, along with right observance of the Sabbath (Isa 58:13), will bring light, righteousness, answered prayer, God's guidance, and Israel's restoration and prosperity (Isa 58:8–12, 14).

Considering the almost constant references to military violence through the prophets and Isaiah to this point, until Isaiah 59, Trito-Isaiah has been remarkably free of such language. However, this changes here. Verses 1–16 again recall the first part of Isaiah, with a withering and vivid attack on Israel's sin, corruption, injustice, and blindness. God sees the complete absence of any righteous ones, and is displeased (Isa 59:15–18). Hence in vv. 17–18, as if embodying Israel's view of God as a "God of hosts," a "man of war," or a "mighty man," God rises and dons his armor of righteousness, the helmet of salvation, vengeance, and zeal. Dressed in the armor of God (cf. Eph 6), God will repay wrath "to his adversaries, repayment to his enemies, to the coastlands he will render repayment" (Isa 59:17–18). This speaks not merely of God's wrath against Israel, but the nations. Because of his wrathfulness, God will be feared from the west, "for he will come like a rushing stream, which the wind of the LORD drives." This is the terror of military onslaught (Isa 59:19). Then Isaiah declares that "a Redeemer will come to Zion, to those in Jacob who turn from transgression"; a text Paul cites of Jesus (Isa 59:20; Rom 11:26–27). In context, one would be forgiven for expecting not a crucified Messiah, but a Redeemer clothed with God's armor subjugating the nations. The outpouring of the Spirit is then predicted (Isa 59:21).

In Isaiah 60, the nations experience darkness, symbolizing defeat and destruction (Isa 60:2). However, they will come to Israel, who now experience God's light and glory (Isa 60:1). Kings will be drawn to the light (Isa 60:3). Israel's people will return (Isa 60:4). Southern Bedouins will come bearing gold, frankincense, good news, praise, flocks, and rams, and will be accepted to worship (Isa 60:5–7). With the darkness referred to earlier in the oracle, and the previous chapter, this could speak of subjugation; the nations coming with tribute to their sovereign who has defeated them. Alternatively, the wealth is bought by the returning people of God, returning from the nations shrouded in darkness and accepted home by God.

The former is more likely, for in the verses that follow, people come from Spain with their wealth (Tarshish), bringing God's people (Isa 60:9). Foreigners rebuild Israel's walls, kings minister to Israel restored after God's wrath, people bring Israel the nations' wealth, and kings are led in procession. These are classic images of bringing prisoners of war (Isa 60:10–11). The nations and kingdoms that do not serve God will perish, "those nations shall be utterly laid waste" (Isa 60:12). This is the language of classic ancient conquest—the easy way or the hard way—fight and be destroyed, yield and be subjugated but intact. Lebanon's wonderful timber will be brought to rebuild God's house, as it was when Solomon built the first Temple of God (Isa 60:13). Israel's oppressors will come in subjugation, bowing at Israel's feet, and Jerusalem will be "the City of the LORD, the Zion of the Holy One of Israel" (Isa 60:14). This is a picture of Israel's hope of a global theocracy, ruled from Zion, with Torah as the world's constitution, and God filling his Temple, and Israel ruling his world. Israel, once forsaken and despised, will be majestic forever (Isa 60:15). She will suckle the nations' milk, nursed by kings' breasts, a humiliating description (for ancients) of the world's sovereigns as breastfeeding women (Isa 60:16). Then there will be the peace Israel yearns for, where there is no longer violence, devastation, or destruction, only salvation and praise (Isa 60:18). No longer will the sun be required, for God will light the world forever (Isa 60:19–20). All humanity will prosper and be righteous, the land secure and God glorified (Isa 60:21–22). This is peace from military rule, which wipes out the "bad guys," and allows the good guys to be free, a pax-Yahweh, so to speak. The vision of a ruler bringing peace from peace and not a military takeover, or through being violently killed without resistance, is simply not in their worldview. Little wonder that even his closest followers did not fully grasp what Jesus was about until after his resurrection.

In Isaiah 61:1–2, in the first person, the prophet cries out that he is the anointed one to bring release to the poor, the brokenhearted, the captives, and the bound. This is a pivotal text in Luke's account of Jesus' ministry (Luke 4:18–21). Luke infuses into it a line from Isaiah 58:6, and cuts off the citation at Isaiah 61:2a, removing "and the day of vengeance of our God." For many scholars, he does so, as his emphasis is on Jesus, the minister to the poor and others in material need. However, this line exists in Israel's Scriptures, and so we have a picture of a figure who will be anointed by God's Spirit, indicating he is a king, a prophet, or a priest, or some combination thereof (e.g. Psalm 110, where the figure is both king and priest). There is a wide range of views on who this person is.[45] It is most likely that this figure would be recognized as an eschatological Theo figure, and understood in accordance with the various views in Israel (the Prophet, a priestly Messiah, a Davidic Messiah/Son of God, Son of Man). However, what really matters is not the specific identity of the figure,[46] but that he is The Expected One. After Christ's resurrection, Christians comfortably harmonized this with the Servant figure, Jesus drawing together in his identity the wide range of expectations, including of the above concepts.

Here, what matters is what he does. His ministry is one of the proclamation of the good news to the poor and liberty to the captives, binding the brokenhearted and releasing from prison the bound, and comforting those who mourn. This speaks of Israel, as Zion indicates in verse 3. While some will push this setting to post-exile, this seems exilic, with the oracle a declaration of the restoration of the nation. So in verse 4, they shall rebuild the nation. It seems a hopeful picture of a gentle Messiah/Servant who will act out of compassion. Yet, verse 2 speaks of the proclamation of the year of the Lord's favor and the day of God's vengeance. The year of the Lord's favor recalls Isaiah 49:8, where the Hebrew *rā·ṣôn* is paralleled with "the day of salvation" for Israel, i.e. release from Babylon. The parallel day of God's vengeance restates this and speaks of God's violent retribution against Israel's enemies. It anticipates the horrifying picture of God the Warrior with his clothes soaked in blood from crushing the nations, as if grapes in

---

45. See Smith, *Isaiah 55–66*, 630–32. Views include Isaiah? Trito-Isaiah? A prophetic figure? Artaxerxes? A Levitical collective? The Servant, his descendant, or disciple? The Messiah (cf. 1QM; Luke 4:18–19)?

46. I see here a recollection of both the messiah figure (esp. Isa 11:1) and the Servant (esp. Isa 42:1–2). Jesus is of course both figures in the New Testament.

THE HOPE OF A DELIVERER ("THEO" = "THE EXPECTED ONE")   93

a winepress (Isaiah 63). While in Luke 4 this line is removed, there is no such removal here—this Anointed One will wield the sword and liberate the people of Israel. Again, we see the centrality of the expectation of violent military action in Israel's hopes of Theo. Thus, it is good news for Israel, for she will be redeemed and her mourning becomes gladness.

Having been liberated, Israel will rebuild its cities (Isa 61:4). In Isaiah 61:5, foreigners and aliens will farm the land. Israel's people will be priests (cf. Exod 19:6) and ministers, and they shall gorge on the wealth of the subjugated nations in joy (Isa 61:5–7). The next verse stresses God's love of justice and repudiation of corruption. God will faithfully make an everlasting covenant with his people, likely recalling the Davidic covenant of Isaiah 55:3. The children of God's people will be known throughout the world, which is now in submission to God (Isa 61:9). The chapter ends in the first person, with the anointed one of Isa 61:1–2, crying out in joy, having been clothed with salvation, righteousness, and God's righteousness, will grow through the nations (Isa 61:10–11).

Isaiah 62 is a powerful picture of the forthcoming salvation of Zion. She will gleam in righteousness to be seen by the nations and their kings (Isa 62:1–2). Her people will be newly named, crowned in beauty, no longer named forsaken or desolate but "My delight in her," and "Married" (Isa 62:3–5). God will make Israel "a praise in the earth" (Isa 62:7). Isaiah 62:8–9 speaks of a future where Israel will never again be subjugated so that enemies and foreigners devour her food and wine, but Israel will enjoy it in God's Temple. God has proclaimed to the end of the earth the salvation of the city (Isa 62:10–12), where people are "The Holy People," "The Redeemed of the Lord," living in "A City Not Forsaken." Little wonder that the restoration of Zion and its complete security lay at the heart of Israel's hopes when Jesus burst on the scene.

If Isaiah 62 is a message of hope for Israel, Isaiah 63 gives a horrific vision of God's ultimate vengeance on the nations. It begins with an awful image of God or his Theo figure (s.a. Isa 61:2b) coming in blood-stained garments "marching in the greatness of his strength." He has crushed the nations as if treading a winepress (Isa 63:2–3). He has done this in anger and wrath, with the lifeblood of the peoples all over his clothes (Isa 63:3). In verse 4, redemption and vengeance are aligned—Zion's glorification in the previous chapter is due to God's redemption, his vengeance, his brutal subjugation of all nations. He has done this alone (vv. 2, 5). He declares: "I trampled down the peoples in my anger; I made them drunk in my wrath, and I poured out their lifeblood on the earth." This is God the Man of War, the Warrior, the LORD of Hosts, the Mighty One, acting decisively to brutally and totally crush the nations so that his clothes are dripping with blood.

As through Israel's writings, redemption, salvation, or whatever word we choose, is consistently, inexorably linked to violent overthrow, whether by God's direct hand or a Theo figure.

In verse 7, this vision abruptly shifts to a recollection of God's *hĕ·sĕḏ*, his "steadfast love," which is recalled by the speaker. It speaks of what God has done for his people, the house of Israel. He loves them, receives them as children, is their savior; he saved and redeemed them (Isa 63:8–9) despite their rebellion (Isa 63:10). What follows recalls the Exodus, another image of military victory over Pharaoh's forces; as God, the "Man of War" (Exod 15:4) led them then, so he will lead them now.

In Isaiah 63:15—64:12, the prophet prays, asking that God look down, and inquiring "where are your zeal and your might?" (v. 15). In light of the previous, this is a prayer for God the Warrior to arise. Despite Israel's failures, he pleads with God to return (Isa 63:17), for adversaries trample his sanctuary, his Temple (Isa 63:18), and it is as if Israel is no longer under God's rule (Isa 63:19). In Isaiah 64:1–3, the prophet cries out that God would tear apart the heavens and descend, shaking the mountains, like a boiling fire, "to make your name known to your adversaries, and that the nations might tremble at your presence!" This is a picture of God descending in brutal power to force Israel's enemies into subjugation. What follows is a passionate appeal to God based on his past actions and despite Israel's sin, to forgive her and act to restore Zion and the temple which lie in ruins (Isa 64:4–12). The destruction of her enemies, the liberation of the city, and the rebuilding of the temple is clearly implied (especially considering the previous chapter).

The twin fates of those who willingly yield to God and those who do not are laid out in Isaiah 65:1–16. Although God has held out his hands to a nation not called by his name (Isa 65:1), he has been rejected—they prefer rebellion, false worship, death, and unclean food (Isa 65:2–5). So God will repay them for their sins and idolatry, another warning of God's wrath (Isa 64:5–8). However, God will bring forth a people from Jacob and Judah and peace will ensue (Isa 64:8–10). Those who forsake God, Zion (my Holy Mountain), who are idolatrous, "I will destine you to the sword, and all of you shall bow down to the slaughter" because of their sin and evil (Isa 64:12). Yet again, we have a picture of God the Warrior, violently destroying the rebellious. In Isaiah 64:13–14, in four parallel couplets, the two fates of God's people and his enemies are laid out: his people will eat, drink, rejoice, and sin for joy; whereas, his enemies (you) will be hungry, thirsty, ashamed, and grieving. This is followed by a statement that God's servants will be blessed, but his enemies cursed and put to death (Isa 64:15–16).

Isaiah 64:17–25 envisages a renewed heavens and earth. In this world, Israel will be a joy, her people a gladness, weeping will cease, children will flourish, lives will be long and full, God's people will build homes and vineyards while enemies will not do so, work will be enjoyed, labor will be productive, children will be born for peace, not war, God will answer, and predators will no longer attack their prey. This is a picture of a nation experiencing the fullness of cosmic shalom. However, considering the previous passages, this is a peace brought to pass by war, a Pax-Yahweh. In Christ, this becomes a peace begotten by peace, or peace despite war.

In Isaiah 66:1–6, God seeks the one who is humble and contrite who trembles at God's word (v. 2). Those who kill animals and bring inferior offerings are punished harshly (vv. 3–4). Those among Israel's people (your brothers) who mistreat God's servants will be put to shame (v. 5). In verse 6, their punishment is pictured with the sound of uproar at the temple as God comes "rendering recompense to his enemies!"—another picture of Theophanic violence against those who oppose God.

In Isaiah 66:7–9, Zion is envisaged as a mother in labor giving birth her children. In verses 10–11, the command is given to rejoice for her, and drink from her breast. This is a picture of God nourishing his people as a mother to a nursing infant. As the people suckle on Jerusalem, peace and the glory of the nations will extend like a river (Isa 66:13, cf. Ezek 40–48). God's people will be comforted in Jerusalem, and his servants will flourish in God whereas the enemies will not (Isa 66:14).

The final section of Isaiah is replete with further references to God coming in violent force against enemies. He begins with God arriving with chariots in blazing fire, anger, and rebuke, to enter "into judgment and by his sword, with all flesh; and those slain by the LORD shall be many" (Isa 66:15–16). Idolaters and eaters of unclean meat will "come to an end together" (Isa 66:17). Representatives of the nations[47] will be gathered and see God's glory (Isa 66:18). God will mark them, and survivors (of a war?) will travel to them to declare God's glory. All Israel's brothers[48] will come as an offering to God and bring offerings to God. Some will be priests and Levites (Isa 66:19–20).

Then God's new heavens and earth will remain, and all flesh shall worship God (Isa 66:23). However, this is the result of a final conflict, for the worshipers will "go out and look on the dead bodies of the men who have rebelled

---

47. It cannot be all peoples, as the survivors are sent to the nations, implying that only some have come.

48. These can be either Jews from the nations, or gentile converts. See Smith, *Isaiah 40–66*, 750.

against me. For their worm shall not die, their fire shall not be quenched, and they shall be an abhorrence to all flesh" (Isa 66:24). Smith writes,

> Verse 24 describes the horrible sight of decaying carcasses of the people whom God has judged in 66:15–16. This gruesome picture might have developed out of the actual sight of the decomposing carcasses of the 185,000 Assyrian troops that were left to rot in the fields around Jerusalem when God defeated the army of Sennacherib (37:36). Later the prophet Jeremiah (7:30–33; 31:40) draws a similar scene, but this time it is associated with the decomposing dead bodies in the valley of Slaughter, where detestable human sacrifices were conducted in the Hinnom Valley. In both cases there were thousands of rebellious people who died and rotted in the field because they refused to trust God. Because there were so many bodies (185,000 Assyrian troops), the birds and the worms could feast on those that were unburied, so the only solution was to burn these bodies to remove the stench and prevent an outbreak of diseases. Such incidents, which the people saw and experienced, seem to provide some of the cultural backdrop for the idea that there is an eternal place of fire and decaying flesh for those who rebel against God.[49]

Here we have a vivid picture of a world at peace because of God's intervention to utterly annihilate those who resist him with violent force. As we come to the Gospel of Mark, it makes complete sense that those who perceived Jesus to be God's anointed would anticipate this being launched at some time or another. They waited in vain. Instead, God's anointed was the one brutally butchered, laid in a grave, the hopes of Israel shattered. Or were they?

Jeremiah

In Jeremiah 23, the hope of a righteous Davidic branch is preceded by God's judgment on the leaders of Israel (shepherds) for their failure to care for the people (Jer 23:1–2). God then gathers the people from the nations and returns them to Israel (Jer 23:3–4). This gathering presupposes the use of force to see them released. Jeremiah then speaks of a golden age, with God raising up a righteous branch of David who will reign wisely with justice and righteousness (Jer 23:5). Thus, Judah and Israel will be saved and safe, and God honored (Jer 23:6). The vision presupposes God acting to release his people through force.

---

49. Smith, *Isaiah 40–66*, 752–53.

Jeremiah 30:9 refers to God raising up a Davidic king. This is preceded by a promise of restoration to the land (Jer 30:1–3) and warning of terrible times of terror in which God will "*break his yoke* from off your neck, and I will *burst your bonds*, and *foreigners* [*zār*] shall no more make a servant of him" (Jer 30:8, emphasis added).[50] This is a short but vivid destruction of God acting with violent military force to overcome Israel's enemies and then establish his king. Ultimately, all Israel's enemies will be "devoured" and enemies exiled, plundered, and preyed upon (Jer 30:16). On the other hand, Israel and Zion will be restored under their own leadership (Jer 30:21). The oracle ends with a further reference to God's wrath and fierce anger (Jer 30:23–24).

In Jeremiah 33 this picture of God acting violently to redeem his people is reinforced. Jeremiah refers to God's destruction of Israel by Babylon including that "they will be *filled with the dead bodies* of the men *I will slay in my anger and wrath*" (Jer 33:4–5). This is followed by the promise of healing, restoration, and Shalom as the people return to the land and her restoration (Jer 33:6–7). This again presupposes that God will act to overthrow the Babylonians and see Israel released. This divinely endorsed military action will bring restoration, prosperity, and peace—all signs of God's favor (Jer 33:8–13). One dimension of this is the future hope of a righteous branch of David's line. He will act justly and righteously, and Judah and Jerusalem will be safe (Jer 33:15–16). The dynasty and the religious cult will never fall (Jer 33:17–18). Note here the fusion of religion and political power (priest and king, cf. the two messiahs of Qumran).

Ezekiel

The image of a Davidic shepherd in Ezekiel 34 includes God's promise to rescue his sheep from the nations and look after them (Ezek 34:10–21). This presupposes God's action to defeat Israel's enemies among whom they are scattered. In verses 23–24, a Davidic shepherd will be set over them by God who will care for them. This will establish peace and prosperity (Ezek 34:25–31). Again, we have the recurring image of a divinely empowered deliverance of the people, and the establishment of a dynasty faithful to God and bringing peace and prosperity. In Ezekiel 34:15–23, Israel is restored and reunited into one nation, free from idolatry. They will be under one Davidic shepherd king forever (Ezek 34:24–25). They will be forever at peace with God and each other (Ezek 34:26–28).

---

50. Here the yoke is Nebuchadnezzar, in particular, and the foreigners, the Babylonians; see Keown et al., *Jeremiah 26–52*, 93.

Ezekiel 34:1–10 catalogs the failure of Israel's leaders who had been poor shepherds. In verses 11–22, God will himself act as shepherd to gather Israel from exile; this likely will involve the subjugation of these nations so his people can be released. Ezekiel 34:23–24 tells of God establishing a Davidic shepherd prince over Israel who will be faithful. In the following verses, Ezekiel talks about God establishing his peace which extends to the animal kingdom, total security from the nations and ample provision ("a covenant of peace"). He mentions that God "will *break the bars* of their yoke, and deliver them from the hand of those who enslaved them," suggesting God acting powerfully against Babylon (v. 27) so that Israel is free from subjugation to the nations (vv. 28, 29). The Theo figure is also mentioned in Ezekiel 37:24–25, with David sole shepherd and king over a restored and unified Israel (vv. 15–23). The people will walk according to God's law and will dwell in the land in eternal peace, with God observed by the nations (vv. 26–28).

An atomistic reading of these texts minimizes the use of violence in literal and specific terms. However, more broadly, the specter of war and violence is infused into all of Ezekiel, including the inevitable sacking of Jerusalem and Judah because of Israel's idolatry, sin, and failed leadership.[51] There are also oracles indicating the destruction of the nations, including the Ammonites, Moab, Edom, Seir (Mount Seir), the Philistines, Tyre, Egypt, Cush, Put, Lud, Arabia, Libya, Assyria, Elam, Meshech-Tubal, Sidon, and Gog (Ezek 25:7, 10–11, 13–14, 16–17; 26:1—28:19, 21–23; 29:4–5, 8–12; 30:4, 6–8, 10–26; 31:1–18; 32:3–32; 35:4–15; 38:1). Throughout Ezekiel, there are also promises of deliverance from exile and restoration, which presuppose military defeat of their oppressor; in particular, Babylon (esp. Ezek 6:8–10; 11:16–25; 20:39–44; 34:11–31; 36:1—37:28; 39:25–29). As such, in the broader context, this peace is achieved through the glorious intervention of God and his agent, with God controlling the ebb and flow of the nations, including politics and war.

Ezekiel 38–39 confirms that his vision involves a Davidic king's military rule. Assuming that this follows the installation of this king, and leaving aside attempts to identify exactly who is in mind and when this will happen, sometime in the indeterminate future (Ezek 38:8), Gog and a series of nations (Meshech, Tubal, Persia, Cush, Put, Gomer, Beth-togamah), will gather to attack Israel and Jerusalem. Because of God's intervention, the enemies will be defeated through earthquakes, sword, pestilence, bloodshed,

---

51. One could say that all of Ezekiel relentlessly warns Israel of her impending violent destruction at the hands of Babylon, based on her sin. But see especially Ezek 5:11–12, 15–17; 6:4–6, 11–12; 7:8, 10–22; 9:5–6; 11:7–12; 12:13–16; 13:11–16; 14:15–23; 16:5–43; 17:16–21; 19:8–9, 12–14; 21:2–4; 22:1–32; 23:13–16, 21–34; 24:9; 33:21–33; 36:18–19.

torrential rain, hailstones, sulfur, and fire—a blend of God's supernatural cosmic intervention and armies (Ezek 38:20—39:6). After this, there will be peace (Ezek 39:7-10). The people of Israel will "*seize the spoil* of those who despoiled them and *plunder* those who plundered them" (Ezek 39:10, emphasis added). It will take seven months to remove the dead of Gog armies from Israel (Ezek 39:11-16), a gross description of utter violent carnage. In Ezekiel 39:17-20, there is a powerful vision of the birds and animals gorging on the bodies, a picture of the complete destruction of the invading hordes. God will then be glorified, and Israel will see God's judgment and acknowledge him (Ezek 39:21-24). The image in Ezekiel 39:25-29 is the end of exile with all God's people in the land, and God's Spirit poured on them, i.e., Shalom. However, this is Shalom through violent carnage.

Daniel

The important "Son of Man" vision of Daniel 7 is set in the context of texts replete with the violent power of monarchs. This is seen in Nebuchadnezzar's preparedness to execute the wise men (Dan 2:12-14) and Darius seeing Daniel thrown to the lions (Dan 6). The demand to worship the enormous idol in Daniel 3 is followed by the attempted execution of anyone who fails to do so. The vision of the statue in Daniel 2:39-45 speaks of kingdoms who execute brutal destructive force, overthrowing and smashing each other. The first kingdom (the head of gold) is Babylon, to whom God had given absolute authority. This is followed by a second (the silver chest and arms), which is inferior.[52] A third kingdom (middle and thighs of bronze) arises. Then, there is a fourth kingdom (legs of iron, its feet of iron and clay). In the explanation, the iron speaks of the strength of the kingdom as iron "breaks to pieces and shatters all things. And like iron that crushes, it shall break and crush all these" (Dan 2:41). However, the kingdom is also brittle (clay) and will not hold together. God will then set up an indestructible kingdom which will "*break in pieces* all these kingdoms and bring them to an end, and it shall stand forever" (Dan 2:44). This is symbolized by a stone that breaks these kingdoms into pieces (Dan 2:45). Scholars debate the identities of the kingdoms here.[53] However, the exact historical referent is not critical to this

---

52. Miller (*Daniel*, 94) suggests that the references to inferiority may refer to the spread of sin in the world. He notes that the two arms may symbolize the two parts of the kingdom. He argues that the second figure is the Medo-Persians (Cyrus).

53. See Goldingay (*Daniel*, 50–51), who discusses the options. The fourth king can be the Greeks. The four kings can all be Babylonian (he lists Nebuchadnezzar II (604–562 BC), Amel-Marduk (Evil-merodach) (562–560 BC), Nergal-šar-uṣur (Neriglissar (560–556 BC), Labaši-Marduk (556 BC), and Nabuna'id (Nabonidus) (556–539 BC), whose son

analysis. What matters is the pictures of successive violent imperial rule into which God's Kingdom led by Jesus emerges. As Jesus assumes "Son of Man" as his preferred epithet, it is against this backdrop that he is to be interpreted. Little wonder they expected violence when he emerged on the scene.

The writing on the wall in Daniel 5 similarly tells of violent overthrow of Babylon by the Medes and Persians. The actual vision is preceded by Daniel's vision of four empires of the world symbolized by wild animals (cf. Rev 13). The vision instantly speaks then of power and predation; the language of ancient kingdoms. As Goldingay acutely puts it, "Each is fierce and dangerous."[54] The first kingdom is a lion with eagle's wings,[55] likely referring to Babylon.[56] The idea of a lion with eagle's wings strikes terror into the heart, as if a lion running on all fours is not enough. The second is a bear, "second only to the lion" as a source of fear to humans in this context.[57] This bear has three ribs in its mouth "which may safely be understood to represent the conquests of the empire. Since the beasts present nations or empires, devouring other beasts would symbolize triumph over them."[58] It is told to "Arise, devour much flesh"—a horrific vision of rapacious military violence. The third is a leopard with four wings of a bird. Again, we have a vision of a predator that can both run and fly; terrifying to its prey. With four wings, it can represent four Persian kings,[59] or as Smith prefers, "the fourfold Greek empire of [Daniel] 8:8; 11:4."[60] The fourth beast is "terrify-

---

Bel-šar-uṣur (Belshazzar) was regent in Babylon at the Medo-Persian conquest). Others have suggested four rulers of Assyria, Persia, or Ptolemaic kings. The range of possibilities suggests that it may be inappropriate to identify the rulers. Smith (*Daniel*, 97–102) notes that some take the fourth. He sees the second as Cyrus, the third as Greece (Alexander), and the fourth as Rome. Looking from the perspective of Jesus' assumption of the title "Son of Man," this makes sense. However, whether that is how the first readers took it is debatable. How they took it depends on the vexed question of dating.

54. Ibid., 161.

55. Goldingay notes, "The features of a lion (v 4) to which the Old Testament appeals are ferocity, strength, destructiveness, courage, rapacity, and fearsomeness." While, the "eagle's key characteristics are speed and rapacity (Hab 1:8; Lam 4:19)" (ibid., 161).

56. See Smith, *Daniel*, 197; Goldingay, *Daniel*, 162.

57. Ibid., 182. He notes a range of possibilities, including Media and perhaps Darius, Babylonian kings, earlier empires, Medo-Persians. Smith (*Daniel*, 198) is adamant this is the Medo-Persians, and this seems to fit best (certainly from the perspective of Jesus' use of "Son of Man").

58. Smith, *Daniel*, 198. He takes them as "Babylon (539 BC), Lydia (546 BC), and Egypt (525 BC)."

59. Goldingay (*Daniel*, 163) sees it as either Persia or Greece.

60. Smith, *Daniel*, 198, 200. He notes that the four heads may refer to the fourfold division of the Macedonian Empire after Alexander's death: 1) Antipater and/or Cassander over Greece and Macedonia; 2) Lysimachus over Thrace and large portions of

ing and dreadful and exceedingly strong" with iron teeth with which "it devoured and broke in pieces and stamped what was left with its feet"—another picture of political dominance and military destruction. Goldingay suggests that if it is Greece that is in mind, it is an elephant, frequently used by Alexander and Antiochus III and especially Antiochus IV (1 Macc 1:17; 3:34).[61] Smith takes it as Rome:

> By the second century BC, Rome had superseded Greece as the dominant world power. The fourth beast, therefore, represents the Roman Empire, symbolized in chap. 2 by the iron legs and feet of the great statue. The incredible might and cruelty of Rome are aptly depicted by Daniel's fourth beast. Just as this monster was "different" from all the others, so the Roman Empire differed from those that had preceded it. Rome possessed a power and longevity unlike anything the world had ever known. Nations were crushed under the iron boot of the Roman legions, its power was virtually irresistible, and the extent of its influence surpassed the other three kingdoms.[62]

Whoever is in mind, we have a picture of political and military domination, which fits a world of colliding imperium.

The crucial vision of Daniel 7, in which is found the Son of Man material and vital to understanding Jesus' ministry as the "Son of Man" (his favorite self-description), speaks of successive violent military and political empires (Dan 7:4).[63] The vision culminates with a picture of God ("Ancient of Days") enthroned (Dan 7:9-10) and the coming of one "like a son of man" with complete authority. The vision involves "*war* against the saints [God's people] and defeating them" (Dan 7:21, emphasis added). The Ancient of Days pronounces judgment in their favor, and they receive "the kingdom" (Dan 7:22). The picture in Daniel 7:13-14 is of one who receives complete authority to rule eternally over all rulers and nations (cf. Dan 7:27). Although violence, war, and political power are not mentioned explicitly, set in the context of the flow of empires through Daniel, the Old Testament, and the ancient political context, it stands to reason that the reader would see here a final overthrow of all nations by God and the establishment of his

---

Asia Minor; 3) Seleucus I Nicator over Syria, Babylon, and large parts of the Middle East, excluding Asia Minor and Palestine; and 4) Ptolemy I Soter over Egypt and Palestine.

61. Goldingay, *Daniel*, 164.
62. Smith, *Daniel*, 201.
63. For example, ripping off the lion's wings, a bear with three ribs in its mouth and the eating of flesh, a beast with iron teeth which "crushed and devoured its victims underfoot . . . its body destroyed and thrown into a blazing fire."

reign through this son of man—is there another way? The vision of the final times involves a time of unprecedented distress (Dan 12:1) suggesting even more of the same sort of destruction. In the ancient world, it is certain that any intervention from God or his expected one would involve the establishment of peace through violent overthrow of the forces of the world.

Daniel 8 also speaks of the succession of the Medo-Persian and Greek empires again with force (Dan 8:6–7, 23–25). Daniel 11 refers to a succession of empires, including the gaining of power through wealth (Dan 11:2), complete sovereignty (Dan 11:3), the breaking up of empires (Dan 11:4), alliances (Dan 11:6), violent war and pillaging (Dan 11:7–19, 21–45), tribute (Dan 11:20), and deification (Dan 11:36–39)—all classic ancient empire concerns.

Hosea

After the initial verses, which establish the setting and the command to Hosea to take the prostitute Gomer as his wife to illustrate Israel's adultery, Hosea begins with God's destruction of Israel for her idolatry. This involves violent devastation, including punishing Jehu's house (Hos 1:4) and the breaking of the bow of Israel (Hos 1:5). Unlike Judah, which will be spared this violence, there will be no mercy for the north (Hos 1:7; 2:1–13). While Hosea 2:1–13 is not directly militaristic, the language is threatening, especially verse 12, where God will "lay waste" the orchards of Israel, and verse 13, where God will "punish" her (cf. vv. 3, 4, 10, 11). Hosea 3:5 envisages Israel's return to seek God and David, their king—indicating a future hope of the restoration of the Davidic monarchy.

The verses preceding Hosea 3:5 speak of restoration implying a cessation of exile, and so in the ancient world, the defeat of enemies (Hos 2:14—3:4). Hosea 4–5 is a relentless attack on Israel. Hosea 6:1–2 speaks of God having "torn us . . . struck us down," again picturing God's destruction and his restoration after two days (a prediction of Jesus' resurrection?). After this, aside from a few spots reminding us of God's love (e.g. Hos 11:1–4), the relentless attack on Israel and Judah continues through Hos 6–12. So, Israel will be destroyed by "one like a vulture" (Hos 8:1)—a vivid picture of death—pursued by an enemy (Hos 8:3), will experience destruction (Hos 8:4) and a whirlwind (Hos 8:7), and will be swallowed up (Hos 8:8), punished, and returned to Egypt (Hos 8:13, cf. 9:6). Judah's cities will be burned and her strongholds devoured (Hos 8:14). She will be plundered by foreign nations (Hos 9:6). The people will be driven out of God's house (Hos 9:15). Her children will be put to death (Hos 9:16). They will be wanderers in the nations (Hos 9:17). Their altars and temple will be destroyed (Hos 10:2). They will be subject to Assyria (Hos 11:5) and pay tribute to her (Hos 10:6). Their king will die (Hos 10:7). The nations will war and gather against them (Hos 10:9-10), her armies defeated and the nation destroyed (Hos 10:13-15), and the cities destroyed by the sword (Hos 11:6). They will be destroyed by God as if he were a wild beast destroying them (Hos 12:7-9). They will know death (Hos 12:14). Their children will be smashed, and their pregnant women ripped open (Hos 12:16)! Can one imagine a more violent, destructive vision? While the hope of a Davidic ruler lacks any definite militaristic overtones, the whole pattern of destruction and the hope of restoration is shrouded in a militaristic world-view. For the ancients, there was no other.

Amos

The hope of restoration of the Davidic monarchy in Amos 9:11-15, which speaks of it being rebuilt "as in the days of old," lacks anything explicitly militaristic, although possession of "the remnant of Edom" could be read as subjugation.[64] Yet, as with the other prophetic books, Amos is built on a premise of military power and force, and most especially the plundering of the northern state for her sin. God is like a lion who roars from Zion (Amos 1:2), bringing violent destruction on the nations, often with the image of fire (see Amos 1:4-5, 7-10, 12, 14; 2:2-3), and upon Judah (Amos 2:5). The thrust of the whole of Amos is that God will bring destruction to Israel too for her sin (Amos 2:13-16; 3:11, 14-15; 4:14; 5:3, 6, 20; 6:11; 7:8-9, 11, 17; 8:3, 9—9:10). The context is Assyria's rise and threat. As such, while military power is not directly mentioned, considering the context, an ancient reader would assume that some form of military intervention is implied in the restoration of Israel and the Davidic monarchy.

Micah

Micah 4, like Isaiah 2, envisages a future time when God will be enthroned in Zion, war will end, and the nations will flow into it, believing in God and following his law (Mic 4:1-5, cf. Isa 2:1-4). Israel and her kingship will be restored (Mic 4:6-8). God will redeem suffering Israel from Babylon, despite the many nations who assemble against her (Mic 4:9-11); they will be defeated as God's people rise up (Mic 4:12-13). In Micah 5, despite the attacks of enemies (Mic 5:1), from Bethlehem in Judah will come a ruler

---

64. Not according to Kaiser, "The Davidic Promise," 103.

(Mic 5:2, cf. Matt 2:6). He will shepherd "his flock" in security by God's strength, and "he shall be great to the ends of the earth. And he shall be their peace (Mic 5:3–5). The Assyrians will no longer threaten Israel when they attack (Mic 5:5–6). This clearly alludes to the Davidic story, and so speaks of a Davidic redeemer figure.

On the face of it, this appears a peaceful rule. However, the wider context of Micah suggests that it should be not be read in this way. War and violence punctuate the oracles. In Micah 1, God comes from heaven, the elements are affected, and Samaria is destroyed to such an extent that there is a massive outpouring of lament (Mic 1:2–11). A conqueror comes to Judah and Jerusalem (Mic 1:12, 14). Exile is coming, meaning invasion by Babylon (Mic 1:16). Woes are announced on Israel's sin (Mic 2:1–2), leading to disaster (Mic 2:3). God will hide his face from the unjust leaders of Israel (Mic 3:1–4) and declares war against the false prophets (Mic 3:5). Because of their false leadership, "Zion will be plowed as a field; Jerusalem will become a heap of ruins" (Mic 3:12).

In what follows the prediction of a ruler born in Bethlehem, Micah says that a remnant of Jacob will be among the nations and will be a lion tearing its prey to pieces and "all your enemies shall be cut off" (Mic 5:7–9). This is followed by God's vengeance on the nation who do not obey (Mic 5:10–15). The desolation of Israel is due to her sin, whereas she should delight in justice, kindness, and humility, rather than burnt sacrifices (Mic 6:6–8, cf. Matt 9:13; 12:7)—amid the images of carnage we find in the Old Testament snippets that point to Jesus' modus operandi, this is one of them. Destruction is again predicted, including desolation, starvation, and famine (Mic 6:13–16). Despite Micah feeling that there is no godly person left (Mic 7:1–6), he trusts in God, for he will bring his vindication and his enemies will be shamed (Mic 7:10). Israel will be extended, and people will come from Assyria and Egypt, but the earth will be desolate (Mic 7:11–13).

In Micah 7:16–17, because of God the shepherd, the nations will be ashamed and will be humiliated and subjugated before God. Again, we have a picture of God acting decisively and violently to redeem his people and to subjugate the nations to him. Micah 5:2–5 indicates the active involvement of his appointed ruler from Bethlehem in Judah—a Davidic messiah.

Haggai

In Haggai 2:23, the post-exilic prophet is commanded to speak to Zerubbabel to tell him that God is about to make him "like a signet ring," for he has chosen him. The ring indicates divine approval and authority, and his position as coregent.⁶⁵ This could indicate a failed prophecy, or that Zerubbabel is representative and a messianic anticipatory figure.⁶⁶ What is important for our study is the preceding verses which speak of God's action to "shake the heavens and the earth, and to *overthrow the thrones* of kingdoms ... *destroy the strength* of the kingdoms of the nations, and *overthrow* the chariots and riders. And the horses and their riders shall go down, every one *by the sword* of his brother" (2:20–22, emphasis added). Earlier in Haggai, we read of God shaking all nations and filling his house with glory (Hag 2:7). Clearly, the context of this appointment of Zerubbabel is the violent military overthrow of Israel's enemies by God. This may involve human agency. In light of the prevailing patterns of religiously endorsed military engagement which led Israel into its exile and return, as elsewhere in Israel's Scriptures, it is likely that Haggai envisages more warfare this time, with Israel and her God destroying her enemies.

Zechariah

The first visions of the book of Zechariah speak of the anger of the Lord toward the nations (Zech 1:14). The four horns of Zechariah 1:18–20 represent the nations that scattered God's people and will not be terrified and thrown down. The picture of the restoration of Jerusalem and the destruction and subjugation of the nations persists (Zech 2:1–13, esp. v .9). God will send the branch (Davidic king), and Israel will be purified and at peace (Zech 3:8–10).

In Zechariah 4, the prophet has a vision of a gold lampstand with seven lamps and two olive trees to the right and left. Zechariah is given an interpretation, including Zerubbabel rebuilding the temple (Zech 4:9). The two olive trees represent the "two *anointed ones* who will stand by the Lord of the whole earth." These could represent the notion of an anointed priest and ruler, something taken up in the Qumran. Little is said at this point of their role. In Zechariah 6:11–13, the prophet crowns Joshua, the high priest. Reference is then made to one whose name is the Branch, who will branch out from this place and build the temple. This could refer to Zerubbabel, or be a messianic prophecy of one to come who will rebuild the temple with the aid of people from far off—or both (Zech 6:15). Aside from rebuilding the temple, there is no detail concerning the various "messianic" roles of Joshua or this branch. Zechariah 1:18–20 indicates that violent military force will be involved.

65. Taylor and Clendenen. *Haggai, Malachi*, 198.
66. Ibid., 200.

The glorious vision in Zechariah 8 of Zion's complete restoration and Shalom includes the rescue of God's people (v. 7). Just as God used foreign nations to punish Israel, he will rescue them, no doubt in a similar manner: destruction. Zechariah envisages people from all nations desperate to come to Jerusalem to worship Yahweh (Zech 8:22-23). As with the other prophets examined above, Zechariah in chapter 9 speaks powerfully of the destruction of Israel's enemies. Tyre's sea power will be destroyed, she will be "*consumed* with fire," Gaza and Ekron will "*writhe* in agony," Ashdod will be occupied by foreigners, the pride of the Philistines "will be *cut off*, and so on (Zech 9:1-8, emphasis added). On the other hand, Zion will welcome in her righteous and gentle king on a donkey (Zech 9:9, cf. Mark 11:7-8; Matt 21:5-7; Luke 19:35; John 12:14-15). Cosmic peace will then be established (Zech 9:10). If verses 9-10 suggest peace, verses 11-13 speak of God freeing his people based on his covenant and rousing the men of Jerusalem for war with Greece. Through the power of Yahweh, who will appear over them, the warriors of Israel will march to victory (Zech 9:14-17).

In Zechariah 10, God is a shepherd who punishes Israel's flawed shepherds, and God himself cares for Israel (vv. 1-3). In verses 4-5, battle imagery is used of the leaders God will bring forth from the nation of Judah. These include two symbols of stability: "the cornerstone" and "the tent peg." "The battle bow" speaks of these leaders being well armed for war. In verse 5, the military metaphor is explicit: "together they will be like *mighty men* trampling the muddy streets in *battle*. Because the Lord is with them, they will *fight and overthrow* the horsemen" (emphasis added). Similarly, in verse 7, the Ephraimites will be "like *mighty men*" (emphasis added), indicating the people will be empowered as well. These leaders will be warrior-rulers, empowered and endorsed by their God. The image of return from exile in Zechariah 10:8-12 presupposes God in some way, overthrowing the enemies of Israel. Further images of the destruction of Israel's enemies are found in Zechariah 11:1-3. Zechariah 11:4-17, an exceedingly difficult passage, includes notions of violence, including slaughter (Zech 11:3-5), people handed over to neighbor and king (Zech 11:6), the removal of three shepherds (Zech 11:8), the eating of "one another's flesh" (cannibalism, Zech 11:9), and the rupture of Judah and Israel (Zech 11:14).

The vision of Zechariah 12 centers on Jerusalem being surrounded by the forces of the world (Zech 12:3) and the city standing firm and confounding her enemies (Zech 12:2-4). The leaders will lead them to great victory (Zech 12:5-6). God will save and shield Judah (Zech 12:7-9). However, this will not be a direct divine intervention, but will involve the engagement of Israel with "the feeblest among them like David" and "the house of David . . . like God, like the Angel of the Lord going before them." Thus, on that day God "will set out to *destroy all the nations* that attack Jerusalem" (vv. 7–9, emphasis added). The image is of a horrendous war in which the nations attack Jerusalem but, empowered by Yahweh and led by the Davidic shepherd king, the nations are defeated. After this, there is an image of weeping over "one they have pierced," which is likely a reference to Jesus (cf. John 19:33–37; Rev 1:7). It is likely, too, that the mourning relates to the horrors of the war that has just occurred. In Zechariah 13, Israel is purified, but violence is vindicated if it involves the removal of idols (Zech 13:2–3).

The vision of Zechariah 14, like chapter 12, involves an international attack on Jerusalem (Zech 14:2) with the city captured, the houses pillaged, the women raped, and half the city exiled. While distasteful to western moderns, this is a classic ancient picture of defeat in war. However, in verse 3, God will go and fight these nations, standing on the Mount of Olives, splitting it, and causing the people to flee. The Lord will then come with his "holy ones," which probably refers to angels.[67] This theophanic vision is one of holy war with God moving against the enemies of Israel. This will see the establishment of God's reign "over the whole earth" (v. 9). Peace comes from glorious military victory led by God and his angelic forces. Jerusalem will then be secure forever (v. 11).

In verses 12–15, Zechariah gives a vivid and disgusting image of the fate of the nations who attack Jerusalem. This includes rotting flesh, eyes, and tongues in horses and people, and panic with the nations turning on each other in frenzied attack. Again, it is not merely a divine intervention but involves Judah fighting in Jerusalem (v. 14). As expected in ancient warfare, tribute is collected from the enemies (v. 14). The complete subjugation of the nations is seen in their annual attendance at worship in Jerusalem at the Feast of Tabernacles (v. 16), with the Lord punishing those who do not attend with drought and plague (Zech 14:17–18). The cooking utensils of Jerusalem are then purified with the gentiles removed: "And on that day there will no longer be a Canaanite in the house of the Lord Almighty" (Zech 14:21). This is the image of a purged nation as it should have been at the Conquest, with God acting with the armies of Israel to defeat and overthrow the gentiles in the land. The whole world will be subject to his rule. Again, it is little wonder that the Jewish observers of Jesus expected him to get busy destroying the gentiles to demonstrate his messiah-ship.

---

67. Smith, *Micah–Malachi*, 279.

Malachi

Malachi includes reference to the destruction of Edom (Mal 1:4–5). It speaks of a messenger who will prepare for God ("me"). Malachi 3:1 refers to one who will come to his temple, "the Lord whom you are seeking and the messenger of the covenant in whom you delight" (cf. Mark 11:15–19). Assuming the two messengers are different, as the structure seems to suggest, then this refers to a messenger who prepares the way for Theo.[68] The coming of these two figures will refine the priesthood and people of Israel (Mal 3:2–5). In Malachi 4:1–6, a day is foreseen which will bring refinement based on Torah (Mal 4:4). Malachi predicts the coming of "the prophet Elijah" who will restore families, a symbol of Shalom (in the Gospels, John the Baptist; see Mark 9:11–13; Matt 11:14; 17:10–12; Luke 1:17). The picture is very destructive, with the day burning "like a *furnace*," the arrogant and evil in fire, the wicked trampled down under the feet, and the warning of the land being cursed if the people do not respond to the Elijah figure. As such, the picture is again of purification through brute force.

The Psalms

In particular, the messianic kingship Psalms make it abundantly clear that Davidic kingship and divinely endorsed military victory over enemies cannot be separated. In Psalm 2, the setting for the coronation is the nations' conspiring, plotting, standing, and gathering together against Israel's king (messiah) and seeking to break free (Ps 2:1–3). Yahweh responds with scoffing, wrathful anger, rebuke (Ps 2:4–5), and the appointing of his king (Ps 2:6–7). God then says to the king to ask him, and he will grant him all the nations as his inheritance and possession (Ps 2:8). The king will rule with an "*iron scepter*" and will "*dash them to pieces* like pottery" (Ps 2:9, emphasis added). These two images speak of violent, forceful subjugation of the nations to the messiah. The rulers of the world are then warned to take the wise route and to serve Yahweh with fear and trembling (Ps 2:10). They are to completely submit to the king ("kiss the Son")[69] to ensure that he is not inflamed with anger with them and destroy them (Ps 2:11). They are warned his anger could flare in a moment. The picture here is of the nations subjugated to Yahweh, either voluntarily or through violent force. It is a threatening scene. Again, the notion of military and violent intervention is assumed. The placement of this Psalm is also critical, as it sets the scene for

---

68. See the discussion in Taylor and Clendenen, *Haggai, Malachi*, 384.
69. See the discussion on the textual issues in Craigie, *Psalms 1–50*, 64.

THE HOPE OF A DELIVERER ("THEO" = "THE EXPECTED ONE") 109

understanding other kingship and messianic psalms; through violence the Davidic king will ultimately triumph.[70]

The concluding verse of Psalm 18 (v. 50) refers to God's salvation brought to his Davidic king, who is "his anointed" (*māšiaḥ*). God shows steadfast love to him and his descendants forever. The Psalm is replete with references to conflict, including salvation from enemies (v. 3), death (vv. 4–5), theophanic cosmic events as God acts (vv. 7–19), God equipping the king for war (vv. 34–35), utter defeat and violent destruction of enemies (vv. 37–42), the sovereignty of the king over the nations so that foreigners come trembling and cringing before him (vv. 43–45), and vengeance and the subjugation of enemies (vv. 47–48). Clearly, the association of violent retributive force and utter destruction sits alongside the notion of the anointed king.

In Psalm 21, the king is blessed by God and trusts in him, and is immovable in God's steadfast love (vv. 1–7). He finds his enemies, and God makes them a "blazing oven" when he appears, "swallows" his enemies in "his wrath," and consumes them with fire (v. 9). The king eradicates the descendants of the enemies from the earth despite their unsuccessful scheming (vv. 10–11), putting them to flight and shooting their faces with arrows (v. 12). Davidic kingship is again associated with God-assisted and enabled destruction.

In Psalm 72, a kingship psalm, military motifs are prevalent. In verse 4, the psalmist prays that the king will "crush the oppressor." In verses 8–11, he will rule the world ("from sea to sea and from the River to the ends of the earth"), and the nations and their rulers will be subjugated to him and will bring tribute (v. 15). In an allusion to the Abrahamic promise of Gen 12:1–3, all nations will be blessed through him and call him blessed (v. 17).

Psalm 110 envisages God (Yahweh) saying to the king (messiah/Adonai) to "sit at my right hand until I *make your enemies a footstool* for your feet" (v. 1, emphasis added) This pictures the king, and ultimately the messiah, being empowered by God ("I make") to subjugate his enemies. In the initial context, it speaks of the Davidic king, but more broadly, the messiah—seen in this Psalm being cited all over the New Testament (e.g. Matt 22:44; Mark 12:36; Luke 20:42; Acts 2:34–35; Rom 8:34; 1 Cor 15:25, 27; Eph 1:20, 22; Col 3:1; Heb 1:3, 13; 2:8; 8:1; 10:12–13; 12:2; 1 Pet 3:22, cf. Matt 5:35; 26:64; Mark 14:62; Luke 22:69; Acts 2:25; 5:31; 7:49, 55–56; Rom 16:20). Psalm 110:1 is a very important passage for Jesus' self-understanding in Mark and the other gospels (Mark 12:35–36 and parr).

---

70. On the relationship of Ps 2 to Ps 1 and the Psalter see Cole, *Psalms 1–2*, 1–45, 82–87.

The subsequent verses envisage the extension of the kingdom of this "Lord" from Zion so that he rules in the midst of his enemies, i.e., across the world (v. 2). Verse 3 explicitly speaks of willing troops arising on the day of battle arrayed in holy majesty. In verse 4, the king is not only a monarch, but a priest, not from the order of the Levites, but of Melchizedek, the priest-king of Genesis 14. In verse 5, the Lord crushes kings "on the day of *his wrath*" (emphasis added). In verse 6, God judges the nations with such brutal force, that he crushes the rulers of the whole earth. This is a picture of international conflict and the king's triumph over every nation. This Psalm, then, again powerfully pictures a military Theo figure who is both priest and king (or two images, cf. Qumran) and is empowered by Yahweh and through whom God subjugates the world to his reign. Here we have the classic ancient alliance of spiritual and political power, something we have seen through the whole Old Testament.

Psalm 132 begins with a prayer to remember David and his suffering on God's behalf and his desire to build him a temple (vv. 1–7). God is urged to come to his dwelling place for David's sake, with priests clothed in righteousness, the people praising, all for David. The psalmist exhorts God not to "turn away from the face of your *anointed one*" (v. 10). The Davidic covenant promising a Davidic king forever is recalled (vv. 11–12). The choice of Zion as God's home is vindicated with blessings of prosperity and salvation for the priests and praise from the people (vv. 13–16). God will make a horn sprout for David, a shining lamp for "my anointed," and the king's enemies will be shamed (vv. 17–18). Implicit here is the defeat of the enemies of David and his descendants—at the time of Christ, Rome would be self-evident.

THE APOCRYPHA, PSEUDEPIGRAPHA, PHILO, JOSEPHUS, AND THE RABBIS

There are a range of views on the nature of Theo ("The Expected One") in the other literature of Judaism.[71] Some lack any interest (below), others have a priestly figure (e.g. Qumran, Testament of Levi), some royal, some have multiple messiahs, some have a Davidic king (e.g. Psalms of Solomon 17; 2 Baruch, Sibylline Oracles 3), some have a transcendent pre-existent kingly

71. See Collins ("Messianism in the Maccabean Period," 101), who sees the development of "transcendent savior figure under God" as the most significant development in Jewish messianism in the second-century BC. He adds that there is not one orthodox notion of the messiah and it usually related to the political attitudes and circumstances of the groups in question. See also Collins, *The Scepter and the Star*, 47; Charlesworth, *The Messiah*, 7; Bokser, "Messianism," 102; Neusner, "Mishnah and Messiah," 275.

figure like the "Son of Man" (1 Enoch, Sibylline Oracles 5, Testament of Judah), and others have a blend (e.g. Philo, some of the Qumran literature). All through the literature, God himself is Theo intervening to bring salvation. The LXX was also produced in this period, and messianic interest is seen in its interpretation of Num 24. Collins, however, indicates this:

> The expectation of a king from the Davidic line, which is dormant for much of the postexilic era, resurfaces after the restoration of native, non-Davidic, Jewish kingship in the Hasmonean period (late second to early first centuries BCE). It then reappears in more than one setting. By the first century CE it can fairly be said to be part of the common heritage of Judaism.[72]

In this section, I will not focus so much on the different features of the messiah figure (Theo) across the literature, but that the intervention of the figure necessarily involved *the use of violent force* on behalf of God and his people. As in the above discussion of the Old Testament, it is not difficult to demonstrate that the intervention of God and/or his agent involved military victory over Israel's enemies.

God as Theo in a Direct Sense

In all the writings, whether there is a human or transcendent Theo figure, God is the ultimate agent of deliverance. He acts directly, or with and/or through, his agent. All expectations involve military overthrow and subjugation of Israel's enemies in some sense.

Some writings lack reference to a human or semi-divine Theo figure, including 1 Esdras, Judith, Additions to Esther, Greek portions of Daniel, 1–2 Maccabees, Tobit, Baruch, and the Epistle of Jeremy.[73] However, in these works, God himself is the Theo figure whose retribution against the nations and restoration of Israel is implied.[74] In Judith, for example, the prayers of 9:7-14 and 16:3-20 speak of God's deliverance to overthrow Israel's

---

72. Collins, *The Scepter and the Star*, 49.

73. Horbury, *Messianism Among Jews and Christians*, 42.

74. Ibid., 42–45. He notes on p. 45 that the so-called messianic "messianological vacuum" in the fifth to second century BC is not watertight: "In sum, therefore, the prayers and predictions in the Apocrypha which have just been considered show that redemption and judgment could be satisfactorily imagined through concentration on the portrayal of God himself as the hero; but they hardly show that a messianic leader was ruled out. It seems indeed not unlikely that divine redemption could have been taken to involve human leadership of the kind which was archetypally depicted in the Pentateuchal narratives of the exodus."

enemies, implying a future hope of violent retribution on the nations and Israel's restoration. Esther 14:8–12 includes a prayer for God's deliverance from enemies, which alludes to a future hope of gentile submission to God.

The blessing of Tobit 13 refers to God's kingdom which lasts through all ages (Tob 13:1), that God afflicts (Tob 13:2), a command to Israel to acknowledge him before the nations (Tob 13:3), that God will gather Israel *from the nations* (13:5, 13), the glorious restoration of Jerusalem (Tob 13:9, 16–17, cf. 13:10), that the nations will see its light and come bearing gifts (Tob 13:11), and curses upon those who conquer Israel (Tob 13:12). In Tob 14:4 it is said that "everything that was spoken by the prophets of Israel, whom God sent, will occur. None of all their words will fail, but all will come true at their appointed times" (NRSV). This is followed by a reference to the danger to Assyria and Babylon and a promise of restoration (Tob 14:4–5). This is followed by the world being converted, abandoning idols, worshiping God, and restored Israel at peace (Tob 14:6–7). While specifics are not given, it stands to reason based on these texts and the prophetic tradition of Israel that Tobit affirms and confirms the prophetic picture of God's deliverance, including his intervention and the subjugation of the nations.

Baruch 4:8 summarizes God's agency in Israel and Jerusalem's destruction and exile as a response to her sin. The neighboring nations are told that this is God's work through the nations (Bar 4:9, 14–16). Then, if Israel repents, God becomes the agent of deliverance from these enemies (Bar 4:18, 21, 23). The nations will see this salvation (Bar 4:24). Baruch 4:25 urges Israel to be patient in her suffering due to God's wrath, knowing that "your enemy has overtaken you, but *you will see their destruction, and will tread upon their necks*" (emphasis added). They will thus experience God's salvation through God's violence and deliverance. The final clause indicates Israel's involvement in this activity. Jerusalem is singled out in Baruch 4:30–36 to be courageous and assured that those who mistreated them will be destroyed and Israel's children returned (Bar 4:36–37) to restored Jerusalem (Bar 5). While muted, the picture is one of God's intervention to take control of his world and establish Israel with force.

In the Wisdom of Solomon (second to first century BC), the righteous will triumph over the ungodly. The Lord will act with contempt toward the unrighteous, will laugh at them, and they will become "dishonored corpses" and an "outrage among the dead forever." God will "dash them speechless to the ground . . . they will suffer anguish" (Wis 4:18). This will be followed by repentance of the unrighteous and their ceasing to exist (Wis 5:3, 13); whereas, the righteous will live on eternally with great reward (Wis 5:15). God will protect his people as a mighty armed warrior laying waste the whole world (Wis 5:17–23). There is no reference to a messiah, but the context speaks of bloodshed and violent overthrow of the enemies of God and his people.

Sirach (second century BC) does not have a specific Theo figure. However, Sirach 10:16 speaks of God laying waste the nations in a sovereign sense. He appoints rulers over every nation and repays them for their words (Sir 17:17, 23). God metes judgment as a warrior on the nations (Sir 35:22–23, cf. Sir 39:23). The writer prays for mercy for Israel and that God would bring fear to the nations by lifting his hand against them (Sir 36:2–3), and crushing the heads of their rulers (Sir 36:12). Joshua is commended for crushing nations (Sir 46:5), affirming the use of force to exterminate the enemies of Israel ruthlessly. This is significant, as Jesus is the new Messiah; however, his modus operandi is completely different.

In Sirach 45:25, the covenant with David, son of Jesse from Judah, is mentioned. In Sirach 47:1–11, reference is made to David and his dealing with lions, bears, killing Goliath through the strength of God, wiping out enemies, and annihilating the Philistines—all by God's power. In verse 11, the writer notes "the Lord exalted his power forever" indicating an ongoing rule. With the references to David's use of force to subdue Israel's historic enemies, this adds up to a Davidic military messiah, albeit implicitly. In Sirach 47:22, it is stated of Solomon that God will never blot out the Davidic family line, indicating an ongoing reign and implying a Davidic messianic future. However, there is no explicit development of Theo's eschatological role.

In 1 Maccabees (second century BC), it is the Maccabean house which is spoken of in salvific and Theo terms. In 1 Maccabees 3:3–9, Judas Maccabees is particularly glorified for his brilliance in battle, leadership, and destruction of the ungodly. In 1 Maccabees 5:62, the Maccabean family has brought "salvation" (*sōtēria*) to Israel, Judas is the savior of Israel (1 Macc 3:21), and Simon is honored for bringing peace (14:4–5). Yet, in 1 Maccabees 2:57, the author refers to David, who "inherited the throne of the kingdom forever," indicating the author's understanding of the ongoing relevance of the Davidic monarchy. The place of war to win Israel's freedom in 1 Maccabees makes it certain that any future conception in 1 Maccabees, explicit or implicit, includes the same pattern of the cleansing of the land through military engagement with "God on our side" (cf. 1 Macc 4:30).

The writer of 2 Maccabees (second century BC) does not reference the messiah. However, in the prayer of 2 Maccabees 1:24–29, the writer speaks of God's uniqueness and deliverance from "every evil." In verses 27–29, he prays that God will gather together his people and set free those who are enslaved to the gentiles. It reads, "let the Gentiles know that you are God. Punish those who oppressed and are insolent with pride," and establish his people in "your holy place," i.e., Jerusalem. In 2 Maccabees 6:14–17, the writer speaks of the Lord waiting patiently to punish the "other nations" when "the full measure of their sins" is complete. This contrasts with God showing mercy to Israel and promising never to desert her. For the writer, God will raise his people up to "everlasting renewal of life" (2 Macc 7:9). This speaks of the ultimate act of God: to save Israel and subjugate the nations.

In conclusion, in these passages above, although a human or semi-divine Theo figure is absent or at best implied, God himself is the Theo figure who will act violently against Israel's enemies. When Jesus came, and it became apparent that he saw himself acting on God's behalf in his ministry, the question of his messianic identity and relationship to God's expected deliverance was natural. If Jesus were a Theo figure in any sense, violent military engagement would be expected, whether directly from God or led by Jesus himself.

Theo as a Human/Semi-divine Messianic Agent of Some Sort

In some writings, mention is made of a human agent, whether transcendent (e.g. Son of Man), a Davidic messiah, or a priestly agent. In each case, it is easy to demonstrate against the wider context and the prevailing worldview, that force would be used to bring about God's purposes. While the details vary, in sum, this purpose is the deliverance of Israel, the return of the exiles, the restoration of the nation (and especially Jerusalem and the temple), the destruction or submission of the gentiles, universal submission to Yahweh, the delivery of the wealth of the nations to Israel, the resurrection, judgment, and an eternal kingdom under God's rule.

Jubilees

The writer of Jubilees (second century BC) upholds the hope of a messiah sprung from Judah. A prince is predicted from Judah who will reign over the sons of Judah. He will cause the gentiles to fear and the nations to quake. He will be the help of Jacob and its salvation, will bring peace, and all those who curse him will be "*rooted out and destroyed* from the earth and be accursed" (Jub 31:18–20, emphasis added). This is clearly based on the scepter and ruler's staff in Genesis 49:10. It involves dominance. There is a reference to a renewal of the earth (Jub 1:29, cf. 23:30).

Assumption of Moses

In the pseudepigraphal Assumption of Moses 10 (first century AD), God's kingdom will appear across creation and the devil will be destroyed (As. Mos. 10:1). A messenger is appointed who will "*avenge them* of their enemies" (As. Mos. 10:2, emphasis added). Then "the Heavenly One" arises and leaves heaven with "indignation and wrath" on Israel's behalf (As. Mos. 10:3). There are theophanic events on earth not unlike the events of Mark 13:24–25 (As. Mos. 10:4–6). Then God acts to "work vengeance on the nations," destroying their idols and bringing happiness and glory to Israel (As. Mos. 10:7–10). The identity of the "messenger" is unclear, and his role in the destruction is also vague. A good case can be made that this is a Theo figure, a messiah.[75] Whatever the identity and role, the coming kingdom will bring war and destruction as is consistent across the literature.

1 Enoch

In the late first-century document 1 Enoch, and particularly chapters 37–71, Theo is known as "the Son of Man," "the Elect One," "The Anointed One," or the "Christ." In 1 Enoch 38:2, a "Righteous One" is revealed and sinners are judged and driven from the presence of the righteous and elect. Kings and the mighty will perish (1 En. 38:5). In 1 Enoch 39:6a, he is the "Elect One" of righteousness and faith. In 1 Enoch 45:4, God's Elect One sits among God's holy people (1 En. 45:5, cf. 39:6a; 40:5), and there is judgment from God and destruction (1 En. 45:6).

In 1 Enoch 46, this figure becomes the "Son of Man." This is obviously influenced by Daniel 7. He has the appearance of a man with a face full of graciousness (1 En. 46:1). He is righteous (1 En. 46:3), will raise up the kings and rulers, and "will loosen the reigns of the strong" and "*break* the teeth of the sinners" (1 En. 46:4, emphasis added). He will put down "kings from their thrones and kingdoms because they do not extol and praise him nor humbly acknowledge when the kingdom was bestowed upon them" and this will be irrevocable (1 En. 46:5–8). In 1 Enoch 48, he is chosen before the creation and will be righteous, a light to the gentiles, and hope for the troubled, and will be the object of worship and bring salvation (1 En. 48:3–5). Again, there is a picture of destruction with the kings of the earth and the strong who possess the land afflicted and destroyed at the hands of

---

75. Horbury, *Messianism*, 58. Others consider it an angel (Collins, *Scepter*, 176), Elijah (Manson, "Miscellanea Apocalyptica," 41–45), or a human messenger, Taxo the Levite (Tromp, *The Assumption of Moses*, 228–31).

God's elect (1 En. 48:8-10). He is also called "His Anointed" or messiah (1 En. 48:10). He is again called the Elect One in 1 Enoch 49:2.

In chapters 51-53, this figure arises and sits on God's throne, causing mountains, hills, angels, and people to rejoice. Mountains of metal are destroyed, and sinners "destroyed before the face of the Lord of Spirits" so that they "perish forever" (1 En. 53:2). In 1 Enoch 52:4, he is again called "His Anointed," who will be "potent and mighty on the earth." He is also called "the Righteous and Elect One" in 1 Enoch 53:6. In chapters 54-55, the angels bring destruction like Noah's flood. In 1 Enoch 56:5-8, war is declared against God's people by the gentile nations and they are destroyed. In 1 Enoch 62, this Elect One or Son of Man is enthroned and worshiped, and "*slays* all the sinners" (emphasis added), *destroys* the unrighteous, delivers the unrighteous to angels for punishment, *executes vengeance* on those who have oppressed God's children and elect and "*his sword is drunk with blood*" (1 En. 62:2, 12, emphasis added). This is a powerful description of horrific violent military destruction. In 1 Enoch 63:8, the unrighteous will experience darkness and shame in Sheol, will be driven from his presence, "and the sword will abide before his face in their midst."

In 1 Enoch 69:26-29, the Elect One is revealed, brings judgment, wipes sinners off the face of the earth and binds them, and is seated in glory (cf. 1 En. 71:14, 17). In 1 Enoch 92:3, the righteous one shall arise; either meaning that he will awake from sleep to act in the present, or it may indicate resurrection. He will be righteous, bring eternal goodness and peace, be gracious to the righteous, grant them eternal righteousness, vanquish sin, and walk in eternal light. While the figure is transcendent and there is no reference to Davidic descent, he brings violent retribution against sinners and the ungodly.

2 Baruch

Late in the first century AD, in 2 Baruch 29:3, the messiah is revealed after a time of terrible woe (2 Bar. 27). The messiah will arise when "all is accomplished" (2 Bar. 29:3). This will be followed by a time of plentiful food (2 Bar. 29:3-8). The messiah will then return in glory (2 Bar. 30:1). The resurrection of the dead will follow. In 2 Baruch 39:7—40:3, after a string of kingdoms, the messiah is revealed, *he convicts the final leader of the time and kills him*, and his reign is forever until the corruption of the world is at an end. This seems to presuppose a progressive transformation of the world which undoubtedly involves the use of force as in 2 Baruch 40:2. In 2 Baruch 72:2, at the climax of a series of good rulers, including David, Solomon,

Hezekiah, and Josiah (2 Bar. 61:1; 63:1; 66:1), and a time of horrendous woe and war (2 Bar. 70), he comes and summons the nations: "some of them he shall spare, and some *he shall slay*" (emphasis added).

Nations will be judged based on how they have treated Israel, and all will be made subject to God's people. The vision includes those who have ruled over Israel being "given up to the sword" (2 Bar. 72:2-6). He will bring "low everything that is in the world" (2 Bar. 73:1). This presupposes the use of force. Peace then follows (2 Bar. 73:1—74:4). However, it is a peace brought by violent subjugation, rather than willing submission.

4 Ezra

Toward the end of the first century AD, in 4 Ezra 7:26-30, the messiah, who has been kept for many ages (pre-existent), is God's son (cf. 4 Ezra 13:52; 14:9). Others will be with him and the survivors will rejoice for four hundred years. He then dies, as does all humanity. This is followed by the general resurrection and judgment (4 Ezra 7:31-44). In 4 Ezra 11:37—12:34, the messiah is a roaring "lion" (cf. Gen 49:9) who overcomes the eagle (Rome) (4 Ezra 11:37; 12:11, cf. Dan 7:4) which has ruled the world with great terror and offended God, so will be destroyed. Thus, the world is freed from its violence (4 Ezra 11:40-46). In 4 Ezra 12:32, the messiah, who has been kept to the end by God, is a Davidic heir and will rebuke the unrighteous for their sin. He judges them, then destroys them (4 Ezra 12:33). In chapter 13, he is "a Man" who arises from the sea and flew on a mountain, and the people of the world war against him, and he destroys them with his breath without the use of a weapon (4 Ezra 13:8-11, 28). Then some come to him peaceably, others sorrowfully and *in bonds* (4 Ezra 13:12-13). In 4 Ezra 13:37-40, Theo is referred to as "my Son" (cf. 4 Ezra 13:32, 37, 52; 14:9, cf. 7:28) who will rebuke the nations for their ungodliness. This will be like a storm. He shall *destroy* them by the law. He will gather a multitude which seeks peace from the scattered northern tribes. In 4 Ezra 13:49, he will "destroy the multitude of the nations that are gathered together" and perform many wonders. This is unquestionably the picture of a violent Theo figure.

Testament of the Twelve Patriarchs

This work was likely written in the Maccabean period, but has Christian interpolations.[76] Some of these documents refer to a Theo figure which is relevant to this discussion.[77]

Testament of Levi

In Testament of Levi 8, the writer has a vision of his anointing as God's priest, and part of this is a hope of a new king who shall arise in Judah and establish a new priesthood "after the fashion of the Gentiles" (T. Levi 8:14–15). In Testament of Levi 18 there is more detail. Theo is a "new priest" to whom God will reveal his word, and he will "execute a righteous judgment upon the earth for a multitude of days." He will be highly exalted as a star, as the light of the sun, will remove darkness and establish "peace in all the earth" (T. Levi 18:1–4). Joy will fill heaven because of him. His priesthood will be wise and extend to the gentiles. He will end sin, and the lawless will cease doing evil (T. Levi 18:9). He will open the gates of Eden, and the saints will eat the tree of life (T. Levi 18:10). He will defeat Beliar, and give power to his people to tread on evil spirits (T. Levi 18:13). Joy will result (T. Levi 18:14).

Violent force is not explicit, although perhaps implied with "He shall effect the judgment of truth over the earth for many days." In the broader context, judgment includes a range of natural disasters (e.g. T. Levi 4:1) and "*hosts of the armies* which are ordained for the work of judgment" (T. Levi 3:3, emphasis added). Reference is made to Levi executing vengeance on Shechem because of Dinah, and the Lord being with him as he does so (T. Levi 5:2, 4–11. This recalls the story of the violent vengeance of Simeon and Levi as they avenged Dinah's rape by tricking and then killing the men from the city and then laying it to waste (Gen 34). Although not stressed, the judgment of the righteous priest will necessarily involve violent force in the minds of the readers.

Testament of Reuben

As in Testament of Levi, in Testament of Reuben 6:8, Theo is an "anointed priest" of Levi to whom the people must draw near and who will bless Israel and Judah and reign as king over the entire nation. Israel must bow down

---

76. Charlesworth, *The Old Testament Pseudepigrapha*, 778.
77. Christian interpolations of Christ include *T. Levi*, 10:2.

before his seed. Reference is made to "*wars* visible and invisible" and his being among Israel as an "eternal king" (T. Reu. 6:12, emphasis added). Thus, alongside spiritual war, no doubt against Satan and his demonic powers, military warfare and violence are presupposed.

Testament of Judah

In Testament of Judah 24, after a time of wrath on Israel's idolatry, a "star from Jacob" (cf. Num 24:17) will arise in peace. He will be marked sinless and by gentleness and righteousness. He will pour out the Spirit. The readers will be God's children. He will be the Branch of God most high (cf. Isa 11:1; Jer 23:5; 33:15; Zech 3:8; 6:12), the fountain of life for all humanity. He will judge the nations and save those who "call on the Lord." It is unclear whether this picture of a peaceful, gentle messiah is a Christian interpolation, or whether this has an image of a non-violent messiah. Again, because of the overwhelming evidence from Israel's literature that violence is part of the fabric of life and any future hope, this involves violent force.

Testament of Gad

In Testament of Gad 8:1, the Lord will raise up a savior for Israel from Judah and Levi. No details are given other than at the end, God's children will depart from them.

Psalms of Solomon

In Psalms of Solomon 17, late first century BC, reference is made to David's everlasting kingship (v. 5). Then, the psalmist refers to the exile and foreign nations which expelled Israel "with force" (v. 6) and destroyed the Davidic monarchy in arrogance (vv. 7–8). As such, God will hunt them down and remove their seed from the earth when a person alien to Israel arises against her (v. 8). God will "repay them according to their sins," "will have no pity on them," and "is faithful in all his judgments that he makes upon the earth" (vv. 9–12). Verses 13–22 summarize the destruction of Israel, Jerusalem, and exile—a time of military annihilation.

As a response, God will raise a Davidic king who will reign (v. 23). God will "undergird him with strength *to shatter unrighteous rulers*" (v. 24, emphasis added). He will cleanse Jerusalem of the gentile oppressors, expel sinners, *rub out* the arrogance of sinners, and "*crush* all their support with an *iron rod*" (v. 26, emphasis added). He will "*destroy lawless nations* by the word of his mouth" (emphasis added). Gentiles will flee (v. 27). He will gather a holy people, his children, who will live in righteousness and justice, who will be scattered across all the earth. "No longer will an expatriate or foreigner dwell among them" (v. 31). The nations will serve under his yoke (v. 32), and they will flow to a restored Jerusalem to see God's glory bearing gifts (v. 33–35). This will yield peace, so that the king will not put his hope in weapons of war and wealth, but will live under God's kingship and show mercy to the nations who are "before him in fear" (vv. 37–38). Verse 39 sing of his greatness as a leader, his purity, justice, mercy, strength, spiritual empowerment, wisdom, righteousness, and strength in God. He will be a righteous and faithful shepherd of God's flock, feeding the people, impartial.

Psalms of Solomon 18 is another song of the messiah. It begins with praise for God's mercy, goodness, concern for the poor, compassionate judgments across the whole world, love, and discipline of Israel. In verse 6, the psalmist prays God would cleanse Israel for the day of mercy, the "appointed day when his messiah will reign." The psalmist pronounces blessing on those born in those days who live "under *the rod of discipline* of the Lord Messiah" which will be conducted in the fear of God, wisdom, righteousness, strength (v. 7). He will lead people to righteous life in the fear of God (v. 8). The focus of Psalms of Solomon 18 is the era of peace that will be inaugurated through the messiah, rather than the means by which he assumes control.

Psalms of Solomon paints a vivid picture of a Davidic king rising up with retributive violent military force on God's behalf against those who oppress Israel, driving them out, and purifying the people (vv. 6–12). Through this he establishes peace. This peace is further amplified in Psalms of Solomon 18. However, as is the pattern across the ancient world (and in much of the world today), peace is established through retributive military force. It is after this that peace is established and maintained through the righteousness and faithfulness of the Davidic Shepherd.

3 Enoch

This book gives a late Jewish view of the messiah. There is a reference to a messiah who is the Son of Joseph and a messiah who is the Son of David. It is unclear whether this is one figure or two. Whichever the case, both will bring war and vengeance on the gentiles, and especially Gog and Magog (3 En. 45:5, cf. Ezek 38–39). The war goes on until God intervenes to win the last battle (3 En. 48). The messiah will save Israel and bring them to

Jerusalem, and the kingdom of Israel from the whole world will eat with the messiah and the gentiles with them (3 En. 48:10). It ends with "the Lord will be King of the whole world."

Sibylline Oracles 3

In Sibylline Oracles 3, in the middle of the second-century,[78] after several chapters glorifying God and challenging idolatrous humanity to worship him as they should, the writer speaks of a holy prince who will arise and "wield the scepter over all the world unto all ages" (Sib. Or. 3:49-50). This will occur when Rome rules over Egypt (v. 46) and "there shall be *inexorable wrath* on Latin men" (v. 51, emphasis added). At some uncertain future point (v. 55), three will arise and "bring ruin on Rome, and all its people shall perish in their own dwellings through fire from heaven (vv. 52-54).

The subsequent oracles speak of godless violent rulers (à la the antichrist, Babylon, cf. Rev 17), God's vengeance, Greek gods and empires at war, and tribulations (Sib. Or. 3:63-285). In Sibylline Oracles 3.386, God will raise up a king who shall "judge each man *with blood* and *flame of fire*" (emphasis added). He will be from a royal tribe and family that never stumbles," i.e., David (Sib. Or. 3:286-93). The historical enemies Assyria, Babylon, Egypt, Gog, Magog, Libya, Asia Minor, Greece, and Rome will be judged and destroyed in a bloody, violent destruction (Sib. Or. 3:295-651).

In Sibylline Oracles 3:652, God will send a king who will relieve the land from war, "some he will slay" indicating the use of violent force (Sib. Or. 3.654). Israel will then be blessed materially (Sib. Or. 3.657-61). There will then be further war against Israel (3:663-67), only to be destroyed by God, including fiery swords from heaven (Sib. Or. 3.669-701) with "all the shameless [being] *washed with blood*" (Sib. Or. 3.696, emphasis added). There will then be glorious peace, with the temple at the center of the earth and people worshiping God, and Israel armed with the weapons of their enemies (Sib. Or. 3.702-31). There will then be judgment, the unrighteous will be consumed, and there will be peace and an eternal kingdom (Sib. Or. 3.741-95). This presents a picture of the violent intervention of God on Israel's behalf.

---

78. Charlesworth, *The Old Testament Pseudepigrapha: Volume 1*, 355. The reference to Christ in Sib. Or. 1.324-85 is clearly a later Christian interpolation; similarly, Sib. Or. Pro 15-25; 2:45-55, 241; 5:256-84; 6:1-25; 7:29-39, 63-75; 8:216-50, 251-336, 484.

Pseudo-Philo

The first-century AD history of Israel Pseudo-Philo includes the anointing of Phinehas at Shilo (LAB 48:2) and of David by Samuel (LAB 59:3). There is no real reference to military destruction.

Apocalypse of Abraham

The Apocalypse of Abraham (first to second century AD) calls the Theo figure "my chosen one" (cf. 1 En. 49:2; 55:4; Isa 42:1; 49:7). After a period of typical apocalyptic woe (Apoc. Ab. 30), God will sound his trumpet, and the chosen one is sent imbued with one measure of God's power and "will summon my people, humiliated by the heathen" (Apoc. Ab. 31:1). Then God's chosen will burn Israel's mockers and rulers with fire in Hades for ceaseless suffering, while God's people rejoice. A gross picture is painted of these people rotting and burning for resisting God and worshiping idols (Apoc. Ab. 31:2–5).

The Dead Sea Scrolls

In the Dead Sea Scrolls, it is disputed whether there is one, two (Priestly, Davidic), or three messiahs. My purpose here is not to resolve this issue, but to explore whether the messiah figure(s) come in violence—a picture of a military messiah.[79]

There is a reference to a prophet who will come and "the Messiahs of Aaron and Israel" (1QS 9:11), suggesting a plurality of messiahs. Elsewhere, there is reference to "the Messiah" (1Q28a II 12). There is also reference to a Davidic messiah, a branch of David and his descendants, to whom has been "given the covenant of the kingship of his people for everlasting generations" (4Q252 V 3–4). Reference is made to Genesis 49:10: "the scepter shall not depart from the tribe of Judah." This monarchy will not be cut off. This is clearly a Davidic kingly figure.

4Q295 V Isaiah speaks of one who will come from the stump of Jesse, a branch of David, and this figure will kill the "Prince of the Congregation *by strokes and by wounds*" (emphasis added). This brings violent force to the fore. Reference is also made to a messiah of Aaron (CD–A XII 23)." In 1 Q28a II 20, the messiah attends a meal and stretches his hands toward the bread. Elsewhere, some will escape but "those that remain shall be *delivered*

---

79. On this question, for example, see Vermes, *The Dead Sea Scrolls in English*, 58–63.

up to the sword when there comes the Messiah of Aaron and Israel" (CD-B XIX 10–11). This same figure is mentioned in CD 14:19, and the iniquity of the people are atoned through meal and sin-offerings (cf. 4Q266 10 I 12). In 4Q246 II 1, he is also called "the Son of God" and "son of the Most High" (cf. Jesus as Son of God). In 4Q521 II 2, the heavens and earth will listen to God's messiah. In what follows, it is not completely clear whether the action is that of the messiah or God. If the messiah is in mind, the poor and godly will experience blessing, the captives will be liberated, the blind and broken healed, and good news preached to the poor (Ps 146:7-8; Isa 61:1). There is no reference here to the use of violent force (cf. Luke 4:18-19).

However, 4Q161 8–10 refers to a branch of David who will arise at the end whom God will uphold with royal clothing. He will rule with a scepter in hand. "*His sword* shall judge [all] the peoples" (emphasis added), indicating the use of force to rule and judge.

In 1Q28b V 18, there may be reference to a messiah. Here he renews the covenant, establishes an everlasting kingdom for his people, judges with justice, causes the humble to be righteous, and raises up the people. The writer then prays,

> may you be [. . .] with the power of your [mouth]. With your scepter may *you lay waste the earth*. With the breath of your lips may you *kill the wicked*. May he give [you a spirit of coun]sel and of everlasting fortitude, a spirit of knowledge and of fear of God. May justice be the belt of [your loins, and loyalt]y the belt of your hips. May he make your horns of iron and your hoofs of bronze.
>
> May you *gore like a bu[ll* . . . and may you *trample the nation]s* like mud in the streets. For God has raised you to a scepter for the rulers be[fore you . . . all the na]tions will serve you, and he will make you strong by his holy Name., so that *you will be like a li[on* . . . *]* you *the prey*, with no-one to give it [back]. Your [fa]st ones will scatter over. (1Q28b V 24–28, emphasis added)[80]

Clearly, this prayer vividly envisages the messiah coming in violence to overcome the enemies of God like a bull and lion.

1Q33 XI 6 refers to Numbers 24:17-19, specifically to a star from Jacob, a scepter from Israel. This person will "*smash* the temples of Moab, it will *destroy* all the sons of Seth" (v. 6, emphasis added). This is followed by further descriptions of the destruction of "the city," being "glorious over our enemies," felling "the hordes of Belial, the seven peoples of futility." They shall be "treated like Pharaoh" and "the chariots in the Red Sea" (vv. 8-9), indicating violent destruction. Ashur will "fall *by the sword*" not wielded

---

80. García and Tigchelaar, "Dead Sea Scrolls," 109.

by a man, indicating God's direct action in this war (v. 11–13, 17, emphasis added). This is a picture of messianic war with God's intervention.

In 4Q174 (4QFlor), reference is made to a Davidic messiah (esp. vv. 10–13). He will establish a temple in which no Ammonite, Moabite, bastard, foreigner, or proselyte shall enter (v. 4). It will never be destroyed by foreigners (v. 5). The messiah will bring rest from enemies (v. 7). Sons of Belial (Satan) will be destroyed (v. 8). He will save Israel (v. 13). The sense is that this messiah will defeat Israel's enemies with force.

In 4Q266, there is an expectation of a messiah "from Aaron and Israel" (2:10, cf. 8:2, 9:10, 29, 14:19; 15:4, 18:8), or a messiah of Aaron (12:22–23). In chapter 1, God has taken Israel into exile, left a remnant in the land, and now she is defiled again. God is long-suffering and has kept a remnant. "Through his Messiah he shall make them know his Holy Spirit" (2:10). In 9:8–9, a star will come from Jacob and a scepter from Israel. He is the "prince of all the congregation." In 9:10, when the messiah comes from Aaron and Israel "the rest shall be *handed over to the sword*" (emphasis added) indicating the use of violence and force to subdue his enemies. This violence is akin to an earlier time when "*the sword avenged* with the *vengeance* of the covenant" (emphasis added) and involves judgment on all who have entered into his covenant and not held fast to its statutes; they will experience "destruction through the hand of Belial" (vv. 11–12b). Wrath will be poured out on the "princes of Judah" (v. 13).

In 11Q13, Melchizedek of Genesis 14 and Psalm 110 fame (cf. Heb 5:6, 10; 6:20; 7:1–2, 10–11, 15, 17), is the Theo figure. The passage begins with the year of Jubilee (vv. 2–4, cf. Lev 25; Luke 4:19). In the last days, captives will be liberated, and hidden teachers from the inheritance of Melchizedek will make them return to liberty (vv. 4–6). On the Day of Atonement on the tenth Jubilee, atonement shall be made for the all the sons of light and those of Melchizedek, for their words. In this year, Melchizedek and his armies of holy ones will stand in the assembly, and God will judge the peoples (vv. 7–11). In verse 13, Melchizedek will "carry out the vengeance of Go[d]'s judgments, [and on that day he will fr]e[e them from the hand of] Belial and from the hand of all the sp[irits of his lot.]." He will be aided by the gods of justice and all the sons of God (v. 14). This will be the day of peace of Isaiah 52:7. The messenger is the anointed of the Spirit in Daniel 9:25. He announces salvation, and comforts and instructs the afflicted forever (vv. 19–20). He frees the people from Belial (v. 25). Again, we have violent force, this time through a Melchizedek Theo figure.

Philo

Philo's infrequent picture of Theo is political (a king) and military. *On the Life of Moses* 1.290 speaks of a man who will arise from Israel who will "rule over many nations," whose kingdom will "increase every day and be raised to the heaven." What follows is Israel devouring many nations, removing their fat to their marrow, who will "*destroy their enemies* with far-shooting arrows" (emphasis added). He will lie down to *rest like a lion*, "fearing no one, but showing great contempt for everyone, and causing fear to all other nations. Miserable is he who shall stir up and rouse him to anger. Blessed are they that bless thee, and cursed are they that curse thee (*Moses* 1.291).

In *On Rewards and Punishment* 95–97, a man will emerge "*leading a host and warring furiously*, who will subdue great and populous nations" (emphasis added). God will assist this man with divine intervention through swarms of wasps "so as to overwhelm their enemies with *shameless destruction*" (emphasis added). He will rule with dignity which causes respect, terror which induces fear, and beneficence which causes good will—these render subjects obedient to their rulers.

Josephus

Josephus does not use messiah of any of the figures of the time. In a passage which is considered a Christian interpolation by many, but is found in all extant passages, Josephus refers to Jesus as the Christ and fulfillment of the prophets (*Ant.* 18.63–64).[81] He also mentions Jesus as the one "called Christ" in relation to James' death in *Jewish Antiquities* 20.200. As such, Josephus shows little interest in a Jewish redeemer figure.

Rabbinic Literature

Although we cannot be sure what aspects of Rabbinic thought applied at the time of Christ, it is still helpful to consider the messianic perspective. There is only one reference to the messiah in the Mishna, in *m. Soṭah* 9.15 W: "With the footprints of the Messiah: presumption increases, and death increases." This tells us little of his role. In prayers, the fourteenth benediction of the Palestinian Eighteen Benedictions includes: "In your great mercy O Yahweh our God, have pity on Israel your people, and on Jerusalem your city, and on Zion the habitation of your glory, and on your temple, and on

---

81. See the discussion in Feldman, "Josephus," 3:990–91.

your dwelling, and on the monarchy of the house of David, the Messiah of your righteousness."[82] The fifteenth benediction of the Eighteen Benedictions, which is likely later than the New Testament period, reads "Let the shoot of David sprout quickly and raise up his horn with thy help, Blessed be thou, Yahweh, that thou dost cause a horn of help to grow." This says little about the messiah's function. The prayers speak of hope for "a new independent state."[83]

In the Targums, a messianic kingdom precedes the resurrection of the dead and the last judgment. The messiah is the center of hope (*Tg. Neb.* on Isa 52:14), but he is hidden due to Israel's failure (*Tg. Neb.* on Mic 4:8). His time is in God's hand (*Tg. Neb.* on Mic 5:1; Zech 4:7; Isa 9:6). The messiah is a Davidic descendant (*Tg. Neb.* Mic 5:1), from Jesse (*Tg. Neb.* Isa 11:1). God empowers him (*Tg. Neb.* on Isa 11:3; Mic 5:3) and *arms for war* (*Tg. Yer. I.* Gen 49:11). He destroys Israel's enemies, such as Gog (*Tg. Jer. I.* Num 24:17), and also the antichrist, who he destroys with his mouth (*Tg. Neb.* Isa 11:4), and he vanquishes the nations (*Tg. Neb.* Isa 10:27; 11:4; 14:29; 42:1; 52:15; 53:7, 11; Jer 23:6; Zech 4:7; 10:4). He will restore peace (*Tg. Neb.* Isa 28:6), the spoils of war will be distributed to faithful victorious Israel (*Tg. Neb.* Isa 53:11), he will bring forgiveness (*Tg. Neb.* Isa 53:4–6, 12), and Israel's sins will fall on gentiles (*Tg. Neb.* Isa 53:8). He will rule over all kingdoms (*Tg. Neb.* Isa 53:3; 16:1; Amos 9:11; Zech 4:7) and will be triumphant over all (*Tg. Neb.* Isa 42:6; Mic 5:3; Isa 28:16; 41:25). Israel will return from exile having been freed by the messiah (*Tg. Neb.* Isa 11:11; 42:7; 53:8; Hos 14:8; Mic 4:6; 5:3).

He is not only king, but prophet and teacher of the law. He makes a new covenant between God and his people (*Tg. Neb.* Isa 42:6). He is anointed by the Spirit (*Tg. Neb.* Isa 42:1) and prophetic (*Tg. Neb.* Isa 11:2). He establishes righteousness (*Tg. Neb.* Isa 42:4) and causes all to submit to the law (*Tg. Neb.* Isa 52:11; 42:7). He throws all sinners into Hell (*Tg. Neb.* Isa. 53:9). There is no real reference to the gentiles being enlightened.[84] He rules in the land cleansed of impurity (*Tg. Neb.* Zech 6:13) with peace and prosperity (*Tg. Neb.* Isa 9:5; 11:6–9; 16:5; 53:2, 5; Hos 3:5; 14:8; Jer 23:6; 33:16). He will rebuild the temple (*Tg. Neb.* Isa 53:5; Zech 6:12). There will be resurrections and other miracles (*Tg. Neb.* Hos 14:8; Isa 53:8; Hab 3:18) with people living long lives (*Tg. Neb.* Isa 53:10). The long-term future of the messiah is not discussed with a focus on the new age that dawns through his kingship.

---

82. van der Woude, "χριστός: Rabbinic Writings," 9:521.
83. Ibid., 9:521.
84. Ibid., 9:524.

Talmud and Midrashim

Both the Talmudic literature and Midrashim frequently refer to the messiah like the Targums with embellishment. Aside from R. Hillel, who believed the messiah had come in the days of Hezekiah (*b. Sanh.* 98b), most agree he is a future figure. The coming of the messiah is preceded by a time of tribulation and woe (e.g., *b. Sanh.* 97a; 98a). He is usually David or David's son, with a range of names such as Shiloh (*b. Sanh.* 98b) among others. The coming of the messiah is often preceded by the announcement of Elijah (Pesiq. Rab. 22, 149a, b). There will be a final attack on Jerusalem by the nations under Rome (Pesiq. Rab. 15, 75b). He will ultimately triumph after a period destroying the enemies with the breath of his mouth (Pesiq. Rab. 37, 163a). The nations that have not enslaved Israel will remain alive and will be subject to him and his people (Pesiq. Rab. 1, 2a). The reign of the messiah will be over all people and will precede God's final kingdom. The dispersed will return (Midr. Ps 147:3; Gen. Rab. 98:9 on 49:11) and gifts will flow into the land from the world (Midr. Ps. 87:6 on 87:5). He will reign in peace and righteousness (*b. Sandh.* 93b) and teach the law (Gen. Rab. 99:11 on 49:11). The Spirit will pour on all flesh (Midr. Ps 14:6 on 14:7) and Israelites will obey the law (Midr. Ps 73:4 on 73:10). Prosperity, peace, and joy will flow (Midr. Ps 147:3 on 147:3). Jerusalem and the temple will be gloriously rebuilt (Exod. Rab. 52:5 on 39:32; Pesiq. Rab. 21, 145a). Sin and sacrifice will end. He is a spiritually endowed human king. For most, his time will end with Gog and Magog attacking Israel.

There is also a messiah who is the son of Joseph or Ephraim of Manasseh, found in the second century AD. He is anointed for military action (Pesiq. Rab. 8 [30a]; Gen. Rab. 99:2 on 48:26). In Setter Eliyyahu Rabba, 18, 97,[85] he leads armies from Upper Galilee to Jerusalem to rebuild the temple and defeat the people surrounding Israel. Gog kills him after forty years of peace, and the Davidic messiah comes and finally destroys Israel's enemies (*Làqach tǫb* בלק [bā·lǎq] on Num 24:17, 129b, 130a). His death is not salvific.

Messianic Movements and the New Testament

Messianic Movements

The writings of Josephus and the New Testament indicate that there were many movements in the period 200 BC–AD 100 which can be considered

---

85. Str-B., 2.297.

"messianic," giving further indication of widespread expectations of a royal liberator.

A series of these occurred in the instability after the death of Herod the Great. Josephus writes of a certain Judas, a son of Hezekiah, who was a leader of a group of robbers (ca. 4 BC),[86] who had been captured by Herod the Great. Judas responded by gathering a mob from around Sepphoris in Galilee, attacking Herod's palace, and seizing the weapons and money to arm his men. He then became violent and terrifying, plundering those he met with the purpose of "an ambition for royal rank" through violence (Josephus, *Ant.* 17.271-72; *J.W.* 2.56). While his target was Herod, it may be that he was also anti-Roman in his intent.[87]

Another movement at a similar time was instigated by Simon of Perea (ca. 4 BC), who had been one of Herod the Great's slaves, with great talent and responsibility. Josephus writes that he was a good-looking tall man (seemingly a prerequisite for messianism). A servant placed a diadem on his head, and others declared him king. He and his men burnt down and plundered the royal palace at Jericho and others of Herod's houses. He was defeated and beheaded by the Roman Gratus and some soldiers (Josephus, *Ant.* 17.275-76; *J.W.* 2.57-59).

The able, tall, and physically impressive shepherd Athronges led another movement (ca. 4-2 BC). He boldly set himself up as a king crowned with a diadem. With four powerful brothers, each with a small band of fellow-revolutionaries, he set about retaining his kingship. He established a council and retained power for a while as self-proclaimed king. He and his supporters killed many Roman and Herodian forces and became violent toward others. Near Emmaus, they attacked a Roman company, killing a centurion named Arius and forty others. Such expeditions continued for a while, but were subdued by Gratus, Ptolemy, and Archelaus (Josephus, *Ant.* 17.278-84; *J.W.* 2.60-65). Josephus also indicates that there were other messianic movements in which people claimed kingship, supported by a bunch of rebels, and caused havoc to both Romans and their fellow Jews (Josephus, *Ant.* 17.285).

In Acts 5:36, reference is made to another rebel, Theudas. Gamaliel refers to him as a man who "rose up, claiming to be somebody, and a number of men, about four hundred, joined him. He was killed, and all who followed him were dispersed and came to nothing." Josephus makes mention of him as a sorcerer (or cheat, *goēs*), a self-proclaimed prophet, who believed he

---

86. This is the date of Evans, *Mark 8:27—16:20*, 306. Dates for the others named come from Evans..

87. Giles, "Messianic Movements," http://douglasjacoby.com/attachments/Mess.Movements.pdf.

could emulate Joshua (Josh 3:14-17, cf. Exod 13:17—14:29; 2 Kgs 2:13-14), and divide the Jordan. He operated when Fadus was Judean procurator (AD 44-46); Fadus intervened, killed many of the men, took Theudas alive, and decapitated him, taking his head to Jerusalem (Josephus, *Ant.* 20: 96-99).[88]

Another rebellion, referenced in Acts 5:37, occurred after the deposing of Archelaus in AD 6. Judas of Gamala, or as Luke describes him, "Judas the Galilean." Luke states that he "rose up in the days of the census and drew away some of the people after him. He too perished, and all who followed him were scattered." Josephus confirms he was a Galilean,[89] who led others, including a Pharisee, Zadok, to revolt. He urged them to have the courage to refuse to pay Roman taxes, to yield only to God and no human ruler, and to fight for liberation, to the death if necessary, believing God would come to their aid.[90] This led to some battles and assassinations across Israel. Josephus credits this uprising as the launch of the fourth philosophy,[91] that of the Zealots, which led to a revolt against Rome, with disastrous results. Judas's sons, James and Simon, were crucified later by Alexander (Josephus, *Ant.* 18:4-10, 23-25; 20:102; *J.W.* 2.118).

In Acts 21:38, some three years after a revolt in Jerusalem which happened in AD 54, Paul is mistaken for an Egyptian Sicarii who staged a revolt and who led four thousand men into the desert. Josephus refers to the Sicarii as those who carried hidden small curved daggers in their cloaks, which they used to assassinate enemies in broad daylight, especially at festivals. This included killing Jonathan the high priest, a deed purportedly instigated by the Governor, Felix, and a certain Doras. This led to other such murders, including in the temple itself (Josephus, *J.W.* 2.254-57; *Ant.* 20.161-64; 186-88). Josephus also refers to the Egyptian Sicarii, who claimed to be a prophet, encouraged a great crowd to join him at the Mount of Olives, and claimed he would cause the walls of Jerusalem to fall, allowing them entry (cf. Jericho, Josh 6). Felix sent troops to attack them, killing four hundred and capturing two hundred, while the Egyptian escaped. Hence, Paul was being challenged as to whether he was this figure (Josephus, *Ant.* 20. 169-72).

Other rebellions came in the period, leading to the Roman War. Josephus refers to Manahem, a son of Judas of Galilee, who led a rebellion in AD

---

88. On solutions to the chronological issues, see Henderson, "Theudas"; Witherington, *The Acts of the Apostles*, 235-39.

89. Although in Josephus, *Ant.* 18.4, he appears to be a Gaulonite, of the city of Gamala. Hence there is some doubt concerning his origins.

90. Today we can understand this type of thinking with Isis, who believe Allah will come to their aid in the holy war to establish radical Islam.

91. The others being Pharisees, Sadducees, and Essenes.

66 (*J.W.* 2.432–48). During the Jewish War, with a band of men, he broke into Herod's armory in Masada and established a small army. He returned to Jerusalem *as king* and leader of the rebellion and siege of Jerusalem. He launched an assault on the city, initially forcing the Romans back to the towers. He killed Ananias, the high priest, and his brother Hezekiah. Although arrayed in royal clothing, he was forced to flee to Ophla, and was eventually defeated, tortured, and killed.

John of Gischala, a son of a certain Levi, is another who led a messianic movement. John was cunning and rash and sought authority (*J.W.* 4.85). He went to Jerusalem to join the rebellion. However, he set up his own movement and sought monarchical power (*J.W.* 4.390). Others repudiated his claim to power, and the rebellion was split (*J.W.* 4.393–94). John was of the view that Jerusalem would not be captured, as it is God's own city (*J.W.* 6.98). He was ultimately captured and imprisoned for life (*J.W.* 6.434).

Simon Bar Giora is also a messianic figure during the time of the war with Rome. He was physically powerful, and joined the rebels in Masada. He then left and set himself in the Judean Mountains, and gathered an army of slaves, robbers, and some of the leaders who submitted to him as their king (Josephus, *J.W.* 4.503–10). He then set himself in Nain and Paran. He was then attacked by the zealots and defeated them and, with an army of twenty thousand, attacked Idumea but was held back. He attacked again, and thanks to the help of an Idumean commander, he took Idumea and then Hebron (*J.W.* 4.511–29). He then ransacked Idumea (*J.W.* 4.534–37). The Zealots then took his wife captive in Jerusalem and Simon responded by torturing those who left the city and demanded that they return his wife, which they did out of fear (*J.W.* 4.538–44). Simon then continued his devastation of Idumea, and again threatened Jerusalem (*J.W.* 4.556–58). John was terrorizing those inside the city. So, Simon was welcomed into the city as "savior and preserver" (*J.W.* 7.575–76). He attacked the temple, but was repelled (*J.W.* 7.578–84). He ultimately surrendered to the Romans after seeking to tunnel his way out of Jerusalem and then dressing as a woman, and was put to death (*J.W.* 6.433–34; 7.21–36). Josephus describes his actions as "bitter and savage tyranny," falsely accusing his fellow Jews (*J.W.* 7.32).[92]

What *all* these movements have in common is the royal appointment, self or otherwise, of *a man of war*. The zealous figure leads a band and seeks to take power by force, either fighting his own people, who have in his mind collaborated with the Romans, and/or the Romans themselves. No doubt

---

92. Evans (*Mark 8:27—16:20*, 425–26) notes other later uprisings, including Lukuas of Cyrene in North Africa (AD 115–116) (see Eusebius, *Hist. eccl.* 4.2.1–5; Dio Cassius, *Roman History* 68.32; 69.12–13), and Simon Bar Kochba (or ben Kosiba; also "Andreas") (AD 132–135) (see ibid., 59.13.3; Jerome, *Ruf.* 3.31).

if any had been successful, they would have established a dynastic monarchy centered on Jerusalem and the temple. Without a doubt, this common thread reinforces that, for many in Israel at the time, a movement inaugurated by a Theo figure would be violent and messy. All these men failed and fell by the sword. It is fully understandable for many to see in Jesus a potential messiah, especially considering his immense spiritual power. Hence, it is against this type of backdrop that the remarkable story of a non-violent Messiah (Jesus Christ) stands in stark relief.

The New Testament

Back-reading from the New Testament, we can see that there were great expectations concerning a messiah. Such a back-reading is, of course, loaded, as Jesus is being interpreted looking backward by people who are biased to read him as a messiah, and a particular type of one. However, even with this in mind, there is strong evidence of *existing expectations* of a Davidic messiah military figure.

The Synoptics

The Synoptics speak of great crowds coming out to hear John the Baptist and Jesus with heightened messianic expectations (e.g. Mark 1). John's declaration that Jesus is greater than he and that he will baptize with the Spirit is messianic. The language of the kingdom is provocative and speaks of an expectation of God's intervention directly or through his Theo agent (Messiah, Son of Man, etc.) to establish God's reign (e.g. Mark 1:14–15; the kingdom parables of Mark 4).

Pharisees and other leaders come to Jesus seeking to understand his identity. Their challenges suggest a presupposed view of a Theo figure, and Jesus was exciting enough for them to challenge him, yet he confounded them and drove them ultimately to kill him. Their request for a sign from heaven likely stems from their desire that Jesus produce some evidence of his Theo-status so that they could support rather than challenge him (Mark 6:11–12).

Encounters with people who recognize Jesus as a "son of David" indicate the presence of the expectation of a Davidic messiah (Mark 10:47–48; 11:10, and parr.). Jesus' debate with the scribes over Psalm 110 shows that the Psalm was, for them, an essential component of first-century expectation

(Mark 12:35–37 and parr.).[93] Indeed, the passage begins with Jesus asking, "How can *the scribes say* that *the Christ is the son of David*?" (Mark 12:35 and parr.; emphasis added). This indicates that the Scribes expected a Christ who is a descendant of David.

In the Olivet Discourse, Jesus speaks of the ongoing expectation of a Christ figure, with many claiming to be the messiah (Mark 13:21–22 and parr.). The high priest's question of Jesus' identity focuses on his messianic status, indicating an expectation Jesus was being interpreted against (Mark 14:61, and parr.).[94] The following verses show Jesus failed to meet those expectations, and this is part of the reason he was killed. The mocking of Jesus on the cross is likely linked to the same expectation, which Jesus was failing to meet in being "hung on a tree" at the hands of the Romans. A true messiah smites Romans and is not killed by their hand without raising arms against them (Mark 15:32, and parr., cf. Gal 3:13; Deut 21:23).

Matthew's presentation of Jesus, in particular, which is generally agreed to be presented from the perspective of reinforcing to Jewish Christians that Jesus is the long-awaited Messiah,[95] presupposes that there was an existing strong tradition which expected a Davidic messiah in Judaism. This is seen in the Davidic emphasis in the genealogy and of Joseph as a descendant of David (e.g. Matt 1:1, 6, 7, 20). People also identify Jesus as the "Son of David," including his entry into Jerusalem (Matt 9:27; 12:23; 15:22; 20:30, 31; 21:9, 15; 22:42).

Similarly, Luke's infancy narrative, which seemingly intentionally stands in continuity to the LXX,[96] emphasizes Jesus' Davidic heritage indicating an existing expectation (Luke 1:27, 32, 69). Accounts of Jesus' birth in Bethlehem support this, with Luke even calling Bethlehem the city of David, rather than Jerusalem as was common in the day (Luke 2:4, 11, cf. Matt 2).[97] Simeon and Anna represent Israel awaiting a Davidic messiah

---

93. Evans (*Mark 8:27—16:20*, 272) notes this is a very "early attestation" of messianic expectations, preceded only by Pss. Sol. 17.21.

94. On this, see ibid., 448–49.

95. See Blomberg (*Matthew*, 34) who notes: "Suggestions for Matthew's Gospel have usually involved apologetic designs to try to convince non-Christian Jews of the truth of the gospel, catechetical purposes (instructions for Christian living, perhaps administered to initiates into the community), encouragement to the church's witness in a hostile world, and deepening Christian faith by supplying more details about Jesus' words and works." Blomberg favors the first option.

96. Marshall (*The Gospel of Luke*, 39) states that "The preface is written in excellent Greek with a most carefully wrought sentence structure, and stands in contrast to the style adopted in the following narrative" whereas at 1:5 "Luke's style changes abruptly from that of the preface to one strongly reminiscent of the LXX" (*The Gospel of Luke*, 51).

97. Harris, *The Davidic Shepherd King*, 71–76.

THE HOPE OF A DELIVERER ("THEO" = "THE EXPECTED ONE") 133

(Luke 2:26). Luke explicitly speaks of people pondering whether Jesus is the Messiah, indicating an expectation (Luke 3:15). The Romans' killing of Jesus is likely due to their concern of an uprising based on anyone who is labeled a messiah, and thus raising messianic fervor and rebellion (e.g. Luke 23:2). The attribution "Christ" across the New Testament indicates Jesus' identity, which recalls the expectation (e.g. Mark 1:1; 8:29, and parr.; Matt 1:18; 2:1).

JOHN

In John, there is direct interest from Levites in Jerusalem who enquire as to whether John the Baptist is the messiah or the Prophet (John 1:20-28; 3:28). The reaction of the first disciples to Jesus interprets their response to him as related to their expectation of the messiah, something Jesus fulfilled (John 1:41).

John 4:25 speaks of Samaritan expectations of a messiah. John 6 portrays crowds who were aware of the feeding miracle and who then sought to make Jesus "king by force." This indicates an expectation of a military figure and interest in Jesus being that person (John 6:14-15). John 7 records Jewish debate over Jesus' descent, focused on whether he was born in Bethlehem—indicating the expectation that the expectation of Micah 5:2 was widespread (John 7:41-42, cf. Matt 2:5-6). The reference to Jewish expulsion of Jews who confessed Jesus as Christ from the synagogue suggests that there was an existing mainstream of Judaism and Synagogue-endorsed expectation, and that in claiming that Jesus was the Christ, this was violated (John 9:22).

In John 10:24, Jesus is directly asked if he is the messiah, with Jesus answering that he is God's Son, leading to the Jewish leaders seeking to kill him (John 10:30). Again, this indicates a preconception of the messiah and sonship which Jesus confounded. Martha's confession draws out that, unlike most others, she perceives that he is this awaited figure (John 11:27). John 12:34 speaks of the Jewish expectation of a messiah who "remains forever" (*menei eis ton aiōna*).[98] The ultimate purpose of the Gospel is that readers who either have no belief in a messiah (gentiles), or those who have a preconceived notion (mainstream Jews), will come to believe in Jesus as Messiah and/or those who already believe, will continue to do so.[99]

---

98. The Greek can translate "remain into the ages", indicating a very long time, or "forever." Either way, there is an expectation of a messiah who remains a long time, rather than dying after a short ministry that had no direct effect on the gentiles.

99. On this verse and the ambiguity of the Greek see the succinct discussion in Köstenberger, *John*, 581-82.

Acts

Acts 2:34 features Psalm 110:1, a Davidic Messianic Psalm, and applies this to Jesus' heavenly session as Lord. In Paul's sermon to the Antiochian synagogue, Paul refers to the blessings of David applied to Jesus, likely indicating that those in the Synagogue understood this expectation (Acts 13:34). He also refers to Psalm 16 as another Davidic Psalm, regarding the resurrection and Jesus (Acts 13:36). James cites Amos 9:11–12, where God rebuilds David's tent in relation to the ongoing work of Christ in the church as it extended among gentiles. These all indicates a preceding prevailing expectation of a Davidic messiah.

Paul

Paul's perspective is interesting, as he speaks of Christ as a Pharisee who is now converted. In Romans 9:5, Jesus is "the Christ," the culmination of a list of privileges afforded the Jewish people. This suggests that Paul had hopes of such a figure, and through his radical conversion has come to realize that Jesus is that one. Despite his being crucified, an anathema to a Jewish perspective on messiah (Gal 3:13; Deut 21:23), Jesus *is* the Christ. In Romans 1:3, which likely forms part of a creedal formulation,[100] Paul introduces his summary of the gospel with Jesus' Davidic descent. This indicates that, for Paul and Roman Christians—Jew and otherwise—this was an integral part of the creedal remembrance of Jesus. Similarly, in 2 Timothy 2:8, Jesus is a descendant of David.

The name "Christ" is Paul's favorite term for Jesus. While some scholars consider that he uses Christ without reference to its original messianic sense, i.e., as a surname for Christ, I would agree with Wright, who argues that this is far from the case.[101] Paul's preference for Christ indicates that Jesus is Israel's Messiah. He is "now" Lord of all the earth, the ruler of God's kingdom, which is growing in the midst of Rome, and the colliding kingdoms of the world.

A COMPOSITE PICTURE OF THEO

While it is precarious to boil down messianic expectations too narrowly, this inquiry has indicated that we can draw together a general composite

---

100. See for example, Dunn, *Romans 1–8*, 5.
101. For example, Wright, *Paul and the Faithfulness of God*, 518–36.

picture of what many in Israel hoped for when this Theo figure came to Israel on behalf of God. Here I will summarize the key strands of hope.

The Coming of the Divinely Empowered Warrior-King Leader

While not all Jewish writings expected a single Davidic messiah in specific terms, most expected God's intervention in some way or another. This would come in the form of God himself acting directly, as in 1 Esdras, Judith, Expanded Esther, Greek portions of Daniel, 1–2 Maccabees, Tobit, Baruch, the Epistle of Jeremiah, and the Sadducees. Alternatively, the expectation centered around a transcendent semi-divine figure such as the Son of Man (and Elect One, Messiah) of 1 Enoch, a Davidic messiah as in the Psalms of Solomon 17, or through a Davidic messiah alongside other messianic figures, such as a priestly messiah as at Qumran.

Where a Davidic messiah, or more transcendent kingly figure such as the Son of Man, is concerned, he would be patterned after the great rulers of Israel and world history, empowered by the Spirit of Yahweh, and be established as king by force (God's or his own). He would overcome Israel's oppressors, liberating Israel, and establish Shalom (below). Here are the key elements.

The Restoration of Israel by Military Force

The general hope appears to be that this Theo figure would in some way rally the people of Israel together, and would lead them into battle against the gentiles, overcoming them, establishing the nation in the land, and liberating the land and people. Israel would be restored to her rightful place, free of foreign rule, living according to the Torah. As such, it is likely that when a Theo figure emerged, he would be expected to establish his credentials through signs, i.e., demonstrations of power. One calls to mind Moses and his staff turning into a snake, his leprous hand, or the string of miracles before Pharaoh. After this, he would be recognized as the Theo figure and would lead Israel's cleansing and restoration.

The Vanquishing of the Gentiles through Military Force

Some degree of repentance and a call from the messiah to turn to Yahweh would not be out of kilter with expectations. However, the real problem to be resolved for Israel was not so much her own sin (which was Jesus' focus), but the gentiles. As I have discussed above, since the exiles in north and south, Israel had been subjugated. The unclean gentiles had violated their faith. Central to their expectation was that the messiah would remove this problem, driving them from the land or forcing their submission to Yahweh. There would appear to be two ways this could happen: voluntary submission (surrender) or military subjugation. After this, the nations would be under God's rule and pay tribute to Israel, living by the law, with pilgrimages to Jerusalem.

The Establishment of Jerusalem and Zion as the Capital of the World

Central to Jewish hope was Jerusalem and the temple on Zion. For the Jew, Jerusalem was the jewel of the world. The temple was the locus of God's presence on earth. The messiah would drive out the gentiles and establish his center for the restoration of the whole world from this point. He would no doubt encourage monotheistic worship of Yahweh, and call the people to war. He would urge gentiles to voluntarily submit to Yahweh with the warning that if they did not, they would be destroyed. He would call for the world to bring tribute to Jerusalem to sustain the monarchy and Yahwism. In that it was unlikely that the world would voluntarily bow the knee to Yahweh, it is likely that a program of military conquest would begin. Most likely it would involve the overthrow of the Romans and, ultimately, a direct assault on Rome. Perhaps he would move north through Lebanon, across Asia Minor, through Greece, and into Rome, where the final conflict would occur. He would no doubt then send forces to all parts of the known world and establish an empire without end.

Law

Central to the new world order would be the Torah. The principles of the law would be the locus of the world. The system of priests, sacrifices, festivals, purity, circumcision, and the Sabbath would continue unabated to ensure the good pleasure of Yahweh. The world would live by the Law of Yahweh or pay the consequences.

The Establishment of Cosmic Shalom

Ultimately God, through Theo, would bring peace to the world. This would be an end of all war as the nations submit to God's reign through his agent. This peace would involve the natural order with the resolution of the problem of the Fall. This peace would be eternal with the righteous granted access to the Tree of Life and eternal life. Evil would be removed from the world.

How It Might Have Looked

Putting it all together, we come up with a scenario like this. Theo is born, as Micah predicted and Jewish scribes expected, in Bethlehem (Mic 5:2). At some point, he would present himself to the people as a miracle-working warrior-leader. Like Moses in Exodus, he would demonstrate that he had divine vindication and authority satisfying the leaders of the nation (Exod 4:1–9, 30–31). They would either rally to him and join him in his mission, or be swept away as infidels. He would call Israel to repentance and refreshed fidelity to the Law, to prayer and fasting in preparation for the final conflict. He would perform signs and wonders to demonstrate that he is imbued with divine power. At some point, he would call the sons of Israel to join him and talk terms with the Romans. How this happened is unclear. Perhaps he would enter Jerusalem and meet with Pilate, talking terms. If so, he would likely urge the gentiles to renounce their idolatry and false value system and yield to Yahweh and the Law. If they resisted, he would launch an assault on them. This may involve divine intervention, as in the moments of Israel's history like the Exodus or the stopping of the sun. Alternatively, he may simply launch a violent attack on the Romans with devastating consequences. As he is Theo, God's agent, his power would be unstoppable and his victory unquestionable.

Then there is the question of what would happen next. The Davidic monarchy only made limited attempts to extend the kingdom. Messianic hope spoke of something much greater—a global kingdom. As such, a messiah figure would likely lead or send spiritually endorsed and empowered armies to move across the Middle East, Asia, North Africa, and Europe, taking the *euangelion* of this Israel-centric kingdom to the nations. As Rome was the seat of imperial rule, he could possibly begin by going north through Tyre and Sidon, across Asia to the west coast, into Greece, and then on to Rome, crossing the Tiber in glory. He would either force Roman subjugation, or he would begin the destruction in the Roman Forum and Palatine.

Over time, the world within the Roman Empire and beyond would submit one way or another.

As he moved through the world, he would conscript young men to join his cause. He would send armies to all corners of the earth, establishing his reign. The fate of all peoples is their response to the command to bow their knee to Yahweh alone and live by Torah. Ultimately, the whole world is at peace under his reign.

Now, as we peruse this hope, we see that there some things missing that might come in handy later. First, although some of the hopes of a transcendent Theo figure speak of a semi-divine figure, because of their fierce monotheism the Jewish people didn't perceive that the messiah would be on par with Yahweh. He would not do things like directly challenge the interpretations of Israel's leaders and reinterpret the law, even reframing some laws completely (e.g. ritual purity in Mark 7; Sabbath, e.g., Matt 12:1–14; Mark 2:23—3:6; Luke 13:10–17). He would not claim to be Lord of the Sabbath (Matt 12:8; Mark 2:28; Luke 6:5) and forgive sin (Mark 2:1–12 and parr.; Luke 7:48–49).

Second, they had little notion of a messiah suffering and dying, certainly not on a cross at the hands of the gentiles; to be hung on a tree was to be cursed (Deut 21:23; Gal 3:13, cf. 1 Cor 1:23). Rather, Theo would be a great warrior who would inflict suffering and would ultimately be a key agent in ending it.

Third, they didn't really see themselves as part of the problem. Sure, there were some in Israel, like those in Qumran, who saw the whole system as corrupted and had established a new community in the wilderness. But overall, the people of Israel saw the gentiles as the problem, and any solution would see them dealt with.

Fourth, they had no comprehension of a solution that did not involve the center of the world being Jerusalem and the nations flowing into it. The idea of the message going out and there being no center except a Christ figure and his people is not in their worldview.

Finally, they did not connect the Servant found in the writings of Isaiah with messiah. Isaiah's Servant Songs, which speak in various ways of a servant of God who would be anointed with the Spirit, be the light to the nations, suffer vicariously, die, and be vindicated, was simply not applied to the messiah. The Son of Man in Daniel 7 was about the messiah, found through the writings that followed the completion of the Old Testament (Apocrypha, Pseudepigrapha). Many passages in the prophets, especially in Isaiah, such as Isaiah 9, 11, and 16, were messianic, but the servant of Isaiah was seen as Israel herself. Become a Jew to be saved.

THE HOPE OF A DELIVERER ("THEO" = "THE EXPECTED ONE") 139

The Problem with This Perspective

As one ponders this scenario, or something similar, one realizes that this strategy is full of holes and problems. First, this strategy does not deal with the problem of human corruption, greed, self-aggrandizement, and so on. The human problem cannot be limited to the good guys (i.e., Jews) and the bad guys (i.e., Romans and everyone non-Jewish). It is a heart issue, and all people and peoples need redemption, including Israel and the gentile world. People would rally to this messiah, but ultimately for personal gain, and not the good of the world or the triumph of good. A solution must still be found to the problem of sin, which corrupts all humanity.

Second, this approach removes all notions of human freedom. All people would be forced to submit or be destroyed. Human history tells us that such submission, where forced, will not hold. Indeed, if it did, it would not be genuine. It would be rule by fear. This has been seen at various points in Christian history, where adherence was imposed either directly or indirectly. This is seen in contemporary times, where religious or philosophical fundamentalism, whether Islam, Hindu, Christian, communism or other, is imposed. It simply does not work.

Third, and relatedly, this messiah would, in reality, be just another despotic megalomaniac utilizing evil, supposedly for good ends. This is self-defeating, as true peace is not begotten by war, but through peace. Indeed, such an approach is corrupted from the first and leads to the triumph of evil. Certainly, there will be times of "peace," but in these will be temporary and the problem will continually reemerge.

Fourth, the whole thing is unworkable. Certainly, if God zapped all the bad guys and made them good from the heart, it could work. Alternatively, God could simply force adherence—but that would not be genuine. In the above scenario, this messiah would have to control a whole world through force. Would humanity allow this to happen? No chance. Such a messiah could only be in one place at one time (remember,s the idea of an omnipresent ubiquitous messiah is not possible with radical monotheism where such attributes are for God alone). How could he simultaneously maintain control over the whole of Europe, the Middle East, Asia, Africa, the Americas, Oceania, and Australasia simultaneously? It is hardly likely that these peoples would be to bring tribute to this king enthroned in Zion for all eternity.

Finally, the idea that the entire world would take on the culture of Judaism is inconceivable. Culture is rooted deeply in the hearts and minds of people. It is possible that the world would take on Sabbath as a day of worship and rest. However, expecting all men to be circumcised and all peoples to yield to the eating laws and ritual purity expectations of Israel, to be prepared to go on pilgrimages to Israel, and to take on the religious calendar of Israel by force, seems inconceivable.

As we come to Mark's Gospel, it is important to hold in our minds the flawed but prevalent idea that God would come in violent force to resolve Israel's problems. He would come as a liberator, a warrior-king who would subdue Israel's enemies. He would overthrow all who stood in his way. When Jesus turns up, and he is considered through the lens of their expectations, one can easily see why they failed to understand him. He simply did not conform to the hopes of the nation. They had a flawed eschatology with false apocalyptic expectations. In Mark's Gospel, even those who traveled with him, observing miracle and miracle and hearing his direct teaching on the nature of his messiahship and discipleship, struggled to grasp what Jesus was about. Many did not get it, and so he was killed. As I will now seek to show, Mark is replete with irony upon irony as Jesus took the expectations, in some ways fulfilled them, and subverted them. This will now be considered in the remainder of this volume and in volume two.

6

The Messiah Revealed (Mark 1:1—8:29)

So far, I have argued that the world at the time of Jesus and Mark's Gospel (ca. AD 30–70) was an ongoing, swirling collision of empires. Seemingly without exception, kingdoms, nations, and tribes contended for resources. War and violence were normal to establish and maintain power. Men sought to conquer, dynasties were established, and empires rose and fell. Israel's dream for God's intervention was consistent with such expectations. She hoped that God would move decisively, set in motion the last days, conquering her enemies, and establishing Israel and her faith at the center of a renewed world. Is there another way?

The first of the extant written Gospels and the essential source for Matthew and Luke, Mark's Gospel, should be read against this sort of backdrop. It is written in the time of Roman dominance and imperial despotism when Israel experienced the power of Rome in, ultimately, its destruction (see chapter 1). In this section, I will begin in Mark 1:1 and consider how Mark's account of Jesus might have looked to those swept up in such expectations. We will see that, from the beginning, Jesus works within the expected framework but subverts it. He is extremely strategic in his approach. In some ways, he meets expectations and excites huge interest. In other ways, he completely lets the people of Israel down as they struggle to understand him. Even his disciples repeatedly fail to grasp what Jesus is about. All the time, he has a carefully conceived plan. It will culminate with his death. However, that is just the beginning.

THE PROLOGUE (MARK 1:1-13)

The Title of the Gospel (Mark 1:1)

Mark starts with these words: "The beginning of the good news about Jesus the Messiah, the Son of God."[1] This is effectively the title of Mark's work.[2] It starts provocatively for anyone familiar with the beginning of the Old Testament in Gen 1:1, using *archē*, meaning "beginning" (cf. John 1:1). For Mark, a new creation had begun, and it has begun in this Messiah.[3] The idea of "beginning" presupposes a continuing story—"wait, there's more!" Mark's Gospel will tell the story, and it goes on to Mark's time, in Rome in the 60s–70s. It goes on for us today.

The verse tells us of the subject matter of the Gospel: "the 'good news' [*eu* = good + *angelion* = news, message] of Jesus the Messiah." For Mark, Jesus is Theo, "the expected one." He has come, and this is his story as told by Mark.[4]

The word for gospel, *euangelion*, has a double background in Israel's story and the Greco-Roman world. First, from the Jewish background, the related verb *euangelizomai* ("preach the good news") is found particularly

---

1. It is debated whether "Son of God" is original. If so, it intensifies the idea of Jesus' divinity and his identification as king in contrast to Caesar, who was understood to be God's son. The phrase is missing in Codex Sinaiticus, Irenaeus, and Origen, and ancient scribes were more prone to add then delete from these sacred documents. As this analysis will argue, the messiah is the key point of Mark. However, a strong argument can be made for its authenticity, with its omission due to scribal error (e.g. Guelich, *Mark 1–8:26*, 6). If original, it would strengthen the case of this book. Son of God would allude in a Jewish sense to Psalm 2:7 and other texts where the king is God's Son. Similarly, in the Roman world, the emperor was often known as the son of the gods. As such, it simply adds to the royalness of the one about whom the good news is coming. It also strengthens the link to Yahweh.

2. Similarly, Edwards (*Mark*, 26) notes that it must be defined by what follows. Contra Guelich, *Mark 1–8:26*, 7. See the excellent discussion in France, *The Gospel of Mark*, 50–51.

3. Similarly, Edwards, *Mark*, 23: "in Jesus a new creation is at hand."

4. I consider it likely that the genitive is objective ("the gospel concerning Jesus Christ") (e.g. Lane, *The Gospel of Mark*, 44–45; Pesch, *Das Markusevangelium*, 75), rather than subjective ("the gospel proclaimed by Jesus Christ") (e.g., Cranfield, *Mark*, 35–36) or both (e.g. See Friedrich, "εὐαγγελίζομαι," 728; Gnilka, *Das Evangelium nach Markus*, 43; Guelich, *Mark 1–8:26*, 9; France, *Gospel of Mark*, 53). However, the genitive relates to the content of Mark's Gospel, which is about Jesus, who is the content of that proclamation. This phrase, then, does not refer to Jesus' proclamation, per se. Jesus did proclaim the good news of the kingdom, but became for Mark the good news. Hence it is best seen as objective (cf. Lane, *Mark*, 44).

in Isaiah of the hope of the glorious victory of God for those in exile in Babylon (e.g. Isaiah 40:9; 41:27; 52:7; 60:6; 61:1, cf. Nahum 2:1).[5]

This hope immediately brings empires, kings, and war to the fore; it is clear that this "good news" includes God's intervention and victory. For example, Isaiah 40:10 reads "Behold, the Lord God comes with might, and his arm rules for him." He will show shepherd-like mercy for Israel (Isa 40:11), but the God who created the cosmos and who controls history (Isa 40:12–26) will act among the nations to bring Israel's redemption. This victory of God for Israel will be achieved by military victory through Cyrus. From the Achaemenid dynasty, he was crowned king of Persia in 558 BC and took Media by a revolt in 550 BC. He overthrew Babylon in 539 BC. This event is recorded in the "Nabonidus" chronicle[6] and Cyrus Cylinder.

Cyrus released the Jews by edict to return to Jerusalem, as Isaiah predicted. He also permitted the reconstruction of the Jerusalem temple (2 Chr 36:22–23; Ezra 1:1–3; 6:2–5).[7] He ruled until AD 530. The first allusion to Cyrus is in Isaiah 40:2–3, where God stirs up "one from the east"[8] who will conquer "at every step" (Isa 41:2–3).[9] Isaiah asks:

> Who stirred up one from the east whom victory comes at every step? He gives up nations before him, so that he tramples kings underfoot; he makes them like dust with his sword, like driven stubble with his bow. He pursues them and passes on safely, by paths his feet have not trod.

---

5. See also 1 Sam 4:17; 31:9; 2 Sam 1:20; 4:10; 18:19, 20, 26, 31; 1 Kgs 1:42; 1 Chr 10:9; 16:23; Pss 40:9; 68:11; 96:2; Jer 20:15.

6. Watts (*Isaiah 34–66*, 147–48) records it thus: "In the month of Tashritu when Cyrus attacked the army of Akkad in Opis on the Tigris, the inhabitants of Akkad revolted, but he [Nabonidus] massacred the confused inhabitants. The fourteenth day Sippar was seized without battle. Nabonidus fled. The sixteenth day Ugbaru, governor of Gutium, and the army of Cyrus entered Babylon without battle. Afterwards Nabonidus was arrested in Babylon when he returned [there]. . . . In the month of Arahsammu, the third day [October 29, 539 BC] Cyrus entered Babylon; green twigs were spread in front of him—the state of peace was imposed on the city (*ANET*, 306)." This is a great example of ancient victory followed by a "peace." See also Herodotus, *Hist.* 1.189–91; however, the account is generally discredited.

7. "Cyrus the Great," 565.

8. As Watts (*Isaiah 34–66*, 102) notes, "Farther east the political pot is boiling. A bright and fearful new name is being whispered in all the world's seats of power. It is the name of Cyrus the Persian, who already reigns over the combined kingdoms of Media and Persia (cf. [Isa] 41:21–29; 42:5–9; 44:24–28; 45:1–7, 9–11; 48:12–15)."

9. Some do not see this as a reference to Cyrus and see the reference to Cyrus as a *Vaticinium ex eventu* (prophecy after the event). However, this is unnecessary.

Isaiah's answer is God (Isa 41:4). As a result, "the coastlands have seen and are afraid; the ends of the earth tremble" (Isa 41:5). The impact is truly cosmic, which is important, because the gospel is now penetrating Rome and beyond. This violent victory will come through Israel, whom God will make "a threshing sledge, new, sharp, and having teeth" that will thresh and crush mountains and hills (Isa 41:15–16).[10] Just as he raised Babylon to "trample rulers as on mortar," he raises Cyrus (Isa 41:25); that this involves war is self-evident. Isaiah is the one who heralds this good news (*euangelizomai*) to Jerusalem (Isa 41:27).

In Isaiah 42:13, "The Lord goes out like a mighty man, like a man of war he stirs up zeal; he cries out, he shouts aloud, he shows himself mighty against his foes." In Isaiah 42:22–25, the prophet uses classic war imagery to speak of Israel, by God's hand, being plundered, looted, imprisoned, and burnt through the battle at exile. But in Isaiah 43, God becomes savior, giving the nations in exchange for Israel (Isa 43:1–13). He will destroy Babylon and the Chaldeans (Isa 43:14). He is the God "who brings forth chariot and horse, army and warrior" (Isa 43:17).

Specifically, in Isaiah 44:28—45:1, Cyrus is named as God's shepherd and anointed. The latter term is *māšîaḥ* (messiah) translated *Christos* (Christ) in the LXX. This term is used in Mark 1:1 of Jesus the Christ. Isaiah writes of him that he will "subdue nations" (Isa 45:1) and through him God will "break to pieces the doors of bronze and cut through bars of iron" (Isa 45:2), and so Israel will experience redemption through war. Tribute, prisoners of war, and worship of Yahweh will flow from the nations, indicating their complete submission to God through the Christ Cyrus's victory (Isa 45:16). This is the language of a new creation (Isa 45:18). The nations' futile idols will be destroyed (Isa 45:20). Every knee will bow and every tongue of the nations will yield to God for salvation (Isa 45:22–25, cf. Rom 14:11; Phil 2:10).

In Isaiah 47, Cyrus's victory will include the utter humiliation of Babylon, the nation consumed by fire (Isa 47, cf. Isa 48:14). Israel will be released (Isa 48:20). The nations and her rulers will come in complete submission to Yahweh (Isa 49:22–23). Isaiah 49:24–26 is a vivid description of God's destruction of Israel's opponents: "I will make your oppressors eat their own flesh, and they shall be drunk with their own blood as with wine. Then all flesh shall know that I am the Lord your Savior, and your Redeemer, the Mighty One of Jacob." God is Israel's warrior-king who will reduce their opponents to cannibalism.

---

10. As Briley (*Isaiah*, 127) notes, "In these verses God makes it clear that he will not only act *on behalf of* Israel, but also that he will prevail over the opposition *through* Israel" (emphasis his).

Isaiah 51 predicts salvation for Zion which has "drunk... the cup of his [God] wrath" (Isa 51:17, cf. 51:20) and experienced "devastation and destruction, famine and sword" (Isa 51:19). This cup of wrath will be handed to "your tormentors," i.e. Babylon, through Cyrus (Isa 51:23).

In Isaiah 52:7, in a song of Israel's redemption, the prophet sings, "how beautiful upon the mountains are the feet of him who brings *good news* [*euangelizomai*], who publishes peace, who brings good news of happiness, who publishes salvation, who says to Zion, 'Your God reigns.'"

In Isaiah 54:2, Israel is to "enlarge the place of her tent" as she will "spread to the right and to the left" and take possession of "the nations" and "people the desolate cities." Again, her victory includes the subjugated nations. Central to this is the everlasting covenant with David (Isa 55:3). He will be a witness, a leader, and a commander for the peoples (Isa 55:4), and nations will run to Israel (Isa 55:5).

Throughout Isaiah 40–55 are also found the so-called Servant Songs. The term "servant" is used throughout these chapters of Israel (Isa 41:8, 9; 42:19; 43:10; 44:1, 2; 44:21; 45:4; 48:20; 49:3). Sometimes it seems to refer to the prophet Isaiah (Isa 44:26). At other times, an individual is servant (Isa 42:1; 49:5–7; 50:11; 52:13; 53:11). It is possible that these refer to Cyrus, who will redeem Israel.[11] However, the vision of this individual transcends the context and so points to an anointed one who will redeem Israel. Jesus is the fulfillment of this figure.

Euangelizomai is also used of one who will come empowered by God's Spirit and who will preach good news to the poor in Isaiah 61:1. Jesus, in his first recorded sermon, applied this to himself, declaring himself God's empowered one who would preach good news to the poor and bring God's salvation (Luke 4:18–19).[12] Hence, the gospel in Isaiah is a message of God's deliverance of his people by war, defeating the Babylonians who have subjugated them, bringing them out of exile, and restoring them to their land with the temple in Zion rebuilt. This liberation will ultimately yield a new heaven and earth (Isa 65–66). *Euangelion* thus speaks of political, military, and spiritual conquest.

In the Greek world, *euangelion* speaks of good news, especially regarding the emperor, such as when his son is born, a wedding occurs, but

---

11. See Watts, *Isaiah 39–66*, 115–17, "Excursus: Identifying the 'Servant of Yahweh,'" for a fuller discussion of options.

12. Sometimes the verb that is related to *euangelion*, *euangelizomai*, is used in a more general sense of bringing news of some sort like victory in battle (see 1 Sam 31:9; 2 Sam 1:20; 4:10; 18:19, 20, 26, 31; 1 Kgs 1:42; 1 Chr 10:9; Pss 39:10; 67:12; Isa 60:6; Jer 20:15. See also Pss. Sol. 11:1).

especially of his victory in war.¹³ Indeed, *euangelion* was the technical term for "news of victory."¹⁴ The herald (*euangelos*) would come from the field of battle by ship, horse, or on foot (like the legendary marathon runner Pheidippides who supposedly dropped dead on delivery). He often carries a letter, to proclaim the victory to the anxiously waiting city.¹⁵ Radiating joy, decked with a laurel, his head crowned, swinging palm branches, he would raise his right hand in greeting, crying "greetings . . . we have the victory."¹⁶ This would lead to great joy, sacrifices, the decoration of temples, athletics events, sacrifices crowned, the honoring of the victor, and the rewarding of the messenger. *Euangelion* was especially associated with the imperial cult: worship of the Roman emperor, who is the savior of the world, the gods incarnate. He is the embodiment of "good news." His birth and birthday, his coming of age, and his ascension to the throne are good news when a new era of peace is established.¹⁷ Often "salvation" in the sense of deliverance from enemies was linked to *euangelion*.¹⁸ Thus, for a Greek or Roman of the time, "good news" suggested the rising of a new "emperor" who would bring victory, salvation, and peace. In a world ruled by seemingly all-powerful Roman emperors, this is highly threatening and politically dangerous.

In the New Testament, *euangelion* is used to refer to God's victory over all opponents, spiritual and worldly, and the setting free of humanity from the exile of sin, judgment, and eternal destruction. Ultimately, it will be the complete deliverance of humanity from all evil rule, illness, death, poverty, and suffering. So, we can see that it has both a spiritual and a political edge.

As argued, Mark was written to Romans. His readers living in the shadow of the almighty Caesar, his administration, and the Forum and Palatine, could not help but make the connection to the Roman world and recognize that Mark is declaring from the beginning that he is bringing the good news of a great ruler. The story must then be read against the prevailing notions of power in Israel, where the Gospel is set, and in Rome, where the emperor holds sway. For Jews, the declaration of the "gospel of Jesus

---

13. See Friedrich, "εὐαγγελίζομαι," 2.710.

14. See ibid., 7.722.

15. See ibid., 7.710–12. The legend of the marathon runner is debated.

16. Ibid., 722.

17. The best example is the famous Priene Inscriptions from 9 BC from near Ephesus: "and since the Caesar through his appearance [*epiphanein*] has exceeded the hopes of all former good messages [*euangelia*], surpassing not only the benefactors who came before him, but also leaving no hope that anyone in the future would surpass him, and since for the world the birthday of the god was the beginning of his good messages." As found in Witherington, *1 and 2 Thessalonians*, 71.

18. Friedrich, "εὐαγγελίζομαι," 722–25.

Christ" suggests that a new "anointed" one is coming, a "new Cyrus." Just as Cyrus delivered Israel, so too this *Christos* would deliver Israel. Considering the context and background presented to this point, the whole idea screams "violent military revolution"!

In addition, by the time Mark was written, Roman Christianity had been established for a good thirty years or so, probably started when Roman pilgrims heard Peter preach at Pentecost and returned home with the *euangelion* (Acts 2:10). In fact, it is possible we know the names of the ones who started it; the apostolic husband and wife couple, Andronicus and Junia (Rom 16:7).[19] Whether or not this is correct, we know that the Roman Church started among the Jews of Rome, and before long they were in conflict over Jesus (*Chrestus*) to the point that Emperor Claudius expelled the Jews from Rome in 49 AD.[20] This suggests that there were a lot of Jews and they were making a real impact; at least enough to disturb the Jewish people and the city and move its emperor to expel them. It is certain that these Roman Christians knew their Old Testament well, familiar with some early version of the Septuagint, the Greek translation of the Old Testament (LXX). As such, they would have got both sides of *euangelion* as clear as a bell. They would have realized Mark was declaring that God's salvation had come to the Jews from their people. They would have recognized that the one Isaiah hoped for in Isaiah 61:1 was here. They would have noted that Mark meant that his story is the good news of a new ruler—one could say "Caesar" Jesus. Mark, as the first written full Gospel, represents the development of the idea of the good news from an oral presentation to a written record.

Right from the first, Mark is set against the common understanding of the dominant understanding of power based on a warrior-king and Empire sustained through military force and political intrigue. As we will see, Mark's presentation sustains this throughout with subversion and irony beginning from the first sentence.

The name "Jesus" needs further comment, recalling the earlier discussion of the first Joshua in chapter 4. The name is Jesus' earthly name, the Greek *Iēsous*, which renders the variations of the Hebrew $y^e hô\cdot šŭ^{aʿ}$ or $y^e hô\cdot šŭ^{aʿ}$ (*Yehoshua* or *Yeshua*). The name means "Yahweh saves," an entirely appropriate name for both the Joshua of the conquest and Jesus. There are a few Joshuas in the Bible, but the first that stands out, of course, is Joshua,

---

19. An idea I came to independently of Bauckham, who argues the same; see Bauckham, *Gospel Women*, 181.

20. See Suetonius, *Claud.* 25.4: "As the Jews were making constant disturbances at the instigation of *Chrestus* (Christ), he expelled them from Rome." Claudius enjoyed making edicts including one in which he promoted public flatulence for good health (Suetonius, *Claud.* 32).

son of Nun, Moses' aide, who became the leader of Israel's army and who took the land of Canaan. He was the ultimate warrior-ruler (not king at this point—he yielded to God as king). He led the people across the Jordan and drove the Canaanites out from the land (see the book of Joshua). The naming of Jesus after him is provocative. If Jesus is Messiah, his name (which in Matthew and Luke is given by God, Matt 1:21; Luke 1:31), is no accident. Surely he would seek to emulate his predecessor and lead the forces of Israel in driving the gentiles out of their land. This time, it would not be the Canaanites, as Joshua son of Nun achieved, but the Romans. More than that, what a great name for the one who, with the aid of the armies of the Lord's angels and people, would not only purify Israel, but the whole world, for Yahweh. Whereas the first Joshua, imbued with Yahweh's power, took the land, the second would take the world.

A second Joshua arguably of significance is the post-exilic high priest Joshua mentioned in Haggai and Zechariah (Hag 1:1, 12, 14; 2:2, Ezra 10:18). Joshua is always mentioned in reference to his father Jehozadak, who was high priest at the time of exile (1 Chr 6:14–15). "This link legitimates Joshua as the proper chief priest to lead worship in the new Temple."[21] Joshua, alongside the governor Zerubbabel, a descendant of David, in obedience to the prophet Haggai, assisted in the rebuilding of the temple after exile. This Joshua, Jesus, would restore the temple after Israel's "exile."[22] Zechariah crowned Joshua, calling him the Branch and recalling the awaited messiah. In Zechariah 3:1, the prophet is shown Joshua the high priest before God's angel and being accused by Satan. God is described as the one who "has chosen Jerusalem." He rebukes Satan. In the vision, Joshua is dressed in filthy garments, likely symbolizing the failure of Israel's priest that led to exile. Joshua is obedient, and is reclothed by the angel in pure vestments and a turban. He is charged to walk in God's ways and, if so, he will "rule my house and have charge in my courts." He is granted the right of access to the celestial court of God.[23] The priests are then described as a sign of something yet to come, i.e., the coming of the Branch—this is clearly a reference to the messiah (Isa 4:2; Jer 23:5; 33:15; Zech 6:12).[24] The coming of the Branch will see Israel's iniquities removed "in a single day" and all Israel will

---

21. Fager, "Jehozadak," 670. Jehozadak was son of former high priest Seraiah (1 Chr 6:14–15), killed by Nebuchadnezzar after the destruction of Jerusalem (cf. 2 Kgs 25:18–21; Jer 52:24–27). He was also brother to Ezra the scribe (Ezra 7:1).

22. See Wright, *Jesus and the Victory of God*, 576–79, who argues Israel was still in exile in the theological sense, even if in the land. While I find it problematic to use the term "exile," his overall point is sound.

23. Stuhlmueller, *Rebuilding with Hope*, 79.

24. Smith, *The Minor Prophets*, Zech 6:12–13.

sit with neighbors in complete safety. In Zechariah 6:10, Zechariah takes silver and gold from exiles and fashions a crown and sets it on Joshua's head. Joshua is told that he is the Branch who will build the temple (Zech 6:12). He shall receive "royal honor and shall sit and rule on his throne" (Zech 6:13).[25] A priest then will rule and, with the king, bring peace.[26] Here then we have the clear notion of the messiah as a crowned king-priest. This is not novel, as Psalm 110:4 indicates that the messiah is a king-priest. This lays the foundation for the two messiahs of Qumran. The name Jesus not only calls to mind Joshua son of Nun, but Joshua the high priest. Jesus fulfills these expectations, coming as a Davidic king, as well as the fulfillment of the hope of a high priest on the throne. His clearing of the temple then takes on a new light in this regard—he is the High Priest coming to act to cleanse the temple. His oracle of forthcoming destruction of the temple in Mark 13 anticipates the destruction of the physical temple, and the establishment of himself as a temple (see John 2:19) and the people of God as a living temple of the Spirit (1 Cor 3:16). It anticipates the writer of Hebrews, who sees Jesus as the High Priest leading the worship of the heavenly sanctuary (Heb 2:17; 3:1; 4:14–15; 5:5, 10; 6:20; 7:26; 8:1; 9:11). The name Joshua, then, is laden with connotations regarding Jesus as deliverer and priest of Israel. In Jesus, these ideas are morphed into a servant priest-king who himself becomes the temple of God and the center of a hope that transcends Israel and her cult[27] but draws in the whole world to faith in God through the new Joshua.

The name "Christ" is the crunch word for this book. While it becomes Jesus' second name and some limit it to this, here it is unarguably referring more to Jesus as Israel's Christ.[28] It is Greek for anointed, and translates

---

25. Smith (*Micah-Malachi*, 218) notes that some see this verse as alternating between Zerubbabel and Joshua: "And he [Zerubbabel] shall build the temple, And he [Joshua] shall put on splendor, And he [Zerubbabel] shall sit and rule upon his throne; And he [Joshua] shall be priest upon his throne; And a counsel of peace shall be between them." While this is possible, Zerubbabel is not mentioned, although perhaps alluded to in verse 13. As such, the emphasis here seems to be on Joshua.

26. Smith (*The Minor Prophets*, Zech 6:12–13) writes of the difficult "both" here: "The reference must be to the concord existing between the offices of priest and king. Only when these two offices were combined in one person could such concord exist (Zech 6:13b)."

27. This is made explicit by John in John 2:19–21. That the Johannine tradition was known by Jesus' opponents is clear from the accusations that Jesus would destroy the temple at Jesus' trial and crucifixion (Mark 14:58; 15:29 and parr.).

28. Guelich, *Mark 1–8:26*, 9. Some limit it to a name here (e.g. Gnilka, *Das Evangelium nach Markus*, 1.43). However, without a doubt, the whole point of Mark is that Jesus is Israel's Christ, albeit not as expected. Mark is telling his story (e.g. Cranfield, *Mark*, 37; Lane, *Mark*, 44; Guelich, *Mark 1–8:26*, 9–10; France (*Gospel of Mark*, 50) notes every use in Mark is titular.

the Hebrew Messiah (or more accurately, *māšîaḥ*, also meaning "anointed"). The term used of a person or people is entirely Jewish, recalling the anointing of priests[29] and, more importantly, kings,[30] in Israel's history.

The hope of Israel rested in such a Messiah to which many Old Testament texts were attached (see the earlier discussion of the expectations of Israel in chapters 5–6). Mark is stating here that Jesus *is* the Messiah. He is thus the culmination of all the hopes of Israel. He is the one who will liberate her. They expect this not to be merely a spiritual release from evil (although this is included in the vision), but a political and military rescue from foreign rule, i.e., a revolution. For any Roman to accept this Jesus is a big call. It is, from the beginning, the story of the king of the world who is not Roman, but Jewish! While there was interest in Judaism among some Romans, there was much distaste for Jews. It is a big thing to go against the flow and let go of one's sense of ethnic privilege. This is especially true when Rome ruled a large portion of the known world.

This verse launches the theme of the Gospel. Mark is the good news of Jesus the Messiah. The whole narrative will be based around the unraveling of what a messiah looks like. Jesus walks a fine line throughout, in some ways meeting expectations, in others, turning the idea upside down.

The "Last" Prophet and Crowner of the King, John the Baptist (Mark 1:2–8)

Mark's account which follows begins somewhat surprisingly. Unlike Matthew and Luke, it does not begin with Jesus' birth and childhood. Nor does it begin with the pre-existent Jesus, as does John. Rather, it begins with the ministry of John the Baptist.[31] Why Mark begins there is a fascinating question.

A clue is found in the quote that Mark begins with, which he says is from Isaiah. Actually, he blends a quote from Malachi 3:1 and Isaiah 40:3, and may also be thinking of Exodus 23:20.[32] If the latter is in mind, the wilderness wanderings of Israel are relevant, as later in the narrative John

---

29. See Lev 4:3, 5, 16; 6:22.

30. See 1 Sam 2:10, 35; 12:3, 5; 16:6; 24:6, 10; 26:9, 11, 16, 23; 2 Sam 1:14, 16; 19:21; 22:51; 23:1; 1 Chr 16:22; 2 Chr 6:42; Pss 2:2; 19:50; 20:6; 28:8; 84:9; 89:38, 51; 105:15; 132:10, 17; Lam 4:20; Dan 9:25, 26; Hab 3:13, cf. 2 Sam 1:21; Isa 45:1.

31. See also, on John the Baptist, Josephus, *Ant.* 18.116–19.

32. See Allison, "Mountain and Wilderness," 565. France (*Gospel of Mark*, 45) notes that this fused text may come from a testimony-collection where the conflation had taken place.

the Baptist will minister in the desert, and Jesus will be tempted there (Mark 1:4, 12). In Exodus 23:20–23, it is written,

> See, I am sending an angel ahead of you to guard you along the way and to bring you to the place I have prepared. Pay attention to him and listen to what he says. Do not rebel against him; he will not forgive your rebellion, since my Name is in him. If you listen carefully to what he says and do all that I say, I will an enemy to your enemies and will oppose those who oppose you. My angel will go ahead of you and bring you into the land of the Amorites, Hittites, Perizzites, Canaanites, Hivites and Jebusites, and I will wipe them out."

If the link is correct, we have here the motif of a Second Exodus. If this were picked up by a first Jewish hearer, they would expect a glorious military campaign with God's supernatural intervention to start. "Pharaoh" Caesar is going to get it! John also represents God's messenger, to bring his message, to which Israel must listen. If they do, God will drive out their enemies; in this case, Rome. Israel will finally be liberated from six hundred years of oppression. As such, it too plays into the hand of the notion of the messiah as a warrior-king.

Both Malachi and Isaiah 40–66 point to the intervention of God. Malachi was written some four hundred fifty years before Jesus' coming, and Isaiah eight hundred or so years before Christ.[33] Some Jews believed that the voice of the prophets had been interrupted after Malachi (Ps 74:9; T. Benj. 9:2; 2 Apoc. Bar. 85:3; 1 Macc 4:46; 9:27; 14:41; Josephus, *Ag. Ap.* 1.41).[34] There was a hope that a "faithful prophet" like Moses would appear, signaling that the "last days" were underway (Deut 18:15–19; 1 Macc. 4:42–46; 14:41; 1QS IX 11).[35] So, when Mark begins this way, he is linking the Old Testament prophets with John the Baptist, stating that the prophets are back. Not only are they back, but the moment all of Israel was holding its breath for is here! The long-awaited messenger of God was on the way

---

33. There are differing views on the dating of Mark, with some scholars seeing all oracles dated from the eighth century BC, while others contend that chapters 1–39 date from the eighth century while chapters 40–55 and chapters 56–66 are dated post-exile (Deutero-Isaiah, Trito-Isaiah). Either way, they are well before Jesus' coming.

34. See Str-B 1.125–34 for evidence that after Malachi, the Holy Spirit (the Spirit of prophecy) went quiet and communicated through an inferior *bat qôl* (cf. Str-B 2.128–34). Qumran was an exception. Concerning the so-called "Silent Years" of the Intertestamental Period, see Pfeiffer, "Israel, History of the People of," 2:919–20; Jeremias, *New Testament Theology*, 80–81. This should not be applied to all Jews but was held by some—see Aune, *Prophecy in Early Christianity*, 103–6; Greenspahn, "Why Prophecy Ceased," 17–35.

35. Lane, *Mark*, 47.

and John, like Isaiah, was there to herald him in. Isaiah, as noted above, heralded in Cyrus "the Christ" who would overthrow the Babylonians and release Israel to live in their homeland free of foreign tyranny. Mark, the gospel-writer, and John the prophet, declare that a new Cyrus is being raised up who will release Israel. In Roman terms, Mark is the *euangelos*, declaring the good news of the victory of God!

There is another reason Mark (and Luke and Matthew) starts with John. There is an interesting parallel in the story of the prophet Samuel and the first kings of Israel, Saul and David. Samuel is the prophet who gives authorization to these kings, anointing them (1 Sam 10:1; 16:12–13, cf. 1 Kgs 1:34–39, 45; 19:15–16; 2 Kgs 9:3, 6, 12). John plays the prophetic role here, anointing the new Davidic king Jesus through baptism in water; God anointing him not with oil, but with the Spirit and God's authorization. Luke will develop this further in his Infancy Narrative (Luke 1–2), in which John the Baptist, like Samuel was born of a barren woman (Hannah and Elizabeth, cf. 1 Sam 16:2–8; Luke 1:7).

In Mark 1:4, John comes. He behaves like a classic prophet (such as Elijah, 2 Kgs 1:8),[36] living in the wilderness (fulfilling Isaiah's "voice of one crying in the wilderness"), wearing camel's hair with a leather belt, living in complete reliance on God, eating locusts and wild honey.[37] He challenged Israel to turn from sin and baptized them, cleansing them.[38] Luke gives more detail, with John bringing the classic prophet's appeal for social justice seen in generosity to the needy (Luke 3:10–14). All of this was in preparation for what is to come, something John was at pains to state.

He predicts that one is coming after him who is far stronger than he,[39] whose sandals he is not worthy to untie and who would baptize people with

---

36. Here we read: "They replied, 'He was a man with a garment of hair and with a leather belt around his waist.' The king said, 'That was Elijah the Tishbite.'"

37. This is also standard material for nomadic life, where people did not hesitate to eat a locust or two (Lane, *Mark*, 51). Locusts were also ritually clean (Lev 11:21–22; *m. Hul.* 3:7).

38. See Dockery, "Baptism," 55–56, who states, "The practice of baptism is widespread. Examples include the Hindu rituals in the Ganges River, the purification ritual in the Babylonian cult of Enki, and the Egyptian practices of purifying newborn children and the symbolic revivification rites performed on the dead. *Baptizō* and related terms were used to define ritual practices in early Cretan religion, Thracian religion, Eleusinian mystery religions and in several gnostic groups and cults." See also Guelich, *Mark 1–8:26*, 17.

39. Scholars debate who this is: 1) God; 2) messiah; 3) Son of Man; 4) Eschatological prophet; 5) Unknown eschatological figure. Most opt for 1–3; I prefer that he senses the messiah is coming. Yet, for John, like all, it is likely that he thinks he will be a warrior-king messiah, which accounts for why he himself gets a little uncertain and sends disciples to check Jesus out (see Matt 11:1–19; Luke 7:24–35). See also the

God's Spirit. While Mark's readers immediately jump to assume this is Jesus and that he is Messiah (cf. 1:1), John's original intent is unclear.[40] Considering the variety of Jewish expectations noted earlier, Guelich suggests five possibilities as to who this prediction refers to; God himself, the Messiah, the Son of Man, the eschatological prophet, or an unknown eschatological figure.[41] To this, we can add that he is simply another prophet, like John, but greatly imbued with power, perhaps akin to Elisha, who had a double portion of Elijah's power (2 Kgs 2:9). Reference to his sandals and baptism by the Spirit suggests a human figure, although this can be literal or figurative. Luke's story indicates that Zechariah, John's father, was expecting a Davidic figure (Luke 1:69), and so it is very possible that John has the messiah in mind. With that said, it not required that John know the exact nature of the one who is coming, only that one is coming. Both Matthew and Luke record that later John sent disciples to Jesus, asking him if he is "the one who is to come," reinforcing an expectation of a human figure (Matt 11:2; Luke 7:20). That John sent emissaries in this way could indicate that he is unclear on whether Jesus meets his messianic expectation.[42]

What hearers thought is also unclear, and has the same range of possibilities. His words may have excited messianic hope, although on its own the term is too vague to narrow down. If anyone heard it messianically, and that is doubtful at this early stage, they likely thought in military terms—if this guy is the messiah, war is coming. Certainly, for Mark's readers, messianism is in mind. However, by the time of Mark's writing, Jesus had completely rewritten what coming as the messiah meant.

For Mark's readers, thirty years after Pentecost, one coming who would baptize in the Spirit would be well understood as the one to initiate the Spirit outpouring that was to come on believers across the empire.[43] Yet, for first hearers, it would be utterly ambiguous. The mention of the Spirit is vital in terms of Jewish hope, as it was believed that, at the culmination of the world, God would pour out his Spirit on all flesh, and that by this Spirit, people would obey God's law and live righteously (e.g. Joel 2:28–32; Ezek 11:19; 36:25–27; 37:14). It recalls Isaiah's dream of a second exodus, when there will be a fresh outpouring of the Spirit (Isa 32:15; 44:3, cf. Isa 63:11,

---

discussion in Guelich, *Mark 1–8:26*, 21–22.

40. For example, Guelich (ibid., 19) sees this as hyperbolic.

41. Guelich (ibid., 22) gives a good range of examples for each.

42. See the discussion in ibid., 23–24.

43. It is argued by some that we should not read Luke into Mark here. However, Luke and Mark are linked three times in the Pauline corpus, including one reference in the undisputed letters (Phlm 24; Col 4:10, 14; 2 Tim 4:11). We can be quite confident that they were missionary co-workers.

14). It would thus excite great hope of God's intervention. What that would look like to hearers would be unclear.

It is important to hold back from projecting ahead at this point and seeing that John is the Elijah figure Malachi anticipated (see Mark 9:12, cf. Matt 11:13; Mal 4:5), the one who would be the bridge between the era of the law and the prophets, and Jesus. Putting ourselves in the place of first-century Jewish listeners, they would get none of this, but would have found John intriguing and exciting. First, with John behaving very like Elijah and Elisha, it would mean that the prophets were back. This must mean that things are heating up again. They would have their religious antennae up! Perhaps John is the messiah (or another savior figure) or a prophet heralding in the messiah. In fact, there is evidence, especially in John's Gospel, that some thought John himself was messiah (John 1:19–24). John quickly puts that to bed, resolute in his proclamation of a coming one who would dwarf him in greatness and power.

Further, it is significant that Israel's eschatological hope was often centered on the wilderness. In Israel's history, God had met the wandering Aramean Abraham in the wilderness (Gen 12:1–3; Deut 26:5), and he had brought Israel through the wilderness to the land. Prophetic hope suggested that "in the wilderness, God's people would again find their true destiny" (Hos 2:14–15; Ezek 20:35–38).[44] Revolutionary leaders were closely connected with the wilderness, including Theudas (Acts 5:36; Josephus, *Ant.* 20.97–98), the Egyptian for which Paul is mistaken (Acts 21:38, *J.W.* 2.258–63), and Jonathan of the Sicarii (*J.W.* 8.437–42). Hooker states that this "suggests that the Messiah may have been expected to appear there (perhaps Matt 24:26), and to repeat the miracles performed by Moses."[45]

It is also intriguing that the Essene community at Qumran, in the wilderness of Judaea, also saw themselves preparing the way for the messiah and God's intervention in Isaiah 40:3 terms (1QS 8:13–14, cf. 9:19–21).[46] Whether John was related to this group is neither here nor there; however, his appearance would excite real interest in Israel—is now the time?

So, when Mark writes in verse 5 that "the whole Judean countryside and all the people of Jerusalem were going out to him," it is not necessarily hyperbolic or surprising.[47] Rather, considering the stunning news that a prophet was in town, and the red-hot expectation of a Theo figure who

44. France, *Gospel of Mark*, 57.

45. Hooker, *The Gospel According to Saint Mark*, 36; cf. France, *Gospel of Mark*, 57–58.

46. France, *Gospel of Mark*, 56.

47. See Witherington, *Mark*, 73 who notes, "This is of course a hyperbolic remark, but its rhetorical purpose is to indicate John's great popularity."

would obliterate the Romans, it is not unlikely that large numbers of the Jewish population came to hear his message, receive baptism, and anticipate what would come next.

Jesus' Coronation, John's Baptism (Mark 1:9–11)

At this point, Jesus himself enters the story.[48] For Mark, this is critical; the one who is Messiah and Son of God, *Yeshua*, the savior is here. The description of his entry is ironical. Clearly, he is the one Mark wants his readers to recognize as the "stronger one" whose sandals John is not worthy to untie and who he will baptize with the Spirit. Yet, he does not come from the Galilean seats of power Sepphoris or Tiberias, or the nation's center, Jerusalem, but comes out of Nazareth.[49] Nazareth! Nazareth was a nothing town in Galilee about an hour (by foot) from Sepphoris.[50] So obscure is it that it is not mentioned in the Old Testament (although Nazarene might be linked, cf. Isa 11:1)[51] or any other Jewish writing. Indeed, it was only after the discovery of an inscription in recent times that doubt concerning its existence has been removed.[52] John gives us some idea of its lack of renown with Nathanael's response to Philip: "Nazareth! Can anything good come from there?" (John 1:46). Archaeological excavations suggest it only had a population of two hundred people![53] Galilee too speaks of provincial antipathy from the south and contrasts with the crowds from Jerusalem and Judea (cf. 14:62, 70; John 7:40–52).[54] The Jordan continues the motif of obscurity.[55]

Yet, for Mark, the savior of the world above Moses, the first Joshua, Caesar, Cyrus, or any other figure one may care to imagine, is from this tiny

---

48. "Now he arrives, as abruptly as Elijah burst on the scene in 1 Ki. 17:1" (France, *Gospel of Mark*, 75).

49. Similarly, Brooks, *Mark*, 42.

50. See Riesner, "Archeology and Geography," 36; Reed, "Nazareth," 951; "Nazareth," 1531; and Mounce, "Nazareth," 500, for more detail on Nazareth. Even though it was on trade routes, the complete lack of mention and its small size suggest it was a backwater.

51. See the discussion in Blomberg, *Matthew*, 70. The term could be a play on the Hebrew *nezer*, meaning "branch," and so is messianic, speaking of a king from David's line (Isa 11:1); it could also be a slang term for someone from a hick town, Nazareth (cf. John 1:46). Further, it might be that "Nazarene" should be understood as "Nazarite." However, this is debated.

52. Riesner, "Archeology and Geography," 36.

53. Ibid., 36.

54. France, *Gospel of Mark*, 34–35, 75.

55. Brooks (*Mark*, 42) notes that the Jordan, only two hundred meters (three hundred twenty kilometers) long, is one of the most overrated rivers in the world.

town in the backwaters of the Empire. Contemporary sagas often have a similar ironical motif. For example, Luke Skywalker in *Star Wars* was born in the obscure distant planet of Tatooine.[56] Frodo Baggins in *The Lord of the Rings* originated in the obscure Hobbiton. Rand al'Thor from the *Wheel of Time* was raised in the small obscure town of Emond's Field.

Jesus appears in, of all places, the Judean wilderness, to be baptized in the Jordan by John (v. 9).[57] No attempt is made by Mark to explain why this should happen (cf. Matt 3:15); he simply came and was baptized. As he came out of Jordan's waters, heaven is torn open, there is a visible manifestation of the Spirit, and an audible voice of God vindicates his son: "this is my Son, whom I love, with him I am well pleased" (1:10–11).[58] The reference to the Spirit descending would be viewed eschatologically as further evidence of the return of God's voice to Israel (above on John).[59] However, whether this meant Jesus is Messiah to observers is unlikely (below).

In Mark's story, it is clear that this is Jesus' anointing as king, i.e., Messiah, the Christ, the anointed one, the Son of God. First, as noted earlier, this parallels Samuel's anointing of David, i.e., a prophet and the new Davidic king (1 Sam 16:12–13).[60] The receipt of the Spirit recalls empowering chosen people for specific tasks (e.g. 1 Sam 16:13; Judg 3:10; 6:34).[61] It also reflects Isaiah's prophecy of a coming eschatological figure in Isa 61:1: "The Spirit of the Sovereign LORD is on me because the LORD has anointed me to preach good news to the poor." Indeed, Luke's Jesus will state that he is the fulfillment of this in the Nazareth synagogue (Luke 4:18–21). It also recalls Isaiah 11:1–2 and the anointing of the messiah: "A shoot will come up from the stump of Jesse; from his roots, a Branch will bear fruit. The Spirit of the LORD will rest on him." Psalms of Solomon 17:37 also associated the Spirit with the coming of the messiah: "And he will not be weak in his days upon his God, because God made him strong by the Holy Spirit."

---

56. See "Tatooine," http://en.wikipedia.org/wiki/Tatooine.

57. Refer to Footnote 55. Similarly, continuing the thread of obscurity, the crowds are mainly from Jerusalem and Judea, but Jesus is from Galilee in the north (see France, *Gospel of Mark*, 75).

58. Some texts have "a voice came from heaven" and others "a voice from heaven." One adds "was heard." For my purposes, the difference is minimal. On these, see Metzger, *A Textual Commentary*, 74.

59. Edwards, *Mark*, 35.

60. On the anointing of kings by God through prophets, see also Samuel and Saul (1 Sam 9:16; 10:1; 15:1, 17); Samuel and David (1 Sam 16:3, 6). The King is thus "the Lord's anointed" (1 Sam 2:35; 12:3, 5; 24:6, 10; 26:9, 11, 16, 23; 2 Sam 1:14, 16; 19:21; 22:51). In some situations, people anoint the king (2 Sam 2:4, 7; 5:3).

61. France, *Gospel of Mark*, 77,

More importantly, it calls to mind the anointing of Isaiah's servant in Isaiah 42:1: "Here is my servant, whom I uphold, my chosen one in whom I delight; I will put *my Spirit on him,* and he will bring justice to the nations" (emphasis added). The servant motif is critical in Isaiah 10:45 and 14:24, and is anticipated here.[62] As France says,

> The servant of Yahweh portrayed in Is. 42:1–4 is a nonviolent figure who achieves justice *(mišpāṭ)* for the nations by patient faithfulness, under the direction of the Spirit of Yahweh... The combination of this text with Ps. 2:7 thus offers a suggestive basis for Mark's presentation of the paradox of a suffering, unrecognised[sic] Messiah.[63]

Of course, Mark writes knowing this and we modern readers know this in hindsight. Whatever the exact Old Testament references he has in mind, the coming of the Spirit upon Jesus here is programmatic. From this point on, although mentions of the Spirit are few (3:29; 12:36; 13:11, cf. 2:8), readers are to assume that everything Jesus does in Luke's story is done in the power of the Spirit (cf. Luke 4:14).[64]

The tearing *(schizō)* of the heavens in v. 11 speaks of the ripping apart of the barrier between heaven and earth, between God and humanity (cf. Isa 64:1, LXX 63:19).[65] Such a rending was common idea in apocalyptic thought (cf. Apoc. Bar. 22.1; T. Levi 2:6; 5:1; 18:6; T. Jud. 24.2; Rev. 4:1;

---

62. Guelich (*Mark 1–8:26*, 33) and others rightly dispute based on lack of evidence those who argue "my son" (*huios mou*) adapts "my servant/child" (*pais mou*) from Isa 42:1 and so is also indicative of the servant; e.g., Jeremias, "παῖς θεοῦ as a Title of Jesus," 701–2. See also Marshall, "Son of God or Servant of Yahweh?" 327–32.

63. France, *Gospel of Mark*, 81.

64. The importance of the Spirit is especially clear in Luke's work, where he expands Mark's account to emphasize the role of the Spirit in Jesus' ministry (esp. Luke 4:14, 18–19; 10:21; Acts 1:2; 10:38). To a lesser degree, Matthew does the same, drawing out the function of the Spirit in terms of Jesus as Servant (Matt 12:18) and in his deliverance ministry (Matt 12:28). For a discussion on the use of *eis* ("to"), of the receipt of the Spirit, see France, *Gospel of Mark*, 77.

65. Edwards (*Mark*, 35) sees here a reference to the descent of the messiah. However, this is the coming of God rather than the messiah or the Spirit. Neither does Christ in Mark 1:10 descend—he ascends from the water and the Spirit descends upon him. Further, the LXX diverges from the Hebrew and Mark, using *aniogō* ("open"), rather than *schizō* and 1:10. It is thus a possible parallel based on the Hebrew. It is hardly a "clear echo" as is commonly claimed (e.g. Witherington, *Mark*, 74). T. Levi 18:6–8, which gives explicit parallels to this, is likely a Christian interpolation. Similarly, T. Jud. 24:1–3; Jos. Asen. 14:3. See also France, *Gospel of Mark*, 77, for examples of heavenly visionary experiences (e.g. Ezek 1:1; John 1:51; Acts 7:56; 10:11; 2 Cor 12:1–4; Rev 4:1; 19:11).

11:19; 19:11).[66] *Schizō* is a powerful term used in the LXX of the division of the Red Sea (Exod 14:21), Moses splitting rock to produce water (Isa 48:21), and the splitting of the Mount of Olives (Zech 14:4). Mark uses it later in 15:38 of the temple curtain's tearing, also symbolically demonstrating the tearing of the divine-human barrier.

The baptismal scene also has powerful echoes of creation. The Spirit as a dove descending on Jesus in the water recalls the hovering Spirit over the watery depths at creation (Gen 1:2–3).[67] God's voice echoes at creation with a series of creational oracles. Here, God speaks again, endorsing his son through whom he will renew creation.[68] For those with ears to hear, the words spoken are pregnant with meaning.[69] "This is my Son," as noted earlier in Mark 1:1, indicates God's endorsement of Jesus as his king. Divine sonship language in the Old Testament was sometimes used of the king.[70] For example, in the formative passage for the Davidic monarchy in 2 Samuel 7:14, God promises this of the Davidic king: "I will be his father, and he will be *my son*." In Psalm 2:7 we read of the king: "You are *my Son*; today I have become your Father." It is likely that this Psalm was used in the coronation of the Davidic king.[71] In Psalm 89:26–27, it is written of the king: "He shall cry to me, 'You are my Father, my God, and the Rock of my salvation.' And I will make him the firstborn, the highest of the kings of the earth." The *Florilegium* from Qumran (4Q174), which draws on Psalm 2 also indicates that the messiah was sometimes known in the first-century circle as God's son.[72]

---

66. Witherington, *Mark*, 74.

67. The Spirit is likened to a dove in Judaism (Str-B 1.124–25) and in *b. Hag.* 15a, it is seen as a dove (see also *Gen. Rab* 2; *Yal.* Gen 1:2). Odes Sol. 24:1 reflects Christian influence.

68. As Hooker (*Mark*, 46–47) notes, for Mark this is not merely the inferior *baṭ qôl* ("daughter of a voice"), a substitute for the prophetic voice. This is the voice of God (similarly, France, *Gospel of Mark*, 78).

69. Some note a parallel with Isa 49:3: "And he said to me, 'You are my servant, Israel, in whom I will be glorified'" (e.g., Edwards, *Mark*, 37). However, there are also clear differences: Israel/beloved Son; in whom/with whom; I will be glorified/I am well pleased.

70. In the Old Testament, it is also used of angels (e.g. Gen 6:2; Job 1:6; Dan 3:25), Israel of Israel's election (Exod 4:22–23; Hos 11:1; Mal 2:10). In other Jewish writings, it is used of angels (1 En. 69:4–5; 71:1; Jub 1:24–25), miracle workers (*b. Taʻ an.* 3:8; 24b; *b. Ber.* 17b; *b. ḥul.* 86a; *m. Taʻ an.* 3:8). In Qumran, the Son of God is connected to the messiah (4QFlor 1:10–14; 1QSa 2:11–12; 4QapocrDan ar). See Bauer, "Son of God," 770.

71. Craigie, *Psalms 1–50*, 64.

72. France, *Gospel of Mark*, 80, 609n31. See also 4Q246 2:1; perhaps 1QSa[28a] 2:11–12. See also Hengel, *The Son of God*, 43–45; Marshall, "Son of God," 770.

THE MESSIAH REVEALED (MARK 1:1—8:29)

In the Greek world, the Egyptian rulers,[73] Alexander the Great,[74] and the Ptolemies[75] were all called the son of god. The Roman emperor Augustus was called *Divi filius*, the Latin for the Greek *Theou huios* ("Son of god").[76]

For readers of Mark, Jesus is thus endorsed as King. He is not merely Davidic king, but the notion is blended with the servant motif—Jesus is the Servant-King! Readers will grasp quickly that this is substantially different from the Theo expectations of Israel. However, this was no doubt well beyond the worldview of first observers.

Note too that God says that Jesus is his "beloved son, with him I am well pleased." This is a ringing endorsement, even before Jesus enters his ministry. A similar statement will be made at Jesus' transfiguration, and his belovedness as son features in the vineyard parable (9:7; 12:6; more on these later). "Beloved" (*agapētos*) calls to mind Gen 22:2, where *agapētos* translates the Hebrew *yā·ḥîd*, indicating Abraham's "one and only, unique" son (cf. Gen 22:12, 16; Judg 11:34). It also potentially recalls the pierced one Israel mourns for (Zech 12:10, cf. Jer 6:26). Matthew also cites Isaiah 42:1–3 of Jesus, using *agapētos* as a translation of *bā·ḥîr*, "chosen one" (LXX, *eklektos*) linking the idea with the Servant. It is possible that this is in mind here, implying Jesus' uniqueness and further linking Jesus as Son (King) and Servant (cf. Mark 9:7; 12:6).[77] However, across the New Testament, *agapētos* is used of one loved by God or others, so this is unclear (e.g. Acts 15:25; Rom 1:7; 1 Cor 4:14; Eph 5:1; Phil 4:1; Jas 1:16; 1 Pet 4:12; 2 Pet 3:1; 1 John 2:7; Jude 3).[78] Regardless, *agapētos* from the beginning sets the theological framework for Christian ethics in which love (*agapē*) will govern Christ's ministry (e.g., 10:21) and Christian life (12:29–31).

First observers would likely make little of this event. First, Jesus is one of a multitude who came to John for baptism. John has spoken of a coming stronger one, but there is nothing to indicate that he recognized this when Jesus came or made known to the crowds that Jesus was that person. Depending on what others saw and heard at the baptism of Christ, there is no reason that Jesus' baptism would be any more special than others. Indeed, that he came and submitted to John's baptism would hardly suggest he is the "stronger one," but subordinate to the baptizer. Mark's readers can

---

73. See Schweizer ("υἱός, υἱοθεσία," 336), who notes that Egyptian gods are described as "son of God," "son of Helios," and "son of Zeus."

74. Schweizer ("υἱός," 336) notes that Alexander was called "son of Ammon," which in Greek is "son of Zeus."

75. Schweizer (ibid., 336) notes the Ptolemies were called "sons of Helios."

76. Schweizer (ibid., 337) details references.

77. See e.g. France, *Gospel of Mark*, 81; Guelich, *Mark 1–8:26*, 34.

78. Hooker (*Mark*, 47) is rightly dubious.

recognize that Jesus comes as a representative Israelite, baptized on behalf of his people.[79] However, for other observers, like all the rest he would be no doubt have been seen as a penitent Israelite (albeit a Galilean) who needed purification for sin.

Second, it is unclear what others saw and heard. Mark writes that "he saw" (*eiden*), the second person singular of *eidon*, which stands in parallel to "he was baptized" (the second person singular of *baptizō, ebaptisthē*). This likely points to a visionary experience of Jesus himself (1:10, cf. Matt 3:16).[80] It is uncertain, then, whether only Jesus or others saw heaven opened and there is no indication that others heard the voice. Certainly, the fact that it is recorded suggests others saw something, or it was Jesus who told them this. Even if others had seen and heard the whole thing, it is most unlikely they would have immediately jumped to the conclusion that Jesus was a Theo figure, let alone the servant-messiah (which no one expected anyway). They may have surmised that Jesus was called and imbued with God's Spirit and approved by God. This would still leave the usual range of possibilities—a prophet? A priest? A king? Elijah? If they heard God's voice and linked "beloved son" to messiah (cf. Ps 2:7), they may have recognized Jesus' messiahship (or theoship). If so, they would likely have anticipated that Jesus would rally Israel for war with Rome. However, it is not likely that they made this connection at this point.

Whatever they understood, they did not fully appreciate who it was that was baptized before them. If we accept Luke 7:18–20 and Matthew 11:2–3 as authentic, even John is not sure. Why would he or anyone grasp that Jesus was a Servant-King? The whole context was shaped by the theological, political, and militaristic expectations of Israel.

Jesus Resists Satan (Mark 1:12–13)

The first event in Jesus' ministry is his being thrust out (*ekballō*)[81] into the desert to be tempted (*peirazō*) by Satan (cf. *peirasmos*, "temptation" in

---

79. E.g., Lane, *Mark*, 54, 57n61, who notes Rabbinic uses of the dove for Israel. See France, *Gospel of Mark*, 75–76, also, for a discussion of ways of interpreting this.

80. Most commentators accept this as a visionary experience of Jesus rather than others (e.g., Witherington, *Mark*, 74; Brooks, *Mark*, 42; Hooker, *Mark*, 45; Guelich, *Mark 1–8:26*, 32). Importantly, "alone" (*monos*) is not used, leaving open the possibility of a broader audience. Matthew (contra Hooker) picks up Jesus as audience: "the heavens were opened to him, and he saw." Luke, however, deletes "he saw" and it is described more openly (Luke 3:21–22).

81. *Ekballō* in Mark is used here for the first time. It has the strong sense of compulsion, most often of expelling demons (1:34, 39, 43; 3:15, 22, 23; 6:13; 7:26; 9:18, 28,

14:38).⁸² The desert in the Scriptures calls to mind a range of situations, including: the chaos of earth before creation (Gen 1:2), Adam and Eve's ejection from the beauty of the garden of Eden (Gen 3:23), the nomadic world of the Patriarchs (e.g. Gen 21:20–21), the place of Moses' "exile" from Egypt (Exod 3:1; Neh 9:21), the wilderness wanderings of Israel (e.g., Exod 15:22), David's flight from Saul (e.g., 1 Sam 23:14), Elijah's flight from Ahab (1 Kgs 19:4), and, in many of these instances, associated faith struggles. The Judean desert is a harsh dry lonely environment, below freezing on a winter's night, sweltering in the day (above 45°C, 113°F.), and is commonly believed to be populated with demons (Deut 32:17, cf. Luke 8:29; Matt 12:43–45) and wild animals (e.g. Isa 13:19–22; 34:13–14; T. Naph. 8.4; Mark 1:13).⁸³ While it will ultimately be a place to meet God and find deliverance (e.g. Isa 11:6–9; 32:14–20; 65:25; Hos 2:18; 2 Bar 73.6), here it has the negative sense.⁸⁴

This forty-day experience theologically calls to mind a range of Old Testament connections, including the flood (Gen 7:12), Moses on Mount Sinai (Exod 24:18), the time the spies were in the land (Num 14:34), Elijah on Sinai/Horeb (1 Kgs 19:8), and the days until Nineveh's destruction (Jonah 3:4).⁸⁵ The notion of forty years also recalls Israel's wilderness experience (Exod 16:35; Deut 2:7), Moses' forty-year "exile" in Midian (Acts 7:23–30), and the period of Philistine domination (Judg 13:1).

The wilderness also recalls Moses' forty days on Mout Sinai (Exod 24:18). Jesus thus, in a sense, embodied Israel and a new Moses. He is tested, as were Adam and Eve (Gen 3) and Israel (Exod 16:4; 20:20; Deut 13:4). While it may merely be an insignificant temporal designation without theological significance,⁸⁶ the links to the Old Testament are tantalizing. It may

---

38, cf. 16:9, 17). Also of Jesus sending a healed man to a priest (1:43), sending people outside a room (5:40), tearing out an eye that causes sin (9:47), Jesus driving people from the temple (11:15), and the tenants throwing the son out of the vineyard (12:8). Here it is not violent and coercive, as Marcus (*Mark 1–8*, 167) suggests, but "something like 'drove... out' (RSV, NRSV, REB) or 'impelled' (NASB)" (see Brooks, *Mark*, 44). The idea is that of divine necessity, not that Jesus was reluctant to go. The "desert" was the place of John's preaching (vv. 3–4); it was also the place of Jesus' temptation. Here it is an historic present tense—see Stein, *Mark*, 62.

82. As Satan is the agent, *peirazō* here must carry the negative sense of tempted (cf. Matt 4:1, 3; Luke 4:2; 1 Cor 7:5; 10:13; Gal 6:1; 1 Thess 3:5; Heb 2:18; 4:15; Jas 1:13–14) rather than test (e.g. Mark 8:11; 10:2; 12:15). See Stein, *Mark*, 64; contra France, *Gospel of Mark*, 85.

83. On the wilderness, see "Desert," 615; Brubacher, "Desert," 338–40; Allison, "Mountain and Wilderness," 563–65; Morgan, "Desert," 927–28.

84. Stein, *Mark*, 63.

85. Also the period of Jesus' resurrection appearances (Acts 1:3).

86. Hooker, *Mark*, 50; Stein, *Mark*, 63.

indicate that, unlike Israel in her forty-year wanderings, Jesus does not fail, but overcomes temptation.[87] It may also add to the Exodus motif, with Jesus being the new Moses. There may be a subtle anticipation of the Transfiguration, where Jesus meets Moses and Elijah on a mountain and becomes God's mouthpiece (9:2–8). People versed in the Old Testament could hardly fail to notice that Jesus succeeds where Eve and Adam fail (Gen 3)—Jesus is the new Adam.[88] Here, we arguably see Jesus fulfilling the history of Israel in his being the Servant-Messiah. Further, Jesus is unthreatened by the wild animals, recalling the pre-Fall creation state and speaking of a new creation (cf. Isa 11:6–9; 65:17–25).[89] He is then served (*diakoneō*) by angels recalling God's provision for Israel and Elijah (Mark 1:12–13; Exod 16; 1 Kgs 19:4–8).[90] It also recalls Psalm 91:11–13, which speaks of God commanding angels to guard the righteous, who will tread on the lion and snake (cf. *T. Naph.* 8.4).[91]

Unlike Matthew and Luke, Mark is not interested in the details of this encounter, only that the battle occurred and that Jesus is victorious.[92] He thus wins his *first* battle as king.[93] This is not a once-for-all defeat of Satan.[94] There remain the ongoing "battles," including the casting out of demons (Mark 3:23, 26), Satan's attempts to divert Jesus' mission (8:33), Christ's death and resurrection, and the gospel preached in the context of Satan's on-

---

87. France, *Gospel of Mark*, 85; Lane, *Mark*, 60; contra Stein, *Mark*, 64.

88. Guelich, *Mark 1–8:26*, 38–39; Marcus, *Mark 1–8*, 168; Turner and Bock, *Matthew and Mark*, 408; contra Stein, *Mark*, 64 who rules it out.

89. Marcus, *Mark 1–8*, 168, 170; Guelich, *Mark 1–8:26*, 39. Lane, *Mark*, 61, and Stein, *Mark*, 64, reject this, and are correct in narrow exegetical terms, in that Mark does not explicitly make the link, However, a reader knowing the Scriptures would likely make the connection. Stein also contends that the wild animals are set against the angels in some way, yet this is not in the text. Jesus is "with" (as implied by the use of *meta* with the genitive *thērion*) the wild animals, and the angels minister to him. There is nothing setting one against the other. France (*Gospel of Mark*, 87) considers the angels protected Jesus, but this is not stated; their service is non-specific. Edwards (*Mark*, 41) rejects the paradise-interpretation because of a lack of parallels, but ironically finds reference here to Nero's persecution, which is even more tenuous.

90. Stein, *Mark*, 64. Marcus (*Mark 1–8*, 168) also notes that this fits the Adamic motif, as a Jewish legend depicts "ministering angels" preparing food and drink for Adam in Eden (*b. Sanh.* 59b). He also notes that *diakonein* can mean worship, and this may be the sense here.

91. Hooker, *Mark*, 51.

92. Stein, *Mark*, 64.

93. Witherington (*Mark*, 77) sees a parallel to Nebuchadnezzar in Dan 4:28–37; however, this is without warrant.

94. Stein (*Mark*, 64) against Robinson (*The Problem of History in Mark*, 26–27); Best, *The Temptation and the Passion*, 3–60.

going resistance across the world until his return (4:15; 13:10). As Lane puts it, "his whole Gospel constitutes the explanation of the manner in which Jesus was tempted."[95] Jesus is thus demonstrated to truly be the Messiah, the Son of God. As Stein puts it:

> Along with [Mark] 1:1–11 the present account portrays Jesus Christ, the Son of God as *announced* by John the Baptist (1:2–8), *anointed* by the Spirit (1:10), *acknowledged* by the divine voice from heaven (1:11), *approved* by testing in the wilderness (1:12–13), and now prepared for his ministry and mission (1:14—16:8) [emphasis added].[96]

Whether he knew the fuller story or not,[97] Matthew and Luke fill out Mark's temptation narrative with fuller accounts of three specific temptations (Matt 4:1–11; Luke 4:1–13).[98] In the first, Jesus, who is hungry through fasting, is tempted to demonstrate that he is the "Son of God" by using his power to provide for himself with the miraculous transformation of stones into bread (Matt 4:2–3). Jesus responds with Deuteronomy 8:3, showing that obedience to God transcends all human need. He is the prototypical Davidic king, fully submitted to God. Second, Satan urges Jesus to throw himself down from the temple, as God will save him.[99] This is a challenge to prove his divine appointment as king. This time he quotes a Psalm of God's salvation (Ps 91:11–12), full of allusions that fit a desert context (see vv. 5, 6, 12–13). In my view, the key to this is the location of the temple on Zion. Were Jesus to do this, all would see it occur, and he would thus be vindicated as Messiah and people would come to him in support of his mission. It is a temptation to prove who he is and begin taking the world with an army. However, Jesus rejects this, quoting Deuteronomy 6:16, which refers to Israel's testing of God at Massah, again in their wilderness wanderings (Exod 17:1–7).

---

95. Lane, *Mark*, 61.

96. Stein, *Mark*, 62–66.

97. See Guelich (*Mark 1–8:26*, 36–37) for various explanations of the relationship of Mark to Matthew and Luke—I consider it likely that Matthew and Luke took Mark's short account and added Q material (cf. Bultmann, *The History of the Synoptic Tradition*, 253–54).

98. This Q material is ordered differently, due to the respective writers' emphases. Matthew places the temptation to yield to Satan and receive the world's kingdoms last, in line with his emphasis on world mission (cf. Matt 28:18–20). Luke places the temple temptation last as part of his emphasis on Jerusalem to which Jesus will journey, and from which the gospel will go global (cf. Luke 24; Acts 1).

99. See Hagner, *Matthew 1–13*, 66, for a discussion of the meaning of the difficult *pterygion tou hierou* ("pinnacle of the temple") in Matt 4:5.

Finally, the devil offers Jesus all the kingdoms of the world if he will bow to him. To do so would, of course, have caused a cosmic rupture, whereby the Godhead would have imploded into cataclysmic disaster, Satan would have recruited Jesus for mass destruction, and together they would have been a force for complete and eternal devastation. It was effectively an appeal to do things the "warrior-king" way. Jesus gives him a short shift, quoting again from the same context in Deuteronomy 6:13.

It can hardly be coincidental that, in both Matthew and Luke's Gospels, Jesus quotes three times from Deuteronomy. He, unlike Israel, stands the test. He has now overcome his first challenge from his ultimate enemy. He will not resort to using his power for himself, proving himself to Israel so that a revolution begins, or of doing things Satan's way. No, he will do it God's way.

Of course, we can see all this as readers considering the whole story and the subsequent Gospel accounts. At the time, no one in Israel knew that Jesus had been sent by the Spirit into the wilderness to contend with Satan. This was a private experience, so it meant nothing concerning Jesus' identity and role. Hence, when Jesus emerged from the desert into ministry, they had little, if any, idea of who he was and what he would do. If he is a prophet, he must preach God's word, as did John and the prophets of old. Even miracles would not necessarily prove he is anything more than another Elijah or Elisha. If he is the messiah, or another Theo figure, he would need to do the same; but, more importantly, he would need to perform signs that demonstrate his credentials, call the sons of Israel to his side, and storm the Romans. If he doesn't do this, he is at best a prophet; alternatively, a false messiah.[100]

JESUS THE DAVIDIC MESSIAH KING REVEALED (MARK 1:14—8:29)

This section is framed by Jesus' proclamation that the kingdom of God is near (Mark 1:14) and the confession by the disciples that Jesus is Messiah, i.e., King (Mark 8:29). Mark 1:16—8:26 involves the calling of disciples and the appointing and sending of apostles (1:16–20; 2:13–17; 3:13–19; 6:7–13). It also gives summary events in Jesus' ministry through a series of miracles,[101]

---

100. It is significant that Jesus is not viewed by contemporary Jews as a prophet, but as a false messiah. See "Why Jews Don't Believe in Jesus," http://www.aish.com/jw/s/48892792.html. For a fuller understanding, see Singer, *Let's Get Biblical*.

101. There are examples of deliverance (Mark 1:23–27; 5:1–41); eight healings, including a fever (1:29–31), leprosy (1:40–45), a paralytic (2:1–12), a withered hand

and preaching and teaching in synagogues and in pithy ambiguous parables.[102] His ministry is set against the backdrop of clashes with institutional Judaism, which have varied, and false expectations of God's intervention.

In this passage, Mark focuses on Jesus' ministry and a range of responses to him. Demons who are cast out by Jesus know from the first who he is, and are silenced or banished (Mark 1:24, 34; 3:11; 5:7). Then there is the consequent spread of his fame, leading to crowds of people (2:4, 13; 3:7–9, 20, 32; 4:1, 36; 5:21, 24, 27, 30, 31; 6:34, 45; 7:33; 8:1, 2, 6) coming for ministry (1:28, 32–34, 45; 2:12; 3:7; 5:41; 7:37). These crowds are from Galilee, but at times include people from Judea, Jerusalem, and gentiles from Tyre, Sidon, Idumea, and across the Jordan (3:7–8).[103]

The crowds are made up of people who come and go from Jesus' ministry, observing some miracles and hearing snippets of his teaching, usually in the form of parables (Mark 4:10–11, 33). Always Jesus is on the move,[104] refusing to be tied down geographically (e.g. Mark 1:35–39), and so most have only seen a snapshot(s) of Jesus. Jesus works hard to reduce the spread of news of his identity, silencing demons and the family of the raised girl (Mark 5:42–43). However, his impact is unstoppable. Jesus' family enter the

---

(3:1–6), a bleeding woman (5:24–34), a Syro-Phoenician woman's daughter (7:24–30), a deaf man (7:31–37), a blind man (8:22–26); healing summaries (1:33–34; 3:7–12; 6:53–56); a resurrection of a sick girl (5:21–43); two feeding miracles: the five thousand (6:30–44) and the four thousand (8:1–10); and "nature miracles," including calming the storm (4:35–41) and walking on water (6:45–52).

102. On preaching and teaching, authoritative in Synagogue, see Mark 1:21–22; 1:35–38; 6:6. Fused through the story are Jesus' clashes with Jewish leaders on a range of issues: forgiveness (2:1–12), table fellowship with sinners (2:15–17), fasting (2:18–22), Sabbath (2:23–3:6), power over demons (3:22–30), ritual purity (7:1–23), and miraculous signs (8:1–21). This leads to an increasing desire to destroy Jesus (3:6). Also, there are a series of kingdom parables (4:1–34).

103. Edwards (Mark, 103) notes that "Galilee, Judea, and Jerusalem were principally Jewish territories; Idumea and Transjordan were mixed Jewish-gentile regions; and Tyre and Sidon were largely if not entirely gentile regions (see Luke 6:17; Matt 11:21–22)."

104. Jesus' movements are: unspecified location beside Sea of Galilee (Mark 1:16–20)—Capernaum (1:21–39)—preaching tour throughout Galilee, no specifics (1:39–45)—Capernaum (2:1–12)—beside the Sea (2:13–22)—through the grainfields (2:23–28)—the Synagogue (Capernaum?) (3:1–6)—unspecified location beside the sea (3:7–12)—up an unspecified mountain (3:13–19)—home (Capernaum?) (3:20–35)—unspecified location beside the sea (4:1–34)—Gerasenes (disputed) on the other side of the lake (4:35—5:20)—to the other side (5:21–43)—Nazareth (6:1–6a)—teaching through unspecified villages (6:6b)—Twelve sent two by two to unspecified locations (6:7–30)—unspecified desolate place (6:31–44)—other side of the lake to Bethsaida (6:45)—up an unspecified mountain (6:46)—across the lake to Gennesaret (6:47–7:23)—Tyre and Sidon (7:24–30)—through Sidon to Sea to Decapolis (7:31—8:9)—Dalmanutha (8:10–21)—Bethsaida (8:22–26).

story a couple of times. They are concerned about his state of mind and seek to seize him (Mark 3:20–21, 31). Jesus is uninterested, considering his disciples his family (Mark 3:31–35). When he returns to his home, there is the uncertainty of his hometown and stubborn unbelief, so Jesus moves on (Mark 6:1–6a).

In Mark 6:14–17 (cf. 8:28), we get insight into who people consider Jesus to be.[105] There are three perspectives given. Some such as Herod consider him John the Baptist raised from the dead. This may be literal[106] for those only aware of Jesus' ministry after John's death. Or, more likely, it is "a rather clumsy but vivid way of expressing a sense of continuity such as is better conveyed in the imagery of the transfer of the 'spirit of Elijah' to his companion Elisha (2 Kgs 2:15)."[107] Others consider him Elijah. A return of Elijah to announce the day of the Lord was expected in some Jewish thought based on his translation to heaven (2 Kgs 2:11) and the prophecies of Malachi 3:23–24 and 4:5–6 (cf. Sir 48:4; Apoc. El. (H) 5.5.32). Others think Jesus is a prophet, like "one of the prophets of old." If so, a new age of prophets has come, and God's intervention is likely imminent. Notably, none of these consider Jesus as the Messiah. As Hooker says, "All three opinions thus attribute high status to Jesus: nevertheless, none of them is adequate."[108]

Then there are the disciples who, alone among the people of Israel, travel with him the whole time, observing his miracles and hearing his teaching. They dialogue with Jesus on the road and in private, hearing his explanations (Mark 4:33–34). They see all his amazing miracles, hear his teaching, and observe the debates. Through it all, however, they wonder at his identity; most especially in Mark 4:41: "Who then is this, that even the wind and the sea obey him?"

It is the thesis of this book that Jesus' goal through these chapters was not to convince all of Israel that he is Messiah—this would excite ideas of revolution (cf. John 6:15). Rather, he sought to convince his close followers of his identity as the Christ. Once they "get it" (Mark 8:29), Jesus will then teach them what this Messiah looks like—a selfless servant who would act only out of love for others and who would die as a sacrifice to save the world—a crucified Messiah. The pattern of his life would become the pattern of their life as they take up their crosses and follow him (Mark 8:34).

---

105. On the singular textual variant *elegen* rather than the plural *elegon*, see Metzger, *Textual Commentary*, 76. He rightly notes that *elegon* is likely original with *elegen*, a copyist adaptation to bring the verb into agreement with the verb "heard" (*ēksousen*). However, the plural introduces the parenthetical section, giving three views on Jesus.

106. Hooker, *Mark*, 159.

107. France, *Gospel of Mark*, 253.

108. Hooker, *Mark*, 159–60.

That this is Jesus' goal is seen in that he is very guarded, keeping his messianic status under wraps. When someone clicked to his identity, he shut them down. We see this with evil spirits who recognize him as "the Holy One of God" (Mark 1:24) or "the Son of God" (3:11-12), and are told to keep this quiet (see also Mark 1:34). In many of Jesus' healings, he asks recipients to keep the healing secret. This includes a healed leper who is only to go to the priest who will pronounce his healing (1:44), the family of the raised girl (5:43), and the healed blind man who is not even to enter his village (8:26). Jesus clearly does not want to excite public messianic excitement. The exception is the man who, delivered of a legion of demons, is encouraged to return to his home to share what God has done for him. He does so, testifying in the gentile region of the Decapolis (5:19-20). Neither does he tell the Syro-Phoenician woman to be silent, sending her to "go your way" (7:30).

This so-called "messianic secret," then, is not evidence that Jesus was not the Messiah and that these limiting texts are placed on his lips later by church or evangelist—an idea made popular by William Wrede and carried on by many biblical scholars.[109] Rather, these texts lie at the center of Jesus' ministry, and he was consciously avoiding becoming caught up as a leader in a political and military uprising. If this were to happen, it would run completely counter to his non-violent intention in coming and seeing the flawed patterns of human power which dominate the world played out yet again. In the Gospels, this is most clearly seen in John's account of the feeding of the five thousand where, after the feeding, the crowd recognizes that Jesus is the long-awaited "Prophet" (Deut 18:15). Jesus then withdraws, perceiving that the crowd of well-fed men (an ideal army) were about to come and make him king by force (John 6:14-15). As Carson writes of this passage in John,

> they had witnessed or heard of Jesus' miracles of healing, and they had been fed from food provided by his miraculous power. Surely nothing could prevent such a person from being the powerful liberator that so many children of Israel longed for.[110]

Jesus' intent, then, was to convince his close followers that he is the Messiah. He set about this task, not by demonstrating his military prowess in violent raids or declaring himself king, like so many false messiahs of the time (see the section "Messianic Movements" in chapter 5 of this volume). Rather, he demonstrated his true messianic credentials through his relentless ministry of selflessness, service, compassion, healing, feeding, calling, and loving.

109. Wrede, *The Messianic Secret*. See for a summary, Tuckett, "Messianic Secret," 797-800.

110. Carson, *John*, 272.

His ministry was genuine. He brought God's love to the lost. Yet, his purpose was to build a messianic community in the world, who would do the work of the kingdom across God's world. He is their ultimate example.

His goal was to gather around him a group of followers who would come to recognize that he was indeed Theo, the Savior of the world, and who would be completely dedicated to serving him (Mark 8:27–30). Even when they did recognize his Messiahship, much to their confusion he immediately commanded them not to tell anyone (Mark 8:30). Rather, he would then educate them on what this means (Mark 9:2—15:47). He would show the world what Theo looks like in Jerusalem, where he would enter as the Messiah come to save, and then die on a cross. This would confound Israel, yet, it would lead to the salvation of many from the nations.

The baptism indicates that the Synoptic Jesus was thoroughly aware of his own identity (Mark 1:11). The Transfiguration, again, demonstrates his Messianic self-awareness (Mark 9:7). The three passion predictions and other hints indicate that he knew he would ultimately be killed in this mission (Mark 8:31–33; 9:30–32; 10:32–34). Jesus clearly believed that his death was essential for the completion of that mission. However, his goal was never to avoid death, but to die to save the world ("as a ransom for many," Mark 10:45). He knew that the essential problem of humanity required a solution, and that his death was it.

In what follows, I will take a detailed look at Mark 1:14–15, and then survey the first half of Mark, skimming 1:16—8:29 and suggesting how Jesus' actions may have looked to first observers. Irony is everywhere when one understands Jesus' real intentions against Jewish expectations. While Mark knows the full story, in the minds of the general populace, if Jesus were Theo (of any sort), he would be a divinely imbued warrior. If he was the Christ, he was a descendent of David who would liberate Israel and take the world for God. He would function like Cyrus, liberating Israel from her new Babylon, Rome (1 Pet 5:13; Rev 14:8; 16:19; 17:5; 18:2, 10, 21). He would establish his reign in and from Jerusalem, and so the world would finally be set right. What we see is a confusing Jesus who is full of power and so seems perhaps to be this Theo, yet will not play the game of thrones correctly, and who will ultimately be killed as a false prophet and messiah.

God's Deliverance is Imminent (Mark 1:14–15)

For Mark, 1:14–15 is undoubtedly programmatic for the gospel and Jesus' teaching. Mark writes: "After John was put in prison, Jesus went into Galilee, proclaiming the good news [*euangelion*] of God. 'The time has come,' he said. 'The kingdom of God is near. Repent and believe the good news!'"

The placement of these verses is critical. They launch Jesus' ministry and set up the "kingdom of God" as the governing leitmotif of the Gospel. The verses provide the content of Mark's *euangelion* ("good news"); namely, that the kingdom of God is near. This is a summary of Jesus' message. The second part of the verse, "repent and believe the good news," calls for the appropriate response to this good news—turn from sin and all false gospels, Jewish, Roman, or otherwise, and believe this new message that God's rule has arrived in his Messiah and Son Jesus. That is, they must bend the knee to this King, this Christ, this Son of Man, this Son of God. They must submit to his rule. From the mouth of Jesus, it is first a clarion call to the Jews. Now, from the pen of Mark, it is a declaration and invitation to the Romans and world—Jesus reigns above all, including Caesar. It is a call to us to do the same.

The first part of Mark 1:14 speaks of the imprisonment of John. The placement is not merely descriptive; it is theological. In the imprisonment of the prophet who inaugurates Jesus, the time of "the prophets" is coming to an end,[111] and the new era in which God's dealings with humanity will be reckoned through his Messiah and Son is inaugurated. Mark gets this. The Roman readers will get this when they read the full account. The first hearers had no idea of the connection. Why would they? Jesus hadn't done anything yet to demonstrate that he is the King. More to the point, it is *God's* kingdom, so God is King!

As noted above, in Mark 1:9 the choice of Galilee for Jesus' proclamation is fascinating. Galilee was the northern-most region of tripartite Israel of Jesus' time; including Judea in the south and Samaria in its center. One might ask why Jesus didn't head to the seat of Jewish power in the south, Jerusalem, or to the Roman regional centers of Sepphoris (an hour walk from Nazareth) or Tiberius (close to Capernaum). Going to these places would make sense if Jesus wanted to quickly assume power, impress those in authority, or begin an assault on the Romans. However, Galilee was ideal as a breeding ground for a revolution; it known for social banditry and revolutionary movements.[112] Jesus, then, looks like a classic messianic pretender. Surely his next step is gathering an army and war. Jesus' approach will be

---

111. That is not to say there are not prophets in the New Testament era, e.g., Agabus (Acts 11:28; 21:10), Judas and Silas (Acts 15:27), and others (Acts 13:1; 1 Cor 12:28, 29; 14:29, 32; Eph 2:20; 3:5; 4:11). However, the era of Jewish prophets ended in John, looking forward to Theo and God's reign. Now it is here. A Christian who prophesies now does so in light of the new covenant.

112. See Riesner, "Galilee," 252–53, and Heard, "Revolutionary Movements," 688–98.

subtler than this. Ultimately, if he is truly Theo, he must go to Jerusalem. He does, but not as expected.

Jesus comes heralding (*kērussō*) the "good news" (again, *euangelion*). The verb *kērussō* was linked to the role of the herald, the *kērux*. The *kērux* was used of the herald in the royal court, and at the service of the state, a position of political and religious significance as the two were intertwined. His role was widespread, including summoning men to the assembly, warriors to battle, and giving official decrees and announcements. All this was to be done with a commanding voice—the more commanding, the better. This herald was the spokesman for his master. His role included religious proclamation, especially in prayer. The *kērux* is found in the LXX, of heralds of kings (Gen 41:43; Dan 3:4; 4 Macc 6:4) and of towns (Sir 20:15).[113] *Kērussō*, the verb used here, speaks of the activity of the herald, meaning "to announce, proclaim, cry aloud, declare." The verb was used in the context of games for the honoring of victors.[114] In the LXX, the term is always used with an official political or religious edge: of official royal proclamation (Gen 41:43; 2 Chr 36:22; Esth 6:9, 11; 1 Macc 10:63–64; Dan 3:4; 5:29) and decrees (2 Kgs 10:20; 2 Chr 20:3; 24:9; 1 Esd 2:1), priestly proclamation (Exod 32:5), messages proclaimed on behalf of Moses (Exod 36:6), military proclamation (1 Macc 5:49), wisdom's proclamation (Prov 1:21; 8:1), good news in Zion (Pss. Sol. 11:1), prophetic proclamation on behalf of God (Hos 5:8; Mic 3:5; Joel 1:14; 2:1, 15; Jonah 1:2; 3:2, 4, 5, 7; Zeph 3:14; 9:9), and future messianic proclamation (Isa 61:1). Here, then, the choice of verb strengthens the idea of an official message from God by his "Herald" and "Prophet" Jesus Christ. As the story unfolds for the disciples, it becomes clear he is more than a mere herald or prophet. He is the ultimate bearer of God's word, greater than Moses and Elijah (Mark 9:2–7). Indeed, as John understands, he is the message (the *logos*, cf. John 1:1, 14).

"The time has come, the Kingdom of God[115] is near" would be utterly provocative considering expectations. In Jewish thought, despite the rebellion of most of the world, God was undoubtedly the king of all. "Kingdom of God" is rare but found in the Old Testament in such places as 2 Chronicles

---

113. See further Friedrich, "κῆρυξ," 683–96.

114. Ibid., 697–98.

115. The phrases "Kingdom of God" (e.g. Matt 6:33; 12:28; 19:24; 21:31, 43; Mark 4:11, 26, 30; 9:1; 10:14, 15, 23–25, 34; Luke 4:43; 6:20; 7:28; 8:1; 9:2; 17:21–22; John 3:3, 5; Acts 1:3; 28:31; 1 Cor 4:20, etc.), "the Kingdom" (Matt 4:23; 8:12; 9:35; 13:19, 38; 24:14; 25:34; Luke 12:32; 19:15; Acts 20:25; 1 Cor 15:24; Jas 2:5), "the Kingdom of their Father" (Matt 13:43); "the Kingdom of Christ and God" (Eph 5:5); "the Kingdom of our Lord and of his Christ" (Rev 11:15); "His Kingdom" (Matt 12:26; 13:41; 16:28; Luke 1:33; 11:18; 12:31, cf. 2 Tim 4:1), and "Kingdom of Heaven" (Matt 3:2; 4:17; 5:3, 10, 19, 30; 7:21; 10:7; 13:11, 33; 18:1; 19:14, etc.) are parallel.

13:8, where "kingdom of the Lord" is used. God is king (e.g., Ps 24:7–10; Isa 6:5). He rules over Israel (e.g. Pss 47:8; 149:2; Isa 33:22; 41:21; 43:15; 44:6; Jer 8:19; Zeph 3:15). He rules over the world as 1 Chronicles 29:11 states: "Yours, O Lord, is the greatness and the power and the glory and the victory and the majesty, for all that is in the heavens and in the earth is yours. Yours is the kingdom, O Lord, and you are exalted as head above all" (cf. Pss 47:2–9; 103:19). His kingdom is eternal (Ps 145:11–13; Dan 4:3, 34). The proclamation "the Kingdom of God is near" cries that God is coming to bring his long-awaited salvation for Israel and the world.

"The time has come" and "near" are ambiguous and provocative. The former literally reads "the time is fulfilled" (*plēroō*, cf. Mark 14:49), speaking of the fulfillment of Israel's hopes of redemption. Salvation history is reaching its pinnacle. The hopes of the prophets are coming to pass. Theo is near. "Near" speaks of closeness, and is ambiguous, perhaps meaning that the kingdom of God is proximate in the person of Jesus, or is close temporally speaking. Likely, the first hearers heard it in the second sense. They would need to see much more to consider Jesus Theo. Together, they would suggest to hearers that the coming of God was imminent. For the Jew, this would mean that the climax of history was at hand, in which God would act decisively, restoring Israel, ending gentile domination, restoring Jerusalem and her temple on Zion as the world's political and religious center, and the world is subjugated to Yahweh and is coming to Jerusalem for worship and tribute. The question for first hearers is, "what is Jesus' role in this?"

From our perspective on the other side of Mark's story, we know that Jesus himself is the key to understanding Mark's account. It is in Christ that the kingdom of God has come. For Mark's Roman readers and believers since that time, Jesus is the Messiah and Son of God (1:1). His identity will be reinforced through the story (8:29; 9:41; 12:35; 14:61–62). He will also be revealed by Mark as Daniel's expected Son of Man (2:10, 28; 8:31, 38; 9:9, 12, 31; 10:33, 45; 13:26; 14:21, 41, 62). He is God's Son (1:1; 3:11; 5:7; 15:39). These christological titles will become entwined in the story of Jesus as God's servant who will give his life as a ransom for sin (Mark 10:45).

However, to first hearers, none of this is yet known. Jesus may merely be another prophetic herald like John the Baptist, proclaiming the forthcoming intervention of God. The details of this intervention would be debated; whether through God's direct action (Zech 14:9, cf. Wis 3:8) or through one of the various Theo figures in Israel's history. He could be a transcendent "Son of Man"-type figure (Dan 7:14, 18, 27), a Davidic messianic kingly ruler born in Bethlehem (2 Sam 7:16; Isa 9:7; 16:5; Jer 23:5–6; Ezek 34:23–24; 37:24; Amos 9:11), a prophet (Deut 18:15), or an Elijah figure (Mal 4:5), etc. Jesus' role as he cried out "The Kingdom of God is near" would excite expectations, but ambivalence would reign.

What would verify that Jesus is more than a prophet, but is Theo, God's expected agent of deliverance? Considering the previous chapters, imbued by God's power, he would establish himself, and then make moves toward violent political and military revolution. This would involve the gathering and preparation of an army of supporters suitable for war. They would be fiercely Yahwistic and potential warriors. He would demonstrate with signs of his credentials as God's chosen deliverer, perhaps like Moses in Exodus or Joshua at Jericho. He would no doubt need to demonstrate spiritual power, as the Romans presented an insurmountable challenge for Israel to overcome merely with military force. She could not win by aligning with other unclean gentiles, but this Theo figure would need to have "God on his side" so that he could overcome the gentiles against insuperable odds. At some point, it would include his partnering with Israel's leadership and directly challenging the Romans. He would rise up as a new Joshua, a new Cyrus, a new Moses, a new David, a Jewish version of Alexander the Great or Caesar, and gather Israel's best. Perhaps over time, gentile nations would yield and join his cause, and he would lead the revolution as God's brilliant and powerful warrior-king. What will genuinely verify him will be success and not defeat. Otherwise, he will be merely another failed messiah among many. Little did Israel and the world know that God had other plans.

Likely, then, this proclamation—"the time is fulfilled, the Kingdom of God is near"—would have been heard as a call to zealous Jews faithful to God who dreamed of his deliverance to ready themselves for war. The moment is near when Israel will be called to arms and empowered by God; he would perform the sort of signs that have been seen in Israel's history (the Passover, the crossing of the Red Sea and Jordan, the sun standing still, and God's intervention). God and his armies would take control of his world at last.

The appeal "repent and believe the good news" sums up the expected response by subjects of the kingdom. Such an appeal is consistent with prophetic proclamation. The prophets classically called people to repent and return or turn back to the covenant (Isa 1:27; 6:10; 9:13; 10:2; 14:27; 31:6; 44:22; 45:22; 55:7; Jer 3:1, 10, 12, 14, 22; 4:1; 5:3; 8:5; 15:7, 19; 19:11; 24:7; 25:5; 26:3; 35:15; 36:3, 7; 44:5; Lam 3:40; Ezek 3:19; 14:6; 18:23, 24, 32; 33:11; Hos 6:1; 14:1, 2; Joel 2:12, 13; Amos 4:6–11; Jonah 3:8; Hag 2:17; Zech 1:3, 4; Mal 3:7). Jesus will do the same. John the Baptist had preached a message of repentance (Mark 1:4), so Jesus on the face of it stood in continuity with John on this point. What Israel would not have seen was how deeply runs this appeal to repent. They were not only to repent of those sins that most acknowledged in Israel: personal sin. Rather, they were to repent of the corporate sin of presumption over their false gospel of militaristic eschatological expectations, their misunderstandings of election, their false trust in military power, and in many instances, their misguided desire to see the gentiles destroyed, i.e., that they were as much of a problem as the rest of the world. And that is the point. When Jesus came, all humanity was swept up in a false understanding of power, whereby one uses superior military power in partnership with divine force to defeat evil. They were blind to the fact that this approach was flawed and corrupt. Jesus came to show another way. Mark's readers would also have to repent of all false gentile gospels, such as the gospel of the imperial cult.

"Believe the good news" has taken on a technical meaning of salvation by faith for many today. However, while this is true, as the New Testament story unfolds (for it is by faith we are saved [e.g., Luke 8:12; Acts 15:11; 16:31; Rom 10:9; Eph 2:8]), for the first hearers it meant something more. It conveyed the thought that the hearer should trust in this announcement that the *kingdom of God is approaching*. Or, better, they should trust in the one who is establishing his reign, *God*! God is coming; he is establishing his sovereignty over the nations, so have faith! Believe! It certainly does not yet mean "trust in Jesus." As Jesus' story unfolds, this is essentially what it means—trust in the King of the kingdom. In other words, yield to his rule and give him complete allegiance.

So, in sum, this announcement would have created tremendous interest and excitement. One can imagine the political leaders of Israel gathering to discuss the preaching of Jesus. Indeed, we see this through the story, as they come again and again to him to observe him, question him, and challenge his authority, and invariably go away confused, frustrated, and infuriated. Ultimately, they will resolve to kill him, as he is clearly no messiah, from the perspective of their expectation, at least. One can picture the young zealots of Judaism gathering, full of excitement at his miracles, inspired by the possibility that this is the moment when they will rise up and smite the Romans. One can understand their later disillusionment. One can imagine the confusion of those closest to him who sought to understand what he was about as he healed the sick, fed the poor, raised the dead, touched the untouchable, partied with sinners, and called the insignificant. They would have been drawn to the depths of love that poured from him. But they would have been baffled by his failure to rise up and lead the revolt that they believed was coming. There was no other way. Or was there? And now to the story, as it plays out from the perspective of the irony of revolution in Mark.

Calling Disciples, Conscription to an Army? (Mark 1:16–20; 2:13–17; 3:13–19)

After the initial summary of Jesus' teaching in Mark 1:14–15, the first thing Jesus does on his return from resisting Satan is to call followers (Mark 1:16–20). I want to suggest how this might have looked to observers.

First, he did not call the hotshots of Israel's politics (like Herod's entourage,[116] the Sanhedrin[117]), or religious leaders (scribes,[118] Sadducees, Pharisees), but called four humble fishermen; two sets of brothers, absolute nobodies, Peter and Andrew, James and John. The identification of the first four as fishermen is useful as it leads into the analogy of evangelism and fishing, "I will make you fishers of people" (cf. Luke 5:1–12). But more than that, these fishermen, unlike the elite of the political and religious society, would make ideal soldiers. These are tough guys who knew what it meant to work and suffer. We see this in Luke's version (Luke 5:5) where they have fished all night and caught nothing. They know what it is to work in a team, the two sets of brothers, as business partners (Luke 5:7). They know what it is to take orders, working under Zebedee (Luke 5:10). We see their devotion as they are found repairing nets (Matt 4:21, cf. Luke 5:2). They are also likely frustrated with Roman rule and the economic struggles they face. For an external observer with the expectations of a military Theo figure, there is a certain logic here; namely, Jesus is calling the sorts of men who would make a great army.

Knowing that Jesus is the Messiah, we can now see what he is doing. Of course, we know looking back that Jesus is not trying to gather a military force at this point, but first observers would potentially make the connection. We know that Jesus selected them because he saw in them their potential to be leaders in the movement. If we accept John and Luke's accounts, he already knew them, as Jesus had healed Peter's mother-in-law before their call (Luke 4:38—5:11), and Andrew had previously been a disciple of John the Baptist (John 1:40–42).

---

116. Although Luke records that Chuza, the wife of Herod's household manager (*epitropos*), was one of his female followers and supports (Luke 8:3). The word *epitropos* was used of governors and procurators, so indicates a man of some standing and means (BDAG 385).

117. One of the Sanhedrin has interest in Jesus, Joseph of Arimathea (Mark 15:43). However, he is not one of the original called disciples.

118. Matthew 8:19 indicates that at least one scribe sought to join Jesus. However, he initiated the moment rather than Jesus, who answered cryptically with a challenge concerning potential homelessness. We have no idea whether the scribe took up the challenge of joining Jesus, the fox without a hole or a bird without a nest. Mark 12:28 mentions another scribe impressed with Jesus, who is pronounced "not far from the Kingdom of God"; however, we know little more of him.

Also provocative is his second call; namely, Levi, a tax-collector, meaning that he worked in the service of Rome (Mark 2:14), who is also known as Matthew (Mark 3:18).[119] Tax-collectors were notorious turncoats, or traitors. They had sold out to the Romans for personal gain. They were despised by their own people, who hated paying taxes. These tax collectors worked for the enemy. They took money from God's people for the unclean.[120] We see this in Luke 19, where Zacchaeus, a tax farmer in charge of many tax collectors, is treated with disdain. By calling a tax collector, Jesus might be perceived to be making the first act of deliverance, saving this man from Roman rule. Of course, we know that Jesus is welcoming this tax collector into the people of God, showing that the kingdom is for the marginalized. Yet, for an observer, this is provocative.[121]

119. Assuming Matthew and Levi are one and the same. Bauckham (*Jesus and the Eyewitnesses*, 108–12) argues that they are not, with Matthew transferring the story of Levi in Mark to Matthew. This leads him to argue that Matthew was not an apostle. However, just why the Gospel writer (who is a follower of Jesus and writes powerfully advocating integrity and repudiates hypocrisy) would do this is beyond me (see the Sermon on the Mount, esp. Matt 5:33–37; 6:2, 5, 16; s.a. 23:28). A far better explanation is that of Hagner (*Matthew 1–13*, 237), who says "We are clearly meant by our passage to know that the tax collector named Levi in the remainder of the Gospel tradition is to be understood to be Matthew (the name that regularly occurs in the listings of the twelve)" (ibid., 238). He correctly adds, "It is, of course, not unusual for individuals in the New Testament to have more than one name. Matthew (abbreviated form of 'gift of Yahweh') may have been the Christian name taken by Levi after his conversion to indicate his new life (cf. Saul-Paul)" (ibid., 238).

120. On tax collectors, see the section "Tax Collectors" in Schmidt, "Taxes," 805–6.

121. From 63 BC, taxes were paid to Rome initially administered by the high priest. This was reduced by Julius Caesar from perhaps thirty-three percent to twelve and a half percent per harvest in 47 BC, aside from sabbatical years (Josephus, *Ant.* 14.202). Herod then took responsibility for this, but in 30 BC was able to gather the funds for himself. After his death, Antipas raised taxes for Rome in Galilee and Perea, while prefect and procurators (probably through the Sanhedrin) took taxes in Judea after AD 6 (Josephus, *J.W.* 2.405). The average tax was likely about three weeks' work per year. For the poor, this was a heavy burden. There were three kinds of taxes: 1) The land tax (*triubutum soli*): taxes on produce, collected by Jewish leaders and representatives annually; 2) The head tax (*tributum capitis*): it included the census (Luke 2:1–5; Acts 5:37), likely about one day's wage per annum (denarius, Matt 22:19–22), and was collected by Jewish leaders and representatives annually; 3) The customs system: tolls and duties collected at ports and city gate tax offices (Mark 2:11), two to five percent of value, "farmed" to the highest bidder who collected for a district, and paid in advance to Rome by the tax collector. These are those mentioned in the New Testament (*telōnai*). Zacchaeus was a chief tax collector (Luke 19:1–10). Tax collectors were universally seen as "sinners" (e.g. Mark 2:15; Luke 15:1). They were considered "robbers" in Rabbinic literature (*m. B. Qam.* 10:2). They are paired with prostitutes (Matt 21:32) and brothel-keepers (Dio Chrysostom, *Disc.* 14.14). Tax farmers were often involved in fraudulent behavior (cf. Luke 3:12–13; Luke 19:8) and were "the embodiment of dishonesty." Tax farmers were repudiated not only for gathering taxes and fraudulent behavior, but for

Accounts are not given of the other seven calls for the remainder of the Twelve Apostles, but the description of several in the list of Mark 3:13–19 is intriguing. Some of the information is clearly just descriptive and clarifying, such as Simon's renaming as Peter, to distinguish the other James as a son of Alphaeus, and that Judas Iscariot would betray Jesus. However, three pieces of information stand out. First, he adds the detail that James and John are nicknamed "Sons of Thunder" (*Boanerges*) (Mark 3:17). Second, he tells readers that the second Simon is the *kananaios*, meaning "Zealot" (Mark 3:18). Thirdly, there is Judas Iscariot, which may mean "Judas the Sicarii." I will look at each briefly.

The ascription "Sons of Thunder" of John and James perplexes scholarship for a few reasons. The first is that the transliteration *Boanerges* does not fit with known Hebrew/Aramaic words. The second is that it is never mentioned again. The third is what it says about them. Regarding the first question of the meaning of the underlying Hebrew/Aramaic, there are a variety of suggestions to resolve the conundrum.[122] However, I prefer to accept Mark's translation as authoritative, and that the root Semitic phrase is lost. The second question of its non-recurrence suggests that this is not a renaming of these two by Jesus, but a nickname. The third question is the primary point of interest for this discussion.

"Sons of Thunder" suggests to some that they are sons of the Greek god of thunder Zeus, and so they are lined up with Zeus's twin sons Castor and Pollux, the Dioscuri. However, in a Jewish and Christian setting, this is very unlikely—although Greek and Roman readers might have made the connection. A better explanation is that this refers to their thunderous zeal. Their enthusiasm is seen on several occasions, twice in Mark's story, and once in Luke's Gospel. First, in Mark 9:38, when they come upon an outsider using Jesus' name in exorcism, they seek to stop that person. This shows their desire for power and to control the Jesus' movement. Jesus overrules them. Second (and more pointedly), in Mark 10:35–45, the two approach Jesus seeking assurance that they will be granted the leading positions after Jesus enters glory (more on this later and the role their mother may have played). Clearly, they have a very high opinion of themselves. Jesus responds by challenging whether they dare to go through what is yet

---

their collusion with Rome. Jesus' association with tax collectors would be controversial and lead to the charge of treason. See Schmidt, "Taxes," 804–6.

122. Guelich (*Mark 1–8:26*, 162) tells us that at least four Hebrew/Aramaic words have been suggested as background: 1) *rēgeš*= "commotion"; 2) *rōgez* = "excitement" or "agitation"; 3) *ra' aš* = "quaking"; 4) *ra' am* = "thunder." The final would seem likely, but does not correspond to *Boanērges*. So, either Mark's translation gives a standard meaning of the underlying phrase now lost to us, or it clarifies an obscure term.

to come; which they likely understood to be war. I will discuss this passage in more detail later; suffice it to say that this request and their response to Jesus demonstrates their zeal, arrogance, and excessive self-confidence to be the greatest warriors of the Twelve in the impending expected conflict (that never eventuated of course). Knowing that the other apostles include Simon, the Zealot, they are clearly full of themselves. Thirdly, in Luke 9:54, after Jesus is rejected by a Samaritan village, John and James seek to call down fire from heaven to destroy it in the manner of Sodom and Gomorrah. They thus believe themselves to be arrogantly capable of such miraculous feats. With all this in mind, it is likely that the nickname relates to their zealous warrior spirit. This fits with Jesus picking young men who would make great warriors.

The description of Simon as the *kananaios* (Cananaean) on the one hand distinguishes this Simon from Simon Peter. On the other hand, it describes him. While the name sounds rather like "Simon of Cana" or "Simon the Canaanite," it rather comes from the Aramaic *qan·ān*, meaning "Simon the enthusiast or zealot."[123] This is confirmed in Luke's redaction of Mark in Luke 6:16, where Simon is called *zēlōtēs* (zealot), avoiding any misunderstanding of the original term (cf. Acts 1:13).[124] The term indicates that he belonged to the group known as Zealots, who were patriots, guerillas, or freedom fighters on Israel's behalf. Of course, for many of the Romans, these revolutionary troublemakers were terrorists—"one man's terrorist is another man's freedom fighter." That being the case, we have a very provocative selection by Jesus; in the Twelve is a man who has strong aspirations to bring down Rome. Some argue that *zēalōtēs* indicates religious fervor only, as the Zealot movement came later. However, as Hengel notes, it is unlikely that the term was ever used in such an innocuous way.[125] Further, by the time of the writing of Mark, the term had "clear political connotations" and as such, likely indicates that Simon was "a fervent nationalist."[126]

Judas Iscariot (*iskariōth*) may also be militarily and messianically suggestive. *Iskariōth* is usually understood as pointing to his being a man

---

123. BDAG 507 notes that his surname Cananean does not indicate that he is from Cana, as claimed Jerome, or that he is a Canaanite, but rather, it is derived from an Aramaic term meaning "zealous one." In Luke 6:15 and Acts 1:13 he is described as *zēlōtēs*. He was likely a member of "the party of the 'Zealots' or 'Freedom Fighters.'" See also the discussion in Bock, *Luke Volume 1:1–9:50*, 545, who notes that Josephus traces their roots to AD 6 (Josephus, *J.W.* 2.217–18; *Ant.* 18.1–10, 23–25).

124. Guelich, *Mark 1–8:26*, 163.

125. It is argued that the term only became political in the lead-up to the Jewish war. However, as Hengel notes in *The Zealots*, 392–94, it is dubious that the term was ever used merely of religious zeal.

126. See Guelich, *Mark 1–8:26*, 162.

from the town of "Kerioth."¹²⁷ However, it is also possible that it derives from *sikarios*, meaning "daggerman, assassin, or terrorist." The Sicarii were "the most extreme group among the Judean nationalists," hostile to Rome, who "did not hesitate to assassinate their political opponents."¹²⁸ They were renowned for carrying hidden daggers and, in crowds, stabbing Jewish collaborators, often in the temple precincts, only to escape untouched (e.g. Josephus, *J.W.* 2.254–57; *Ant.* 20:162–65, 185–87). They were thus hit-and-run assassins; ideal characters for a James Bond movie. The Sicarii are mentioned in Acts 21:38 from around AD 54,¹²⁹ when Paul is mistakenly taken for an Egyptian revolutionary who led four thousand men of the Sicarii (translated "assassins" in ESV, LEB, NKJV; "terrorists" in NIV) (cf. Josephus, *J.W.* 2.261–63; *Ant.* 20.168–72). Paul understandably quickly removed any such associations, describing himself as a "Jew from Tarsus, in Cilicia, a citizen of no mean city" (Acts 21:39). It could be then that Judas is a radical revolutionary. Perhaps this explains in part his betrayal of Jesus; perhaps he simply ran out of patience waiting for Jesus to move or hoped to incite Jesus (or God) into action.¹³⁰

As noted above, one of the disciples is a tax collector (Levi, Matthew),¹³¹ a sellout to the Romans, who walks away from his "sin" and would follow Jesus (Mark 2:14; 3:18; Luke 5:27–28; 6:15; Matt 9:9; 10:3). It is interesting to ponder how he and the violently anti-Roman zealot Simon got on in those initial days. One can imagine some very interesting conversations in the early days of their acquaintance. It shows how Jesus sought to reconcile enemies.

Finally, we should note the number of apostles: twelve, associated in Israel's history with the twelve tribes of Israel (Gen 49:28; Exod 24:4; 28:21). In the account of Joshua's invasion, the twelve tribes are strongly emphasized (Josh 3:12; 4:2–4, 8–9, 20). Not only is Jesus named after the great Joshua, who led the glorious invasion of Canaan, overthrowing all the Canaanites and other "-ites" and establishing Israel in Palestine, but this new

---

127. Some readings of John 6:71 (also John 6:12, Text D) interpret "Iscariot" as "from Kerioth" (*apo karuōtou*). However, this is to be rejected through the range of texts that support Iscariot, among other arguments; see Metzger, *Textual Commentary*, 184.

128. BDAG 923.

129. Witherington, *Acts*, 661.

130. We see this type of thinking with ISIS, who appear to believe that if they begin storming the Middle East, Allah will come to their aid and enable them to establish a Jihadist Empire, which will eventually encompass the world. See "Daily Mail: ISIS Map of the World, Plan for Global Domination," http://myocn.net/daily-mail-isis-map-world-plan-global-domination/. See also "The ISIS Map of the World," http://www.dailymail.co.uk/news/article-2674736/ISIS-militants-declare-formation-caliphate-Syria-Iraq-demand-Muslims-world-swear-allegiance.html.

131. Assuming Matthew and Levi are one and the same; see footnote 119.

Joshua chose twelve men to be on his team. Further, he chooses a group of strong young men, one who has repented of being a traitor to Israel turning against Rome, a couple who are known for their thunderous passion, and at least two others who are likely freedom-fighters "heaven bent" on the overthrowing of Roman rule. The whole thing put together looks highly provocative—surely this is a reconstitution of Israel, and attack on Rome by Jesus and his messianic band is imminent.

One can perhaps see why the Herodians, the Sanhedrin, and the other leaders of Israel watched Jesus closely. Jesus' behavior was highly provocative. Any Romans in the know would also be interested, although Jesus would have to gain a great deal of momentum before being perceived as a threat. Evidence suggests he never got to that point, and the Romans had to be lent on quite strongly to have Jesus put to death. This they did for political expediency.

Jesus' Miracles and Teaching: Demon-Possessed, Prophet, or Messiah?

As noted above, the section concerns the journey of the disciples to the point where they grasp that Jesus is Messiah at Caesarea Philippi in Mark 8. Jesus' ministry is directed at bringing the kingdom of God, restoring the world to the direction of God's great dream and project. The disciples struggle to understand him, and Jesus patiently reveals to them that he is the Messiah.

This section contains a sequence of miraculous encounters and teaching. While it is customary to divide Jesus' ministry between teaching and miracles, both point in the same direction. They are visual (miracles) and oral (teaching) glimpses into the nature of the kingdom. Indeed, it is probably a mistake to separate Jesus' teaching and miracle ministry, as they are fused together—he taught through parable and miracle; word and sign. What makes Jesus stand apart is his power and authority (Mark 1:22, 27).

One interpretation of Jesus' miracles that comes from the scribes is that Jesus is an emissary of Beelzebul performing miracles by his power. Beelzebul (also Beelzebub) is another epithet for Satan or the devil. Originally, Beelzebul is a Hebrew term, and may imply "lord of the flies," "lord of the dung heap," "lord of the flame," or "lord of the heavens"). It was also employed for the deity ("prince of Baal") of the Philistine city of Ekron (1 Kgs 1:2–3, 6, 16). Beelzebul features in the Pseudepigraphal Testament of Solomon, where he is the "prince of demons" or demonic "king," or the "ruler of the spirits of the air and the earth and beneath the earth" who contends against God's people (T. Sol 3:6; 6:1, 9; 16:3, 5, cf. Eph 2:2).[132] In Mark, he is also the "prince of demons"—clearly, Satan is in mind. The accusation is that Jesus is effectively a demonically possessed wizard who can manipulate the powers of darkness to achieve his goals. However, Jesus refutes this, stating that this would be suicidal for his purposes, for "how can Satan cast out Satan?"

Further, a kingdom divided and pitted against itself will fall, as will a household. Here, Jesus articulates one of the basic principles of the survival of a kingdom in any situation—if it becomes beset with civil war, it will self-destruct, weakening itself and becoming vulnerable to conquest. Israel knows this from bitter experience during the civil war between the north and south, after the death of Solomon—this resulted in Israel being torn in two (Israel and Judah) under Jeroboam and Rehoboam (1 Kgs 12:1–24).[133] Mark's Roman readers would remember the bloody civil war following Julius Caesar's death, ending with Octavian gaining the ascendency and the Roman Empire being formed.[134] Immediately following Nero's death, there would be another brutal period of internal conflict which saw four emperors (including Nero) within a year (AD 69). Those following Nero included Galba, who was murdered by the Praetorian Guard; Otho, who committed suicide after defeat by Vitellus at the Battle of Bedriacum; and Vitellus, who was murdered by Vespasian's troops so Vespasian could assume power. Jesus' words would, in a sense, be fulfilled later in Mark, as one of his own, Judas, betrayed him and caused his death. But for the resurrection, his kingdom would have fallen. Israel itself became divided not long after Jesus' death, with the Zealot solution winning the day, revolt against Rome, and Israel's destruction. Reference to households divided may call to mind the clash over the high priesthood between Aristobulus II and Hyrcanus II, which led to the end of Israel's "golden age" and Roman rule in 63 BC.[135]

In verse 27, Jesus repudiates the explanation of the scribes, speaking of his mission as the binding of a strong man and the plunder of his house. Here, the "strong man" alludes to Satan, and Jesus' ability to overpower him. As Stein puts it, "The kingdom of Satan is not self-destructing from within but is being invaded from without, and the liberation of its captives is taking place because Jesus is stronger than Satan (3:27) and has brought the kingdom of God (1:15)."[136] This does not refer to a particular event in Jesus' ministry, such

---

132. On Beelzebul, see further Meeks, "Beelzebul"; Edwards, *Mark*, 120.
133. Similarly, see Stein, *Mark*, 183.
134. See Osgood, *Caesar's Legacy*.
135. Stein, *Mark*, 183.
136. Ibid., 184.

as his temptation in the desert, but speaks of his whole ministry, which sees the defeat of Satan who binds up humanity, as the kingdom extends, first, through his own ministry, and through that of his disciples. Jesus thus casts aside the idea that his ministry is demonic; it is God's power breaking in to loosen the hold of the demonic over God's world. For Mark, as for Paul in Ephesians 6:10-18, the war is not between world kingdoms, but God against Satan and his demons. This is the real battle. Victory is not won through the violence of warring armies leaving destroyed cities and countries, raped women, and corpses everywhere. It is won by the power of God's unbreaking reign through his spoken word, healing by touch and word, the feeding of the poor, the forgiveness of the sinner, the setting free of the oppressed, and ultimately, through the death and resurrection of the King.

Rather than being demon-possessed (a ludicrous clutching at straws by the scribes throughout this section of Mark), Jesus is behaving very much as a prophet, moving from town to town preaching and refusing to be tied down. Like Jesus, the prophets of old performed many miracles. Moses can be credited with around forty miracles, including his three initial signs to the Jewish leadership, the ten plagues on Egypt, and a range of others, including the defeat of enemies, guidance, natural events, provision, encounters with God, judgment, and healing.[137] In doing his miracles, Jesus is very reminiscent of Moses. But does it imply that *he* is Theo?

The first Joshua was also a miracle worker. He was involved in Moses' intercessory war victory miracle (Exod 17:8-13), was with Moses at the

---

137. Miracles of Moses include: 1) Three initial vindication signs for Israel (Exod 4:30): a) staff becoming a snake (Exod 4:2-3), b) his hand becoming leprous and then restored (Exod 4:6-7), and c) Nile water becoming blood (Exod 4:9); 2) ten signs before Pharaoh (Exod 7:9); staff (above; Exod 7:10); 3) Egypt's plagues: a) Nile to blood (Exod 7:14-25); b) frogs (Exod 8:1-15); c) gnats (Exod 8:16-19); d) flies (Exod 8:20-32); e) livestock death (Exod 9:1-7); f) boils (Exod 9:8-12); g) hail (Exod 9:13-35); h) locusts (Exod 10:1-20); i) darkness (Exod 10:21-29); j) death of the firstborn and Passover (Exod 11:1—12:32); 4) Exodus (Exod 12:33-42); 5) guidance by pillar and fire (Exod 13:17-22); 6) crossing of the Red Sea and destruction of Pharaoh's forces (Exod 13:17—14:31); 7) bitter water made sweet (Exod 15:22-27); 8) manna and quail (Exod 16:1-36); 9) water from the rock (Exod 17:1-7); 10) victory over the Amalekites (Exod 17:8-16); 11) Sinai and the Law three times (Exod 19:1—23:20; 24:12—31:18; 34:1-28); 12) land promised (Exod 23:20-33); 13) plague on Israel for idolatry (Exod 32:35); 14) direct speech with God (Exod 32:7-23); 14) radiant face (Exod 34:29-35); 15) God's glory on tent of meeting (Exod 39:34-38); 15) Aaron and Miriam leprous and healing (Num 12:1-16); 16) intercession that saves Israel but brings generations who die in the wilderness (Num 14:1-38); 17) the land opens and fire falls to kill Korah's rebels (Num 16:1-50); 18) Aaron's staff buds (Num 17:1-13); 19) water from rock (Num 20:2-13) ; 20) the bronze serpent heals the snake-bitten (Num 20:4-9). There is also a military victory (e.g. Num 21:1-3, 21-30, 31-35; 31:1-54; Deut 2:26-37; 3:1-22).

giving of the law (Exod 24:13; 32:17),[138] led Israel into the land through the Jordan (Josh 3:6—4:18), prayed and oversaw the destruction of Jericho (Josh 5:13–27), prophetically recognized Aachen's disobedience (Josh 6:6–26), led the victory over Ai (Josh 8:1–29), caused the sun to stand still, giving Israel victory over the Amorites (Josh 10:1–14), and can be credited with other military victories (Josh 10:16—11:23; 12:7–24).[139] Surely Jesus, like his namesake who performed great military miracles in particular, at some point would emulate his ancestor and lead Israel to God-ordained military victory over the Romans who had taken the land?

Elijah performed eight recorded miracles, including miracles of provision, a resurrection, the defeat of enemies, weather miracles, direct speech with God, and translation to heaven.[140] Elisha, with the double anointing of the same Spirit, performed twice as many miracles as Elijah, sixteen,[141] including feeding and provision, judgment, healing infertility, one resurrection, healing, prophecy, and others.[142] Jesus, in performing miracles (albeit many of them) at the least indicates to the common Israelite the return of the prophets. But is he Theo?

There are no recorded miracles of John the Baptist, so Jesus performing miracles may have excited greater messianic expectation and

---

138. This is disputable, as Exodus 24:15 only mentions Moses going up the mountain; however, it is likely that Joshua was with him while the elders remained behind with Aaron and Hur, who were to resolve disputes. Joshua was also with Moses on his return (Exod 32:17).

139. These victories are listed after those of Moses, indicating Joshua's esteem as God's agent of military victory. Further, he is vindicated as God's chosen in Deuteronomy 31:14–29.

140. Miracles of Elijah: 1) God's provision through ravens (1 Kgs 17:6); 2) flour and oil for widow of Zarephath (1 Kgs 17:8–16); 3) raising of widow's son (1 Kgs 17:17–24); 4) defeat of the prophets of Baal (1 Kgs 18:20–40); 5) prayer brings rain (1 Kgs 18:41–46); 6) strengthened for forty-day trip (1 Kgs 19:1–8); 7) God speaks to Elijah (1 Kgs 19:9–18); 8) translation to heaven (2 Kgs 2:11).

141. That the numbers of Elisha's miracles are twice those of Elijah is not likely a coincidence, as he purportedly received twice the spiritual empowering of Elijah (see 2 Kgs 2:9).

142. Miracles of Elisha: 1) purification of bad water (2 Kgs 2:19–22); 2) killing of abusers by bears (2 Kgs 2:23–25); 3) oil provided for widow (2 Kgs 4:1–7); 4) conception of Shunamite woman (2 Kgs 4:8–17); 5) raising of Shunamite's son (2 Kgs 4:18–37); 6) purification of stew (2 Kgs 4:38–44); 7) feeding one hundred people with twenty loaves of barley and fresh ears of grain (2 Kgs 4:42–44); 8) Naaman healed of leprosy (2 Kgs 5:1–14); 9) Gehazi gets leprosy (2 Kgs 5:15–27); 10) axe head floats (2 Kgs 6:1–7); 11) heavenly chariots of fire revealed (2 Kgs 6:8–23); 12) foresees assassination attempt (2 Kgs 6:32–33); 13) predicts God's provision of food (2 Kgs 7:1–20); 14) prediction of famine and restoration of land (2 Kgs 8:1–6); 15) prediction of Ben-hadad's recovery then death (2 Kgs 8:7–15); 16) prediction of defeat of Syria (2 Kgs 13:14–19).

speculation—although as noted previously, he may still be seen merely as a prophet (not that such a perspective is demeaning; it is a great honor). It was expected that the coming age would include miraculous signs of healing (Isa 56:10; 57:18–19; 58:8; Jer 15:19; 30:17; Ezek 47:12; Hos 6:1; Amos 9:14; Mal 4:2; 3 En. 48D.10; Sib. Or. 1.350, 353; 8.206, 272;[143] T. Zeb. 9.8; T. Ad. 3.1). This would include the deaf hearing (Isa 29:18; 35:5), the blind seeing (Isa 29:18; 35:5, cf. Isa 42:16), the lame walking (Isa 35:6), and the mute speaking (Isa 35:6). The Servant would open the eyes of the blind (Isa 42:7). Jesus certainly excelled in such miracles, performing a wide range of them. However, on their own, they did not necessarily suggest to Israel that he was Theo and not merely a prophet, and especially so when we remember that people only saw snippets of these miracles. He would need to do much more to convince the crowds. For the disciples, who saw them all, the eureka[144] moment would come sooner.

Most particularly, he would need to provide a vindication of his claims to the Jewish leadership (the Sanhedrin especially). Moses proved his credentials to Israel's leadership with his three signs; the staff to snake, the leprous hand, and the water turned to blood. He confirmed them with the plagues and the Exodus itself. Joshua did so as he led Israel into the land, splitting the Jordan and leading the supernatural demolition of Jericho (which Jesus would visit before Jerusalem—more on this later). Elijah demonstrated his power over the prophets of Baal. It is this type of sign the Pharisees likely seek. Jesus' refusal indicates that he had no desire to excite messianic and revolutionary expectations (Mark 8:11–12, cf. Matt 12:38–39; 16:1–4; Luke 11:16, 29–30; John 2:18–22; 6:30). These calls for a sign often came after amazing miracles, like the feeding of the five thousand (Mark 8:1–10; Matt 15:29–39) or casting out demons (Luke 11:14–15). This confuses many contemporary readers, who ask, "aren't these signs enough?" The problem is that signs don't prove Jesus' credentials. He needs to demonstrate, like Moses, Joshua, and Elijah, that he is God-approved and sent. The miracles are not sufficient for those seeking to assess Jesus' credentials, but for Jesus, they are enough. They demonstrate what the kingdom of God is all about: selfless service, love, and compassion to restore. It is not about violent revolution. We know this now, but the leaders expected something to draw them in.

Further, like Moses before Pharaoh, or Elijah before Ahab, if Jesus were a Theo figure, he would demonstrate before the Roman authorities that

---

143. These Sibylline Oracle references are likely Christian interpolations.

144. A eureka moment is a sudden unexpected discovery. It comes from the Greek *heurēka* and is linked to Archimedes, who supposedly said "eureka" when he saw the water level rise in a bath, helping him understand displacement. See "Eureka Effect," https://en.wikipedia.org/wiki/Eureka_effect.

he was God's deliverer. His power would be seen in military victories. He would lead the armies of Israel, either directly or with guidance and intercession. However, Jesus showed no interest in this. When before Pilate, he did nothing of the sort, and went to his death without any attempt to resist.

The prophets were also teachers and preachers, bringing God's word to Israel. Moses brought the Law, and Joshua was with him (Exod 24:13; 32:17). The later pre-exilic prophets in the ninth to sixth centuries BC bought God's word of renunciation, especially to leaders,[145] against idolatry,[146] social justice,[147] repentance,[148] warning of exile,[149] and future restoration.[150] The post-exilic prophets in the sixth to fifth centuries BC called for faithfulness to God and Torah,[151] the rebuilding of Jerusalem and temple,[152] and future restoration.[153]

Jesus' teaching spoke of God's imminent intervention (e.g., Mark 1:14; 9:1; Matt 4:17; Luke 10:9–11; 11:20; 17:20–21), his concern for social justice (e.g., Mark 10:21; 12:42–44; Matt 6:1–4; 11:5; Luke 4:18; 6:20–26; 14:13; 16:19–31), his call for repentance (e.g., Mark 1:15; Matt 4:17; 11:20–21; 12:41; Luke 5:32; 13:3–5), and his rebuke of Israel and her leaders (esp. Matt 23:1–36; Mark 12:1–12; Luke 11:37–54). None of this would necessarily excite messianic expectations. More likely it would lead to Jesus being seen as a prophet with much in common with Isaiah, Jeremiah, and the other prophets—which is, in fact, what we see in Mark's summary of people's view of Jesus in Mark 6:15; 8:28. Likely they would consider that Jesus' coming, like John

---

145. E.g., Isa 1:10; 28:7; Jer 1:18; 2:8, 26; 5:31; 10:21; 14:15; 23:1–40; 27:9—28:17; Ezek 7:26; 13:1–23; 22:23–31; 34:1–10; Dan 9:12; Hos 4:1—5:14; Mic 3:1–12; Nah 3:18; Zeph 1:8; 3:4, cf. Mal 1:6—2:9.

146. E.g., Isa 2:8; 10:11; Jer 8:19; 10:5–16; Ezek 6:1–14; 8:10; 14:3–7; 16:36; 18:6, 12, 15; 20:7–8, 16, 18, 24, 31, 39; 22:3–4; 23:7, 30, 37, 39, 49; 33:25; 36:17; 44:10–12; Hos 4:17; 8:4; 10:6; 11:2; Mic 1:7.

147. E.g., Isa 1:21, 23, 27; 3:14–15; 5:7; 10:2; 59:8, 15; Jer 5:28; Ezek 9:9; 16:49; 18:12; 22:29; Hos 10:13; Amos 2:6–7; 4:1; 5:7, 11–12; 8:4, 6; Hab 1:4.

148. E.g., Isa 1:27; 6:10; 10:2; 31:6; 44:22; 45:22; 55:7; Jer 3:12, 14, 22; 4:1; 5:3; 15:7, 17; 18:11; 25:5; 26:3; 35:15; 36:3, 7; 44:5; Lam 3:40; Ezek 3:19; 14:6; 18:30, 32; 33:8–11; Hos 6:1; 12:6; 14:1, 2; Joel 2:12–13; Amos 4:6–11; Jonah 3:8.

149. E.g., Isa 5:13; 39:6, 7; Jer 13:19; 20:4–6; 21:7, 10; 22:25; 25:9, 11; 27:8–22; 28:14; Ezek 12:3–11; Amos 5:5, 27; 6:7; 7:11, 17; Mic 1:16; 4:10.

150. E.g., Isa 1:26; 24–27; 40–66; Jer 15:19; 27:22; 29:14; 30:3, 17–18; 31:23, 31; 32:44; 33:6–11, 26; 50:19; Ezek 16:53; 34:11–31; 36:22–38; 39:25; Dan 9:25; Hos 6:11; 7:1; Joel 2:25; 3:1; Amos 9:11–14; Zeph 2:7; 3:20, cf. Zech 9:12.

151. E.g., Zech 1:3–6; Mal 1:6—2:16; 3:6–18.

152. E.g., Hag 1:2–11; Zech 1:16; 2:4–13; 6:12–13; 8:3–16; 8:9.

153. E.g., Hag 2:5–9, 20–23; Zech 1:17; 2:9; 3:1–5; 8:20–23; 9:9—10:12; 12:1—14:21; Mal 4:1–6.

the Baptist, was a pointer that God was soon to intervene, either directly or through a Theo figure. Jesus' authoritative teaching and rebuke of Israel and its leadership would excite great interest, but would be ambiguous. Indeed, for the leaders, it excited antagonism, for a true Theo would vindicate himself before them, join forces with them, and make his move on Rome.

For the disciples who traveled with Jesus, the miracles and teaching had a cumulative effect. Over time, because of the amazing array of miracles Jesus performed, it dawned on the disciples that Jesus was more than a prophet. He was the Messiah. They had the advantage of seeing every miracle, and Jesus explaining all that he taught in private (Mark 4:34). Yet, there is no indication at any point that they had any sense that Jesus was anything but a political and military Davidic messiah. That is because this was their expectation, and the deeper purposes of Jesus were beyond them.

Jesus and Israel's Leaders

Through the narrative of Mark 1:14—8:29, Jesus clashed continually with Israel's leaders. As noted earlier, this puts Jesus in continuity with the prophets of old who challenged Israel's king, priests, false prophets, and elders. Understanding Jesus' clash with Jewish authorities, considering the Jewish expectations of Theo, is critical. Piecing together expectations of a God-sent redeemer in Israel as we have, it becomes apparent that people would expect Theo to marshal the leaders together for the God-endorsed revolution and the subjugation of those who opposed him as he launched his assault. His inner circle would be composed of Israel's leaders rather than merely a ragtag bunch of Galilean fishermen, tax collectors, and nationalistic Jews. He would produce supernatural signs for them verifying his creditials as God's anointed sent for the task of liberating Israel. They would not be his target; rather, his end game should be the Romans. So, if Jesus is Messiah, Daniel's Son of Man, the Prophet, or Elijah, or any other of the expected Theo figures, the leaders expected he would respond to their inquiries for his identity and performing signs, and they would support him as he led the assault on the Romans.

Again, Moses is the ideal prototype of this. When he returned to Egypt from the Midian wilderness, he was armed with his three signs for the Jewish leadership (staff-snake; leprous hand; Nile-blood), as previously discussed (Exod 4:1–9). Aaron, Moses' brother, a Levite, and so a priest (Exod 4:14) was sent by God to meet Moses at Sinai, and after showing Aaron the signs, Aaron joined Moses (Exod 4:27–28). Moses and Aaron then gathered "all the elders of the people of Israel" (Exod 4:29) and Aaron, as Moses' mouthpiece, spoke on Moses' behalf, while Moses performed the signs (Exod 4:29–30). The response in Exodus 4:31 is critical: "and the people believed; and when they heard that the LORD had visited the people of Israel and that he had seen their affliction, they bowed their heads and worshiped." The "elders" are clearly the leaders of Israel.[154] Here they acknowledge that Moses and Aaron, prophet and priest, are indeed God's agents for their deliverance. It is likely that the Jewish leaders would expect the same.

Gathering and convincing the Jewish leaders at the time of Jesus would have been no easy feat because of the fragmentation of Israel's leadership. We can identify a range of them, including Herod's retinue, the Sanhedrin, Sadducees, Pharisees, Essenes, and priests. Some of these leaders may be a target of any Theo figure; namely, those that did not oppose Rome but syncretized the faith to Greco-Roman values and collaborated.

Leaders a Theo Figure May Oppose

THE HERODIANS

It is likely that Jesus, as a legitimate Theo figure, would have been expected to reject and destroy the Herodian dynasty. Most particularly, Herod and his family were despised and seen as puppets of Rome. The Herodian dynasty ruled from around 37 BC to AD 100.[155] Herod the Great's (37–4 BC) father Antipater II was an Idumean (Josephus, *J.W.* 1.123; *Ant.* 14.8). Through his father's support of Rome, Herod became governor of Galilee from 47 to 37 BC, dealing with threats like the messianic pretender Ezekias (Josephus, *Ant.* 14.159; *J.W.* 1.204). Herod was appointed King of Judea by Antony, Octavius, and the Senate after a trip to Rome in which he wooed them. By ancient standards (some might say modern ones, in some contexts), Herod the Great was a very clever politician (Josephus, *Ant.* 14.370-89; *J.W.* 1.274-85, cf. Strabo, *Geogr.* 26.2.46; Tacitus, *Hist.* 5.9). He captured Galilee and Jerusalem in 37 BC, married a Hasmonean, and killed Antigonus, ending Hasmonean rule (Josephus, *Ant.* 14.439—16.26; *J.W.* 1.16.7—18.3; Dio Cassius 49.22). His power was clearly gained with Roman support. He was brutal, as the slaughter of the children of Bethlehem indicates (Matt

---

154. Elwell and Beitzel ("Elder," 679) define the elder as a "person who, by virtue of position in the family, clan, or tribe; or by reason of personality, prowess, stature, or influence; or through a process of appointment and ordination, exercised leadership and judicial functions in both religious and secular spheres in the ancient world, both among biblical and nonbiblical peoples."

155. Including 1) Herod the Great (47–4 BC); 2) Archelaus (4 BC–AD 6); 3) Philip the Tetrarch (4 BC–AD 34); and 4) Herod Antipas (4 BC–AD 39).

2:1–18).¹⁵⁶ The historicity of this is questioned by some, but is consistent with Herod's brutality, and the ancient game of thrones where despots were paranoid, and opponents (even babies) should be wiped out, whatever the collateral damage.¹⁵⁷ Jews despised him for being an Idumean and for his relationship with the Romans. He greatly favored his supporters (as at the banquet in Mark 6) and brutally oppressed his enemies (Josephus, *Ant.* 15.1–2; *J.W.* 1.358–60). When Octavius gained control, Herod traveled to Rhodes, and his kingship was affirmed. Enamored with Greek culture, he sent his sons to Rome for their education, and to be received by Caesar. He also violated Jewish law, introducing Greek games, building theaters, amphitheaters, and hippodromes (Josephus, *Ant.* 15.267–76; 17.10.3; *J.W.* 2.39–45). His favor in Rome is reflected in Augustus granting him substantial territories in Trachonitis, Batanea, Auranitis, and Zenodorus, the tetrarchy of Perea, and making Syrian procurators responsible to him. Herod built a temple for Augustus in Zenodorus as a response (Josephus, *Ant.* 15.354–64; *J.W.* 1.398–400, 404–6, 483–84). He also began the rebuild of the Jerusalem temple (20/19 BC–AD 63; Josephus, *Ant.* 15.380–425, cf. John 2:20). He had ten wives, meaning that the final ten years of his reign were marked by great rivalry for political succession (Josephus, *Ant.* 17.19–22; *J.W.* 1.561–63). While he reduced taxation in this time, he was repudiated by many for his love of Greco-Roman culture and religion (Josephus, *Ant.* 15.365–72; 16.58–65). One can easily see why Herod was despised.¹⁵⁸

After much intrigue, Herod was ultimately succeeded by Archelaus (4 BC–AD 6), and he gave little reason to improve the populace's view of the Herodians. Archelaus was the son of Herod and a Samaritan Mathace, and succeeded Herod as ethnarch of Idumea, Judea, and Samaria, hoping to ultimately become king. He treated Jews and Samaritans brutally, once killing three thousand pilgrims at an uprising at Passover. His viciousness is indicated by Matthew 2:20–23, where Joseph avoids his territories on his return from Egypt (cf. Josephus, *J.W.* 2.111–13). He replaced the high priest Joazar with his brother Eleazar, and then Jesus, son of See. He divorced and

---

156. See Hagner (*Matt 1–13*, 37), who notes that the number killed was likely around twenty, as the population was likely one thousand. This was greatly exaggerated in the early church, with Byzantine tradition suggesting fourteen thousand, and Syrian tradition at sixty-four thousand.

157. As Hagner notes in *Matt 1–13*, 37: "that Herod could perpetrate such a horrendous act is consistent with what history has recorded about him. His ruthlessness knew no bounds when it came to protecting his throne, as can be seen in the oft-mentioned example of the execution of his wife Mariamne and his own sons Alexander and Aristobulus in AD 6 or 7, and thereafter his son Antipater (Josephus, *Ant.* 16.392–94; 17.182–87). And this is but a token of his atrocities."

158. For more detail, see Hoehner, "Herodian Dynasty," 318–21.

remarried| Glaphyra, daughter of the Cappadocian king Archelaus and former wife of his half-brother Alexander, in violation of the law (Josephus, *Ant.* 17.339–41; *J.W.* 2.114–16). This led to great unrest, which he quelled oppressively. This led to his banishment to Gaul in AD 6 as Jews, Samaritans, and his brothers petitioned Augustus. Idumea, Judea, and Samaria were reduced to one imperial province with each region under its own prefect; e.g., Pontius Pilate (Josephus, *Ant.* 17.339–54; *J.W.* 2.111–18; Strabo, *Geogr.* 16.2.46; Dio Cassius 55.27.6).

Archelaus was succeeded by Philip the Tetrarch (4 BC–AD 34), who ruled over the northeastern regions of Herod's sphere (Gaulanitis, Auranitis, Batanea, Trachonitis, Paneas and Iturea [Luke 3:1; cf. Josephus, *Ant.* 17.9.4; *J.W.* 2.6.3]). He rebuilt and enlarged Paneas, renaming it "Caesarea Philippi" in his own and Caesar's honor. This town is vital to this discussion, it being where Jesus is professed to be Messiah (below, Mark 8:27; Matt 16:13). He also rebuilt and enlarged Bethsaida, renaming it "Julias" in honor of Julia, Augustus's daughter (Mark 8:22–26; Luke 9:10). He was well-liked (Josephus, *Ant.* 18.106–8). He married Herodias's dancing daughter Salome, who was pivotal in the story of John the Baptist's death (Mark 6:17–29 and parr, cf. Josephus, *Ant.* 18.5.2).

At the time of most of Jesus' life (Matt 2:22), Herod Antipas (4 BC–AD 39) the younger brother of Archelaus ruled Galilee and Perea. He rebuilt Sepphoris (ca. AD 8–10), only seven kilometers (four miles) from Nazareth. It is possible that a young Jesus worked there as a carpenter (Matt 6:3) with his father, Joseph. Although, if Matthew's Gospel is trusted, Joseph may have avoided anything any of the Herods was involved in after the attempt on Jesus' life as a baby. Antipas also built Tiberias in the pattern of a Greek polis, a work completed in AD 25, and other possible places Jesus worked. His first marriage was a political alliance with the daughter of Aretas IV, the daughter of the Nabatean king. However, he divorced his Nabatean wife and married Herodias, his brother Antipas's ex-wife (Josephus, *Ant.* 18.116–19).[159] This slight against Aretas would come back to haunt him later.

His marriage led to John the Baptist's rebuke based on the law (Lev 18:16; 20:21). He had John beheaded in AD 31 or 32 (Luke 6:14–29; Matt 14:1–12; Luke 9:7–9). As the people highly regarded John, this further incited hatred for the Herodians. Antipas considered Jesus to be John resurrected (Luke 6:14–16; Matt 14:1–2; Luke 3:19–20; 9:7–9). Luke records that Antipas sought to see Jesus, but Jesus withdrew (Luke 9:9). Jesus warned the disciples to avoid Herod's teaching (Mark 8:15). According to Luke, Antipas

---

159. On the identity of Herodias's first wife, see Hoehner, "Herodian Dynasty," 323–24.

did get to see Jesus during his trial, and hoped to see him perform a sign. However, Jesus was silent, and after his soldiers mocked him, Herod sent him back to Pilate (Luke 23:7-11, cf. Acts 4:27). Luke also records that, on one occasion, Herod sought to kill him, but Jesus sent a message to "that fox" concerning his miracles and his impending death (Luke 13:31-35).[160]

There is ample evidence that the Herodians were extremely unpopular in the general populace. Any Theo figure would surely be expected at some point to target him along with the Romans. In Jesus' case, he had good personal reason to attack Herod Antipas. First, in accepting Matthew's account, Antipas's father Herod the Great had massacred the children of Bethlehem, seeking to kill Jesus, and driving him and his family away from Bethlehem to Egypt (Matt 2:1-19). Second, Antipas had put to death Jesus' close relative and baptizer, the great prophet John (Mark 6:14-29; Matt 14:1-12). Third, Antipas wanted to kill Jesus (Mark 3:6; Luke 13:31). However, Jesus shows no interest in allying with Antipas or attacking him. Rather, he repudiated the Herodians sent to question him (Mark 12:13-17 and parr.), avoided Herod (Luke 9:9), warned people against him (Mark 8:15), and refused to answer him when Antipas met him (Luke 23:7-11).

Mark's explanation of Herod's killing of John the Baptist plays an important narrative function in presenting "King" Herod in stark contrast to Jesus, Messiah and Son of God. Herod is described as the king (*ho basileus*, Mark 6:14). Jesus is the true king, although the term is never used of him, likely because of its negative associations (at least in regards to Jesus as king). Jesus is totally subservient to his God, whereas Herod is Rome's puppet and defied God and his law. Herod exercised his power by sending (*apostellō*) and seizing (*krateō*) John coercively (Mark 6:17). In the previous pericope, Jesus sent (*apostellō*) his apostles with no provision to preach, heal, and deliver (Mark 6:7). Antipas's arrest of John is the stuff of despotic paranoid rule (Mark 6:17-18). Jesus' sending is the stuff of the upside-down kingdom God was advancing through him. John's crime was merely to proclaim God's word, speaking out against the illegal and unethical practices of the king. John's critique cuts to the heart of Israel's view of marriage as the center of human society and life (Gen 1:27; 2:24), and its repudiation of incestual relations. Jesus will uphold Israel's view of marriage in Mark 10:1-12. Herod's taking of Philip's wife is also an example of his abuse of power. Jesus plays no such games with women or others. He endorsed faithful marriage and repudiated divorce (again, 10:1-12). Herodias plays the role of the wife of an ancient king, ever involved in political machinations, plotting and scheming to advance her and her family's status. However, she

---

160. For more on the Herodians, see Hoehner, "Herodian Dynasty," 317-25.

had to overcome Herod's respect for John, whom he liked to listen to, despite John greatly perplexing (*polla ēporei*) him (Mark 6:19–20).[161] Further, "he protected him" (*synetērei auton*), suggesting he actively ensured John's safety, likely against Herodias's attempts to have him removed.

In what looks like a brilliant set-up based on Herodias's recognition of Herod's lusts, her daughter danced for Herod and excited his passions to the point that he was prepared to do anything she wanted. The context is a classic example of ancient political hospitality; a (no doubt elaborate) banquet to which *only the elite* are invited—the nobles, military commanders, and leading people (*prōtos*, cf. Mark 9:35; 10:31) of Galilee (6:21). Luke's Jesus repudiates such a banquet, urging a Pharisee and host to invite the marginalized to a meal and then giving the Parable of the Great Banquet, in which God invites all, including those at the edge, to his cosmic feast (Luke 14). Here Antipas's guests are served by a retinue of servants, whereas Jesus and his disciples are not to be served, but to serve others (Mark 9:35–37; 10:42–45). In the previous passage, Jesus' disciples went to serve without provision (Mark 6:7–12).

In the passage that follows, the disciples return from their ministry of service, and are urged by Jesus come with him to a desolate place and rest and find space from their hectic work to eat (6:30–31). However, the crowds recognize and follow. Jesus does not turn them away, but, like Herod, he holds a banquet (6:32–33). Jesus, moved by compassion for the crowd, who are like sheep without the protection and provision of the shepherd, feeds them first from God's word (6:34). Then he holds a banquet for the crowds of five thousand men (and who knows how many women and children).[162] Invited are the poor and destitute who have come seeking God's word and touch. The "prominent people" are not to be seen—they are at Antipas's party. Jesus, like Herod, provides, but the meal is simple (bread and fish) and multiplied by God, yet "all are satisfied" (6:42). There are no dancers mentioned. Herodias' dance was no doubt highly provocative, so that Herod

---

161. The verb *aporeō* (perplexed) is used elsewhere of the women's confusion at the tomb (Luke 24:4), of the disciples' confusion concerning who would betray Jesus (John 13:22), Festus's uncertainty of what to do with Jesus (Acts 25:20), and Paul's perplexed state (2 Cor 4:8; Gal 4:20). It speaks of real uncertainty and confusion.

162. The Greek is not *anthrōpos* which could be inclusive and equal the total five thousand. Rather, Mark uses the plural of *anēr*, man, indicating that this is the number of men. Matthew 14:21 notes that there were "five thousand men, besides women and children," indicating a massive crowd. France (*Gospel of Mark*, 168) suggests this could indicate only men were present. However, Matthew's version calls this into question. The population of Capernaum and Bethsaida at the time was only two to three thousand each (Witherington, *Mark*, 220; Lane, *Mark*, 231; Marcus, *Mark 1–8*, 413), so this indicates Jesus' massive popularity.

and his guests were "pleased" (v. 22). Likely, this means (at least in part) that they were aroused. This led to Herod's foolish offer to give Herodias whatever she wanted, "up to half of my kingdom" (v. 23)—here is a foolish leader whose mind is in his trousers. In all the Gospels, Jesus is not interested in sexual relationships, illicit or otherwise; he does not treat women as sexual objects. Rather, he repudiates sexual immorality, which is anything that violates sexual relationships in the context of heterosexual faithful monogamous marriage (Mark 7:21; 10:11-12, 19, cf. Matt 5:27-32; 15:19; 19:9, 18; Luke 16:18; 18:20).

Herodias and her mother ignored all sorts of other things they could have claimed from Herod's offer, and seized the opportunity to have John killed. Despite his horror and held by his honor to keep his promise, Antipas ordered John to be killed (vv. 26-28). The beheading of John contrasts Antipas with Jesus. Again, he sent (*apostellō*) an executioner to do his bidding—to act with violence and behead John. This again vividly contrasts with Jesus' sending of the Twelve, not to behead and kill, as one might expect from a military messiah, but to heal and restore. Jesus came to end violence and restore, Herod perpetuates it. The violence is horrific—a beheading and the head served on a platter (cf. Eddard Stark's beheading in "Game of Thrones"). Finally, it is noteworthy that John's disciples come and take John and bury him. Later, when Jesus the true king is ruthlessly killed, there are no disciples to come for his body. It takes a courageous Sanhedrin member Joseph of Arimathea to do so (15:42-47). Jesus shows no interest in wooing the Herodians.

Nor does Jesus show interest in attacking Herod and avenging the death of John. Such an act would be socially appropriate and honorable for a member of John's family. Indeed, with a well-fed army of five thousand men, Jesus was well-positioned to storm Antipas. It is also likely that many of these men harbored zealous desires to overthrow Rome and rid the country of the Herodians. As Edwards states:

> Rural Galilee was a stronghold of the Zealot movement (Acts 5:37). The Zealot movement was founded in AD 6 by Judas *the Galilean*, who hailed from Gamala in the hills to the east of Bethsaida (Josephus, *War* 2.118). Two of his grandsons, Menahem and Eleazar, perished in the battle for Masada in the early 70s of the first century (*War* 2.433; 7.253). Even before Judas, the independent sentiments of Galilee had resulted in stiff resistance against Herod the Great prior to his accession of the throne in 37 BC, and when he died in 4 BC Sepphoris in Galilee revolted against the transferal of his throne to his sons. Josephus, who commanded the forces in Galilee in AD 66-67 against

Vespasian, speaks of the valiant resistance of Galilee against the Roman invasion. Galilee—and particularly this part of Galilee which lay within eyeshot of Gamala—was, in other words, the spearhead of freedom movements against Rome, and particularly of the Zealot movement.[163]

Indeed, it is likely that many of these men were drawn to the second Joshua with his twelve "mighty men" because they sensed in him the possibility of a revolution. The idea of a shepherd in Mark 6:34 also has potential military overtones, often used of a "Joshua-like military hero who would muster Israel's forces for war . . . It is, in other words, a metaphor of hegemony, including military leadership and victory."[164] Edwards suggests that "the wilderness commotion was aflame with messianic fervor, and that the crowd hoped to sweep Jesus up as a guerrilla leader" (cf. John 6:14-15).[165] However, this is not Jesus' plan; he will not "march to a populist and militarist drumbeat. He will not be a militant-messianic shepherd of the sheep."[166] Rather, he chooses to feed the crowds, providing spiritual food (the word, cf. Matt 4:4; Luke 4:4) and physical food (bread and fish), and moving on to find others.

The Sadducees

Neither is Jesus interested in working with the Sadducees or directly challenging their rule. As part of the elite, many of the Sadducees were collaborators with Rome. The Sadducees repudiated fate (Josephus, *Ant.* 13.173), rejected the immortality of the soul (Josephus, *Ant.* 18.16), and rejected the oral law, concerned only with the Torah (Josephus, *Ant.* 13.297; 18.16). The Gospels and Acts also indicate that they rejected resurrection (Mark 12:18-27; Matt 22:23-33; Luke 20:27-40; Acts 4:2; 23:6-8) and the existence of angels and spirits (Acts 23:8). They were influential mainly among the rich and those of status (Josephus, *Ant.* 13.298; 18.17). They were political expedients. Josephus records that when they took up a position as a magistrate, they took on the ideas of the Pharisees to gain popularity (Josephus, *Ant.* 18.17). They were extremely harsh on offenders (Josephus, *Ant.* 20.199). The high priest Annas was a Sadducee, and perhaps others were as well (Josephus, *Ant.* 20.199). Matthew's John the Baptist encounters them

---

163. Edwards, *Mark*, 194.

164. Edwards, *Mark*, 191; see Num 27:17; 1 Kgs 22:17 (also 2 Chr 18:16); Jer 10:21; Ezek 34:5; 37:24; Nah 3:18; Zech 13:7; Jdt 11:19.

165. Ibid., 195.

166. Ibid., *Mark*, 195.

with vitriol, branding them with the Pharisees as a "brood of vipers," calling for them to repent and warning them of forthcoming wrath (Matt 3:7–10). They came to Jesus with the Pharisees, requesting a sign. Jesus refuses, other than offering the sign of Jonah, which points to the resurrection. He then warns his disciples against the Pharisees' teaching (Matt 16:1–12). With the Sanhedrin and Temple authorities, they strongly opposed the nascent Christian movement in Jerusalem (Acts 4:1–3; 5:17).

As collaborators with the Romans and with a flawed theology, any genuine Theo figure would likely target them. However, just as they showed only scant interest in Jesus, Jesus shows no interest in attacking them or drawing him to his side. Instead, he critiqued them severely (Matt 3:7). He refused their requests for a sign (Matt 16:1), warning people of their false teaching (Matt 16:6, 11–12), and demolished them in public theological debate (Mark 12:18–27 and parr.).

The Priests

As with others who collaborate with Rome, Jesus shows little interest in taking on the priests of Israel. Many of the priests were Sadducees, and many were Roman appointees. By the first century AD, the priestly power had waned from its zenith in the mid-second century BC. While the priesthood was mainly genealogical in the first half of the first century AD, Herod the Great (37–4 BC) usurped the appointment of the high priest, whose power waned. After Herod's death, the high priest worked more closely with the Roman authorities. This indicates that most were from the Sadducees, who were more prone to collaborate with Rome. Under Rome, the high priest's influence was greater, with control of the Temple, the priesthood, Sanhedrin, and had Roman support with the power to collect taxes.[167] The high priest at the time of Christ was Joseph Caiaphas (AD 18–36/37; Matt 26:3, 57; Luke 3:2; John 11:47; 18:13–14, 24, 28, cf. Annas, Luke 3:2). He is a politically savvy character, wanting Jesus' death for the sake of Israel (John 11:50). Also, mentioned in the Gospels and Josephus are the "chief priests" (*archiereis*) (Luke 19:47; 20:19; 22:2, 4, 52; 23:4–5, 10, 13; 24:20; Josephus, *J.W.* 2.236–341). Josephus names them alongside the Sanhedrin as "men of power," indicating their importance. Under the high priest, they likely had oversight of the cult, temple, treasury, and other priests and Levites. They

---

167. On the priesthood, see Green and Hurst, "Priest, Priesthood," 634–36.

may have been Sanhedrin members (Mark 14:53; Luke 22:66).[168] Many of the priests, too, would likely be targets of any genuine Theo figure.[169]

Jesus' response to the priests is, at times, positive, urging some whom he healed to present to priests to confirm their healing, and see them reinstituted into fellowship (Mark 1:44 and parr.; Luke 17:14). He also endorsed the behavior of priests at the time of David (Mark 2:26 and parr.). However, he also tacitly critiques the priests and Levites in the parable of the Samaritan (Luke 10:31–32). He also predicts that the priests, along with other Jewish leaders, will be complicit in his death (Mark 8:31; 10:33; Matt 16:21; 20:18; Luke 9:22; 19:47; 22:2–4; John 18:3). Their concerns over the crowds at his entry and his authority are disregarded (Mark 11:27; Matt 21:15–16; 21:23–27; Luke 20:1, 19), and with other Jewish leaders, they are ruthlessly critiqued, especially in the Parable of the Tenants (Mark 12:1–12 and parr.). Despite the chief priests gathering false witnesses (Mark 14:55–59 and parr.), Jesus made no move to defend himself against the high priest's charges and mocking (Mark 14:60–65 and parr.; John 18:19–24), when they bound him and brought him to Pilate (Mark 15:1–5 and parr.) or when the priests and other leaders incited the people to call for the release of Barabbas and Jesus' crucifixion (Mark 15:7–15 and parr.; John 19:1–16). All in all, Jesus had no desire to include the Sadducees in his plans or oppose them.

The Sanhedrin

The Sanhedrin, made up of seventy-one members in Jerusalem,[170] by the end of the Maccabean period was "wide spread in the Greek literature for the supreme Jerusalem council."[171] It was convened by the high priest, and included in its membership chief priests, elders (Matt 26:3; 27:1; 28:11–12),[172]

---

168. See further ibid., 636.

169. Not all. Take, for example, Zechariah, the father of John the Baptist, who is portrayed very positively (Luke 1:5–25).

170. The idea of seventy can be tracked back to Numbers 11:16 (cf. Josephus, *J.W.* 2.482; Let. Arist. 46–50; *m. Sanh.* 1:6; Luke 10:1).

171. Twelftree, "Sanhedrin," 728. He also notes that the term can refer to any judicial body, or even the assembly room (Luke 22:66). Josephus uses it for the Jerusalem council (Josephus, *Ant.* 14.167–80; *Life* 62). He also uses it for five districts and the councils created by Gabinius in Israel (Josephus, *Ant.* 14.89–91). Elsewhere in Greek literature, it was used of councils from various contexts. Mishnah sources suggest that there were multiple Sanhedrins, giving rise to a range of theories. However, these reflect later developments (see p. 729).

172. By New Testament times, the Sanhedrin consisted of priests and lay members of the nobility. Twelftree ("Sanhedrin," 731) notes, "From observing the synonyms for these elders we learn that they are leading men of the people (Luke 19:47; Josephus, *Life*

scribes (Acts 5:34; 23:6; Josephus, *Ant.* 18.17; *J.W.* 2.411), leading citizens, Sadducees, Pharisees, and others (Matt 26:59; Mark 14:55; 15:1; Luke 22:66; John 11:47; Acts 5:21; 6:12; 22:30; 23:20; 23:28). The dominant group in the Sanhedrin were the priests and Sadducees (cf. 1 Macc 7:33; 11:23; 14:28).[173] The key player was the high priest who presided over the council (Matt 26:57; 27:41; Mark 14:54; Acts 5:17; 24:1; 1 Macc 14:44; Josephus, *J.W.* 2.301, 316–42; *Ant.* 20.200, 251; *Ag. Ap.* 2.194). The high priest was a political appointment or hereditary. Another important participant was the captain of the temple (Acts 4:1). There was also a secretary (Josephus, *J.W.* 5.532). As such, it was dominated by Israel's priestly aristocracy and Sadducees (cf. Acts 4:1; 5:17; Josephus, *Ant.* 20.199). The one positive light from the Sanhedrin in the Synoptic story is Joseph of Arimathea who, while apparently making little attempt to defend Jesus before the Council, courageously sought his body from Pilate (Mark 15:43–46; Luke 23:50–53). When before the Sanhedrin, Jesus did not seek to impress them with signs or draw them to his cause. He said little, and what he did say caused them to react viciously, mocking him and beating him and sending him to Pilate, hopefully to be sentenced to death (Mark 14:62–65; 15:1).

The Romans

Surely a Theo figure would, at some point, make moves toward the Romans. Yet, in the leadup to the Passion, aside from one cryptic discussion about paying taxes to Caesar (12:14–17), the Romans do not feature. In Mark's Passion Narrative, even when before Pilate and among Roman soldiers, Jesus shows no interest in challenging Rome. Indeed, as I will discuss later, Jesus is remarkably silent going to his death, without raising so much as a whimper (15:1–41). Aside from Pilate, the only Roman of significance is the centurion who oversaw Jesus' execution, but then becomes the only person in the Markan narrative to genuinely confess Jesus' divine sonship at the cross (15:39, cf. 15:44–45). The first fruit of the nations yielding to Christ is seen in this man's confession. Matthew and Luke add to Mark's story the account of the Roman centurion who sends to Jesus for healing. Jesus defies social protocol and heads to the centurion's house. He does not refuse the centurion's request or launch an assault on him, but agrees to serve the gentile, healing his servant. Jesus was prepared to give a sign to those who were genuinely seeking his help. He then commends the centurion for

---

194), the leading men of Jerusalem, the powerful and the dignitaries (Josephus, *J.W.* 2.316, 410; *Life* 9).''

173. Witherington, *Mark*, 383.

his outstanding faith, which transcends what he had found in Israel (Matt 8:5–13; Luke 7:1–10). Luke also adds details of the Roman historical context (Luke 2:1; 3:1) and one reference to Pilate's brutality (Luke 13:1). At no point does Jesus shows the slightest inclination to launch an assault on the Romans. He is just not that sort of messiah.

Leaders a Theo Figure Would Potentially Work With

Other Jewish leaders would seem likely to be targeted positively by a genuine Theo figure; particularly the Pharisees, who held tightly to Israel's law and traditions, the Essenes, who sought purity and challenged Israel's corrupt religious system, and the Zealots, who wanted to overthrow Rome.

THE PHARISEES

The Pharisees are the most frequently mentioned Jewish leaders in the Gospels, mentioned eighty-eight times. Alongside the Sadducees and Essenes, Josephus regarded the Pharisees as one of the three key Jewish religious parties (Josephus, *Life* 10). He himself speaks of following their teaching (Josephus, *Life* 12, 21). They had a strong interest in Jewish law (Josephus, *Life* 191). Unlike the Sadducees, they accepted a wider body of law, including the Torah, the rest of the Old Testament, and the oral law (Josephus, *Ant.* 13.297, cf. Josephus, *Life* 191; *Ant.* 17.41). They had a strong concern for reason (Josephus, *Ant.* 18.3). They were concerned with food laws and despised delicate food (Josephus, *Ant.* 18.3). They rejected table fellowship with sinners (Mark 2:16 and parr.; Luke 15:2). They maintained hand washing protocols before eating (Mark 7:3, 5; Luke 11:38). They fasted regularly (Mark 2:18 and parr.; Luke 18:12). They practiced tithing carefully (Matt 23:23; Luke 11:42; 18:12). They were deeply concerned with protecting the prohibition against work on the Sabbath (Matt 12:2; Mark 2:24; Luke 6:2, 7; 14:1–3). They believed in a balance of fate (predestination) and human volition (Josephus, *Ant.* 13.172). They may have accepted the immortality of the soul and believed in eternal reward and punishment based on the goodness of a life lived (Josephus, *Ant.* 18.3). In Acts, Luke notes their concern for circumcision (Acts 15:5) and their affirmation of resurrection and acceptance of spiritual forces (Acts 23:6–8). They had a high regard for the elderly among them (Josephus, *Ant.* 18.3). They lived to please God (Josephus, *Ant.* 13.289). They advocated more moderate punishment for offenders (Josephus, *Ant.* 13.293–94). They repudiated divorce to varying degrees (Mark 10:2–12; Matt 19:3–12; John 8:3). Due to their virtue, they

THE MESSIAH REVEALED (MARK 1:1—8:29)

were greatly popular and persuasive among the general populace who followed their prescribed patterns of worship (Josephus, *Ant.* 13.298; 18:3). They opposed Herod and Caesar on occasion (Josephus, *Ant.* 17.41–46).

Jesus' response to the Pharisees is consistently negative, as was John the Baptist, who labeled them a "brood of snakes" and warned them of God's wrath (Matt 3:7). They constantly challenged Jesus, criticizing him for a range of things. These included breaking table fellowship law and eating with tax collectors and sinners (Mark 2:16; Matt 9:11; Luke 5:30; 7:39; 15:2); refusing to fast (Mark 2:18; Matt 9:14; Luke 5:33); being empowered by Satan in his deliverance ministry (Matt 9:34; 12:24); harvesting and eating on the Sabbath (Mark 2:24; Matt 12:2; Luke 6:2); breaking hand-washing protocols at meals (Mark 7:1–5; Matt 15:1–2; Luke 11:38); pronouncing forgiveness (Luke 5:17–21); healing on the Sabbath (Luke 6:7; 14:3); and his disciples at the entry to Jerusalem (Luke 19:39). They also challenged Jesus' understanding of marriage and divorce (Mark 10:2; Matt 19:3) and the coming kingdom (Luke 17:20). Matthew's Jesus also expected greater righteousness from Christ's disciples than the Pharisees (Matt 5:20).

John notes other points of Pharisee engagement with Jesus frequently (John 4:1; 8:3, 13; 9:13–17, 40). Jesus' response is not to woo them, but to warn others of their teaching (Mark 8:15; Matt 16:6, 11–12; Luke 12:1), to consistently engage them in theological debate, to rebuke them, challenge their theology and authority, and warn them of God's judgment (Matt 21:33–46; 22:41–46; 23:2–36; Luke 11:38–54; 16:14–15; 18:10–11). Their requests for a vindicating sign were constantly rejected; absolutely so in Mark (Mark 8:11–12). In Luke and, at other times, in Matthew, the future resurrection (the sign of Jonah) is offered as the only sign (Matt 12:38–39; 16:1–4; Luke 11:16, 29–30). Not surprisingly, with Jesus seeming to almost provoke them with his relentless critique and violation of their way of understand Yahwism, they seek to trap and kill him (Mark 3:6; 12:13; Matt 12:14; 22:15, 34; Luke 6:7; 11:53; John 7:32; 7:45–52; 11:46–57; 12:19; 18:3). Matthew also records that they tried to stop any possibility of claims to Jesus' resurrection (Matt 27:62). Luke has some positive moments, where Pharisees warn Jesus of a Herodian death plot (Luke 13:31), and Jesus shares table fellowship with Pharisees (Luke 7:36; 11:37; 14:1). John, too, speaks of the spiritual development of Nicodemus from blindness to discipleship (John 3:1–15; 7:50; 19:39).

In Acts, Luke speaks of the clemency of Gamaliel (Acts 5:34) and Pharisee involvement in circumcision disputes in the church (Acts 15:5). Paul was also a Pharisee before his conversion (Acts 23:6; 26:8; Phil 3:5). However, Jesus made no effort to identify with the Pharisees and draw them to his cause. Rather, he antagonized them, even naming them alongside the despised Herod, as people to be rejected (Mark 8:15). Hardly what would be expected of a Theo figure seeking support to overthrow Rome.

The Scribes

While portrayed as a unified group in the Synoptics, the scribes (*grammateus*)[174] or lawyers (Luke 10:25) were recognized as authoritative legal teachers of Judaism who functioned as officials and advisors to the key leadership groups in Israel. They were likely concerned with legal proceedings, enforcement of Judaism's custom and law, and business related to their function.[175] They are sometimes partnered with: priests and often chief priests (Mark 11:27; 14:1, 43, 53; Matt 2:4; 21:15; Luke 5:30;[176] 6:7; 9:22; 19:47; 20:1, 19; 22:2, 66;[177] 23:10), elders (Mark 11:27; 14:43, 53; 15:1, 31; Luke 9:22; 20:1; 22:66; Acts 4:5; 6:12), the Sanhedrin (Mark 15:1;[178] Luke 19:47;[179] Acts 4:5;[180] 6:12[181]), and the Pharisees (Mark 2:16; 7:1; Matt 5:20; 12:38; 15:1; 23:2, 13, 15, 23, 25, 27, 29, 34; Luke 5:21; 11:53; 15:2; Acts 23:9[182]). Likely, there were then scribes associated with each group.

They first appear in Mark in 1:22, where Jesus the teacher is compared to the scribes—he teaches with authority, whereas the scribes do not. This likely refers to the scribes' pattern of passing on teaching as a recital of tradition learned from others.[183] We find this type of thing in the Mishnah, in the pattern "R. XXX says, . . ."[184] Jesus, on the other hand, taught with direct,

---

174. Also used in Acts 19:35 of a town clerk, and in 1 Cor 1:20 inclusively of scribes from a Greco-Roman and Jewish sense. The terms here are fluid and, with the balance of Jewish and Greek/Roman concerns over the cross (cf. 1 Cor 1:22–23; 2:6), is probably inclusive.

175. Saldarini ("Scribes," 1015) limits their function to priestly; however, across the Synoptics, there are scribes associated with a range of Jewish leadership groups and likely indicates legal functionaries with each group. Some may have functioned cross-group, e.g., Sanhedrin and Pharisee.

176. Here they are described as "their scribes," suggesting that they are associates or officials of Pharisees in this instance.

177. In this text, the elders are made up of scribes and chief priests.

178. Described as "the whole council."

179. Described as "the principle men of the people."

180. Described as "their rulers."

181. The elders and scribes here may have been members of the Sanhedrin.

182. Described as "the scribes of the Pharisee's Party," indicating that some scribes are Pharisees, cf. Luke 5:30.

183. E.g., Hooker, *Mark*, 63.

184. So, for example, on divorce in Deut 24:1, something important for interpreting Mark 10:1–12 we read:

authoritative interpretation, not concerned with the scribal tradition. The scribes are also found in Mark 2:6, 16, questioning Jesus' teaching on his capacity to forgive and eating with sinners (s.a. 7:1, 5). Their interpretation of Jesus' miraculous ministry is demonic (3:22, previous section). Jesus predicts they will play a part in his death (8:31; 10:33).

Significantly, they appear mostly in narratives concerning Jerusalem, except Mark 2:6; 9:14. However, these scribes may have been Jerusalem lawyers following Jesus and observing him to feed back to their leaders in Jerusalem. There are positive notes, such as when the role of a scribe as a learned guide is endorsed (Matt 13:52; 23:34). Sometimes their interpretation of prophecy is at least partially endorsed (Mark 9:11; Matt 2:4; 17:10).[185] Scribes are also recognized as teachers, even if inferior to Jesus' authoritative teaching (Mark 1:22; Matt 7:29). One seeks to join Jesus (Matt 8:19), another asks him (legitimate?) questions (Mark 12:28, 32), while on another occasion some congratulate his answers (Luke 20:39).

Likely, as with the Pharisees, they are unified as a group in the Synoptic writers' minds because of their general opposition to Jesus alongside other Jewish religious leaders.[186] This includes many of the same concerns as the Pharisees including forgiveness of sin (Mark 2:6; Matt 9:3; Luke 5:21), table fellowship with sinners (Mark 2:16; Luke 15:2), Jesus' supposed Satan-empowered ministry (Mark 3:22, cf. 9:14), eating cleanliness protocols (Mark 7:1, 5; Matt 15:1), Sabbath healing (Luke 6:7), the demand for a sign (Matt 12:38), and indignation over the entry to Jerusalem (Matt 21:15). They regularly come to Jesus enquiring of him with a goal to incriminate him (Mark 12:28, 32; Luke 11:53; 20:1; John 8:3). With the elders, priests, and Sanhedrin they are seen as conspirators in Jesus' death (Mark 8:31; 10:33; 11:18; 14:1, 43, 53; 15:1, 31; Matt 16:21; 20:18; 26:57; 27:41; Luke 9:22; 19:47; 20:19; 22:2, 66; 23:10). With the Pharisees, they are targets of Jesus' at times devastating critique (Mark 12:35, 38; Matt 23:2–34; Luke 20:46). Jesus is not interested in gaining their support.

A. He who delivers a writ of divorce from overseas must state, "In my presence it was written, and in my presence it was signed."

B. *Rabban Gamaliel says*, "Also: He who delivers [a writ of divorce] from Reqem or from Heger [must make a similar declaration]."

C. *R. Eliezer says*, "Even from Kefar Ludim to Lud."

D. *And sages say*, "He must state, 'In my presence it was written, and in my presence it was signed,' only in the case of him who delivers a writ of divorce from overseas,

E. "and him who takes [one abroad]."

185. Matthew seems to affirm that the Jewish scribes recognized rightly the birthplace of the messiah (Mic 5:2). However, while the expectation of Elijah is endorsed, their failure to recognize John the Baptist as "Elijah" is negative.

186. See further Saldarini, "Scribes," 1015.

The Essenes

Although there are attempts by some scholars to make links between John and Jesus' movements with the Essenes, the group is not mentioned in the Gospel accounts or wider New Testament. Jesus shows no interest in allying with them and there is no known interaction with them. This suggests that the Essenes did not consider Jesus a figure worthy of interest, nor did Jesus seek their support.

Summary

It is apparent that Jesus showed no interest in drawing Israel's leadership together for a great conquest of the land and world. Neither did Jesus show favor to one group or the other. All of them were treated with the same disdain when they encountered Jesus. It seems Jesus saw the Jewish religious leadership as profoundly corrupt. Like all of Israel, however, they were invited to join his new movement, but they almost universally rejected Jesus, and he made no effort to include them in his plans. The only exception in Mark is possibly Jairus, whose daughter Jesus healed (5:21–43)[187] and Joseph of Arimathea (15:42–47). More broadly, there is Nicodemus (John 3:1–15; 7:50; 19:39) and one or two others (e.g. Matt 8:19). However, these are people who encountered Jesus and showed interest in him for healing, because of his miracles and teaching, and after his death. There is no effort on Jesus' part to draw any of them to his cause.

Jesus' response to the Sanhedrin, including the high priest, other priests, Pharisees, Sadducees, the Romans, and others, in his final trial and its aftermath, is fascinating when one considers what one might expect. Surely, in his final hour, he would make his move and call them to the "great war to end all wars." We will discuss the bitter irony in the Passion narrative later; suffice it to say here that Jesus is clearly uninterested in garnering their support. Nor is he prepared to launch a military assault on Israel's opponents, as one would expect.

Despite clearly knowing that he would be arrested in Jerusalem at the instigation of these leaders, Jesus unswervingly headed to Jerusalem to face death (Mark 8:31; 9:31; 10:33). While aware that Judas would betray him, Jesus made no move to stop him, and in John's Gospel urges him to do it quickly (Mark 14:18–21 and parr; John 13:25). When arrested, he did not

---

187. The naming of Jairus could indicate that he is an eyewitness, or part of the subsequent Christian movement, see Bauckham, *Jesus and the Eyewitnesses*, 39–55.

attempt to resist, rebuking those who did in Matthew, and in Luke healing one of his arrestors (Mark 14:43–47; Matt 26:47–56; Luke 22:50).

When before the Council, answering the charges of the high priest, despite what are clearly trumped-up charges (Mark 14:55–61 and parr.), Jesus remained silent. When directly asked by the high priest whether he is Messiah, Jesus answered affirmatively and yet provocatively, speaking of his being seated at the right hand of God himself. Yet, he then did nothing to back up his affirmation (Mark 14:61–62 and parr.). Rather, he is completely passive as he is spat upon, mocked as a false prophet, and beaten, all without resistance (Mark 14:65 and parr.).

When the leaders bring him to Pilate, he does nothing to stop them (Mark 15:1 and parr.). When asked by Pilate if he is king of the Jews, he answers cryptically and does nothing to resist further charges (Mark 15:2–5 and parr.). In Luke's account, before Herod, Jesus is again passive, despite being abused, accused, mocked, and his kingship parodied (Luke 23:6–12). Surely, if he is God's Theo agent, he will launch an assault on Pilate to demonstrate his authority and power—similarly when facing Herod, the Roman turncoat and puppet king (in Luke's account, Luke 23:6–12).

When the leaders of Israel infiltrated the crowd and encouraged them to call for Barabbas's release and Jesus' crucifixion, Jesus stood passively without response (Mark 15:6–15). During the violent mockery of his claims to kingship by the Roman soldiers and flogging, he remained inactive (Mark 15:16–20). When crucified and raised on the cross, with the leaders and others mocking him and challenging him to use his power to save himself, he made no defense and died tamely (Mark 15:24–37). Jesus completely repudiated working with any of the Jewish leadership.

Even after his resurrection, one might have expected Jesus to appear in the center of Jerusalem and call the leaders of Israel to his cause and launch an assault on all who opposed him. Jesus' appearances were intermittent and scattered, to a few of his closest followers across Israel and Syria. Accounts of these appearances were hardly enough to convince the leaders of Israel that Jesus was genuine. If he were, he would appear to them rather than his own followers, away from the seats of power.

Ultimately and significantly, Jesus did appear to one person from the Jewish leadership, the Pharisee Saul of Tarsus, who quickly grasped what Jesus was really about and became arguably the critical player in the expansion of the faith to the gentiles.

The Moment of Truth: The Disciples Recognize Jesus Messiah (Mark 8:27–29)

The climax of the first half of Mark is Mark 8:29, when Peter, speaking on behalf of the other disciples, states "You are the Christ [*Christos*]." The whole of the narrative to this point has led to this moment. Mark 1:1 launches the motif of Jesus as Christ, or Messiah, and Son of God—here for the first time it is realized by Jesus' closest followers. Phase one is then complete. The servant-king, who was inaugurated by John the prophet, vindicated by God the Father and empowered by the Spirit, is declared (1:9–11). The one who will finally and ultimately vanquish God's antagonist the devil (1:12–13) and lies at the heart of the establishment of the kingdom of God (1:14) is here made known. All the preaching, teaching, miracles, the clashes with Jewish leaders, the relentless service across Israel on behalf of her poor oppressed people desperate for God's intervention, healing, and justice, has finally achieved its first goal. Jesus' purpose had reached its first climax; phase one was over. Finally, his disciples "got it." Just as the man in the preceding passage at Bethsaida had been healed of his blindness, the spiritual blindness has been lifted off the disciples (Mark 8:22–26). Jesus is the long-awaited Messiah.

The setting could not be more appropriate: Caesarea Philippi. The town was previously called Panias (or Paneion, Paneas), dedicated to the god Pan (Polybius, *Hist.* 16.18.2)—indeed, the remains of a temple of Pan remain in the ruins today, including niches cut into a cliff around a cave. The area was gifted to Herod the Great by Augustus in 20 BC, who passed it onto Philip, the tetrarch of Trachontis, who founded the actual city in AD 2, built it, and renamed it "Kaisereia" in honor of Caesar Augustus (Josephus, *Ant.* 17.189; 18.28; *J.W.* 2.168). It was the seat of Philip's power. Hence it was named Caesarea "Philippi," a name also used to distinguish it from other cities called Caesarea, e.g., Caesarea Maritima.[188] The very name then calls to mind Roman and Herodian power against which Jesus is to be understood.

On the way to this town, Jesus asks his disciples who people consider him to be, recalling Mark 6:14–16, where Mark records various views. They report that some believe him to be John the Baptist rebooted, e.g., Herod Antipas (Mark 6:14, 16). Others consider him Elijah, fulfilling Malachi's hope of a figure after Elijah who would restore the families of Israel before the day of the Lord (Mal 4:5). This makes sense because of Jesus' miracle-working ministry, which recalls the miracles of Elijah. Thirdly, some consider him to be one of the prophets, no doubt implying the likes of Isaiah, Jeremiah, Ezekiel, etc. His challenge to the Jewish leadership and concern

---

188. See Kutsko, "Caesarea Philippi," 803; DeVries, "Caesarea Philippi," 208.

for social justice would call to mind their ministries. What each of these have in common is that Jesus is considered a prophetic figure, and no more.

Finally, Jesus asks the disciples directly who they consider him to be. One can imagine Jesus holding his breath as he asks, "do you get it yet?" Up to this point, he is clearly becoming frustrated with their inability to grasp his identity. Their incomprehension and his frustration are seen in Mark 4:41, when the disciples are terrified in the storm, and Jesus calms the wind and waves challenging their fear and unbelief. Their response is amazement and query, rather than an admission that Jesus is Messiah—"who then is this that even the wind and sea obey him?" Somewhat bizarrely in the following encounter, a man infested with a legion of demons recognizes Jesus as the Son of God. The disciples remain blinded.

This is followed by a series of sensational demonstrations of power, including the amazing exorcism of the legion-possessed man (Mark 5:1-20), the healing of a bleeding woman and the raising of a dead girl (5:21-43), the apostles empowered to heal and deliver evil spirits (6:7-13), the feeding of the five thousand with twelve baskets remaining (6:30-44), and Jesus walking on water (6:45-51). And yet, the disciples remain uncertain. Rather than responding to Christ's walk on the sea with the recognition that he is Messiah and God's Son, they are filled with fear and incomprehension at the meaning of the feeding miracle (6:52).

They should, by this stage, be joining the dots and realizing that Jesus was more than a prophet. After all, the feeding miracle called to mind creation, Jesus multiplying the food to an astonishing degree. It also recalled God's provision through Moses of manna in the wilderness for Israel as they traveled to the Promised Land (Exod 16:31-36). It recalled and transcended Elisha's feeding of one hundred men with twenty barley loaves and fresh grain (2 Kgs 4:43). His outrageous provision miracles surely testified that the disciples were with someone greater than Moses and Elisha.

They had then seen him heal a gentile women's daughter (Mark 6:24-30). While Jesus is somewhat reluctant, the breaking down of ethnic boundaries points to an ultimate cosmic purpose to call all peoples to him (13:10; 14:9). He then healed a deaf man (6:31-37) and performed a second feeding miracle, this time of four thousand people with seven loaves and a few small fish (8:1-10).[189] This miracle appears to occur in the region of the Decapolis, gentile territory, suggesting that non-Jews and Jews are in attendance. Thus, Jesus breaks Jewish table fellowship limitations, sharing food

---

189. Four thousand is likely the total number, including women and children, as *tetrakischilioi* is likely inclusive (unlike *anēr* at the five thousand miracle). The fish are *ichthydion*, the diminutive of "fish" (*ichthus*), indicating very small fish, like sardines. See further Edwards, *Mark*, 229-32.

among gentiles, and all with unwashed hands. Again, we see the cosmic scope of the gospel in Mark, anticipating later gentile mission. And again, Jesus is motivated by compassion—the driving force for his use of power. The need is real, the crowds without food for three days and a long walk from home. Seven baskets are left over. Yet, Jesus' warning against Herod and the Pharisee's false understandings of messiah are then misunderstood as a critique of the disciples' failure to bring bread. Clearly, this should not be an issue to the disciples, as God will provide when they are short of food. Jesus' frustration is patent in 6:17–21, drawing their attention to the twelve and seven baskets left over after the feeding miracles (6:19).

While it is always tenuous to attach too much symbolism to numbers in the biblical story, here twelve and seven are significant. As noted earlier, twelve points to the tribes of Israel—Jesus is constituting a new Israel around his person. The seven arguably speaks of completion, and points perhaps to creation—Jesus inaugurating a new creation event. Alternatively, it could speak of completion and point to the gentile mission.[190] The two ideas are not mutually exclusive; it may point to the completion of Jesus' mission of the formation of a new humanity and the new creation.

Despite what is staring them in the face, the disciples remain spiritually deaf and blind. The healings of the deaf and blind men, which leads to the revelation at Caesarea Philippi, represent Jesus' hope for the disciples—that their spiritual blindness to his person and mission would also be healed. In the confession, this is partially seen as they recognize that Jesus is Messiah. In what follows, it will become clear that, while they know Jesus is Messiah, their understanding (hearing and seeing) is still partial—they don't know what it really means. The unique double healing of the blind man of Bethsaida takes on new significance. Their confession will be part one of their healing. From this point on, they will recognize the Messiah, but only in a shadowy way. They still run with the false expectations of the Pharisees and Herod, who believe that the messiah will inaugurate a war with Rome and other gentile nations. Jesus must continue to teach them, affecting their spiritual healing and understanding. This will come in what follows. It will not be complete until the resurrection.

It is significant that it is Peter who spoke up on behalf of the apostles. As Papias later indicated and as Bauckham has so persuasively argued in recent times, he is the key source for this gospel (see chapter 1 of this volume).[191] In a sense, then, Mark is Simon Peter's story. Throughout the

---

190. Brooks, *Mark*, 126; Witherington (*Mark*, 236) notes seven commandments in the Noahic covenant and seventy gentile nations (Gen 9–10). Lane (*Mark*, 274) notes the seven Hellenistic Jewish leaders in Acts 6.

191. See Bauckham, *Jesus and the Eye-Witnesses*, 202–39.

Gospel, he is tied up in everything, sometimes positively, more often failing to respond correctly. He is full of bravado, and yet always misses things. He is the first disciple mentioned and called (Mark 1:16). Jesus is initially based at his house in Capernaum, where he heals his mother-in-law and many others. Likely, this home continued to be the base for his work (Mark 2:1).[192] It is Peter who is named among those who searched for Jesus in the wilderness after the healings, and tells Jesus that everyone is looking for him. Jesus tells him it is time to leave; his mission is way bigger than Capernaum (Mark 1:26–38). Peter is named first among the Twelve and renamed "Rock" (Mark 3:16). With the sons of thunder, he is a part of Jesus' inner circle, they alone allowed to see the raising of Jairus's daughter (Mark 5:37–43). This is a great privilege, as they see the fullness of Jesus' power over death. It is no surprise, then, that Peter speaks on behalf of the disciples, saying out loud what they were all thinking: "You are the Messiah."

Immediately after the confession, Peter will be directly rebuked by Jesus for his complete misunderstanding of Jesus' mission (8:32–33). Again, he and the other two members of Jesus' inner circle; James and John, will be with Jesus as he is transfigured, and Peter will be completely at a loss as to what to do. So he proposes building tents for Moses, Elijah, and Jesus (9:2–5). He speaks up when the disciples are concerned over their eternal state in the rich ruler account (10:28) and when the fig tree dies (11:21). Peter, with James, John, and Andrew, triggered and listened to the Olivet Discourse (Mark 13:3). It is Peter who boldly states that he will never deny Jesus, but fails dramatically (Mark 14:29–31, 54, 66–72). He, James, and John all boldly claim that they will never fail him (cf. Mark 10:39, below). They are with him in Gethsemane and do just that, failing to stay awake with Jesus as he prays in agony and is then arrested (14:33–42). It is Peter who is singled out by the risen Christ to be told by the women of Jesus' resurrection, and that he will again see Jesus in Galilee (16:7). By the time of Mark, Peter is an old man who has become the figurehead of Christianity. He is likely in Rome in prison, facing death, or has recently been put to death. Readers would know this. The power of his story is critical—he embodies the movement from conversion to disciple with all his foibles.

The confession that Jesus is the Christ speaks of Jesus as the long-awaited Davidic Messiah, a king from the line of David who, imbued with the Spirit, will bring Israel's redemption from the gentiles. He will effect a new Exodus, a new conquest, the completion of their time of exile, the liberation of Zion in Jerusalem, the establishment of Jerusalem and the temple

---

192. Jesus returns to Capernaum, and it is reported that he is *en oikō*, which can be rendered "at home." Presumably, it is the home of Peter (cf. 1:29). See Edwards, *Mark*, 74. It can also be a general house or Jesus' own home, e.g., Stein, *Mark*, 116.

as the world's political, economic, and religious capital, into which will flow the nations in homage, worship, and tribute. He will lead the people of God in triumphal victory, subduing every nation.

In light of the expectations discussed earlier in this book, without doubt, their realization that Jesus is Messiah meant war. The tough fishermen, the sons of thunder, Simon the Zealot, Judas the Sicarii, and the others, were no doubt quivering with a mixture of expectation and fear at what lay before them. Now that the cat was out of the bag, surely now was the time. The assault on Pilate, the Fortress Antonia,[193] and the Praetorium,[194] was coming. Surely, the next part of their journey was a march to Jerusalem to war.

As we will see in the next chapters, this is far from what Jesus had in mind. Yet, we should not hold it against the disciples that they were full of false expectations at this moment. After all, that is all that they knew. They were shaped by the false premises of their world, ideas that had their genesis in the heart of hell itself. They were victims of years of misinterpretation of the Scriptures and the Apocryphal and Pseudepigraphal writings of Israel. They were misled by the yeast of the Pharisees, Herod, and, indeed, all the scholars of Israel. The true Jesus was embedded in the Old Testament, but amidst a sea of texts that cried out, "Theo is coming, and it will mean war and glorious victory over the gentiles"! It will only be when they are looking back at his ministry and crucifixion through the prism of the resurrection that they will understand it fully. So, to Mark 8:30—16:8 and part two of the revelation of Jesus Messiah, we now turn.

193. The Fortress Antonia was a renovation by Herod of the Hasmonean fortress the Baris (built by Hyrcanus I, 135–105 BC; cf. Josephus, *Ant.* 15.403–9—on the site of Nehemiah's Tower of the Hundred, Neh 3:1) northwest of the Temple mount in honor of Mark Anthony, hence the name (see Batey, "Jerusalem," 560; Chilton, Comfort, and Wise, "Jewish Temple," 1168). A Roman legion (five thousand men) was placed there (see Josephus, *Ant.* 20.192; *J.W.* 5.244–45; Acts 21:31–32; Rapske, "Roman Governors of Palestine," 980). During the Jewish war, it was captured with the Roman garrison massacred in AD 66 (see Josephus, *J.W.* 2.325–28; see in Guelich and Evans, "Destruction of Jerusalem," 274). Most Roman soldiers were in Caesarea Maritima to on the western coast, and so an assault there would also seem appropriate. See also Hall ("Tower of Antonia," 274), who notes that it reached seventy cubits high (thirty-two meters; one hundred three feet) and was effectively a palace, including baths, courtyards, and troop quarters (see also Josephus, *J.W.* 5.237–47).

194. Pixner ("Praetorium," 477) notes that it is most likely that the Jerusalem Praetorium (the seat of the Roman governor) was not at the Fortress Antonia, but perhaps Herod's Upper Palace. Alternatively, it may be at another site on the western "slope of the Tyropoeon valley, just opposite the SW corner of the temple enclosure." This may be at the site of the old Hasmonean Palace, "at the very edge of the Upper City" (Josephus, *J.W.* 2.344). Herod used this palace (*J.W.* 1.443; *Ant.* 229) and the Romans took it over after AD 6. Jesus was tried at the Praetorium, wherever it was (Matt 27:27; Mark 15:16; John 18:28, 33; 19:9). See also Riesner ("Archeology and Geography," 43), who notes that the palace was built by Herod from 20 BC on (Josephus *J.W.* 5.156–83).

Bibliography

Allen, Leslie C. *Psalms 101–150 (Revised)*. WBC 21. Dallas: Word Inc., 2002.
Allison, Dale C., Jr. "Mark 12.28–31 and the Decalogue." In *The Gospels and the Scriptures of Israel*, edited by Craig A. Evans and W. Richard Stegner, 270–78. JSNTSup 104. SSEJC 3. Sheffield: Sheffield Academic, 1994.
———. "Mountain and Wilderness." In *DJG* 563–65.
"Ancient Rome." http://www.britannica.com/EBchecked/topic/507905/ancient-Rome.
Aune, David E. *Prophecy in Early Christianity and the Ancient Mediterranean World*. Grand Rapids: Eerdmans, 1983.
Batey, Richard A. "Jerusalem." In *DNTB* 559–61.
Bauckham, Richard. *Gospel Women: Studies in the Named Women in the Gospels*. Edinburgh, UK: T&T Clark, 2002.
———. *Jesus and the Eyewitnesses: The Gospels as Eyewitness Testimony*. Grand Rapids: Eerdmans, 2006.
Bauer, David R. "Son of God." In *DJG* 769–75.
Best, Ernest. *The Temptation and the Passion: The Markan Soteriology*. SNTSMS 2. Cambridge: Cambridge University Press, 1965.
Bimson, John J., et al. "The Parthian Empire." In *New Bible Atlas*, 99. Electronic edition. Wheaton, IL: InterVarsity, 2000.
Blomberg, Craig L. *Jesus and the Gospels: An Introduction and Survey*. Leicester, UK: Apollos, 1997.
———. *Matthew*. NAC 22. Nashville: Broadman & Holman, 1992.
Bock, Darrell L. *Luke Volume 1:1—9:50*. 2 Volumes. BECNT. Grand Rapids: Baker Academic, 1994.
Bokser, Baruch M. "Messianism, the Exodus Pattern, and Early Rabbinical Judaism." *The Messiah: Developments in Earliest Judaism and Christianity*. Minneapolis: Fortress, 1992.
Brett, Michael. "Berber People." https://www.britannica.com/topic/Berber.
Briley, Terry R. *Isaiah*. 2 Volumes. CPNIVC. Joplin, MO: College Press, 2000.
Brooks, James A. *Mark*. NAC 23. Nashville: Broadman & Holman, 1991.
Brubacher, Gordon. "Desert." In *EDB* 338–40.

Bultmann, Rudolf. *The History of the Synoptic Tradition*. Rev. ed. Translated by J. Marsh. New York: Harper & Row, 1963.
Bunson, Matthew. "Dacia." In *ERE* 165–67.
Carson, Don A. *The Gospel According to John*. PNTC. Grand Rapids: Eerdmans, 1991.
Champlin, Edward. *Nero*. Cambridge: Harvard University Press, 2003.
Charles River Editors. *The Minoans and the Mycenaeans: The History of the Civilisations that First Developed Ancient Greek Culture*. Online: CreateSpace, 2016. Kindle edition.
Charlesworth, James H., ed. *The Messiah: Developments in Earliest Judaism and Christianity*. Minneapolis: Fortress, 1992.
———. *The Old Testament Pseudepigrapha*. Vol. 1. New York: Yale University Press, 1983.
Chilton, Bruce D., P. W. Comfort, and Michael O. Wise. "Temple, Jewish." In *DNTB* 1167–83.
Cole, R. Dennis. *Numbers*. NAC 3B. Nashville: Broadman & Holman, 2001.
Cole, Robert Luther. *Psalms 1–2: Gateway to the Psalter*. HBM 37. Sheffield: Sheffield Phoenix, 2012.
Collins, Gerald G. "Crucifixion." In *ABD* 1:1207–10.
Collins, John James. "Messianism in the Maccabean Period." In *Judaisms and Their Messiahs at the Turn of the Christian Era*, edited by J. Neusner, et.al., 97–110, Cambridge: Cambridge University Press, 1987.
———. *The Scepter and the Star—The Messiahs of the Dead Sea Scrolls and Other Ancient Literature*. ABRL. New York: Doubleday, 1995.
Cotterell, Arthur. *A History of Southeast Asia*. Singapore: Marshall Cavendish International, 2014.
Craigie, Peter C. *Psalms 1–50*. WBC 19. Dallas: Word Incorporated, 1998.
Cranfield, Charles E. B. *The Gospel According to St Mark*. CGTC. Cambridge: Cambridge University Press, 1966.
Crenshaw, James L. *Old Testament Wisdom: An Introduction*. Louisville, KY: Westminster John Knox, 1998.
"Cyrus the Great." In *BEB* 1:565.
"Daily Mail: ISIS Map of the World, Plan for Global Domination." http://myocn.net/daily-mail-isis-map-world-plan-global-domination/.
Day, John. "Dragon and Sea, God's Conflict With." In *ABD* 2:228–31.
———. "Rahab." In *ABD* 5:610–11.
Debevoise, Neilson C. *A Political History of Parthia*. Chicago, IL: University of Chicago Press, 1938.
"Desert." In *BEB* 1:615–16.
DeVries, LaMoine F. "Caesarea Philippi." In *EDB* 207–8.
Dockery, David S. "Baptism." In *DJG* 55–58.
Dunn, James D. G. *Romans 1–8*. WBC 38A. Dallas: Word Incorporated, 1998.
Edwards, James R. *The Gospel According to Mark*. PNTC. Grand Rapids: Apollos, 2002.
Elwell, Walter A., and Barry J. Beitzel. "Elder." In *BEB*.
"Eureka Effect." https://en.wikipedia.org/wiki/Eureka_effect.
Evans, Craig, A. *Mark 8:27—16:20*. WBC 34B. Dallas: Word Incorporated, 2001.
Fager, Jeffrey A. "Jehozadak." In *ABD* 3:670.
Farmer, William R. *The Gospel of Jesus: The Pastoral Relevance of the Synoptic Problem*. Louisville: Westminster John Knox, 1999.

Feldman, Louis H. "Josephus." In *ABD* 3:981–98.
Flower, John E., et al. "Spain–History." http://www.expatfocus.com/expatriate-spain-hi story?gclid=CNeSwNrcttICFYwDKgodLuoB6w.
Foster, Paul. "Q Source." In *LBD*.
France, Richard Thomas. *The Gospel of Mark: A Commentary on the Greek Text*. NIGTC. Grand Rapids: Eerdmans, 2002.
———. *Jesus and the Old Testament*. London: Tyndale, 1971.
Friedrich, Gerhard. "εὐαγγελίζομαι, εὐαγγέλιον, προευαγγελίζομαι, εὐαγγελιστής." In *TDNT* 2:707–37.
———. "κῆρυξ (ἱεροκῆρυξ), κηρύσσω, κήρυγμα, προκηρύσσω." In *TDNT* 3:683–96.
García, Florentino Martínez, and Eibert J. C. Tigchelaar. *The Dead Sea Scrolls: Study Edition*. Vols. 1 and 2. Leiden, NY: Brill, 1997–1998.
Giles, Glenn W. "Messianic Movements of the First Century." https://www.douglasjacoby.com/wp-content/uploads/2005/03/Mess.Movements.pdf.
Gnilka, Joichim. *Das Evangelium nach Markus*. 2 Vols. EKK 2.1–2. Zürich: Benzinger, 1978.
Goldingay, John. *Daniel*. WBC 30. Dallas: Word Incorporated, 1998.
Grant, Michael. *Nero*. London: Weidenfield and Nicolson, 1970.
Green, Joel B., and Lincoln Hurst. "Priest, Priesthood." In *DJG* 633–36.
Greenspahn, Frederick E. "Why Prophecy Ceased." *JBL* 108 (1989) 17–35.
Griffen, Miriam T. *Nero: The End of a Dynasty*. London: B. T. Batsford, 1984.
———. "Nero." In *ABD* 4:1076–81.
Grousset, René. *The Empire of the Steppes: a History of Central Asia*. Translated by Naomi Walford. New Brunswick, NJ: Rutgers University Press, 1970.
Guelich, Robert A. *Mark 1–8:26*. WBC 34A. Waco: Word Incorporated, 1989.
Guelich, Robert A., and Craig A. Evans. "Destruction of Jerusalem." In *DNTB* 273–78.
Haas, Jonathan., et al. "Power and the Emergence of Complex Polities in the Peruvian Preceramic." *Archaeological Papers of the American Anthropological Association* 14.1 (2005) 37–52.
Hagner, Donald A. *Matthew 1–13*. WBC 33A. Dallas: Word Incorporated, 1998.
———. *Matthew 14–28*. WBC 33B. Dallas: Word Incorporated, 1998.
Hall, John F. "Tower of Antonia." In *ABD* 1:274.
Hall, Robert G. "Circumcision." In *ABD* 1:1025–31.
Harris, Sarah. *The Davidic Shepherd King in the Lukan Narrative*. LNTS 558. London: Bloomsbury, 2016.
Harrison, et al. "Spain." https://www.britannica.com/place/Spain.
Hartin, Patrick J. "The Gospel of Thomas." In *LBD*, n.p. Logos edition.
Heard, Waren. J. "Revolutionary Movements." In *DJG* 688–98.
Henderson, J. Jordan. "Theudas." In *LBD*, n.p. Logos edition.
Hengel, Martin. *The Son of God: The Origin of Christology and the History of Jewish-Hellenistic Religion*. London: SCM, 1976.
———. *The Zealots*. Translated by D. Smith. Edinburgh: T&T Clark, 1989.
Hoehner, Harold W. "Herod, Herodian Family." In *BEB* 1:963–74.
———. "Herodian Dynasty." In *DJG* 317–24.
Hoglund, Kenneth G. "Cyrus." In *EDB* 305.
Holland, Richard. *Nero: The Man Behind the Myth*. Stroud, UK: Sutton, 2000.
Hooker, Morna D. *The Gospel According to Saint Mark*. BNTC. London: Continuum, 1991.

Horbury, William. *Messianism Among Jews and Christians: Twelve Biblical and Historical Studies*. London: T&T Clark, 2003.
Horsley, Richard A., and John S. Hanson. *Bandits, Prophets, and Messiahs: Popular Movements at the Time of Jesus*. Minneapolis: Winston, 1985.
Hucker, Charles O., and Hoklam Chan. "China." https://www.britannica.com/place/China.
"The ISIS Map of the World." http://www.dailymail.co.uk/news/article-2674736/ISIS-militants-declare-formation-caliphate-Syria-Iraq-demand-Muslims-world-swear-allegiance.html.
Jeremias, Joachim. *New Testament Theology*. Translated by J. Bowden. New York: Scribner's, 1971.
———. "παῖς θεοῦ as a Title of Jesus." In *TNDT* 5:701–5.
Johansen, Bruce E. *The Native Peoples of North America: A History*. New Brunswick, NJ: Rutgers University Press, 2005.
Jones, David A. *Old Testament Quotations and Allusions in the New Testament*. Bellingham, WA: Logos Bible Software, 2009.
"Julia Agrippina." http://www.britannica.com/EBchecked/topic/9818/Julia-Agrippina.
Kaiser, Walter C., Jr. "The Davidic Promise and the Inclusion of the Gentiles (Amos 9:15 and Acts 15:13–18): A Test Passage for Theological Systems." *JETS* 20.2 (June, 1977) 97–110.
Keay, John. *India: A History*. London: HarperCollins, 2010. Kindle edition.
Keown, Gerald L., et al. *Jeremiah 26–52*. WBC 27. Dallas: Word Incorporated, 1998.
Keown, Mark J. *Congregational Evangelism in Philippians: The Centrality of an Appeal for Gospel Proclamation to the Fabric of Philippians*. Milton Keynes, UK: Paternoster, 2008.
———. *Philippians*. EEC. Bellingham, WA: Lexham, Forthcoming.
———. *What's God Up To On Planet Earth: A 'No-Strings Attached' Explanation of the Christian Message*. Eugene: Wipf and Stock, 2011.
Kitchen, Kenneth A. "The Exodus." In *ABD* 2:702–3.
Klein, William W., et al. *Introduction to Biblical Interpretation: Revised and Expanded*. Nashville: Thomas Nelson, 1993.
Knight, George Angus Fulton. *Servant Theology: A Commentary on the Book of Isaiah 40–55*. ITC. Rev. ed. Grand Rapids: Eerdmans, 1984.
Köstenberger, Andreas J. *John*. BECNT. Grand Rapids: Baker Academic, 2004.
Kuan, Jeffrey K. "Shalmaneser." In *EDB* 1195–96.
Kutsko, John. "Caesarea Philippi." In *ABD* 1:803.
La Sor, William Sanford, et al. *Old Testament Survey: The Message, Form, and Background of the Old Testament*. Grand Rapids: Eerdmans, 1982.
Lane, William L. *The Gospel of Mark*. NICNT. Grand Rapids: Eerdmans, 1974.
Legarda, Benito, Jr. "Cultural Landmarks and their Interactions with Economic Factors in the Second Millennium in the Philippines." *Kinaadman (Wisdom): A Journal of the Southern Philippines* 23 (2001).
Lightfoot, Joseph Barber, ed. *Saint Paul's Epistle to the Philippians*. Classic Commentaries on the Greek New Testament. London: Macmillan, 1913.
"List of Parthian Kings." https://en.wikipedia.org/wiki/List_of_Parthian_kings.
Major, John S., and Constance A. Cook. *Ancient China: A History*. New York: Routledge, 2017. Kindle edition.
Malitz, Jurgen. *Nero*. Translated by Allison Brown. Oxford: Blackwell, 2005.

Mandell, Sara R. "Hasmoneans." In *EDB* 555–56.
Manson, Thomas Walter. "Miscellanea Apocalyptica." In *JTS* 56 (1945) 41–45.
Marcus, Joel. *Mark 1–8: A New Translation with Introduction and Commentary*. AB 27. New Haven, CT: Yale University Press, 2008.
"Mark (name)." https://en.wikipedia.org/wiki/Mark_(name).
Marshall, I. Howard. *The Gospel of Luke: A Commentary on the Greek Text*. NIGTC. Exeter, UK: Paternoster, 1978.
———. "Son of God or Servant of Yahweh? A Reconsideration of Mk 1, 11." In *NTS* 15 (1968–1969) 327–32.
Mathews, Kenneth A. *Genesis 1–11:26*. NAC 1A. Nashville: Broadman & Holman, 1996.
McRae, John R. "Caesarea Maritima." In *DNTB* 176–77.
Meeks, Charles. "Beelzebul." In *LBD*, n.p. Logos edition.
Metzger, Bruce Manning. *A Textual Commentary on the Greek New Testament, Second Edition*. 4th rev. ed. London: United Bible Societies, 1994.
Miller, Stephen R. *Daniel*. NAC 18. Nashville: Broadman & Holman, 1994.
Morgan, D. F. "Desert." In *ISBE* 1:927–28.
Mounce, Robert H. "Nazareth." In *ISBE* 3:500–501.
Myers, Ched. *Binding the Strong Man: A Political Reading of Mark's Story of Jesus*. Maryknoll, NY: Orbis, 1988.
Nash, Scott. "Gallio." In *EDB* 481.
Naylor, Phillip C. *North Africa: A History from Antiquity to the Present*. Rev. ed. Austin, TX: University of Texas Press, 2009.
"Nazareth." In *BEB* 2:1531.
"Nero." http://www.britannica.com/EBchecked/topic/409505/Nero.
Neusner, Jacob. "Mishnah and Messiah." In *Judaisms and Their Messiahs at the Turn of the Christian Era*, edited by J. Neusner, et al., 265–82. Cambridge: Cambridge University Press, 1987.
"Ofonius Tigellinus." http://www.britannica.com/EBchecked/topic/595454/Ofonius-Tigellinus.
Oliver, Neil. *A History of Ancient Britain*. London: Weidenfeld & Nicolson, 2011. Kindle edition.
"Only Gold." http://www.onlygold.com/tutorialpages/value_of_gold.asp.
Origen, "Origen against Celsus." In *ANF* 4, 395–669.
Osgood, J. *Caesar's Legacy: Civil War and the Emergence of the Roman Empire*. Cambridge: Cambridge University Press, 2006.
"Ozymandias." http://www.online-literature.com/shelley_percy/672/.
"Parthia," http://academic.eb.com/levels/collegiate/article/Parthia/58588.
"Pergamum, Pergamos." In *BEB* 2:1644–65.
Pesch, Rudolf. *Das Markusevangelium*. 2 Vols. HTKNT 2.1–2. Freiburg, Germany: Herder, 1979.
Pfeiffer, Charles F. "Israel, History of the People of." In *ISBE* 2:908–24.
Pixner, Bargil. "Praetorium." In *ABD* 5:477–79.
Porter, H. "Parthians." In *ISBE* 2251–53.
"Power Corrupts; Absolute Power Corrupts Absolutely." http://www.phrases.org.uk/meanings/absolute-power-corrupts-absolutely.html.
Rapske, Bruce M. "Roman Governors of Palestine." In *DNTB* 980–84.
Reddish, Mitchell G. *An Introduction to the Gospels*. Nashville: Abingdon, 1997.

Reed, Jonathan L. "Nazareth." In *EDB* 951.
Riesner, Rainer D. "Archeology and Geography." In *DJG* 33–46.
———. "Galilee." In *DJG* 252–53.
Robinson, G. L., and R. K. Harrison, "Isaiah." In *ISBE* 1:1495–508.
Robinson, James M. *The Problem of History in Mark*. SBT 1/21. Naperville, IL: Allenson, 1957.
Rooker, Mark F. *Leviticus*. NAC 3A. Nashville, TN: Broadman & Holman, 2000.
Russell, Bertrand. *Why I Am Not a Christian, and Other Essays on Religion and Related Subjects*. New York: Clarion, 1957.
Saldarini, Anthony. J. "Scribes." In *ABD* 5:1012–16.
Schmidt, Thomas E. "Taxes." In *DJG* 804–6.
Singer, Tovia. *Let's Get Biblical: Why Doesn't Judaism Accept the Christian Messiah?* RNBN Publishers, 2010.
Smith, Gary. V. *Isaiah 1–39*. NAC 15A. Nashville: Broadman & Holman, 2007.
———. *Isaiah 40–66*. NAC 15B. Nashville: Broadman & Holman, 2009.
Smith, James E. *The Minor Prophets*. OTSS. Joplin, MO: College Press, 1994. Logos edition.
Smith, Ralph L. *Micah–Malachi*. WBC 32. Dallas: Word Incorporated, 1998.
Flower, John E., et al. "Spain–History." http://www.expatfocus.com/expatriate-spain-history?gclid=CNeSwNrcttICFYwDKgodLuoB6w.
Stein, Robert H. *Mark*. BECNT. Grand Rapids: Baker Academic, 2008.
Strange, James F. "Sepphoris." In *ABD* 5:1091.
Stuart, Douglas K. *Exodus*. NAC 2. Nashville: Broadman & Holman, 2006.
Stuhlmueller, Carroll. *Rebuilding with Hope: A Commentary on the Books of Haggai and Zechariah*. International Theological Commentary. Grand Rapids: Eerdmans, 1988.
Subrahmanyam, Sanjay., and Muzaffar Alam, et. al. "India." https://www.britannica.com/place/India.
"Tatooine." http://en.wikipedia.org/wiki/Tatooine.
Taylor, Bayard. *A History of Germany*. New York: Perennial, 2016. Kindle edition.
Taylor, Richard A., and E. Ray Clendenen. *Haggai, Malachi*. NAC 21A. Nashville: Broadman & Holman, 2004.
Taylor, Vincent. *The Gospel According to St. Mark*. 2nd ed. London: Macmillan, 1966.
Thornton, Russell. "Population History of Native North Americans." In *A Population History of North America*, edited by Michael R. Haines and Richard H. Steckel, 9–51. Cambridge: Cambridge University Press, 2000.
"Tiberius." http://www.britannica.com/EBchecked/topic/594862/Tiberius.
Tromp, Johannes. *The Assumption of Moses: A Critical Edition with Commentary*. SVTP 10. Leiden, Netherlands: Brill, 1993.
Trost, Travis D. "Parthia." In *LBD*, n.p. Logos edition.
Tuckett, Christopher M. "The Current State of the Synoptic Problem." In *New Studies in the Synoptic Problem: Oxford Conference, April 2008: Essays in Honour of Christopher M. Tuckett*, edited by P. Foster, et al., 9–50. Leuven, Belgium: Peeters, 2011.
———. "Messianic Secret." In *ABD* 4:797–800.
Turner, David., and Darrell L. Bock. *Matthew and Mark*. CBC 11. Carol Stream, IL: Tyndale, 2005.
Twelftree, Graham H. "Sanhedrin." In *DJG* 728–32.

van Der Woude, Adam Simon. "χριστός: Rabbinic Writings." *TDNT* 9:521–27.
van Iersel, B. M. F., and J. Nuchelmans. "De zoon van Timeüs en de zoon von David: Marcus 10, 46–52 gelezen door een grieks-romeinse bril."*Tijdschrift voor Theologie* 35 (1995) 107–24.
Vermes, Geza. *The Dead Sea Scrolls in English*. Rev. 4th ed. Sheffield, UK: Sheffield Academic Press, 1995.
Watts, John D. W. *Isaiah 34–66*. WBC 25. Dallas: Word Incorporated, 1998.
Wenham, Gordon J. *Genesis 1–15*. WBC 1. Dallas: Word Incorporated, 1998.
———. *Genesis 16–50*. WBC 2. Dallas: Word Incorporated, 1998.
Westermann, Claus. *Isaiah 40–66*. Translated by D. M. G. Stalker. Philadelphia: Westminster, 1969.
"Why Jews Don't Believe in Jesus." http://www.aish.com/jw/s/48892792.html.
Witherington, Ben, III. *1 and 2 Thessalonians: A Socio-Rhetorical Commentary*. Grand Rapids: Eerdmans, 2006.
———. *The Acts of the Apostles: A Socio-Rhetorical Commentary*. Grand Rapids: Eerdmans, 1998.
———. *Christology of Jesus*. Philadelphia: Fortress, 1990.
———. *The Gospel of Mark: A Socio-Rhetorical Commentary*. Grand Rapids: Eerdmans, 2001.
Wrede, William. *The Messianic Secret*. Translated by J. C. Grieg. Cambridge: James Clarke, 1971
Wright, N. Tom. *Jesus and the Victory of God*. COQG 2. London: Society for Promoting Christian Knowledge, 1996.
Wright, R. B. "Psalms of Solomon: A New Translation and Introduction." In *The Old Testament Pseudepigrapha and the New Testament: Expansions of the Old Testament and Legends, Wisdom, and Philosophical Literature, Prayers, Psalms and Odes, Fragments of Lost Judeo-Hellenistic Works*. Vol. 2. New Haven: Yale University Press, 1985.
———. *Paul and the Faithfulness of God*. COQG 4. Minneapolis: Fortress, 2013.
"Xiongnu People." https://www.britannica.com/topic/Xiongnu.

Author Index

Allen, Leslie C., 207
Allison, Dale C., Jr., 150, 161, 207
Aune, David E., 151, 207

Batey, Richard A., 206, 207
Bauckham, Richard, 147, 175, 200, 204, 207
Bauer, David R., 158, 207
Beitzel. Barry J., 154, 208
Best, Ernest, 162, 207
Bimson, John J., 32, 207
Blomberg, Craig L., 9, 132, 155, 207
Bock, Darrell L., 162, 177, 207
Bokser, Baruch M., 110, 207
Brett, Michael, 33, 207
Briley, Terry R., 144, 207
Brooks, James A., 155, 160, 161, 204, 207
Brubacher, Gordon, 161, 207
Bultmann, Rudolf, 163, 208
Bunson, Matthew, 32, 207

Carson, Don A., 167, 208
Champlin, Edward, 7, 208
Chan, Hoklam, 20, 21, 23, 210
Charlesworth, James H., 110, 118, 121, 208
Chilton, Bruce D., 206, 208
Clendenen, E. Ray, 108, 212
Cole, R. Dennis, 80, 208
Cole, Robert Luther, 109, 208

Collins, Gerald G., 128
Collins, John James, 110, 111, 115, 208
Comfort, P. W., 206, 208
Cook, Constance A., 21, 22, 210
Cotterell, Arthur, 28, 29, 208
Craigie, Peter C., 108, 158, 208
Cranfield, Charles E. B., 6, 142, 149, 208
Crenshaw, James L., 66, 208

Day, John, 88, 208
Debevoise, Neilson C., 32, 208
DeVries, LaMoine F., 202, 208
Dockery, David S., 152, 208
Dunn, James D. G., 134, 208

Edwards, James R., 6, 142, 158, 162, 180, 191, 192, 203, 205, 208
Elwell, Walter A., 154, 208
Evans, Craig A., 128, 132, 206, 207, 208, 209

Fager, Jeffrey A., 148, 208
Farmer, William R., 208
Feldman, Louis H., 125, 209
Flower, John E., 39, 209
Foster, Paul, 9, 209, 212
France, Richard Thomas, 142, 149, 150, 154, 155, 156, 157, 158, 159, 160, 161, 162, 190, 209
Friedrich, Gerhard, 142, 146, 170, 209

AUTHOR INDEX

García, Florentino Martínez, 80, 209
Giles, Glenn W., 128, 209
Gnilka, Joachim, 142, 149, 209
Goldingay, John, 99, 100, 101, 209
Grant, Michael, 7, 209
Green, Joel B., 193, 194, 209
Greenspahn, Frederick E., 151, 209
Griffen, Miriam T., 7, 209
Grousset, René, 30, 209
Guelich, Robert A., 142, 149, 152, 153, 159, 160, 162, 163, 177, 206, 209

Haas, Jonathan, 44, 209
Hagner, Donald A., 163, 175, 187, 209
Haines, Michael R., 212
Hall, John F., 206, 209
Hall, Robert G., 72, 209
Hanson. John S., 210
Harris, Sarah, 132, 209
Harrison, R. K., 15, 212
Hartin, Patrick J., 9, 209
Heard, Warren. J., 169, 209
Henderson, J. Jordan, 129, 209
Hengel, Martin, 158, 177, 209
Hoehner, Harold W., 187, 188, 189, 209
Hoglund, Kenneth G., 15, 209
Holland, Richard, 7, 209
Hooker, Morna D., 154, 158, 159, 160, 161, 162, 166, 198, 209
Horbury, William, 111, 115, 210
Horsley, Richard A., 210
Hucker, Charles O., 20, 21, 23, 210
Hurst, Lincoln, 193, 194, 209

Jeremias, Joachim, 151, 157, 210
Johansen, Bruce E., 44, 210
Jones, David A., 85, 87, 210

Kaiser, Walter C., Jr., 103, 210
Keay, John, 24, 25, 26, 27, 210
Keown, Gerald L., 97, 210
Keown, Mark J., 1, 5, 210
Kitchen, Kenneth A., 34, 210
Klein, William W., 10, 210
Knight, George Angus Fulton, 87, 210
Köstenberger, Andreas J., 133, 210
Kuan, Jeffrey K., 16, 210
Kutsko, John, 202, 210

La Sor, William Sanford, 210
Lane, William L., 142, 149, 152, 156, 160, 162, 163, 190, 204, 210
Legarda, Benito, Jr., 28, 210
Lightfoot, Joseph Barber, 7, 210

Major, John S., 21, 22, 210
Malitz, Jurgen, 7, 210
Mandell, Sara R., 75, 211
Manson, Thomas Walter, 155, 211
Marcus, Joel, 161, 162, 190, 211
Marshall, I. Howard, 157, 158, 211
Mathews, Kenneth A., 47, 48, 211
McRae, John R., 211
Meeks, Charles, 180, 211
Metzger, Bruce Manning, 156, 166, 178, 211
Miller, Stephen R., 99, 211
Morgan, D. F., 161, 211
Mounce, Robert H., 155, 211
Muzaffar Alam, 27, 212
Myers, Ched, 211

Nash, Scott, 18, 211
Naylor, Phillip C., 34, 35, 37, 211
Neusner, Jacob, 110, 208, 211
Nuchelmans, J., 213

Oliver, Neil, 38, 39, 211
Osgood, J., 180, 211

Pesch, Rudolf, 142, 211
Pfeiffer, Charles F., 151, 211
Pixner, Bargil, 194, 211
Porter, H., 32, 211

Rapske, Bruce M., 206, 210
Reddish, Mitchell G., 8, 211
Reed, Jonathan L., 155, 212
Riesner, Rainer D., 155, 169, 206, 212
Robinson, G. L., 15, 212
Robinson, James M. 162, 212
Rooker, Mark F., 50, 212
Russell, Bertrand, 212

Saldarini, Anthony, 186, 212
Schmidt, Thomas E., 175, 176, 212
Singer, Tovia, 164, 212

Smith, Gary V., 84, 87, 92, 95, 96, 212
Smith, James E., 100, 101, 212
Smith, Ralph L., 107, 149, 212
Steckel, Richard H., 212
Stegner, W. Richard, 207
Stein, Robert H., 161, 162, 163, 180, 205, 212
Strange, James F., 53, 212
Stuart, Douglas K., 49, 212
Stuhlmueller, Carroll, 148, 184
Subrahmanyam, Sanjay, 27, 212

Taylor, Bayard, 39, 40, 41, 42, 43, 212
Taylor, Richard A., 108, 212
Taylor, Vincent, 212
Thornton, Russell, 44, 212
Tigchelaar, Eibert J. C., 80, 209
Tromp, Johannes, 115, 212
Trost, Travis D., 32, 212

Tuckett, Christopher M., 9, 167, 212
Turner, David, 162, 212
Twelftree, Graham H., 194, 212

van Der Woude, Adam Simon, 126, 213
van Iersel, B. M. F., 213
Vermes, Geza, 122, 213

Watts, John D. W., 84, 143, 145, 213
Wenham, Gordon J., 46, 213
Westermann, Claus, 86, 213
Wise, Michael O., 208
Witherington III, Ben, 129, 146, 154, 157, 158, 160, 162, 178, 190, 195, 204, 213
Wrede, William, 167, 213
Wright, N. Tom., 134, 148, 213
Wright, R. B., 213

Scripture Index

OLD TESTAMENT

Genesis

1	86
1:2	158, 161
1:2–3	158
1–11	47
1:27	189
2	142
3	46, 48, 161, 162
3:15	77
3:16	46, 77, 79
3:23	161
4	48
4:1–6	46
4:1–16	57
4:23–24	47
6–9	24, 48
6:1–5	47
6:2	77, 158
6:4	85
6:5–7	47
7:12	161
9–10	204
10:6–11	35
10:8–9	85
11:1–9	47
12:1–3	52, 109, 154
14	110, 124
18:8–11	47
21:20–21	161
22:2	159
22:12	159
34	118
34:24–29	50
35:21	77
35:41	77
37–50	48
37—Exod 15	34
41:43	170
49:1	76, 77
49:8–12	79
49:9	117
49:10	77, 79, 95, 114, 122
49:10–12	76, 77
49:11	126
49:11–12	79
49:28	178

Exodus

3:1	161
3:14	49
4:1–9	137, 185
4:2–3	181
4:6–7	181
4:9	181

Exodus (*continued*)

4:14	185
4:22–23	77, 158
4:27–28	185
4:29	185
4:29–30	186
4:30	181
4:30–31	137
4:31	186
7:9	181
7:10	181
7:14–25	181
8:1–5	181
8:16–19	181
8:20–32	181
9:1–7	181
9:8–12	181
9:13–35	181
10:1–20	181
10:21–29	181
11–16	50
11:1—12:32	181
12	48
12:33–42	181
12:42	77
12:43–49	49
13:17–22	181
13:17—14:29	129
13:17—14:31	181
14:21	158
15:1–21	48
15:3	85
15:4	94
15:22	161
15:22–27	181
16	162
16:1–36	181
16:4	161
16:31–36	203
16:35	161
17:1–7	163, 181
17:8–13	181
17:8–15	51, 80
17:8–16	181
17:16	76
19:1—23:20	181
19:2	50
19:6	93
20:1–7	49
20:13	49, 57
21	49
21:12–15	49
21:15–17	50
21:18–27	49
21:25	47
22:19	50
23:20	150
23:20–23	151
23:20–32	51
23:20–33	181
24:4	178
24:12—31:18	181
24:13	182, 184
24:15	182
24:18	161
31:16	50
32	51, 70
32:5	170
32:7–23	181
32:17	182, 184
32:35	181
24:29–35	181
34:1–28	181
35:2	50
36:6	170
39:34–38	181
40:9–11	77

Leviticus

4:3	150
4:5	150
4:16	150
6:22	150
11:21–22	152
18:16	188
20:2	50
20:4	50
20:7	50
20:9	50
20:9–16	50
20:10–20	50
20:21	188
20:27	50

24:14	50	24:17	78, 80, 119, 126, 127
24:14–16	50	24:17–19	80, 123
24:16	50	24:17–24	77
24:17	49, 50	24:20	80
24:21	49, 50	25	51
24:23	49, 50	25:5	50
25	124	25:8	50
26	49	25:19	77
27:29	50	26:61	50
		27:17	192
		30:4–9	77
		31:1–20	51

Numbers

		31:1–54	181
1:51	50	31:7–8	50
11:16	194	31:17	50
11:26	77	35:16–24	49
12	51	35:30–32	49
12:1–16	181		
13:33	47		
14:1–38	181		

Deuteronomy

14:34	161		
15:32–26	51	2:7	161
15:35–36	50	2:26–37	181
16:1–50	181	5:7	57
17:1–13	181	6:13	164
20:2–13	181	6:16	163
20:4–9	181	8:3	163
21:1–3	51, 181	13:4	161
21:6	50	13:5–10	50
21:21–30	181	17:1–7	50
21:21–35	51	17:12	50
21:31–35	181	18:15	167, 171
22:1	80	18:15–19	151
22:3–4	80	18:20	50
22:5–6	80	21:18–22	50
22:8–12	80	21:23	132, 134, 138
22:13–20	80	22:1	50
22:21–35	80	22:22–25	50
22:36—24:25	80	24:1	198
23:21	77	24:7	50
23:22	80	25:19	77
23:24	80	26:5	154
24	80, 111	28	49
24:7	77, 78, 80	30:4–9	77
24:7–8	81	31:14–29	182
24:8	80	32:17	161
24:8–9	80		

Joshua

1:1–9	52
1:14	85
2	52
3:1–8	52
3:6—4:18	182
3:12	178
3:13–17	52
4:2–4	178
4:4–9	52
4:8–9	178
4:15–24	52
4:20	178
5:1–9	52
5:9–12	52
5:13–27	182
6	52, 129
6:2	85
6:6–26	182
7	52, 54
8	52
8:1–29	182
8:30–35	52
9	52
10	53
10:1–4	182
10:16—11:23	182
10:20	54
10:30	54
11	53
11:6–8	53
11:6–9	53
11:16	54
11:23	54
12:7–24	182
13:1–5	54
3:14–17	129

Judges

1	55
1:2	55
1:4	55
1:17–23	56
1:19	55
1:19–20	55
1:21	55
1:27–36	50, 55
2:1–5	55
2:11–13	56
2:14	56
2:14–15	56
2:15	56
2:16	56
3:7	56
3:8	56
3:9–10	56
3:10	156
3:11	56
3:12	56
3:12–14	56
3:15	56
3:15–29	56
3:30	56
3:31	56
4–5	50
4:1	56
4:1–16	57
4:2	56
4:2–3	56
4:3	56
4:4–24	56
5:13	56
6–7	82
6–8	50
6:1	56
6:1–6	56
6:6	56
6:7—8:27	56
6:34	156
8:28	56
8:33–35	56
9	57
9:1–4	57
9:5	57
9:6	57
9:7–12	57
9:23–24	57
9:56	57
10:6	56
10:7	56
10:8–9	56
10:10	56

11:1—12:7	56	9:22–23	60
11:34	156	10:1	152, 156
13:1	56, 161	10:19	58
13:2—16:31	56	10:21–22	60
14–16	50	10:26	60
17	57	10:27	60
17–19	57	11	60
18:1	57	11:12–15	60
19	58	12:3	150, 156
19:1	57	12:5	156
20	57	13–15	60
20:18	57	13:1–15	60
20:23	57	13:3–7	60
20:28	57	13:23	60
21:25	57	14:23	60
23:8–39	50	14:32–33	80
		14:47–52	60
		15:1	156

1 Samuel

		15:1–9	60
		15:7–9	80
1	58	15:17	156
1—2:11	58	16	50
2:7–10	77	16–31	61
2:10	150	16:2–8	152
2:12–36	58	16:3	156
2:35	150, 156	16:6	61, 150, 156
3	58	16:7	61
3:1	58	16:12–13	152, 156
3:7	58	16:13	156
3:19	58	17	50, 61
3:21	58	17:26	61
4	50	17:33	61
4–5	58	17:34–36	61
4:1	58	17:44–47	61
4:17	143	17:51	85
7	58	19:5	61
8:1–3	58	18	61, 85
8:6	58	18:7	61
8:7–9	58	18:8–12	62
8:10–18	58	18:13–13	62
8:19–20	58	18:17	62
8:21–22	58	18:24–25	62
9:15–16	60	18:27–29	62
9:2	60	18:30	62
9:6	60	19:1–17	62
9:9–11	60	21:11	62
9:16	156	22:10	62
		22:10–19	60

1 Samuel (continued)

23:1–6	62
23:7—24:22	62
23:14	161
24	64
24:6	150, 156
24:10	150, 156
26	64
26:1–25	62
26:9	150, 156
26:11	150, 156
26:16	150, 156
26:23	150, 156
27:2–12	62
27:8–9	62
27:11	62
28	60
28–29	62
30	62
30:26–31	64
31:1–4	61
31:9	143, 145

2 Samuel

1:14	150, 156
1:15	62
1:16	150, 156
1:20	143, 145
1:21	150
2–4	62
2:4	156
2:7	153
3:2	65
3:3	65
4:10	143, 145
5	62
5:3	156
5:13–15	62
5:17–25	62
6	63
7:1–2	63
7:5–16	63
7:11–14	77
7:14	77, 158
7:16	171
8	63
8:9–10	63
8:14	63
8:14—9:14	63
10	63
11	63
12	63
13–18	63
13:28–29	65
18:9–15	65
18:19	143, 145
18:20	143, 145
18:26	143, 145
18:31	143, 145
19:21	150, 156
20	64
20:1–5	63
20:3	62
20:8–10	64
21:1–3	60
21:2–3	64
21:5–9	64
21:15	64
22	64
22:15	64
22:18–43	64
22:28–32	77
22:38–43	64
22:51	150, 156
23:1	150
23:1–5	77
23:8	85
23:8–39	64
23:9	85
24:8	64
24:18	64

1 Kings

1:2–3	179
1:5–10	65
1:6	65, 179
1:11–53	65
1:16	179
1:34–39	152

1:42	143, 145
1:45	152
3	66
4	66
4:20–26	66
4:24	66
4:25	66
4:29–34	66
5:1–12	66
5:13	67, 77
8	67
9:10	66
9:15–19	67
9:20–21	67
9:22	66
9:23	67
9:26–28	66
9:28	66
10:1–10	67
10:11–12	66
10:14–15	68
10:15–16	68
10:16–25	68
10:17–22	68
10:22	67
10:23	68
10:23–25	68
10:27–40	69
11:1–13	68
12:1–7	69
12:1–24	180
12:21–24	69
12:25–33	70
14:25–28	71
15:6	70
15:8–22	70
15:27–30	70
15:28	70
15:29	70
16:9–12	70
16:15–18	70
16:21–23	70
17:4	70
17:6	182
17:8–16	182
17:9–15	70
17:17–24	182
17:40	70

18:20–40	182
18:41–46	182
19:1–3	70
19:1–8	182
19:4	161
19:4–8	162
19:8	161
19:9–18	182
19:15–16	152
19:15–18	70
20:1–43	70
21	70
21:9–14	50
22	70
22:17	192

2 Kings

1:8	152
2:9	153, 182
2:11	166, 182
2:13–14	129
2:15	166
2:19–22	182
2:23–25	70, 182
3:4–27	70
4:1–7	182
4:8–9	182
4:18–37	182
4:38–44	182
4:42–44	182
4:43	203
5:1–14	182
5:15–27	182
6:1–7	182
6:8–21	182
6:8–23	70
6:32–33	182
7:1–20	182
8:1–6	182
8:7–15	70, 182
8:20–22	71
8:20–24	70
8:28–29	71
9:1–3	70

2 Kings (continued)

9:1–13	70
9:3	152
9:6	152
9:12	152
9:14–28	71
10:20	170
11:1–21	71
12:17–19	71
12:20–21	71
13:14–19	182
14:5–6	71
14:7	71
14:8–14	70
14:19–20	71
15:10	70
15:14	70
15:19	70
15:25	70
15:29	70
15:29–31	50
15:30	70
16:3	71
16:5–18	71
17	70
17:1–6	16
18:9—19:37	71
18:10–11	16
18:13—19:36	16
21:19	71
23:29–30	71
23:33–35	71
24:1–2	71
24:1–17	33
25	71
25:1–30	16
25:18–21	148

1 Chronicles

1:10	35, 85
3:2	65
5:24	85
6:14–15	148
7:2	85
10:9	143, 145
11–29	61
11:11–12	85
16:22	15
16:23	143
27:6	85
29:11	171

2 Chronicles

6:42	150
13:8	170–71
18:16	192
20:3	170
32:1–22	16
36	16
36:22	170
36:22–23	15, 50, 143

Ezra

1	50
1:1	15
1:7–8	15
3:7	15
4:3	15
4:5	15
5:13–17	15
6:3	15
6:14	15

Nehemiah

3:1	206
9:21	161

Esther

6:9	170

Job

1:6	158
1:7	77
9:13	88
26:12	88

Psalms

1	109
2	109, 158
2:1–3	108
2:2	77, 150
2:4–7	108
2:6–7	108
2:7	142, 157, 158, 160
2:8	108
2:9	108
2:10	108
2:11	108
16	134
18	109
18:3	109
18:4–5	109
18:7–19	109
18:34–35	109
18:37–42	109
18:43–45	109
18:47–48	109
18:50	78, 109
19:50	150
20:6	150
21	109
21:1–7	109
21:9	109
21:10–11	109
21:12	109
24:7–10	171
24:8	85
28:8	150
39:10	145
40:9	143
47:2–9	171
47:8	171
67:12	145
68:11	143
72	109
72:4	109
72:8–11	109
72:5	78
72:7	78
72:15	109
72:17	109
74:9	151
77:16–20	88
84:9	150
87:4	88
89:1	88
89:26–27	77, 158
89:38	150
89:50	78
89:51	150
91:5	163
91:6	163
91:11–12	163
91:11–13	162
91:12–13	163
96:2	143
103:19	171
105:15	150
110	92, 109, 124, 131
110:1	109, 134
110:2	110
110:3	78, 110
110:4	110, 149
110:5	110
110:6	110
132	110
132:1–7	110
132:10	110, 150
132:11–12	110
132:13–16	110
132:17	150
132:17–18	110
145:11–13	171
146:7–8	123
149:2	171

Proverbs

1:21	170
8:1	170

Isaiah

1–39	81, 82
1:4–7	81
1:9–10	81
1:10	184
1:21	184
1:23	184
1:24–27	184
1:25	81
1:26	184
1:26–27	81
1:27	172, 184
1:28	81
1:31	81
2	103
2:1–4	103
2:4	81
2:8	184
2:9–22	81
3	81
3:2	85
3:14–15	184
3:25	81
4	81
4:2	76, 148
5	81
5:5	81
5:7	184
5:8–10	81
5:13	184
5:13–15	81
5:22	85
5:25–30	81
5:26–30	81
6:5	171
6:10	172, 184
6:11–13	81
6:13	76
7:30–33	96
9	138
9:4–5	82
9:5	126
9:6	85, 126
9:6–7	82
9:7	76, 78, 82, 171
9:10—10:4	82
9:13	172
10:2	172, 184
10:5–19	82
10:11	184
10:20–34	82
10:21	85
10:27	126
10:45	157
11	82, 128
11:1	76, 82, 92, 119, 126, 155
11:1–2	156
11:2	82, 126
11:3	82, 126
11:4	82, 126
11:5–9	82
11:6–9	126, 161, 162
11:10	82
11:10–12	82
11:11	126
11:13–14	82
11:14–16	82
13:3	85
13:4–5	82
13:9	82
13:15–16	82
13:18–19	82
13:19–22	161
14:1–3	82
14:3–4	82
14:9	82
14:11	82
14:19	82
14:24	157
14:25	82–82
14:27	172
14:30	83
15:1	82, 83
15:9	83
16	138
16:4–5	82
16:5	76, 126, 171
16:7	83
16:13–14	83
17:1–2	83
17:9	83
18:7	83
19:4	83

19:15–17	83	34:8–15	83
19:18–25	83	34:13–14	161
20	83	35:1–10	83
21:1–10	82	35:5	183
21:11–17	83	35:6	183
21:17	85	36:1—37:38	16
22	83	37:36	96
22:5–11	83	39:6	184
23:1–18	83	39:7	184
24	83	40	83
24:1	83	40–55	83, 145
24:3	83	40–66	151, 184
24:10	83	40:2	83
24:12	83	40:2–3	143
24:21	83	40:3	83, 150, 154
24:21–22	83	40:9	143
25	83	40:9–11	84
25:6–8	83	40:10	84, 143
25:9	83	40:11	84, 143
25:10	83	40:12–17	84
26:1–21	83	40:12–26	143
26:4	83	40:17–22	84
26:11	83	40:23–24	84
26:12	83	40:28–31	84
26:13–15	83	41	84
27:1	83	41:2	84
27:12	83	41:2–3	143
28:2	83	41:3	144
28:6	81, 83, 126	41:4	84
28:7	184	41:5	144
28:16	126	41:8	84, 145
29:1–4	83	41:9	84, 145
29:5–8	83	41:5–13	84
29:18	183	41:15–16	144
30:27–28	81	41:17–20	84
30:27–29	83	41:21	171
20:30–33	83	41:21–24	84
30:7	88	41:21–29	143
31:1–3	83	41:25	84, 126, 144
31:4	83	41:27	84, 143, 144
31:6	172, 184	42:1	122, 126, 145, 157
31:8–9	83	42:1–2	92
32:1	78	42:1–3	159
32:15	153	42:1–4	157
33:22	171	42:1–9	84
34	83	42:4	126
34:2	83	42:5–7	145
34:4	83		

Isaiah (continued)

42:5–9	143
42:6	85, 126
42:7	126, 183
42:10–12	85
42:13	144
42:14	85
42:15–16	144
42:15–17	85
42:16	183
42:18–25	85
42:19	145
42:22–25	144
42:24–25	85
43	85, 144
43:1–4	86
43:1–13	144
43:5–11	86
43:10	145
43:14	86, 144
43:15	171
43:17	86, 144
43:18—44:5	86
44:1	145
44:2	145
44:3	153
44:6	171
44:6–8	86
44:9–20	86
44:21	145
44:21–25	86
44:22	172, 184
44:24–28	143
44:25	15
44:26	145
44:27–28	86
44:28	71
44:28—45:1	144
45:1	15, 71, 77, 86, 144, 150
45:1–7	143
45:2	144
45:2–7	86
45:4	145
45:7–9	143
45:9–10	86
45:11–13	86
45:14–17	86
45:16	144
45:18	144
45:20	144
45:20–21	86
45:21–23	86
45:22	172
45:22–25	144
45:23	86
46	86
46:1–2	86
46:3–10	86
46:13	87
47	144
47:1–5	87
47:3	87
48	83
48:12–15	143
48:14	144
48:20	144, 145
48:21	158
49	87
49:3	145, 158
49:4–6	87
49:7	122
49:8	87, 92
49:9	87
49:10–11	87
49:13	87
49:14–15	87
49:16–21	87
49:22	87
49:22–23	144
49:23	87
49:24	85
49:24–26	88, 144
49:25	85
50	88
50:4–11	88
50:8	88
50:11	145
51	145
51:1–8	88
51:9	88
51:10	88
51:11	88, 126
51:11–12	88
51:17	88, 145

51:19	88, 145	59:8	184
51:20	88, 145	59:15	184
51:22	88	59:15–18	90
51:23	145	59:17–18	90
52:1–12	88	59:19	91
52:7	124, 143, 145	59:20	91
52:13	145	59:21	91
52:13—53:12	89	60	91
52:14	126	60:1	91
53:2	126	60:2	91
53:3	126	60:3	91
53:4–6	126	60:4	91
53:5	126	60:5–7	91
53:8	126	60:6	143, 145
53:9	126	60:9	91
53:10	126	60:10–11	91
53:11	126, 145	60:12	91
53:12	126	60:13	91
54	89	60:14	91
54:1–3	89	60:15	91
54:2	145	60:16	91
54:4–10	89	60:18	91
54:11–12	89	60:19–20	91
54:13–14	89	60:21–22	91
54:15–17	89	61:1	123, 143, 145, 147, 156, 170
55	89		
55:3	78, 93, 145	61:1–2	77, 90, 92, 93
55:4	89, 145	61:2	92, 93
55:5	145	61:3	92
55:7	172, 184	61:4	92, 93
55:7–13	89	61:5	93
56–66	90	61:5–7	93
56:1	90	61:8	93
56:2	90	61:9	93
56:3–5	90	61:10–11	93
56:6–7	90	62	93
56:9–12	90	62:1–2	93
56:10	183	62:2	93
57:18–19	183	62:3–5	93
57:20–21	90	62:4	93
58	90	62:5	93
58:6	90, 92	62:7	93
58:6–7	90	62:8–9	93
58:8	183	62:10–12	93
58:8–12	90	63	93, 93
58:13	90	63:2	93
59	90	63:2–3	93
59:1–16	90	63:5	93

Isaiah (continued)

63:7	94
63:8–9	94
63:10	94
63:11	153
63:14	153–54
63:15	94, 95
63:15—64:12	94
63:17	94
63:18	94
63:19	94
64:1	157
64:1–3	94
64:4–12	94
65:1	94
65:1–16	94
65:2–5	94
64:5–8	94
64:8–10	94
64:12	94
64:13–14	94
64:15–16	94
64:17–25	95
65–66	145
65:17–25	162
66:1–6	95
66:2	95
66:3–4	95
66:5	95
66:6	95
66:7–9	95
66:10–11	95
66:13	95
66:14	95
66:15–16	81, 95, 95
66:17	95
66:18	95
66:19–20	95
66:23	95
66:24	96

Lamentations

3:40	172, 184
4:19	100, 150

Jeremiah

1:18	184
2:8	184
2:26	184
3:1	172
3:10	172
3:12	172, 184
3:13	172
3:14	184
3:22	172, 184
4:1	172, 184
5:3	172, 184
5:28	184
5:31	183
6:26	159
8:5	172
8:19	171, 184
10:5–16	184
10:21	184, 192
13:19	184
14:15	184
15:7	172, 184
15:17	184
15:19	172, 183
18:11	184
19:11	172
20:4–6	184
20:11	85
20:15	143, 145
21:2	16
21:7	16, 184
21:10	184
22:24	16
22:25	184
23	96
23:1–2	96
23:1–8	77
23:1–40	184
23:3–4	96
23:5	76, 96, 119, 148
23:5–6	171
23:6	96, 126
24:1	16
24:7	172
25:1	16
25:5	172, 184

25:9	16, 184	46:2	16
25:11	184	46:13	16
26:3	172. 184	46:26	16
25:9	16	46:28	16
27:6	16	49:30	16
27:8	16	50:17	16
27:8–22	184	51:30	85
27:20	16	51:34	16
28:3	16	52:4	16
28:11	16	52:12	16
28:14	16, 184	52:28–30	16
29:1	16	52:24–27	148
29:3	16		
29:9—28:17	184		
29:21	16		

Ezekiel

30:1–3	97		
30:8	97	1:1	157
30:8–11	77	3:19	172, 184
30:9	97	5:11–12	98
30:12	77	5:15–17	98
30:16	97	6:1–14	184
30:17	183	6:4–6	98
30:21	97	6:8–10	98
30:23–24	97	6:11–12	98
32:1	16	7:8	98
32:18	85	7:10–22	98
32:28	16	7:26	184
33	97	8:2	77
33:4–5	97	8:10	184
33:6–7	97	9:5–6	98
33:8–13	97	9:9	184
33:12–26	77	11:7–12	98
33:15	76, 119, 148	11:16–25	98
33:15–16	97	11:19	153
33:16	126	12:3–11	184
33:17	78	12:13–16	98
33:17–18	97	13:1–23	184
34:1	16	13:11–16	98
35:11	16	14:3–7	184
35:15	172, 184	14:6	172, 184
36:3	172, 184	14:15–23	98
37:1	16	16:5–43	98
39:1	16	16:36	184
39:5	16	16:49	184
39:11	16	16:53	184
43:10	16	17:16–21	98
44:5	172, 184	17:22–24	77
44:30	16		

Ezekiel (continued)

18:6	184
18:12	184
18:15	184
18:23	172
18:24	172
18:30	184
18:32	172, 184
19:8–9	98
19:12–14	98
20:7–8	184
20:16	184
20:18	184
20:24	184
20:31	184
20:35–38	154
20:39	184
20:39–44	98
21:2–3	98
22:1–32	98
22:3–4	184
22:23–31	184
22:29	184
23:7	184
23:13–16	98
23:21–34	98
23:30	184
23:37	184
23:39	184
23:49	184
24:9	98
25:7	98
25:10–11	98
25:13–14	98
25:16–17	98
26:1—28:19	98
26:7	16
26:18–19	16
26:21–23	98
29:4–5	98
29:8–12	98
30:4	98
30:6–8	98
30:10	16
30:10–26	98
31:1–18	98
32:3–32	98
33:8–11	184
33:11	172
33:21–33	98
33:25	184
34	97
34:1–10	98, 184
34:5	192
34:10–21	97
34:11–22	98
34:11–31	98, 184
34:15–23	97, 98
34:20–31	77
34:23–24	76, 78, 97, 98, 171
34:24–25	97
34:25–31	97
34:26–28	97, 98
34:27	98
34:28	98
34:28–29	98
34:29	98
35:4–15	98
36:1—37:28	98
36:17	184
36:18–19	98
36:22–38	184
36:25–27	153
37:14	153
37:15–23	98
37:21–28	77
37:24	76, 171, 192
37:24–25	78
38–39	98, 120
38:1	98
38:8	98
38:20—39:6	99
39:7–10	99
39:11–16	99
39:17–20	99
39:21–24	99
39:25	184
39:25–29	98, 99
40–48	95
44:10–12	184
47:12	183

Daniel

1:1	16
1:18	16
1:21	15
2	101
2:1	16
2:12–14	99
2:28	16
2:39–45	99
2:41	99
2:44	99
2:45	99
2:46	16
3	99
3:1–28	16
3:25	77, 158
3:4	170
4:1	16
4:3	171
4:4	16
4:28–37	16, 162
4:34	171
5	100
5:2	16
5:11	16
5:18	16
5:29	170
6	99
6:28	15
7	77, 99, 101, 115, 138
7:4	101, 117
7:9–10	101
7:13	77
7:13–14	77, 101
7:14	171
7:18	171
7:21	101
7:22	101
7:27	101, 171
8	102
8:6–7	102
8:8	100
8:23–25	102
9:12	184
9:25	124, 150, 184
9:26	77, 150
10:1	15
11:2	102
11:3	102
11:4	100, 102
11:6	102
11:7	76
11:7–9	102
11:20	102
11:21–45	102
11:36–39	102
12:1	102

Hosea

1:4	102
1:5	102
1:7	102
2:1–13	102
2:3	102
2:4	102
2:10	102
2:11	102
2:12	102
2:13	102
2:14–15	154
2:14—3:1	103
2:18	161
3:3–5	77
3:5	78, 102, 126
4–5	102
4:1—5:14	184
4:17	184
5:8	170
6–12	102
6:1	172, 184
6:1–2	102
6:11	184
8:1	102
8:3	102
8:4	102
8:7	102
8:8	102
8:13	102
8:14	102
9:6	102

Hosea (continued)

9:15	102
9:16	102
9:17	103
10:2	103
10:6	103
10:7	103
10:9–10	103
10:13	184
10:13–15	103
11:1	77, 158
11:1–4	102
11:5	103
11:6	103
12:7–9	103
12:14	103
12:16	103
14:5–8	77
14:8	126

Joel

1:14	170
2:1	170
2:12	172
2:12–13	184
2:13	172
2:15	170
2:25	184
2:28–32	153

Amos

1:2	103
1:4–5	103
1:7–10	103
1:12	103
1:14	103
2:2–3	103
2:5	103
2:6–7	184
2:13–16	103
3:11	103
3:14–15	103

4:1	184
4:6–11	172, 184
4:14	103
5:3	103
5:5	184
5:6	103
5:7	184
5:11–12	184
5:20	103
5:27	184
6:7	184
6:11	103
7:8–9	103
7:11	103, 184
7:17	103, 183
8:3	103
8:4	184
8:6	184
8:9—9:10	103
9:11	78, 126, 171
9:11–12	134
9:11–14	184
9:11–15	103
9:14	183

Jonah

1:2	170
3:2	170
3:4	161, 170
3:5	170
3:7	170
3:8	172, 184

Micah

1	104
1:2–11	104
1:7	184
1:12	104
1:14	104
1:16	104, 184
2:1–2	104
2:3	104
3:1–4	104

3:1–12	184	3:4	184
3:5	104, 179	3:14	170
3:12	104	3:15	171
4	103	3:17	85
4:1–5	103	3:20	184
4:3	81	9:9	170
4:6	126		
4:6–8	103		
4:8	77, 126	## Haggai	
4:9–11	103		
4:12–13	103	1:1	148
5	103	1:2–11	184
5:1	103, 126	1:12	148
5:2	104, 133, 137, 199	1:14	148
5:2–5	104	2:2	148
5:3	126	2:5–9	184
5:3–5	104	2:7	105
5:5–6	104	2:17	172
5:7–9	104	2:20–22	105
5:10–15	104	2:20–23	184
6:6–8	104	2:23	78, 104
6:13–16	104		
7:1–6	104		
7:10	104	## Zechariah	
7:11–13	104		
7:16–17	104	1:3	172
		1:3–6	184
		1:4	105, 172
## Nahum		1:14	105
		1:16	184
2:1	143	1:17	184
3:18	184, 192	1:18–20	105
		2:1–13	105
		2:4–13	184
## Habakkuk		2:9	105, 184
		3:1	148
1:4	184	3:1–5	184
1:8	100	3:8	119
3:13	150	3:8–10	105
3:17–19	77	4	105
3:18	126	4:7	126
		4:9	105
		6:10	149
## Zephaniah		6:11–13	105
		6:12	119, 126, 148, 149
1:8	184	6:12–13	184
2:7	184	6:13	126, 149

Zechariah (continued)

6:15	105
8	106
8:7	106
8:9	184
8:20–23	184
8:22–23	106
9	106
9:1–8	106
9:9	106
9:9—10:12	184
9:9–10	106
9:10	106
9:11–13	106
9:12	184
9:14–17	106
10:1–3	106
10:4	126
10:4–5	106
10:5	106
10:7	106
10:8–12	106
11:1–3	106
11:3–5	106
11:4–17	106
11:6	106
11:8	106
11:9	106
11:14	106
12	106
12:1—14:21	184
12:3	106
12:2–4	106
12:5–6	106
12:7–9	106, 107
12:10	159
13	107
13:2–3	107
13:7	192
14	107
14:2	107
14:3	107
14:4	158
14:9	107, 171
14:11	107
14:12–15	107
14:14	107
14:16	107
14:17–18	107
14:21	107

Malachi

1:4–5	108
1:6—2:9	184
1:6—2:16	184
2:10	77, 158
3:2–5	108
3:7	172
4:1–6	184
4:2	78, 183
4:4	108
4:5	154, 172, 202

NEW TESTAMENT

Matthew

1:1	61, 132
1:6	132
1:7	132
1:18	133
1:20	132
1:21	54, 148
2	62, 132
2:1	133
2:1–18	187
2:1–19	189
2:4	198, 199
2:5–6	133
2:6	104
2:20–23	187
2:22	188
3:2	170
3:7	193, 197
3:7–10	193

3:15	156	11:14	108
3:16	160	11:21–22	165
3:17	85	12:2	196, 197
3:18	175	12:7	104
4:1	161	12:8	138
4:1–11	163	12:1–14	138
4:2–3	163	12:14	197
4:3	161	12:18	157
4:4	192	12:18–21	85
4:5	163	12:23	132
4:17	170, 184	12:26	170
4:21	174	12:28	157, 170
4:23	170	12:38	198, 199
5:3	170	12:38–39	183, 197
5:10	170	12:43–45	161
5:19	170	13:11	170
5:20	197, 198	13:19	170
5:21	51	13:33	170
5:27–32	191	13:38	170
5:30	170	13:41	170
5:33–37	175	13:43	170
5:35	109	13:52	199
6:1–4	184	14:1–2	188
6:2	175	14:1–12	188, 189
6:3	188	14:21	190
6:5	175	15:1	198, 199
6:16	175	15:1–2	197
6:33	170	15:19	191
7:21	170	15:22	132
7:29	199	15:29–39	183
8:5–13	13, 196	16:1	193
8:12	170	16:1–4	183, 197
8:19	199, 200	16:1–12	193
9:3	199	16:6	193, 197
9:9	178	16:11–12	193, 197
9:11	197	16:13	188
9:13	104	16:21	194, 199
9:14	197	16:28	170
9:27	132	17:10	199
9:34	197	17:10–12	108
9:35	170	18:1	170
10:3	178	19:3	197
10:7	170	19:3–12	196
11:1–19	152	19:9	191
11:2	153	19:14	170
11:2–3	160	19:18	191
11:5	184	19:24	170
11:13	154	20:18	194, 199

Matthew (continued)

20:20	71
20:21	132
20:30	132
21:5–7	106
21:9	132
21:13	90
21:15	198, 199
21:15–16	194
21:23–27	194
21:31	170
21:32	175
21:33–46	197
21:43	170
22:15	197
22:19–22	175
22:23–33	192
22:34	197
22:41–46	197
22:42	132
22:44	109
23:1–36	184
23:2	198
23:2–34	199
23:2–36	197
23:13	198
23:15	198
23:23	196, 198
23:25	198
23:27	198
23:28	175
23:29	198
23:34	198, 199
24:14	170
24:46	154
25:34	170
26:3	193, 194
26:46–56	201
26:52	74
26:57	193, 195, 199
26:59	195
26:64	109
26:67	88
27:1	194
27:27	206
27:30	88
27:41	195, 199
27:62	197
28:11–12	194
28:18–20	163

Mark

1:1	133, 141, 142, 142–50, 144, 153, 158
1:1–11	163
1:1–13	142–64
1:1—8:29	141–206
1:2–3	83
1:2–8	150–55
1:3–4	161
1:4	151, 152
1:5	154
1:9	156
1:9–11	155–60
1:10	157, 160
1:10–11	156
1:11	85, 157
1:12	151
1:12–13	160, 160–64, 162
1:13	161
1:14	164
1:14–15	131, 168
1:14—8:29	164–206
1:14—16:8	163
1:16–20	164, 174–79
1:16—8:26	164
1:16—8:29	168
1:23–27	164
1:24	165
1:28	165
1:29–31	164
1:32–34	165
1:34	160, 165
1:35–39	165
1:39	160
1:40–45	164
1:43	160, 161
1:45	165
2:1	205
2:1–12	138, 164, 165

SCRIPTURE INDEX

2:4	165	4:26	170
2:6	199	4:30	170
2:8	157	4:33	165
2:10	171	4:33–34	166
2:11	175	4:34	185
2:12	165	4:35–41	165
2:13	165	4:35—5:20	165
2:13–17	164, 174–79	4:36	165
2:13–22	165	4:41	166, 203
2:14	175, 178	5:1–20	203
2:15	175	5:1–41	164
2:15–17	165	5:7	165, 171
2:16	196, 197, 198, 199	5:19–20	167
2:18	196, 197	5:21	165
2:18–22	165	5:21–43	165, 200, 203
2:23–28	165	5:24	165
2:23—3:6	138, 165	5:24–34	165
2:24	196, 197	5:27	165
2:26	194	5:30	165
2:28	138, 171	5:31	165
3:1–6	165	5:37–43	205
3:6	165, 189, 197	5:40	161
3:7	165	5:41	165
3:7–8	165	5:42–43	165
3:7–9	165	5:43	167
3:7–12	165	6:1–6	165, 166
3:11	165, 171	6:6	165
3:11–12	167	6:7	189
3:13–19	165, 174–79, 176	6:7–12	190
3:15	160	6:7–13	164, 203
3:16	205	6:7–30	165
3:17	175	6:11–12	131
3:18	175, 178	6:13	160
3:20–21	166	6:14	189, 202
3:20–35	165	6:14–15	167
3:22	160, 199	6:14–16	202
3:22–30	165	6:14–29	189
3:23	160, 162	6:15	166, 184
3:26	162	6:16	202
3:27	180	6:17	189
3:29	157	6:17–18	189
3:31–35	166	6:17–21	204
3:32	165	6:17–29	188
4:1	165	6:19	204
4:1–34	165	6:19–20	190
4:10–11	165	6:21	190
4:11	170	6:22	191
4:15	163	6:23	191

Mark (continued)

6:24–30	203
6:26–28	191
6:30–31	190
6:30–44	165, 202
6:31–37	203
6:31–44	165
6:32–33	190
6:34	165, 190, 192
6:42	190
6:45	165
6:45–51	203
6:45–52	165
6:46	165
6:47—7:23	165
6:52	203
6:53–56	165
7:1	198, 199
7:1–5	197
7:1–23	165
7:3	196
7:5	196, 199
7:21	191
7:24–30	165
7:26	160
7:30	167
7:31–37	165
7:31—8:9	165
7:33	165
7:37	165
8:1	149, 165, 170
8:1–10	165, 183, 203
8:1–21	165
8:2	165
8:6	165
8:10–21	165
8:11	161
8:11–12	183, 197
8:15	188, 189, 197, 198
8:22–26	165, 188, 202
8:26	167
8:27	188
8:27–29	202–206
8:27–30	168, 202
8:28	166, 184
8:29	133, 164, 166, 171, 202
8:30	168
8:30—16:8	206
8:31	171, 194, 199, 200
8:31–33	168
8:32–33	205
8:33	162
8:34	166
8:38	171
9:1	170, 184
9:2–5	205
9:2–7	170
9:2–8	162
9:2—15:47	168
9:7	159, 168
9:9	171, 178
9:11	199
9:11–13	108
9:12	154
9:14	199
9:18	160
9:28	160
9:30–32	168
9:31	200
9:35	190
9:35–37	190
9:38	160, 176
9:41	171
9:47	161
10:1–12	189, 198
10:2	161, 197
10:2–12	196
10:11–12	191
10:14	170
10:21	159, 184
10:28	205
10:31	190
10:32–34	168
10:33	171, 194, 199, 200
10:35–45	176
10:39	205
10:42–45	190
10:45	168, 171
10:47–48	131
11:7–8	106
11:10	131
11:14	108

11:15	161	14:65	201
11:15–19	108	14:70	155
11:17	90	15:1	195, 198, 201
12:1–12	184, 194	15:1–5	194
12:6	159	15:1–41	195
12:8	138, 161	15:2–5	201
12:13	197	15:6–15	201
12:13–17	189	15:7–15	194
12:14	197	15:16	206
12:14–17	13, 195	15:16–20	201
12:15	161	15:24–37	201
12:18–27	192, 193	15:29	149
12:28	174, 199	15:31	198
12:29–31	159	15:32	132
12:32	199	15:38	158
12:35	132, 171, 199	15:39	13, 171, 195
12:35–37	109, 131	15:42–47	191, 200
12:36	109, 157	15:43	174
12:38	199	15:43–46	195
12:42–44	184	15:44–45	13, 195
13:3	205	16:7	205
13:10	163, 203	16:9	160
13:11	157	16:17	160
13:21–22	132		
13:24–25	115		
13:26	171	Luke	
14:1	198, 199		
14:9	203	1–2	58
14:18–21	200	1:1	9
14:21	171	1:1–4	10
14:29–31	205	1:5	132
14:33–42	205	1:5–25	194
14:38	161	1:7	152
14:41	171	1:17	108
14:43	198, 199	1:27	132
14:43–47	201	1:31	148
14:49	171	1:32	61, 132
14:53	194, 198, 199	1:33	170
14:54	195	1:69	132, 153
14:55	195	2:1	13, 196
14:55–59	194	2:1–5	175
14:55–61	201	2:4	132
14:58	149	2:11	132
14:60–65	194	2:26	132
14:61	132	2:32	85, 87
14:61–62	171, 201	3:1	13, 188, 196
14:62	109, 155, 171	3:2	193
14:62–65	195		

Luke (continued)

3:10–14	152
3:12–13	175
3:15	132
3:19–20	188
3:21–22	160
4	93
4:1–13	163
4:2	161
4:4	192
4:14	157
4:18	90, 184
4:18–19	90, 123, 145, 157
4:18–21	92, 156
4:19	124
4:28—5:11	174
4:34	170
5:1–12	174
5:2	174
5:5	174
5:7	174
5:10	174
5:17–21	197
5:21	198, 199
5:27–28	178
5:30	197, 198
5:32	184
5:33	197
6:2	196, 197
6:5	138
6:7	197, 198, 199
6:14–16	188
6:14–29	188
6:15	177, 178
6:16	177
6:17	165
6:20	170
6:20–26	184
7:1–10	196
7:18–20	160
7:20	153
7:24–35	152
7:28	170
7:36	197
7:39	197
7:48–49	138
8:1	170
8:3	174
8:12	173
8:29	161
9:2	170
9:7–9	188
9:9	188, 189
9:10	188
9:22	194, 198, 199
9:35	85
9:54	177
10:1	194
10:9–10	184
10:21	157
10:25	198
10:31–32	194
11:14–15	183
11:16	183, 197
11:18	170
11:20	184
11:29–30	183, 197
11:37	197
11:37–54	184
11:38	197
11:38–54	197
11:42	196
11:38	196
11:53	197, 198, 199
12:1	197
12:31	170
12:32	170
13:1	196
13:3–5	184
13:10–17	138
13:31	189, 197
13:31–35	189
14	190
14:1	197
14:3	197
14:13	184
15:1	175
15:2	196, 197, 198, 199
16:14–15	194
16:18	191
16:19–31	184
17:14	194
17:20	197
17:20–21	184

17:21–22	170
18:10–197	197
18:12	196
18:20	191
19	175
19:1–10	175
19:8	175
19:15	170
19:35	106
19:39	197
19:46	90
19:47	193, 194, 198, 199
20:1	194, 198, 199
20:19	193, 194, 198, 199
20:37–40	192
20:39	199
20:42	109
20:46	199
22:50	201
22:2	193, 198, 199
22:2–4	194
22:4	193
22:52	193
22:66	194, 195, 198
22:69	109
23:2	13, 133
23:4–5	193
23:6–12	201
23:10	193, 198, 199
23:13	193
23:7–11	189
23:50–53	195
24	163
24:4	190
24:20	193

John

1:1	142, 170
1:14	170
1:19–24	154
1:20–28	133
1:40–42	174
1:41	133
1:46	155
1:51	157
2:7	159
2:18–22	183
2:19	149
2:19–21	149
2:20	187
3:1–15	197, 200
3:3	179
3:5	170
3:28	133
4:1	197
4:25	133
6	133
6:12	171
6:14–15	133, 167, 192
6:15	166
6:30	183
6:71	178
7	133
7:32	197
7:40–52	155
7:41–42	133
7:45–52	197
7:50	197, 200
8:3	196, 197, 199
8:12	87
8:13	197
9:5	87
9:13–17	197
9:40	197
9:22	133
10:22	73
10:24	133
10:30	133
11:27	133
11:46–57	197
11:47	193, 195
11:48	13
11:50	193
12:14–15	106
12:19	197
12:34	133
13:22	190
13:25	200
18:3	194, 197
18:13–14	193
18:19–24	194
18:24	193
18:28	193, 206

John (continued)

18:33	206
19:1–16	194
19:9	206
19:12	13
19:15	13
19:33–37	107
19:39	197, 200

Acts

1	163
1:2	157
1:3	161, 170
1:13	177
2:10	147
2:25	109
2:34	134
2:34–35	109
4:1	195
4:1–3	193
4:2	192
4:5	198
4:27	189
5:17	193, 195
5:21	195
5:31	109
5:34	195, 197
5:36	128, 154
5:37	129, 175, 191
6	204
6:12	195, 198
7:23–30	161
7:49	109
7:55–56	109
7:56	157
10:11	157
10:38	157
11:28	169
12:12	6
12:25	6
13:1	169
13:34	134
13:36	134
13:47	87
15:5	196, 197
15:11	173
15:25	159
15:27	169
15:37	6
15:39	6
16:31	173
17:24–25	85
18:2	7
18:12–17	18
19:35	198
20:25	170
21:10	169
21:31–32	206
21:38	129, 154, 178
21:39	178
22:30	195
23:6	195, 197
23:6–8	192, 196
23:8	192
23:9	198
23:28	195
24:1	195
25:20	190
26:8	197
26:18	85
26:23	85, 87
28:31	170

Romans

1:3	61, 134
1:7	159
8:33	88
8:34	109
9:5	134
10:9	173
11:26–27	91
14:11	86, 144
16:20	109
16	7
16:7	147

1 Corinthians

1–4	1
1:20	198
1:22–23	198
1:23	138
3:16	149
4:14	159
4:20	170
7:5	161
7:18	72
10:13	161
11:18	1
12:28	169
15:24	170
15:25	109
15:27	109

2 Corinthians

4:8	190
12:1–4	157

Galatians

1:15	87
3:13	132, 134, 138
4:20	190
6:1	161

Ephesians

1:20	109
1:22	109
2:2	180
2:8	173
2:20	169
3:5	169
4:11	169
5:1	159
5:5	170
6	90
6:10–18	181
6:17	87

Philippians

2	3
2:1–4	1
2:6–8	1
2:10	86, 144
2:15–16	1
3:5	197
3:16	87
4:1	159
4:1–3	1

Colossians

3:1	109
4:10	6, 153

2 Thessalonians

1:10	87

Philemon

24	6, 153

1 Thessalonians

3:5	161

2 Timothy

2:8	61, 134
4:1	170
4:11	153

Hebrews

1:3	109
1:13	109
2:8	109
2:17	149

Hebrews (continued)

2:18	161
3:1	149
3:14–15	149
4:12	87
4:15	161
5:5	149
5:6	124
5:10	124, 149
6:20	124, 149
7:1–2	124
7:10–11	102
7:15	102
7:17	102
7:26	149
8:1	109, 149
9:11	149
10:12–13	109
12:2	109

James

1:13–14	161
1:16	159
2:25	170

1 Peter

3:22	109

4:12	159
5:13	6, 168

2 Peter

3:1	159

1 John

2:7	159

Jude

3	159

Revelation

1:7	107
1:16	87
2:12	87
2:16	87
4:1	157
5:5	61
11:15	170
13	100
14:8	168
17	121
19:15	87

APOCRYPHA AND PSEUDEPIGRAPHA

Tobit

13	112
13:1	112
13:2	112
13:3	112
13:5	112
13:9	113
13:10	112
13:11	112
13:12	112
13:13	112
13:16–17	112
14:4	113
14:4–5	112
14:6–7	113

Judith

9:7–14	111
11:19	192
16:3–20	111

Additions to Esther

14:8–12	112

Wisdom of Solomon

3:8	171
4:18	112
5:3	112
5:13	112
5:17–23	112

Sirach

10:16	113
17:17	113
17:23	113
20:15	170
35:22–23	113
36:2–3	113
36:12	113
39:23	113
45:25	113
46:5	113
47:1–11	113
47:11	113
47:22	113
48:4	166

Baruch

4:8	112
4:9	112
4:14–16	112
4:18	112
4:21	112
4:23	112
4:24	112
4:25	112
4:30–36	112
4:36–37	112
5	112

1 Maccabees

1	50, 72
1:1–9	14
1:17	101
2	72
2:42–48	73
2:48	73
2:57	113
2:66–68	73
3–4	73
3:3–9	73
3:21	113
3:34	101, 113
3:55	73
4:30	113
4:42–46	151
4:46	78, 151
4:56–59	73
5:14–23	74
5:49	170
5:55	74
5:62	113
6:18–63	74
7:1–5	74
7:26–50	74
7:33	195
8:1–16	12
8:1–32	74
9:1–22	74
9:23–31	74
9:27	151
9:32–73	74
10:1–17	74
10:25–50	74
10:60–64	170
11:23	195
14:4–5	113
14:28	195
14:41	151
14:41–43	74
14:44	195
16:11–17	74

2 Maccabees

1:24–29	113
1:27–29	113
6:14–17	113
7:9	114

4 Maccabees

6:4	170

Apocalypse of Abraham

30	122
31:1	122
31:2–5	122

Hebrew Apocalypse of Elijah

5.5.32	166

Assumption of Moses

10:1	115
10:2	115
10:3	115
10:4–6	115
10:7–10	115

2 Baruch

27	116
29:3	116
29:3–8	116
30:1	116
30:2	116
39:7—40:3	116
61:1	117
63:1	117
66:1	117
70	117
72:2	117
72:2–6	117
73:1	117
73:1—74:4	117

1 Enoch

37–71	115
38:1	78
38:2	115
38:5	115
39:6	78, 115
40:5	78, 115
45:4	115
45:5	115
45:6	115
46	115
46:1	115
46:1–4	77
46:3	115
46:4	115
46:5–8	115
48	115
48:2	77
48:3–5	115
48:8–10	116
48:10	76, 116
49:2	78, 116, 122
49:4	78
51–53	116
51:5	78
52:4	76, 116
52:6	78
52:9	78
53:2	116
53:6	78, 116
54–55	116
55:4	122
56:5–8	116
61:5	78
61:8	78
61:10	78
62	116
62:1	78
62:2	116
62:5–9	77

62:12	116
63:8	116
69:4–5	77, 158
69:26–29	116
71:1	158
71:14–17	116
71:17	116
92:3	116
105:2	77

3 Enoch

45:5	120
48	120
48:10	121, 183

4 Ezra

7:26–30	117
7:27	77
7:28	117
7:29	77
7:31–44	117
11:37	117
11:37—12:34	117
11:40–46	117
12:11	117
12:32	76, 78, 117
12:33	117
12:37–40	117
13	77
13:8–11	117
13:12–13	117
13:28	117
13:32	117
13:37	77, 117
13:49	117
13:52	77, 117
14:9	77, 117
32:18	76
32:29	76

Joseph and Aseneth

14:3	157

Jubilees

1:24–25	77
1:29	114
23:30	114
31:18–20	114

Letter of Aristeas

46–50	194

Odes of Solomon

24:1	158

Psalms of Solomon

11:1	145, 170
17	119–120
17:5	119
17:6	119
17:7–8	119
17:8	119
17:9–12	119
17:12	78
17:13–22	119
17:21	78, 132
17:23	119
17:24	119
17:26	119–120
17:27	120
17:31	120
17:32	76, 120
17:32–34	78
17:33–35	120
17:37–38	120
17:39	120
18	120
18:6	120
18:6–12	120
18:7	120
18:8	120

SIBYLLINE ORACLES

Pro. 15–25	121	3:663–67	121
1:324–85	121	3:669–701	121
1:350	183	3:696	121
1:353	183	3:702–31	121
2:45–55	121	3:741–95	121
2:241	121	4:654	121
3	110, 121	5	115
3:46	121	5:108–110	78
3:49–50	121	5:256–84	121
3:51	121	6:1–25	121
3:52–54	121	7:29–39	121
3:55	121	7:63–75	121
3:62–285	121	8:206	183
3:285	78	8:216–50	121
3:288–93	121	8:251–336	121
3:295–651	121	8:272	183
3:652	121	8:484	121
3:652–55	78		

TESTAMENTS OF THE TWELVE PATRIARCHS

Testament of Benjamin

5:2	78
9:2	151

Testament of Gad

8:1	119

Testament of Judah

24	119
24:1	78
24:2	157
24:4	76
24:5	77, 78
24:13	157

Testament of Levi

2:6	157
3:3	118
4:1	118
5:1	57
5:2	118
5:4–11	118
8	118
8:14–15	118
10:2	77
18:1–4	118
18:6	157
18:6–8	157
18:9	118
18:10	118
18:13	118
18:14	118

Testament of Naphtali

8:4	161, 162

Testament of Reuben

6:8	118
6:12	119

Testament of Zebulun

9:8	126

Testament of Adam

3:1	183

Testament of Solomon

3:6	180
6:1	180
6:9	180
16:3	180
16:5	180

DEAD SEA SCROLLS

1Q13	124
1Q28a	122, 123, 158
1Q33	133
1QM	92
1QS	76, 77, 78, 122, 151, 154, 158
1QSa	77, 158
4Q16	123
4Q52	76
4Q174 (4QFlor)	76, 78, 124, 158, 166
4Q246	77, 78, 123, 158
4Q252	76, 77, 78, 79, 122
4Q266 (Damascus Document, CD)	76, 77, 78, 122, 123, 124
4Q285	77, 78
4Q295	122
4Q521	123
4QApocrDAn ar	158
11Q13	124

JOSEPHUS

Against Apion

1.41	151
2.194	195

Antiquities

11.304–47	14
13.172	196
13.173	192
13.211	74
13.293–94	196
13.297	192, 196
13.298	192, 197
14.8	186
14.54–79	13
14.89–91	194
14.159	186
14.167–80	194
14.202	175
14.370–89	186
14.439—16.26	186
15.1–2	187
15.267–76	187
15.354–64	187
15.365–72	187
15.380–425	187
15.403–409	206
16.58–65	187
16.392–94	187, 197
17.19–22	187

17.41	196	\multicolumn{2}{l}{**The Wars of the Jews**}
17.41–46	197		
17.182–87	187	1.53	74
17.189	202	1.123	186
17.224–27	188	1.204	186
17.271–72	128	1.274–285	186
17.275–76	128	1.358–60	187
17.278–84	128	1.398–400	187
17.285	128	1.404–406	187
17.339–341	188	1.483–84	187
17.339–354	188	2.39–45	187
18.1–10	177	2.56	128
18:3	196, 197	2.57–58	128
18.4	129	2.60–65	128
18.4–10	129	2.93–100	188
18.16	192	2.111–13	187
18.17	192, 198	2.111–18	188
18.23–25	129, 177	2.114–16	188
18.28	202	2.118	129, 191
18.63–64	125	2.168	202
18.106–108	188	2.217–18	177
18.116–19	150, 188	2.236–341	193
18.289	196	2.237–47	206
20.96–99	129	2.250	7
20.97–98	154	2.254–57	129, 178
20.102	129	2.258–63	154
20.153	7	2.261–63	178
20.154–57	7	2.301	195
20.161–64	129	2.316	195
20.162–65	178	2.316–42	195
20.168–72	178	2.325–28	206
20.169–72	129	2.344	206
20.185–87	178	2.405	175
20.192	206	2.410	195
20.195	7	2.411	195
20.199	192, 195	2.432–48	129
20.200	125, 195	2.433	191
		3.4	53
		4.282	194
Life		4.503–10	130
		4.511–29	130
9	195	4.534–37	130
10	196	4.638–44	130
12	196	5.156–83	206
21	196	5.532	195
65	53	6.433–34	130
191	196	7.21–36	130
194	195	7.32	130

7.253	191	7.578–84	130
7.575–76	130	8.437–42	154

PHILO

Life of Moses

1.290	78, 125
1.292	125

On Rewards and Punishments

95	78
95–97	125

Pseudo-Philo (LAB)

59:3	122

www.ingramcontent.com/pod-product-compliance
Lightning Source LLC
Chambersburg PA
CBHW050344230426
43663CB00010B/1987